Professional Communication at Work

D0148819

This text prepares future professionals for success in the workplace through identifying interpersonal communication skills and strategies and exploring when, how, and why to use them. Informed by academic research, professional literature, and author Joseph L. Chesebro's own experiences, the text explores and demonstrates the skills that have facilitated Chesebro's own students to find work and to succeed in their professional lives.

Offering a very practical focus on such topics as handling conflict and giving dynamic presentations, *Professional Communication at Work* also covers essential interpersonal communication skills that are often not discussed, such as:

- Using networking when job hunting;
- Earning a good reputation as a new employee;
- Using storytelling and questions more often;
- Developing coaching relationships with the best senior employees in our workplace;
- Practicing and developing new skills on our own; and
- Using workplace politics in a positive and constructive way to accomplish our goals.

Utilizing the approach of a supportive communication coach, *Professional Communication at Work* will help readers gain a variety of practical communication strategies they can apply to contribute to success in their own careers.

Joseph L. Chesebro is Associate Professor of Communication at The College at Brockport, New York. Joe has taught for 19 years in the areas of interpersonal and organizational communication, including courses in workplace communication and training and development. During his 14 years at The College at Brockport he has served as department chair and been awarded the Chancellor's Award for Excellence in Teaching as well as the Academic Advisement Award.

Professional Communication at Work

Interpersonal Strategies
for Career Success

Joseph L. Chesebro

Routledge
Taylor & Francis Group

NEW YORK AND LONDON

First published 2014
by Routledge
711 Third Avenue, New York, NY 10017

and by Routledge
2 Park Square, Milton Park, Abingdon, Oxon OX14 4RN

Routledge is an imprint of the Taylor & Francis Group, an informa business

© 2014 Taylor & Francis

The right of Joseph L. Chesebro to be identified as author of this work has been asserted by him/her in accordance with sections 77 and 78 of the Copyright, Designs and Patents Act 1988.

All rights reserved. No part of this book may be reprinted or reproduced or utilised in any form or by any electronic, mechanical, or other means, now known or hereafter invented, including photocopying and recording, or in any information storage or retrieval system, without permission in writing from the publishers.

Trademark notice: Product or corporate names may be trademarks or registered trademarks, and are used only for identification and explanation without intent to infringe.

Library of Congress Cataloging-in-Publication Data

Chesebro, Joseph L.
   Professional communication at work : interpersonal communication for a better workplace / by Joseph L. Chesebro.
      pages cm
   Includes bibliographical references and index.
   1. Communication in organizations.   2. Interpersonal communication.
3. Business communication.   4. Interpersonal relations.   I. Title.
   HD30.3.C457 2014
   650.101'4—dc23
   2013050274

ISBN: 978-1-13-801419-0 (hbk)
ISBN: 978-1-13-801418-3 (pbk)
ISBN: 978-1-315-77273-8 (ebk)

Typeset in Sabon
by Apex CoVantage, LLC

Contents

Preface

I wrote this book as if I were sitting beside the reader and acting as a supportive communication coach. I chose content based on what I thought would be most useful in helping you (1) get jobs, (2) establish yourselves well in a new workplace, (3) better understand how to analyze problems that occur in the workplace, (4) appreciate a wider array of communication skills and strategies you may use to address workplace challenges, (5) accomplish something meaningful, even if there are obstacles in your place, and (6) improve your interpersonal communication skills and apply them to various types of workplace situations. I've tried to keep things conversational to make the reading more enjoyable. And while I certainly apply theory and research, I've done it with a very practical focus, always mindful of addressing the question of "so why is this important and how can it help me in the workplace?" I hope you find this book to be no-nonsense, realistic, and a sourced with helpful advice for communicating more effectively with others in your workplace.

Acknowledgments

I'm thankful to far too many people to single out each one here, but I will mention a few.

First, I want to thank Linda Bathgate at Routledge for seeing potential in this project and for her support and encouragement at every step of the process. I also want to thank her team: Ross Wagenhofer (and before him, Julia Sammaritano), Elanor Pike, Denise File, and everyone else.

I also want to thank my mom, Mike, and everyone else in my family for all of their support and encouragement over the years.

I also want to thank all of my friends, teachers who were a huge influence, colleagues who are a lot of fun and who covered for me while I took a semester off to write this, my band mates, the many musicians out there who have provided the soundtrack of my life, and of course, the many current and former students who have put up with me over the years!

And, of course, thanks to my wife, Jen, and kids, Emily and Carter, for being the best, period. It's a blast being your husband and father!

To sum up, I'll borrow from a phrase I heard from Bruce Springsteen on one of my bootlegs and simply thank you all for being my window into the grace of the world . . .

Chapter 1

Communication and Organizations

Why Does Communication "Go Wrong" So Often?

It seems so simple: We say something, and someone else, using presumably the same language as us, receives the message correctly. We take the communication process much for granted in this way, and we get stressed and angry when it doesn't work like this. By the time we're done looking at all of the parts of the communication process, you likely will see why it would make more sense for us to be surprised when the process works, as opposed to when it doesn't work (Richmond & McCroskey, 2009). First, we will define communication. In actuality, there are about as many definitions as there are communication teachers, so I'll simply pick the one that I think best captures the process, one provided by Richmond and McCroskey (2009, p. 20):

Communication is the process by which one or more people stimulate meaning in the mind of another using verbal and nonverbal messages.

Several aspects of this definition are worth noting. The idea of **process** is that communication is dynamic and ongoing, meaning that it is continuous, and we are stimulating meaning in others' minds (and they are stimulating meaning in ours) even when we are not trying to communicate. Suppose you walk into a room to give a presentation. Communication does not start when you start your presentation, it starts as soon as others in the room pay enough attention to you to draw inferences from your behavior, even if you are not verbally communicating with them. At the same time, they may be communicating various messages to you, regardless of whether they are speaking to you. In this sense, communication is an ongoing process.

Notice that we stimulate meaning in others' minds using both verbal and nonverbal messages. Verbal messages primarily communicate the **content** dimension of our message, while nonverbal messages communicate the **relationship** dimension of our message. This relationship dimension is an implied statement of our relationship with the recipient of the message—what we think of the person and of our relationship with him or her. We can communicate warmth and closeness, coldness and distance, or various relational messages in between those two extremes. The relationship dimension is critical because it helps the receiver determine how to interpret the verbal content of our message. And it helps us as communicators by enabling us to tell someone how to interpret the message without spelling it out. Suppose we're in a meeting and after a colleague proposes an idea, we say "that was interesting."

The verbal aspect of our message is the literal content "that was interesting." But from the receiver's perspective, how should that message be interpreted? Was it genuine, sarcastic, dismissive, or something else? In these situations, we do our best to interpret the meaning correctly based on the way the message is delivered non-verbally (or the relational content of the message). Pause for a moment to consider the various ways you could vary your nonverbal behavior when saying "that was interesting" in order to change the relational dimension of the comment. For example, if you sincerely found the idea interesting, how would you deliver the message differently than if you found the idea to be silly and off-the-wall, or if you wanted to be dismissive of the idea? These questions hint at the importance of the relational dimension that is at play each time we communicate. For another perspective on the importance of relational messages, think of a time when you experienced a misunderstanding using electronic communication (email or texting) and had to explain yourself. Unless we use emoticons or spell out how a message should be interpreted, the relational dimension of these messages often is lacking, and that can create problems for us. The same is true when we communicate in-person without carefully considering the relational messages we are sending.

The next aspect of our definition of communication, **stimulating meaning**, also is important because of the high standard we have to achieve to truly communicate. It is not enough to talk, we also must make sure we are heard and understood. It's not what we say, it's what the other person hears. In other words, if we have not stimulated the desired meaning in another person's mind, then we are doing little more than blowing hot air. If we focus only on what we have to say, our focus is on talking. To communicate effectively, we instead need to focus on the meanings other people are gaining from our verbal and nonverbal messages. This is challenging because meanings for words reside within people. If 20 different people read or hear the word "fun," each of those people may have a different meaning for "fun" in their minds. We have to take this into account when we are trying to stimulate our meanings in another person's mind, and use terms that will be meaningful to the other person, regardless of what they mean to us.

And here is where we begin to see why there might be communication problems in the workplace (or elsewhere). Let's take a fairly simple example, making a request. Say that you are a supervisor in a retail store and you tell a subordinate to "take care of a customer" who is in another section of the store, and appears to be in need of assistance. In your mind, "take care of the customer" really means "do anything that is needed to make sure the customer has a great experience on your watch, and comes back again." But the meaning in your subordinate's mind is different. To your subordinate, "take care of the customer" may mean as little as "ask the person if help is needed, answer questions, and ring the customer up." This difference may end up mattering little, but it could be important if the customer needs the kind of help that requires the subordinate to exercise ambition or initiative. For example, you may have had the experience of going into a store looking for a something important, only to find that it wasn't available. This nonavailability can be communicated in a variety of ways. Unfortunately, it may be communicated with an indifferent "no we don't have that" or "it's out of stock," with little additional information. Say you encountered this response from the subordinate above. It's frustrating because you have to ask a string of follow-up questions to get any useful information from the employee ("When will it be back in stock?" "Can you do anything else to locate it?" "Would another store have it?"). But . . . from the employee's perspective, he or she "took care of the customer," and therefore, honored the supervisor's wishes.

So to recap, you gave a simple command to a subordinate, not involving any complex language, yet it is clear to you that the subordinate did not follow through on your wishes to "take care of the customer." It is an example of failing to stimulate the desired meaning in the mind of the employee. In this case, it happened because the two of you had different meanings for "take care of the customer." This is just one of the many ways we can experience a failure to communicate successfully with someone. Below I outline a model of communication, and in each element of the model, there is potential for the communication process to be disrupted.

A Model of Communication (and All That Can Go Wrong When We Communicate!)

The model I am about to cover (see Figure 1.1) is in most communication textbooks, and it is covered during the first week of many communication courses. To be honest, I used to find it tedious to teach it. But over the years I've come to appreciate the model as a blueprint of everything that has to go right in order for us to be able to communicate successfully. From this perspective, it is much more fascinating, because several things have to happen to enable successful communication. And yet every day, without thinking about it or noticing it, these things do happen, almost instantaneously, and we do succeed. This is impressive. Still, the failures we encounter

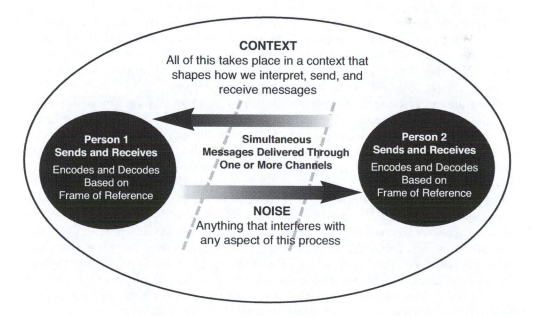

CONTEXT
All of this takes place in a context that shapes how we interpret, send, and receive messages

Person 1 Sends and Receives
Encodes and Decodes Based on Frame of Reference

Simultaneous Messages Delivered Through One or More Channels

Person 2 Sends and Receives
Encodes and Decodes Based on Frame of Reference

NOISE
Anything that interferes with any aspect of this process

Figure 1.1 Model of Interpersonal Communication

are highly frustrating and often costly, so it is worth our time to explore the many ways in which a problem with one or more parts of the process help lead to disrupted communication.

The Communicators. The communication process involves **individuals who simultaneously send and receive messages.** Sending messages involves a process known as *encoding,* and receiving messages involves a process known as *decoding.* **Encoding** involves taking the meaning we want to convey and putting it into the form of a message (involving both verbal and nonverbal aspects) that will help us accomplish our goal. Although we typically don't consciously think about the encoding process, we actually make a number of important decisions when encoding. We consider our goal and determine what words to use and when to use them, and we determine how we will deliver the message nonverbally (which means determining expressions, gestures, posture, vocal tone, pauses, and several other nonverbal cues). Again, while we likely have thought very carefully about these decisions when we had to deliver very important messages, most of the time we do this "on-the-fly," without consciously thinking about each of these elements of encoding.

Decoding involves similar procedures, also typically performed with little conscious awareness. We receive a message from someone and have to decide what it means. This involves considering the literal verbal content, and also any relational cues that accompany it (in other words, the content and relational elements of the message). We have to use the other person's expression, posture, gestures, vocal tone, and so on to correctly infer meaning from his or her message. As with encoding, we typically do this very quickly with little conscious awareness (unless the occasion motivates or requires us to be more deliberate in decoding the message). At the heart of both the encoding and decoding processes is the need to bridge the gap between the meaning that is in our own minds and the meaning in the minds of others. For example, the meaning of "communication" in my mind is different than the meaning of "communication" in your mind. So as I encode my thoughts into messages in each chapter, I continually have to consider the gap between our meanings, and how I best can bridge it. This is no different than when each of us communicates with others each day. The gap that I keep referring to exists because we each approach communication situations with a different *frame of reference.*

Our **frame of reference** is the perspective we bring to a communication situation. It is unique to us and continually evolving, as it has been informed by our personality, self-concept, and the accumulation of our own life experiences. It includes our thoughts, values, attitudes, expectations, and so on. Nobody has a frame of reference that is identical to our own, so the challenge of encoding is to package the meaning in our minds in a way that will successfully stimulate the desired meaning in the mind of a person whose frame of reference is different from our own. This is why communication experts continually stress the importance of being other-oriented, or of being sensitive to our listener's perspective, so we better can reach her and stimulate meaning in her mind. The better we consider our desired audience and their frame of reference, the better we can tailor the message to them and succeed in accomplishing our communication goal. The significance of being other-oriented becomes more clear when we consider our experiences as listeners. Just consider a time when a physician's message either succeeded or failed in fitting your frame of reference. In the latter case, the physician may have talked "above" by using confusing terminology, and possibly delivering the message too quickly. Examples like this, in which a communicator fails to tailor a message to the listener's frame of reference, can be very frustrating for listeners. To better understand frames of reference, we will examine an important element that helps shape our frames of reference: schemas.

A **schema** is the framework that helps us organize our knowledge. Schemas can be thought of as sort of mental "filing cabinets" that are organized in a way to help us access concepts. We have many schemas, and each schema is a cluster of information that is related to a particular concept. For example, consider your schema for the concept of "football." Readers who know little about football will have little to no schema for the concept. Those who know a great deal about football will have a complex and detailed schema. It likely will include several subcategories, for concepts such as famous players, different offensive and defensive formations, types of plays, the various positions on each team, memorable games and plays, statistics (of both team and individual players), different teams, the rules, and so on. Notice that most of these subcategories could have subcategories of their own. For example, the category of "types of plays" can be broken down into numerous categories based on what type of play is best for what type of game situation. If you think of your own areas of interest (maybe music, literature, television, a different sport, your job), you can begin to think of how your knowledge of these areas is organized into various schemas. One of the goals of this book actually is to help you develop your schema for interpersonal communication in the workplace.

The concept of schema becomes important when we consider the role that schemas play in the communication process. Consider the football example above. Imagine you are in a conversation with two people about football, Casey, who has a very well-developed schema for football, and Pat, who has little to no schema for it (assume you have a well-developed schema for football). How will they respond differently, based on their schemas for the topic? As you use football terminology, Casey will be able to "fit" what you are saying into the well-developed schema. Casey will be able to follow you and converse on the topic without too much effort. However, your terminology will be "above Pat's head," as Pat has no schema to enable recognition of the football terminology you are using. Thanks to this absence of schema, as far as Pat is concerned, you might as well be speaking a different language. Casey will be more likely to remember what you said (as it will be easy to fit into the existing schema), while Pat will be less likely to remember, unless he devotes effort to learning the terminology you are using, and how it fits together, so that he can begin building his own schema for football. And this brings us back to the important challenge of tailoring our messages to the listener's frame of reference. If we want our listeners to accurately interpret and remember what we are saying, we should try to use terminology that they can incorporate into their existing schema, or if they lack a schema, we should try to "attach" our information to schema that they already possess. For example, if we were discussing football with Pat (who has little to no schema for it) and wanted him to better understand the concept, we should explain or discuss football in terms that Pat will understand (because he has a schema for them). In other words, we would use analogies, metaphors, or examples to link new concepts to Pat's existing schema. We could start simple, by explaining some of the positions, rules, and objectives, and then build from there. Conversely, with Casey we should expect to use football terminology, as we otherwise would be "dumbing" it down to someone with such a well-developed football schema. The trick is to make sure we are communicating in a way that complements our listener's schema.

The above examples demonstrate the role our frame of reference plays in the encoding and decoding processes. To the extent our frame of reference overlaps with that of the listener, we will have more common ground and in some ways it will be easier to stimulate the desired meaning in the listener's mind. And if we lack that common ground (overlap in frame of reference), it will take more effort to tailor our message so that it fits our listener's frame of reference.

The Message and Channel. The meaning we wish to convey to our listener is delivered in the form of our **message**. As mentioned, it contains both verbal and nonverbal components, and communicates both content and a sense of our relationship with the listener. The message is delivered via a particular **channel**. Common channels include face-to-face, phone, email, text messages, video conferencing, among others. Note the different ways in which our choice of channel can influence the process of communication. There are aspects of channels that can make it more or less difficult to communicate with others, and each channel has its own quirks. In addition, it is worth considering the match between the message we're trying to send and the channel we use, as certain channels may be a better fit for certain types of messages.

Noise. **Noise** is anything that interferes with the message we are trying to send, and may be physical or psychological in nature. **Physical noise** is anything external to us that interferes with the message. It could be actual noise (a coworker's music, construction outside, etc.) or a function of the channel we choose (static on a phone line, delays in web or video conferencing). A newer type of physical noise comes in the form of text messages people get while they already are communicating with someone (such as when students text during class, or employees text during important meetings). When we communicate and want to receive what the other person is saying, it is important to do what we can to eliminate physical noise.

But even if we eliminate any physical noise, it is much more difficult to address any psychological noise that might be present in the situation. **Psychological noise** is internal within us, and may include our mood, physiological state (we may be too tired or too hungry to pay attention to someone), emotions we are experiencing, our own attitudes about the subject or the person with whom we are talking, or other thoughts or feelings that might distract us or prevent us from paying attention. This helps explain why it is difficult to communicate with someone in a variety of situations, such as when we are anxious about something, when we are experiencing conflict with someone, or when we do not have a very good relationship with someone. Each of these issues will be explored in future chapters.

Noise (psychological in particular) presents a serious challenge to our ability to communicate effectively to others. Stop for a minute and consider how difficult it is to identify times during our day when we are free from some kind of distracting physiological noise. Therefore, when we communicate, it is important to consider any psychological noise the listener may be experiencing. Even though we may not be able to control the noise, if we can take it into account, we may be able to adjust our message in a way that enables us to break through it. Suppose we need to discuss something with a coworker and stop down to her office. Even if she is avoiding work by daydreaming, when you arrive she likely will be thinking about something. And if she is making progress on something, she may not want get sidetracked. These may serve as sources of noise as you try to get her to transition to the topic you wish to discuss. Simple gestures like asking if it is a good time to talk or asking how she is doing can help give you a sense of whether it is a good time to bring up your issue. At worst, you can set aside a time that would work better for both of you. Doing this will help make it *your* time, in the sense that both of you will work to eliminate noise so you can focus on the meeting. This may sound basic and obvious, but it is not uncommon to see coworkers come into offices at the wrong time and encounter fellow employees who are distracted by psychological noise (and possibly frustrate their coworker by serving as an additional source of noise). Given all of the competing demands on our listeners' attention, it is in our best interest to do what we can to take noise into account when trying to stimulate meaning in their minds.

Interdependence. So far our discussion of the communication process has had a very individual focus. We have considered how a message sender encodes meaning and sends a message through a channel while trying to account for any noise in the process. When we communicate interpersonally in real-time (as opposed to experiencing a delay with email, text, etc.), we also are listening to another person at the same time, and trying to decode what he or she is saying. As we decode the person's message, we are adjusting the message we are encoding and sending (and the person is adjusting his or her message in response to ours). Because of this mutual influence that communicators exert on each other, they are said to be **interdependent**.

Context. The communication process occurs within a particular **context**, which comprises the physical setting we are in, as well as the history and current state of our relationship with the other communicators. The context in which we communicate has the potential to exert a considerable amount of influence on the choices we make when communicating. The same individual likely will behave differently when in a church, bar, classroom, airport, library, and so on. In each context there are socially created constraints that influence how most people act in each of these settings. In addition, we likely will communicate differently when we are among strangers, acquaintances, good friends, and intimate partners. And we will communicate differently depending on whether we like or dislike the other communicators. All of these elements converge to create the context that shapes our communication with others. In this book we will explore communication in business and professional contexts, and with people in a variety of roles (coworkers, supervisors, subordinates). In the second half of this chapter we will discuss important characteristics that shape our communication in these contexts.

Before we explore the organizational context, it is important to review the parts of the communication process and consider all of the things that have to go right in order for us to successfully communicate with someone. We have to take the meaning that is in our mind and encode it verbally and nonverbally into a message that will enable a person with a different frame of reference to decode it and gain the meaning we intend for her to gain. In the process we have to choose a channel that fits our message, our goal, and any constraints placed on us. We also may have to overcome noise. Finally, we have to conform to the context in which we are communicating. Think of all that can go wrong during different stages in the process.

We may have trouble encoding for a variety of reasons: anxiety, fatigue, distraction, the complexity of the meaning we're trying to convey, and so on. These issues may be independent and stem from our mood or they may be interdependent and based on our relationship with the person, or something the person just said to us. Any such encoding problems can result in a message that is verbally or nonverbally flawed. We may use words that are unclear or inappropriate, or nonverbal expressions that convey the wrong message and make it difficult for the listener to decode. Even if we do craft a good message, the channel through which we choose to send it may be a poor fit for it. For example, we may carefully craft an email message in which we are critical of a coworker, but in spite of our best efforts, it may be quite easy for him or her to read different things into it (the lack of nonverbal cues opens the message to a broader range of interpretations when it is being decoded, so we have sacrificed precision by using email). But suppose we actually get all of this right: We encode the meaning verbally and nonverbally into a good message that we convey using an appropriate channel. We still are very dependent on the other person to hold up his end of the process. He may be distracted by noise and not even pay enough attention to receive your message. Any type of distraction that applied to encoding above also can apply to decoding (anxiety, the relationship between the two of you, his focus on what he plans to say next rather than what you are saying now). And if he does receive the message successfully, he will interpret it with a frame of reference that is different from yours, so he may gain a different meaning than you intended from the verbal and nonverbal aspects of the message. Clearly, communication is a precarious process that is vulnerable to disruption during each stage. We could succeed at every stage but one and still fail to stimulate the desired meaning in our listener. This explains why my colleagues Richmond and McCroskey (2009) suggest that it might be more appropriate to be surprised when the process does work, as opposed to being taken aback when it fails to work. And yet in spite of all of this potential for failure, we routinely and successfully perform this process every day, with split-second timing and little conscious awareness of everything that is involved in the process. It is impressive to consider how quickly we work through noise, find the right words and nonverbal expressions, and are able to recognize an overlap between the frames of reference of ourselves and our listeners. And now that we have a more well-developed schema for the communication process, as we do encounter communication problems, we will be in a better position to consider what might have gone wrong. And ideally, we can be more wary and avoid potential problems or mistakes.

The Workplace as Our Communication Context

I mentioned above that our focus in this book would be on communication in the business and professional workplace. With that in mind, this overview will be guided by the following question: What aspects of the organizational context shape our interpersonal communication in important ways? We will review a number of factors that have been identified by Richmond and McCroskey (2009) and others (see Table 1.1). As I cover each of these, consider the ways in which organizational life is different from the world of school, and some of the problems this may create for newer employees. We will explore some of those differences later in this chapter.

Table 1.1 Key Elements of the Organizational Context

Systems: groups of interdependent individuals

Roles: expectations for our performance based on our job description

Rules: formal expectations of how to handle situations

Norms: informal expectations that have emerged over time

Formal networks: chain of command; how people are supposed to be connected and messages are supposed to flow

Informal networks: how we're really connected and how messages really flow

Culture: the way a group thinks and behaves

Resources: possessions, perks, salary, services

Organizational environment: larger context for the organization

Systems. Organizations are **systems,** in the sense that members in organizations are interdependent, meaning that they influence, and are influenced by, each other. In addition, systems are characterized by the familiar phrase that the whole is greater than the sum of its parts. In fact, this is a main reason for organizing—a group working together can accomplish something greater than a collection of individuals who are working on their own. For example, consider music and bands. Imagine the following individual players: a saxophone player with a jazz background, an acoustic guitar player with a unique style informed by being brought up both in Africa and the United States, a young bass player studying jazz in school, a violin player with a bluegrass and classical background, and a funky drummer with a jazz-fusion background. Twenty years ago, if I had asked you to imagine what they might sound like, it might have been challenging. The five members represent a range of influences that we don't typically see overlap (violin and saxophone; jazz, African, bluegrass, and classical). However, we are well aware that this lineup, in the form of Dave Matthews Band, has been highly successful with this formula (they were the most successful touring act from 2000–2010). When they play, what they create is something that is far greater than a collection of individual parts. Similarly, in organizations, there is a potential to create something greater than the sum of our individual efforts. An additional aspect of systems is that as people leave the system or as new people are introduced to the system, the system will be changed. Sometimes the change will be minor, sometimes major. Continuing with the musical example, when bands lose or gain members, their music sometimes changes in significant ways, even though the difference may only be inspired by the addition or subtraction of one member. And consider live performances. Anyone who has ever been to a live performance is aware of the ways in which the addition of a crowd makes for a special occasion that is entirely different from listening to music on our own. In organizations, shifts in personnel can change the character of the system, whether for better or worse. And as we will learn in a later chapter, as new people come into an organization and have the potential to change it, it can be a challenge to maintain an organization's culture. This helps explain why the organization system is one factor that will shape our communication in the organizational context.

Roles. Our communication in organizations also is shaped by the **role** that we are asked to play. Our role in the organization is shaped by our job description

(Richmond & McCroskey, 2009). Our role also means that we cannot simply be ourselves in organizations, at least in terms of acting how we would outside of work. While most people understand this and I fear that I'm being too obvious, I think most of us probably have worked with people who do not effectively separate their personal life from their professional life. In a sense, at work we have to play a role, not unlike an actor or actress (with less glamour of course). Flight attendants can't complain to fliers about how they're tired from a long flight and just want to get home. Waiters and waitresses can't tell parents what they really think about their messy obnoxious kids. We cannot say what we really want to say to that rude customer. We also might encounter more subtle role conflicts. A sales person may be uncomfortable calling households during the evening and imposing. Those in banking or insurance may struggle with having to deny a loan or claim to someone who seems deserving. Those in health care may struggle to maintain professional distance when they want to express greater empathy for their patients. The concept of role conflict is important because it has been linked to a number of important outcomes, including less happiness, perceived health, and job satisfaction (Schaufeli, Bakker, van der Heijden, & Prins, 2009); emotional exhaustion (Kirk-Brown & Wallace, 2004); burnout (Kirk-Brown & Wallace, 2004; Schaufeli et al., 2009); and less effective job performance (Katz & Kahn, 1978). Similarly, role ambiguity, or not having a clear sense of one's role in the organization, also has been linked to negative outcomes, such as job performance (Tubre & Collins, 2000). In a comprehensive analysis of many research studies, Jackson and Schuler (1985) identified some of the following outcomes of not knowing our role clearly, or experiencing internal conflict because of our role: less job satisfaction, less commitment, less involvement, greater chance of leaving, more tension or anxiety, and less effective performance. Results like these point to the importance of finding careers and organizations that fit us well, and of making sure that we have a clear understanding of our role, as these are important elements that shape our communication in organizations.

Rules and Norms. **Rules** are the formal expectations for how we are to perform our job. They usually are clarified in an employee handbook. **Norms** are "established patterns or standards accepted by most members of the organization" (Richmond & McCroskey, 2009, p. 5). They might be thought of as habits that people or the organization have fallen into that others are expected to follow. Some may be so solidified that they might as well be formal rules. However, while rules are clearly stated, norms present a challenge to new employees, as they often will not be formally stated or mentioned anywhere (because employees have come to take them for granted, so they wouldn't think of writing them down or posting them). In spite of this informality, the sanctions for violating them can be serious. Suppose those with seniority are allowed certain perks—certain parking spaces, leaving early, and so on—and that a new employee unknowingly were to take advantage of one or more of the perks. Although no formal rule exists, the new employee will be viewed negatively by coworkers. This presents an important challenge for new employees. On one hand, we need to know the unwritten norms that nobody mentions to them. On the other hand, the rules are unwritten and nobody mentions them! We will discuss this dilemma in detail in the chapter on organizational culture.

Formal and Informal Networks. In addition to formal/informal rules and norms, organizations also contain both formal and informal networks. Networks are based on how employees are linked and therefore shape the flow of information throughout the system. The **formal network** is represented by the official organizational chart. It represents the official hierarchy of who reports to whom, or the chain of command. In the process, it clarifies status differences between different departments and levels within the structure. The formal network is what is spelled out for you when you receive training or written materials as a new employee. This information will help you better understand how things should be done. Of course, you probably know that in most organizations, there is the way things *should* be done and the way things *are* done. This is similar to the difference between the formal network and the informal network. The **informal network** has nothing to do with the organizational chart and everything to do with "who really is talking to whom and about what" (Richmond & McCroskey, 2009, p. 27). It is based on informal personal relationships and who knows who, as opposed to the arbitrary configuration of the organizational chart. For example, anyone on the lowest levels in an organization could have different kinds of relationships with those at higher levels (they may be friends, former classmates, lovers, in-laws, play a sport together, their kids may go to the same daycare center or school, etc.). Therefore, the informal network has a number of important implications that new employees should keep in mind. First, while there is a formal hierarchy that follows the organizational chart, there can be an amount of unseen hierarchy that is based on the informal network. For example, in some offices, a supervisor may have less informal power than a well-liked and respected employee who has been at the organization a long time. As a result, some employees who have little formal status may have considerable informal status within the informal network. Another implication is that information can travel faster through the informal network. Picture a senior manager sending out a directive that has to travel through various levels of bureaucracy versus his secretary sending it through formal channels, but then calling a couple of friends in varying positions. The informal network will operate much more quickly (notice how gossip travels fast). As with informal norms, it is important for new employees to be sensitive to the presence of the informal network. We will examine ways to accomplish this in the chapter on organizational culture.

Culture. According to Richmond and McCroskey (2009), "**culture** is the way a group thinks and behaves" (p. 8). It should be no surprise that, when we consider the ways organizations are systems with formal and informal rules, norms, and networks, each organization is likely to take on a character of its own. An organization's culture comprises the members' shared behaviors, attitudes, and assumptions (Schein, 2004). It can be challenging for a new employee to adapt to a new organizational culture. Even within the same profession, different organizations can have different cultures. One hospital's culture will differ from another's. Two outlets of the same restaurant chain may have different cultures. Even departments within the same organization can have distinctly different cultures. In the chapter on culture we will explore how cultures form and evolve, and also how new employees can adjust to new cultures.

Resources. Life in organizations is made much more interesting by the exchange of different types of **resources**. We briefly will discuss tangible resources and social resources. Tangible resources include actual possessions, such as salary, benefits, budget allocations, office space and location, furniture, and so on. Social resources include credibility, reputation, connections, relationships, and so on. Many of the things we will talk about later in this book involve issues related to the exchange of resources. For example, for every one of the examples of both types of resources I provided above, pause and consider how each could be linked to disagreements, conflicts, or political maneuvering. I will discuss this in greater detail in the chapters on these topics.

Organizational Environments. As open systems, organizations interact with their **environment.** These interactions can affect our organizations and therefore the context in which we communicate. Tosi, Mero, and Rizzo (2000) identify a number of groups that may influence an organization's environment, including competitors, unions, suppliers, public pressure groups, government agencies, and investors or shareholders. In addition, they suggest that environments may be relatively stable (change little over time) or volatile (change a great deal). Consider some present-day climates affecting businesses. The recent financial crisis had an effect on consumers and on different businesses. For example, some types of businesses may have seen a drop in customers, while other businesses may have had trouble starting up due to challenges receiving credit. Or consider how real estate agents were at the mercy of regional and national trends beyond their control. In education, we sometimes see our graduate program enrollments increase as people try to enhance their credentials for the challenging job market. My point in using these examples is fairly serious: *It is possible to do everything I advise in this book to perfection, to be a great employee and great leader, and still lose a job or be in a failed organization, due to environmental factors beyond anyone's control.* Life sometimes is arbitrary and unfair. Fortunately though, many of the skills that are focused on helping you succeed in these situations also can help you bounce back and respond to the challenges you encounter. If you continue to network even after you have a job, you may be able to reach out to others for help. If you've tried to be coached and to learn from those with more experience, you will have a more informed perspective to help you weather career challenges. And many of the skills we will explore also will help you in many settings beyond the organization. In other words, there still are ways to maximize your chances of "landing on your feet" when you face adversity.

Part of your challenge in organizational life will be to appreciate the ways in which the professional world is different from the academic world, so that you can avoid making mistaken assumptions about the professional world. In this next section we will explore some of these differences.

How Organizational Life Is Different From the Way We Are Taught in School

I have to admit that as a college teacher, I cringe when I hear students or others use the phrase "real world" to describe life outside of the college environment. Nobody likes to think that they go to work in a "fake" world! But I do get it. There are important differences between the two "worlds," and it is important that students learn these differences. For example, consider the testimony of Alexandra Levit, a young professional who found the differences between school and the corporate world to be so striking and stressful that she wrote a book to help graduating students adjust to the changes:

> We're comfortable with the concept of school. We know how the story goes: if you work hard, you get good grades and everyone is happy. The business world, however, is another animal entirely. Politically motivated and fraught with non-sensical change, the corporate world is not a natural fit for graduates who leave school expecting results from a logical combination of education and effort. Suddenly, the tenets of success we were taught since kindergarten don't apply, because getting ahead in the business world has nothing to do with intelligence or exceeding a set of defined expectations. In our first corporate jobs, we come up against in greater detail rules no one ever told us about. We feel lost.
>
> (2009, p. 17)

In this section we will explore some of these differences between the world of school and the world of work (see Table 1.2). As I cover each of these, please understand that I am not criticizing students, but rather the system that sometimes shapes their behavior in ways that are less than conducive for a smooth transition to the professional world.

According to Jeffrey Pfeffer (1992), if we want to succeed in the workplace, we have to unlearn some of the lessons we learned in school. He suggests that "The first lesson is that life is a matter of individual effort, ability, and achievement" (p. 17). In school, if we work hard, do the reading, study, attend class, pay attention in class, perform well on standardized tests, and so on, things will work out. If our classmates do the same, things will work out for them too. And if our classmates do poorly, it will not affect our grade. In other words, in school we usually are independent from our classmates. They don't affect us and we don't affect them. However, in organizational life we often are very interdependent with our

Table 1.2 School vs. the "Real World"

School	"Real World"
Success depends on individual effort, ability, and achievement.	Success depends on the efforts of both ourselves and our coworkers.
There are clear right/wrong answers and we receive them immediately.	We often don't learn of the consequences of decisions until long after they're made, and even then, the results can be ambiguous.
Students passively focus on information they're told to learn.	Employees proactively have to seek out information that helps them solve specific problems.
Effort and hard work usually produce tangible results (good grades), or a teacher is considered unfair or arbitrary.	Hard work and the best ideas are not always rewarded.
Resources are not limited (there is no limit on available "A" grades, and if there is, the teacher is considered to be unfair).	Resources are limited. Not everyone can have all of the rewards.

coworkers. We can do our job very well, but if others don't know what they are doing, or if they fail to do their job, the whole office or organization can suffer. To picture this, imagine a football team in which one lineman does his job poorly. Everybody else will be affected. As Pfeffer puts it, "Most situations in organizations resemble football more than golf" (p. 17). As a result, in organizations, employees have to cooperate with each other much more than classmates in school. In fact, notice that in schools, cooperation sometimes can be considered cheating.

Some may see an exception to this in schools, in the form of the group or team project. Typically these involve small groups of students who are asked to complete a fairly significant assignment, usually due at the end of the semester. I cannot back this up with research, but based on complaints I consistently hear from students, these group projects are frustrating for many students. Part of the problem is that projects like these make students experience the kind of interdependence they will face in the workplace. In projects like these, it is not good enough to excel independently. Others in the group have to succeed for the entire group to succeed. In fairness to these frustrated students, though, while there are aspects of these projects that may increase student interdependence, they still fail to mimic actual organizational life. First, according to Michaelsen, Bauman Knight, and Fink (2004), part of the problem with group projects is that students rarely spend enough time in groups to learn to work as a unit, so they only may go through the initial stages of the team-building process. Even if students are given some time to work together in class, it rarely amounts to more than a few hours. And then, unlike in the professional world, students have to scramble to find additional times that fit their schedules. This can be challenging and, as a result, groups likely don't spend a great deal of time together outside of class. And when teams do meet outside of class, it often is to quickly divide up the work so that team members can work independently on the project. So while there are teams, they often do not get to develop a sense of togetherness. Another concern students have with teams is accountability. In other words, "Why do the people who didn't do anything get the same grade as I did?" While it is good for students to learn interdependence though group projects, this lesson often gets obscured when they see nonperformers rewarded with good grades. Or from another perspective, these students may be getting a very realistic taste of organizational life.

The second lesson Pfeffer (1992) suggests we need to unlearn is that there are right and wrong answers. Students are presented with clear-cut problems and upon completing them get fairly quick feedback from the instructor or the book on whether or not the answers are correct. Even when instructors take a long time to give feedback, getting tangible feedback in a few weeks still is more swift and clear than waiting in organizations for months or longer for feedback that might be quite ambiguous. And there is no single person in an organization that can serve the instructor role and identify the exact consequences of our answer. As Pfeffer (1992) suggests, "the consequences of our decisions are often known only long after the fact, and even then with some ambiguity" (p. 18). Because organizational members work in a system in which they are interdependent with their coworkers, the quality of an answer to a problem may depend on how others are solving their own problems. For example, Larkin and Larkin (1994) discuss an incident in which they were trying to improve efficiency and the flow of work in a bus garage. They suggested having a large board with hooks for all of the drivers' keys. The drivers could come in, sign the board, and take their keys. This would be much more efficient than having to go to the supervisor to get the keys, and it would free up the supervisor to do other things. Sounds like a good solution, right? It probably would have scored well on a test. In spite of the benefits of their suggestion, Larkin and Larkin were surprised that the supervisor resisted it, even though they kept persisting with the idea. Finally, the frustrated supervisor said "Look, if they get their keys off of that board instead of coming to me, how will I know if they're drunk?" While Larkin and Larkin's idea might have led to a high grade on a paper or exam, because there were other factors at play in the workplace their idea had an important fundamental flaw. So while answers given in school can be met with a fairly clear and immediate response, in the workplace the results of our ideas often are more elusive and ambiguous.

Beyond Pfeffer's examples, I have identified a few additional ways in which the workplace is different from the classroom. Following from Pfeffer's second lesson, it is worth noting that in school, students focus on learning information for the sake of learning information, while in the workplace information is used to solve problems. And when students are encouraged to solve problems, they often are guided in a step-by-step manner. For example, in one course, I asked students to convert their assignment to pdf format before uploading it to the course website. Before doing this, I did an Internet search to make sure it would be possible for students with any kind of computer platform to do this (Mac or PC). Within a few short minutes, it was clear to me that, between available freeware and conversion websites, this was possible. But because I wanted to see if my students would take it upon themselves to learn how to convert their documents, I did not tell them how to go about doing the conversion. Although many students were able to convert their documents, several did not, and many came to the next class saying they could not convert their documents. This enabled us to have a discussion about how to handle obstacles and problems in the workplace. In fairness to the students, there are many seasoned professionals who might have given up too. During our discussion, rather than admonishing students for not successfully converting their documents, my focus was on how the workplace requires a different kind of problem-solving approach than school.

As I discussed earlier, and as Levit (2009) mentioned, in the workplace, outcomes can be quite arbitrary. Intelligence and hard work do not necessarily lead to desired outcomes. Layoffs happen to good people. There is no guarantee that the best idea will be accepted by others. Good organizations can fail. In school, students usually do not tolerate instructors that seem arbitrary. At the very least, they complain and give negative evaluations, and in some cases they complain to other faculty or the administration. For some things in organizations (harassment, etc.), employees are able to appeal to higher offices. But often, they cannot. They need a kind of resilience and resourcefulness that is not always necessary for students to succeed.

Another difference between schoolwork and work involves the dichotomy of reactive/proactive. In school, students learn react to whatever the teacher does. The teacher structures the course, assigns readings and deadlines, usually controls class discussions, and so on. There is little ambiguity and students are expected to respond within these boundaries. As a result, this encourages a passive student culture. If a teacher is unclear or fails to explain something sufficiently, students are more likely to ask peers for help and complain amongst themselves than they are to persist with the teacher until he or she teaches effectively. At times I have been surprised with concerns mentioned on my teaching evaluations, and my first thought has been: "I wish you had mentioned this to me earlier in the semester, I agree and would have tried to change things." In fairness to students, they are not encouraged to take this kind of initiative. Instructors sometimes lose patience with persistent questions, and there is little focus on doing things that enhance the welfare of the entire class. And even when students are permitted some discretion, such as with final assignments that require independent work and problem solving, they often are required to stay within carefully crafted boundaries, and therefore are not encouraged to exercise a great amount of judgment and creativity. In organizations, employees often are encouraged to take initiative and do things that help the organization. And when presented with problems, they often know the desired end result and are expected to take steps to address them. Employees have to decide what information is worth reading, who they should consult, and so on. These are the types of decisions students don't always get to make in their courses.

Finally, resources operate differently in schools than in the workplace. In most courses, the number of "As" available to students is not limited, so individual work will lead to the appropriate reward. But in organizations, there often is competition for budget allocations, specific positions, and resources. Not everyone will receive the best office location, a salary increase, the largest departmental budget, a desired work assignment, or a promotion when only a few positions are available. As a result, in organizations there is more incentive to compete for these kinds of things, and the resulting political climate requires an approach and skill set that students rarely need to navigate their courses. We will explore these challenges more in the chapter on navigating organizational politics.

So how might school look if it was altered to more accurately reflect the way things work in the workplace? There are a variety of answers to this question, and they might include some of the following. In addition to grades being based on individual performance, they may be linked to the performance of ongoing teams, or even to the performance of the entire class. This would increase interdependence. Students also may be assigned to different roles. Teachers likely would give complex assignments with greater ambiguity and flexibility for problem solving. They might explain a general desired outcome and leave it to students to decide how to best reach that outcome, while offering facilitation (rather than lecturing) along the way. Rather than assigning readings, teachers may provide suggestions or a general list, and encourage students to take initiative to locate whatever information they need to work on the project. On one hand, students would be frustrated by the ambiguity, lack of direction, "fuzzy" assessment, and the fact that their grade is partially linked to the performance of other students. On the other hand, when those same students entered the workplace, they might feel better prepared. But until the educational landscape changes in this direction, it is important for students to realize some of the ways in which the workplace shapes communication differently than the classroom.

So What Are We Covering in This Book, and Why?

In this book I've done my best to cover topics and skills that are most likely to help you navigate the professional workplace. In the first two chapters I provide a foundation of information about communication and individuals in the workplace. The second section (Chapters 3–5) is about becoming a new member of an organization and adjusting to it. In Chapter 3 we discuss *Networking* as a means of finding jobs and getting ahead in those jobs. In Chapter 4 we focus on *Organizational Culture*, how cultures form and change, and how to adjust to a new culture. In Chapter 5 we discuss *Credibility* and how to earn and keep it in the workplace. In the next section we address communication skills that are an important element of success in the workplace. Chapter 6 is about establishing and maintaining good *Working Relationships* with coworkers. Chapter 7 focuses on *Nonverbal Communication*, Chapter 8 on three important *Verbal Skills* (message framing, storytelling, and using questions effectively), and Chapter 9 on *Perceptive Listening*. The final section focuses on various advanced processes that rely heavily on the foundations and skills provided by earlier sections. The next two chapters are about handling differences of opinion in the workplace, with Chapter 10 focusing on *Disagreement and Negotiation* and Chapter 11 focusing on *Conflict*. In Chapter 12 we explore the process of *Coaching and Being Coached*. In Chapter 13 we put everything together and examine the very complex process of *Navigating Organizational Politics*. And finally, in Chapter 14 we focus on *Giving Good Presentations*. My goal is that once you've read this book, you have a much more informed perspective about important dynamics in the workplace, and that you have gained some ideas for how to address some of the most common communication challenges you will face in your own workplaces.

Getting the Most Out of This Book

This book provides general information to give you greater perspective about communication in the workplace, and in many chapters I discuss various workplace communication skills. In order for you to benefit as much as possible and actually improve your skills, there are a few things you should keep in mind and apply whenever you are reading a section (in this book or in any other) about skill improvement.

First, realize that you are trying a new skill, and one that likely will be replacing behaviors you've engaged in for at least a decade, if not longer. Do not expect the skill to work immediately. I often see students try a skill once, find that it's awkward and after concluding that it doesn't work very well, they return to more familiar and comfortable behaviors that may be less effective. If we used this same approach with driving, most of us would not have a license, and instead would be riding bikes around. Learning a new skill is awkward and takes time. When I drove on the road for the first time, it was in my grandmother's huge car (in this case, the stereotype was true), and I was going slow enough to earn a long line of cars behind me. Being told to look further down the road rather than right in front of the car was like a revelation. So when you try out new skills, remember this, and avoid giving up after only one try. It's possible you never will grow to feel comfortable using a particular skill. Not all techniques are a good fit for everyone. But don't deprive yourself of a potentially useful skill by giving up too soon.

So other than allowing for a slow start, how should we work on a skill? My advice usually is to **try a skill in a low-risk environment**, around those with whom we are comfortable. By low-risk environment, I mean that the consequences for failure are minimal. For example, if you want to work on assertiveness, do it the next time a group of friends is deciding where to eat, where to go out, or what movie to see. In a setting like this, even if you fail miserably, (1) people probably won't notice, and (2) nothing bad really happens. If you make any progress at all, you will have made it easier to try the next time. Eventually, you can work your way "up" to more challenging situations. Instead of trying the skill with friends, you could try it with acquaintances or strangers. You could start doing it with outcomes you care more about, but which still present a low-risk situation. As you work your way up, realize that setbacks do not have to be permanent, and remember that it takes time to develop a new skill.

Finally, I want to discuss an additional challenge that comes with trying to learn a new skill. Over the years, I've noticed that people can be taught specific steps to performing a skill, and yet still do the skill poorly, even after some practice. For example, take customer service when someone is making a purchase and you are at the register. We can outline a detailed set of steps to follow: greet the customer, take the items, scan the items, and after the customer has paid, offer them a friendly goodbye. Some organizations even get more specific, and tell their employees exactly what to say in these situations: "Did you find everything ok?" "How was your visit?" And yet no matter how intensely we train someone to follow these steps, some simply will provide poor customer service. Think of times when you clearly knew someone was following a specific script, or when you and your coworkers were following one. A clearly defined set of steps does little to guarantee that the overall performance of a skill will be effective. What is missing is the third element that you should keep in mind when learning skills: *attitude*. In the example above, someone could perform the steps, but miss the entire attitude that is key to effective customer service: doing whatever it takes to make sure that the customer had a positive overall experience. So as you encounter discussions in this book about how you can improve various communication skills, note that I emphasize attitude far more than specific steps you can follow. In fact, in most cases I've tried to avoid giving you the kind of skill building "recipe" lists that are a feature of many communication self-help books. Besides the fact that steps won't give you a sufficient sense of how to perform a skill, they have additional problems. First, it is difficult to memorize steps in a way that you can recall them when you need to apply them. Second, even if you could, if all you know are steps, then if a step does not work as you expect, you will be stuck, unless the list is made increasingly complicated with "what if this happens" substeps (like a convoluted flow chart).

Instead I focus on attitude, along with a few general techniques that might work in various situations. This gives you some ideas, but much greater flexibility to think for yourself and make informed judgments about how to approach various situations. For example, if you focus more on the attitude of ensuring that a customer has had a great experience, but you are not restricted to a script or specific steps, then you can be yourself, exercise more creativity, and you are more free to think "on-your-feet." Think of times when you have received excellent customer service. Chances are that the person was exercising some personal judgment and being responsive to your unique situation, and that the person might have used an entirely different approach if faced with a different type of challenge, yet with the right attitude. So as you learn about various skills in this book, try to focus on the overarching attitude behind those skills. The attitude will be easier to remember and will serve you far better than a memorized but empty list of steps.

References

Jackson, S. E., & Schuler, R. S. (1985). A meta-analysis and conceptual critique of research on role ambiguity and role conflict in work settings. *Organizational Behavior and Human Decision Processes, 36,* 16–78.

Katz, D., & Kahn, R. L. (1978). *The social psychology of organizations.* New York, NY: Wiley.

Kirk-Brown, A., & Wallace, D. (2004). Predicting burnout and job satisfaction in workplace counselors: The influence of role stressors, job challenge, and organizational knowledge. *Journal of Employment Counseling, 41,* 29–37.

Larkin, T., & Larkin, S. (1994). *Communicating change: How to win support for new business directions.* New York, NY: McGraw-Hill.

Levit, A. (2009). *They don't teach corporate in college: A twenty-something's guide to the business world.* Pompton Plains, NJ: Career Press.

Michaelsen, L. K., Bauman Knight, A., & Fink, L. D. (2004). *Team-based learning: A transformative use of small groups in college teaching.* Sterling, VA: Stylus.

Pfeffer, J. (1992). *Managing with power.* Boston, MA: Harvard Business Press.

Richmond, V. P., & McCroskey, J. C. (2009). *Organizational communication for survival: Making work work* (4th ed.). Boston, MA: Allyn & Bacon.

Schaufeli, W. B., Bakker, A. B., van der Heijden, F.M.M.A., & Prins, J. T. (2009). Workaholism, burnout and well-being among junior doctors: The mediating role of role conflict. *Work & Stress, 23,* 155–172.

Schein, E. (2004). *Organizational culture and leadership.* Hoboken, NJ: Jossey-Bass.

Tosi, H. L., Mero, N. P., & Rizzo, J. R. (2000). *Managing organizational behavior.* Hoboken, NJ: Wiley.

Tubre, T. C., & Collins, J. M. (2000). Jackson and Schuler (1985) revisited: A meta analysis of the relationships between role ambiguity, role conflict and job performance. *Journal of Management, 26,* 155–169.

Chapter 2

Individuals in Organizations

In Chapter 4 we will discuss the ways in which organizational cultures bond people who share common values. But even in a very cohesive culture, organizations still are collections of individuals with their own unique personalities and attitudes. Each of us will mesh better with some personalities than with others. And while this can make the workplace more interesting, it also can make it more challenging and frustrating. In this chapter we will explore some of the key individual differences that help shape most workplaces.

Personality and Traits

We will begin by considering a big question: How did our coworkers get that way? Although the answer to this question can and has filled many books, I will be considerably more brief. First, if everyone were acting the same way, then we could say that organizational factors like culture, rules, and so on are exerting the greatest force on behavior (Tett & Burnett, 2003). But often, organizational forces leave room for considerable variety in our behavior. For example, no policy or norm may exist on how to handle disagreements, treat other coworkers, or manage employees. In these cases, employees will be more free to exhibit individual differences, and much of the time their personality will shape their behavior. Our **personality** is a collection of **traits**, which are enduring predispositions to behave in a particular way (Richmond & McCroskey, 2009). Researchers have identified traits to describe all kinds of predispositions, including assertiveness, aggressiveness, extroversion, and so on. Researchers have debated about the causes of traits (nature vs. nurture), but many believe that both factors interact to influence the development of our traits (Magnusson, 1988). A helpful way to reconcile these two factors is to consider the ways in which they interact, and the ways **nature** sets the boundaries within which **nurture** operates.

Take shyness as an example. Some of us are born with a strong predisposition to be shy, and others with a predisposition to not be heavily shy. These groups form the two extremes of the continuum with respect to the trait. For most people (the group in the middle of the continuum), the predisposition to be shy will be much more moderate. The shyness they exhibit will depend more on situational factors. In some situations they will be shy, while in others they will not. Most traits follow this profile: Some people are high on a trait, some low, and most are in a group comprised of moderately low—neutral—moderately high. To a great extent, these predispositions can be linked to brain structures that are present at birth (Beatty,

McCroskey, & Heisel, 1998; Gray, 1982). These traits influence our perception of our environment and shape the behaviors we display in response to our environment. The amount of influence the environment will have in a given situation depends on the strength of our trait. For example, if we are highly shy, the situations we are in will have less influence. We will be likely to be shy around friendly people, unfriendly people, strangers, family, and so on. In a similar fashion, if we are very low on the trait of shyness, we will exhibit a lack of shyness in a variety of situations: around strangers, friends, friendly people, less friendly people. So when will the situation have more influence on our behavior? For those who are less extreme and more moderate on a given trait, their behavior with respect to that trait will be determined more by situational factors than the trait. So if we are moderately shy, the amount of shyness we exhibit will be more dependent on the situation. Our shyness will be less consistent across situations. In some settings and with some people, we will be more shy, and in other situations we will be less shy. This is how our genetically shaped traits set the parameters within which situations will operate.

This may lead you to think that the environment will have an influence on all but our strongest traits. However, those traits which are the strongest for us (we score very high or low, and not in a moderate range) are the ones that will be most noticeable to others, and be most likely to define our personality to others. For example, consider four characteristics: friendliness, emotional stability, assertiveness, and sense of humor. Suppose we are moderate on sense of humor, assertiveness, and friendliness. Whether we exhibit these behaviors will depend highly on the situations we encounter, so our level of humor, assertiveness, and friendliness will vary from situation to situation. Because these will not necessarily be highly consistent across situations, people will not be likely to apply any of those three labels when thinking of our personality. But suppose we score very low on emotional stability (we're impulsive, may have outbursts, etc.). Because we will be more likely to display this behavior across different types of situations, to others it will define our personality more strongly than the other three characteristics. So even though different situations and environments will influence three of these four characteristics, the ones that the situation doesn't influence as much are the ones that define our personality to those who are familiar with how we act in different situations. An exception will be if people see us in only one context (such as work). Their view of us will be based solely on how we act in that context. So when we consider the collection of traits that strongly predispose our behavior (like emotional stability in the above example) and help shape our personality the most, it becomes more clear that the environment does not have a considerable impact on our personality overall, but it may play a role in how people view us if they only see us in one specific setting.

In spite of the influence of traits, we do interact with our environments. According to Magnusson (1988), we are involved in a continuous ongoing interaction with our environment. We influence our environment and our environment influences us. We interpret events in our environment and act based on those interpretations. This means that the personality we bring into our workplace will shape our perceptions of our workplace, and influence how we respond to it. In the process, we may alter our workplace, which in turn will influence our subsequent behavior. In the next section we will consider some prominent personality characteristics that interact with our workplace.

To make this review of individual differences flow more smoothly, I first will discuss traits that are more concerned with our outward behavior toward others. Following these characteristics, I will discuss characteristics related to our more inward focus on ourselves and our actions. In between these, I will discuss the ways in which emotional intelligence has both external and internal elements.

Individual Differences We Display

The "Big Five" Model

Because so many personality traits have been identified, researchers have attempted to collapse them into smaller general dimensions that can combine in various ways to form more specific traits. The most prevalent among these is known as the "**Big Five**" model and consists of the following five factors: extraversion, agreeableness, conscientiousness, emotional stability, openness to experience (Luthans, 1998). **Extraversion** involves the extent to which someone is talkative, sociable, and so on. **Agreeableness** is the extent to which someone is easy going, cooperative, and so on. **Conscientiousness** involves being dependable, hard working, and focused on achievement. **Emotional stability** is the extent to which someone is secure, and able to regulate his or her emotions. **Openness** to experience is concerned with an enjoyment of learning about new things, willingness to consider new perspectives, and so on. Notice how these five factors capture many dimensions of personality and can be combined in different ways. If you think of different types of people you know, you can imagine how they each might have a unique profile based on variations in these factors.

A considerable amount of research has examined workplace outcomes related to each of these five personality factors. In discussing outcomes, I will distinguish between intrinsic and extrinsic success (Judge & Kammeyer-Mueller, 2007). **Extrinsic success** involves tangible outcomes, such as promotions, higher salaries, more positive evaluations. **Intrinsic success** involves perceived outcomes, such as satisfaction with our job or career. Of the five personality factors in the "Big Five" model, although there have been exceptions, conscientiousness most consistently has been linked to intrinsic and extrinsic success, across different types of jobs (Judge & Kammeyer-Mueller, 2007). Even when conscientiousness was measured in childhood and work outcomes were measured later in life, it predicted intrinsic success (job and life satisfaction) (Judge, Higgins, Thoresen, & Barrick, 1999). Those who are conscientious are more apt to set goals for achievement and remain committed to them (Barrick, Mount, & Strauss, 1993). Those who are emotionally stable are more satisfied with their jobs, careers, and lives, and emotional stability also has been linked to extrinsic success (Judge & Kammeyer-Mueller, 2007). Extroversion also is positively related to extrinsic and intrinsic career success (Judge & Kammeyer-Mueller, 2007). Even when outcomes were measured 20 years after participants' sociability first was measured, sociability correlated slightly with earnings (Harrell & Alpert, 1989). The relationship between openness to experience and outcomes is inconsistent (Judge & Kammeyer-Mueller, 2007). This suggests that in some positions openness may be conducive to success, but that in other positions it may be a hindrance. The relationship between agreeableness and outcomes is more negative. It typically negatively predicts extrinsic success and is less consistently related to intrinsic success (Judge & Kammeyer-Mueller, 2007). For an example related to extrinsic success, being more agreeable was related to lower salary and job level, and fewer promotions for American and European executives (Boudreau, Boswell, & Judge, 2001).

So what can we take from these findings, many of which are inconsistent? There is enough of a pattern to suggest that conscientiousness, emotional stability, and extraversion are linked to intrinsic and extrinsic career success. This makes intuitive sense. Having high expectations and acting on them, while acting in emotionally appropriate ways and being sociable with others, tends to be valued in most positions. Being open to experience can be good, in terms of trying to learn about new ideas, but it may be problematic if one resists sticking with "the way we do things around here." And while it is easy to envision benefits of being agreeable, it is possible that those who are agreeable are not sufficiently proactive in helping their organization change and improve. They may be very worthy employees who stay at a particular level, but when we define success as salary increases and promotions, they might not appear to be as successful.

Given the benefit of extroversion and the fact that this book is focused on communication behavior, we now will focus on the extent to which individuals are predisposed to communicate often or reluctantly.

Willingness to Communicate

Our **willingness to communicate** is our "predisposition to initiate communication with others" (Richmond & McCroskey, 2009, p. 71). People who are outgoing and talkative have a high willingness to communicate, while those who exhibit shy behavior are considerably less willing to communicate. At least in the American workplace (and culture in general), a low willingness to communicate can be problematic. We may mistakenly assume that a quiet person is less knowledgeable or that the person don't like those around them. In fact, there are a few reasons someone may be less willing to communicate that have little to do with either of these assumptions. Instead, they involve additional traits. As each of these are covered, remember that we are referring to a consistently low willingness to communicate, and not those times when we all occasionally exhibit shy or quiet behavior.

One explanation for a low willingness to communicate is **introversion**, which is at the other end of the continuum from extraversion. Although introversion is associated with shy and quiet behavior, it actually is about how sensitive individuals are to sensory stimuli. Sensory stimuli might be sounds, noises, other people. For example, introverts likely will notice the leaky faucet, while extroverts may not. Introverts become physiologically aroused more easily from sensory stimuli, while extroverts are much slower to experience the same arousal. So to maintain optimal (moderate) arousal levels, introverts may avoid stimuli in some situations, while extroverts may seek out more stimuli. To translate these differences into the kinds of communication behavior we observe, consider an example. Imagine heading into a meeting with about 12 people sitting around a conference table. Prior to the meeting, people are hanging out and socializing. An introvert will be perceptive of more stimuli in this environment than an extrovert. The introvert may notice the conversations, the noise of one person removing lunch from a bag, an overhead light that is flickering just slightly, one person tapping his pencil on the table, another person flipping through a book, another texting, another on the phone. To a person who is picking up on all of this, it is a lot to take in. An extrovert will not be as sensitive to all of this. The room may seem quiet, with not much going on. So how does all of this relate to behavior? The extrovert will want to seek people out, and therefore will be more outgoing, talkative, and exhibit the kinds of behaviors we associate with extroverts. And introverts will display introverted behavior, by keeping to themselves, being less outgoing and sociable. But notice how these behaviors are based on physiological arousal, and not on the person's feelings toward others.

A different factor that can explain a low willingness to communicate is **communication apprehension,** or the "fear or anxiety associated with real or anticipated communication" (Richmond & McCroskey, 2009, p. 73). Notice that this fear is associated with real or anticipated communication. Most of us have experienced at least some communication apprehension, whether we were nervous about a speech, awkward conversation, or other situations. We may have been nervous both before and during the event. But those who consistently experience this fear or anxiety across different situations and with different types of people experience communication apprehension as a trait. It can be hard to appreciate this if we do not have this anxiety, but to these highly apprehensive people, the fear of communication is just as real and legitimate as the fear others have of snakes, spiders, and other things. For these people, jobs requiring a great deal of communication can be difficult, and these individuals may gravitate toward positions that do not require as much interaction with others. It is important to point out that communication apprehension is not related to intelligence and does not mean that a person is quiet because of negative feelings toward another person. Therefore it would be a mistake to assume that a person who consistently is quiet with others is less intelligent or that he or she dislikes others.

Individuals also may be less willing to communicate because of a lack of **self-perceived communication competence** (McCroskey & McCroskey, 1988). This does not mean that they actually are less competent, just that they perceive themselves to be less competent. For those with this perception, it makes sense that they would not be eager to spend a considerable amount of their time talking with others.

So what conclusions should you draw about why your friend, family member, or coworker always is quiet? Because you only are observing outward behavior, it would be premature to "diagnose" someone as being introverted, highly apprehensive, or having a lack of self-perceived competence. Various questionnaires are used to more accurately assess why someone exhibits shy behavior. But you can realize that this quiet behavior is not necessarily related to intelligence. You also should notice that pushing these people to communicate more is not likely to increase their willingness to communicate (it may have the opposite effect). Instead, you can realize that quiet people may be more comfortable communicating in environments that are not sensory rich or "busy." It also can help to have established a good working relationship with the person, which could help reduce the person's anxiety and/or give him or her greater confidence to communicate with you.

At this point we will transition to some orientations that can have implications for our success in organizations.

Organizational Orientations

There are many ways to classify employees, and if you do a web search, you will find that they often come with cute names. However, they often are meaningless, in the sense that, rather than being supported by research, they exist to attract clients for organizational consultants. However, a set of orientations identified by Presthus (1962) has been validated by researchers (Goodboy & McCroskey, 2008; McCroskey, McCroskey, & Richmond, 2005; McCroskey, Richmond, Johnson, & Smith, 2004; Pruden, 1973). Although this group of orientations has not received much research attention over the years, between the validation they've received and the fact that they resonate with employees who recognize these types in their organizations, it is worthwhile to briefly discuss each of the three orientations: upward mobiles, indifferents, and ambivalents. According to Presthus (1962), these orientations represent how people adjust to bureaucratic organizations.

Upward Mobiles

These employees have a positive orientation to work and to their organization. Upward mobiles have high morale and job satisfaction, show deference to their superiors, and are eager to help the organization succeed (Tosi, Mero, & Rizzo, 2000). Richmond and McCroskey (2009) suggest that upward mobiles may be less tolerant of those who are not as focused on helping the organization, or in other words, "people they consider to be 'losers' " (p. 83). According to Richmond and McCroskey, communication with upward mobiles is fairly straightforward, in the sense that they predictably are focused on helping the organization succeed. It can be helpful to communicate with them by framing things in terms of how something benefits the organization.

Indifferents

Compared to upward mobiles, indifferents have a different outlook in the sense that they are in it solely for the paycheck (Richmond & McCroskey, 2009; Tosi, Mero, & Rizzo, 2000). Presthus (1962) suggests that the majority of employees are indifferents and that for them, work is a means to achieving resources to make their time away from work more satisfying. According to Tosi et al. (2000), they are more focused on leisure, do not consider their job to be a meaningful part of their life, tend to be alienated at work and not committed to the organization, and are withdrawn psychologically from their organizations. Still, they can contribute meaningfully to the organization and may do a perfectly good job in their position. According to Richmond & McCroskey (2009), communication with indifferents is best centered around life outside of work (family, leisure, etc.), and not the kinds of things you would discuss with an upward mobile.

Ambivalents

These employees are less predictable than upward mobiles and indifferents. Their adjustment to organizations is more dysfunctional, and they are thought to be introverted, anti-authority, and are likely to feel that the organization gets in the way of allowing them to accomplish their work (Pruden, 1973). As a result, ambivalents often will be highly critical of the organization (Richmond & McCroskey, 2009). Yet because they can be highly skilled and reach accomplishments on their own, at other times they may be content. This lack of consistency can be frustrating for their coworkers. According to Richmond & McCroskey (2009), the safest topic of discussion with ambivalents is criticism of the organization, and anything else you say may be used against you the next time they are venting to someone.

Research findings have tended to confirm these orientations as outlined by Presthus (1962). Upward mobiles are more likely to have a higher rank and be satisfied with their job, while being less alienated (Pruden, 1973), be viewed as more credible by coworkers (McCroskey et al., 2004; McCroskey et al., 2005), less manipulative (Machiavellian), and more nonverbally expressive (immediate) (Goodboy & McCroskey, 2008). Indifferents and ambivalents tend to be more alienated (Pruden, 1973), less satisfied with their job (Goodboy & McCroskey, 2008; McCroskey et al., 2004), and viewed as less credible by coworkers (McCroskey et al., 2004; McCroskey et al., 2005) and more manipulative, or Machiavellian (Goodboy & McCroskey, 2008). One area of difference is that ambivalents are likely to hold a higher rank within the organization than indifferents (Pruden, 1973).

Although the literature on these orientations is limited, it consistently points to the ways in which upward mobiles exhibit healthier adjustment to their organizations than ambivalents or indifferents. McCroskey, McCroskey, and Richmond (2005) suggest three additional orientations might be worth considering: authoritarian personality, achievement orientation, and Machiavellianism. We will cover these below.

Authoritarian Personality

According to Richmond & McCroskey (2009), **authoritarians** are oriented to structure and rules. They respect hierarchy and expect others to follow suit. If they are in a position of power, they expect others to recognize their authority and do as they say. And in turn, they respect the authority figures above them. As a result, it is best not to resist authoritarians, as they may have trouble accepting your resistance constructively (Richmond & McCroskey, 2009). The key with them is to respect the chain of command and their authority.

Machiavellianism

Why do some of our coworkers always seem to get their way? This trait is named after Nicoli Machiavelli, who in his book *The Prince* outlined how one could become a leader using a variety of tactics that many would consider to be manipulative. The term "**Machiavellian**" has come to represent the type of person who is willing to manipulate others in order to get what he or she wants. It should be of no surprise that Machiavellians (high machs) demonstrate less ethical behavior in organizations (Hegarty & Sims, 1978; Mudrack, 1993). High machs are less likely to engage in organizational citizenship behaviors that benefit their organization, but they will engage in citizenship behaviors that benefit coworkers (Becker & O'Hair, 2007). The reason for this is that they are motivated in part by impression management (Christie & Geis, 1970), and helping coworkers helps them make a good impression on others, that they then can manipulate for personal gains (Becker & O'Hair, 2007). High machs actually are flexible communicators (Martin, Anderson, & Thweatt, 1998) and are able to use a variety of strategies to achieve their goals (Grams & Rogers, 1990).

So on one hand, we have someone who will be highly manipulative. On the other hand, these individuals are skilled socially and often make good impressions. This leads to the question of how we can spot the high machs in our organizations. According to Richmond and McCroskey (2009), it will be easier to spot a moderately high mach than a high mach. They suggest that the moderately high mach will have manipulative tendencies, but not be as effective as high machs, so their manipulation will be easier to spot. In contrast, high machs are harder to spot. Richmond and McCroskey (2009) suggest looking for the following "symptoms":

> They seem to get what they want without being pushy, they get people to do things for them that those people would not do for others, they rarely look as if they are manipulating, they generally are well liked by others in the organization, and they usually do well in the organizational environment.
>
> (p. 87)

Richmond and McCroskey (2009) also raise the issue of how we should communicate with these people who manage to get what they want, while still being friendly and well-liked. Their advice, in a nutshell, is to be careful and when possible, delay. In being careful they suggest making sure all details are ironed out, and that you make sure what you are doing is in your best interest. The benefit of delaying is that the high mach simply may move on to another "target."

We now will explore an additional element of personality that can help explain success in the workplace.

Proactive Personality

Those who are highly **proactive** "identify opportunities and act on them, show initiative, and persevere until they bring about meaningful change" (Seibert, Crant, & Kraimer, 1999, p. 417). It can be thought of as a combination of conscientiousness and extroversion (Judge & Kammeyer-Mueller, 2007). Rather than reacting to their organization, these individuals help lead change by addressing problems, helping transform the organization's missions, and in general try to have an impact on their organization. They are more likely to seek job and organizational information, seek mentors, and demonstrate persistence when faced with career obstacles (Seibert et al., 1999). Later in this book I will discuss the importance of taking initiative, and in essence I will be recommending that you be as proactive in your workplace as possible, as being proactive is linked to a number of positive workplace outcomes. It is positively related to job performance (Crant, 1995) and involvement in community service activity (Bateman & Crant, 1993). Proactive employees also establish quality relationships with supervisors and experience greater job satisfaction (Li, Liang, & Crant, 2010). They also engage in more organizational citizenship behaviors, which are behaviors that are not formally required or rewarded, but nonetheless benefit the organization and its members (Li, Liang, & Crant, 2010). Being proactive is positively related to innovation and career initiative, which in turn influence salary growth, earnings, promotions, and career satisfaction (Seibert, Kraimer, & Crant, 2001).

Achievement orientation is somewhat similar to proactive personality, though it does not appear that researchers have compared the two. High achievers work hard not for the organization, but to fulfill their own personal goals (though the organization often will benefit from their efforts) (Richmond & McCroskey, 2009). Richmond and McCroskey (2009) add that high achievers may be overworked, put too much pressure on themselves, and blame themselves too harshly when something does not work out. Their biggest challenge may be saying "no" to more work, and avoiding taking on too much work or responsibility. Given this possibility, Richmond and McCroskey (2009) suggest that when communicating with high achievers, it is best to use praise and to take care to help them avoid taking on more work than they can handle. We now will turn our attention to a type of person who uses very different means to pursue success in organizations. We now will explore a more general orientation toward communication that can help explain success in the workplace.

Sociocommunicative Orientation

What different communication styles do people have? Researchers have offered a variety of models, but one of the most useful focuses on our **sociocommunicative orientation** and style (Richmond & Martin, 1998). Sociocommunicative orientation is how we view our own communication, while sociocommunicative style is how others view our communication. To keep things simple, from this point forward, I will use the label SCS in this section. Our SCS comprises two dimensions: *assertiveness* and *responsiveness*. Assertiveness involves making requests, standing up for ourselves, and keeping others from taking advantage of us, all without taking advantage of others (Richmond & McCroskey, 2009). Responsiveness is when we are focused on others in interactions, are aware of others' thoughts, feelings, and communicate accordingly (Richmond & McCroskey, 2009). SCS also involves what has been labeled *versatility* or *flexibility*, which is the ability to adjust our style and adapt to different communication situations (Richmond & McCroskey, 2009). For example, when directing others we may need to assert ourselves strongly, but then switch to responsiveness if someone expresses a concern. Those who are less versatile are more likely to struggle to adapt as smoothly to different types of communication demands.

When we consider the ways assertiveness and responsiveness can intersect, we can see four distinct communication styles, each of which has been identified by Richmond and McCroskey (2009). Although we tend to fall into a style, it is possible to exhibit other styles. So if you recognize yourself as falling into one style, it does not mean that you are incapable of demonstrating other styles. *Drivers* (high assertiveness, low responsiveness) are comfortable directing others and asserting themselves. According to Richmond and McCroskey (2009), they may bee seen as pushy, dominating, strong willed, and decisive. Often they will be well suited for leadership roles which involve directing and delegating to others. *Amiables* (low assertiveness, high responsiveness) are other-oriented and well suited for positions in which they can serve, support, and help others. *Analyticals* (low assertiveness, low responsiveness) are less outgoing and more withdrawn than other types, and may be well suited for technical positions, such as engineering. Although their communication skills may not impress others, these individuals may benefit by focusing more on their task than on communicating with others. *Expressives* (high assertiveness, high responsiveness) are considered to be skilled communicators thanks to their ability to balance different types of skills. But Richmond and McCroskey (2009) argue that, rather than focusing on any one style as "the best," it is more worthwhile to appreciate the need to be flexible with our styles. So in some situations, being a driver might be ideal, while in others, being amiable or analytical might be advantageous. Just from reading this chapter, you can envision the type of versatility needed to communicate with diverse personality types, such as ambivalents, high achievers, those who are less willing to communicate, extroverts, Machiavellians, indifferents, those who are less conscientious or emotionally stable, and so on. Because of the importance of being able to demonstrate various styles, if you are less comfortable with a given style, it may be worthwhile to practice employing it, using the skill practice recommendations I outlined in Chapter 1.

We now move on to an individual difference that involves some external behavior and also internally focused ability.

Bridging the Gap Between External and Internal

Emotional Intelligence

Although it had been discussed by researchers, the concept of **emotional intelligence** (EI) moved beyond the academic realm and burst onto the scene with Daniel Goleman's (1995) popular book *Emotional Intelligence*. Since then, scholars have tried to define and measure emotional intelligence, and to sort through the claims that EI is a cure-all for everything. Reviewing research on emotional intelligence is difficult for a few reasons. First, it has been defined in different ways. More important, because many measures exist, and no specific measure has gained prominence, it is difficult to compare the results of research articles in which different measures of emotional intelligence were used. Below I've attempted to outline some of the most useful aspects of emotional intelligence.

Zeidner, Matthews, and Roberts (2004) suggest that the most widely accepted definition of emotional intelligence is "the ability to monitor one's own and others' emotions, to discriminate among them, and to use the information to guide one's thinking and actions" (Salovey & Mayer, 1990, p. 189). Mayer and Salovey (1997) suggest that there are four elements of emotional intelligence: *perceiving emotions* (our own and others'), **using emotions** to guide our thinking, **understanding** how emotions operate, and **managing** our emotions to pursue goals. Each element involves a set of tasks that range from relatively easy to relatively difficult. *Perceiving emotions* involves being able to identify how we are feeling in general, as well as being able to identify emotions in other people. More advanced skills in this area involve being able to express emotions accurately, and to assess between others' honest dishonest expressions of emotion (whether someone is faking an emotion). In the area of *using emotions to guide thinking,* easier tasks might involve using emotions to direct our attention to important information, while more complicated emotional tasks might involve altering our mood to respond more appropriately to issues or problems. For example, a more emotionally intelligent person may be more likely to decide to not handle a disagreement until he or she has calmed down, while others might not be so thoughtful with respect to their anger. Basic tasks related to *understanding emotions* may begin with the ability to label emotions appropriately, and then to recognize what the presence of certain emotions may mean. More advanced abilities may involve being able to navigate sometimes competing feelings (love and hate) or blends of feelings (jealousy and affection). At the more advanced level, individuals also can recognize transitions from one emotion to a different emotion. Easier abilities related to *emotional management* include being open to experiencing different types of feelings (positive and negative), and range to more advanced abilities like the skill of monitoring our emotions and the role they play in our interactions. The most advanced ability involved with this element is the skill of managing emotions in ourselves and others.

To appreciate the value of emotional intelligence in the workplace, consider this very brief survey of the emotional demands we may face at work: stress from coworkers, deadlines, setbacks, not knowing how something will work out, dealing with the stress your coworkers are experiencing; competition for resources, trying to persuade others, adjusting to the culture, or taking orders from a supervisor or other coworkers. The ability to recognize emotions, use them when making decisions, understand emotions, and regulate emotions (ours and others') can help us navigate these situations more effectively. Therefore, it is no surprise that emotional intelligence is associated with many positive workplace outcomes, including some of the following: greater pay raises, higher rank, higher peer and supervisor ratings of interpersonal facilitation (think "people person") (Lopes, Grewal, Kadis, Gall, & Salovey, 2006); advancement and organizational achievement (Dulewicz & Higgs, 1998); positive work attitudes and altruistic behavior (Carmeli, 2003); the ability to cope with workplace stress (Oginska-Bulik, 2005); and transformational leadership (Gardner & Stough, 2002).

We now will shift our focus to two individual differences that are related to how we perceive ourselves and our environment.

Individual Differences in Our Internal Focus

Core Self-Evaluations

There are a number of traits that explain our evaluations of ourselves. According to Judge and Hurst (2007):

> **Core self-evaluations** is a broad concept representing the fundamental evaluations that people make about themselves and their functioning in their environment. Individuals with positive core self-evaluations appraise themselves in a consistently positive manner across situations; such individuals see themselves as capable, worthy, and in control of their lives. Individuals with negative core self-evaluations, in contrast, tend to view themselves as less worthy than others, dwell on their failures and deficiencies, and see themselves as victims of their environment.
>
> (p. 159)

Judge, Locke, and Durham (1997) suggest that there are four traits that primarily form the core of our self-evaluations (see Table 2.1): *self-esteem*, generalized *self-efficacy*, *emotional stability*, and *locus of control*. *Self-esteem* is the value we place

Table 2.1 Core Self-Evaluations

Self-esteem	The value we place on ourselves. High self-esteem means we have a healthy sense of our self-worth.
Self-efficacy	Our sense that we can cope, perform, and accomplish meaningful things. High self-efficacy means we believe we can succeed at something.
Emotional Stability	Being emotionally secure. High emotional stability means we are emotionally steady and do not experience excessive mood swings.
Locus of Control	Our belief of whether we can exert control over various aspects of our lives.

on ourselves, or our self-worth (Judge et al., 1997). *Self-efficacy* is our ability to "cope, perform, and be successful" (Judge et al., 1997, p. 80). The higher our sense of efficacy, the more we expect that we will be able to succeed. *Emotional stability* involves being emotionally secure and steady. *Locus of control* is the extent to which individuals believe they can exert control over various aspects of their lives. One's locus of control can fall on a continuum from highly external to highly internal. Someone with an external locus of control will believe that he or she has little control over events in his or her life. It is out of her hands, and she can do little about it. He was fired because the boss had it in for him. Or others may have failed to do their part of the project sufficiently, and he was blamed for it. Either way, it is not this person's fault. Things happened because of events beyond his control. A person with an internal locus would see herself as having much greater control over events. She was fired because she made some mistakes on a major project. She should have done a few things differently. If others didn't deliver on their part of the project, she should have followed up more aggressively with them, as it was within her power to do so.

An internal locus of control can be problematic when one assumes he can control things that are beyond his control. The person can put too much pressure on his shoulders. In my professional experience, I also have noticed problems related to an external locus of control. If a person does not believe she can control events, then when the person makes a mistake, in her mind, it is because of external factors (others didn't do their part; the supervisor was not supportive enough, etc.). By placing all of the responsibility on external factors and denying personal responsibility, in addition to annoying coworkers, she is depriving herself of an opportunity to learn from mistakes that may have been made. If she did not make any mistakes (in her mind), then there is no need to learn from mistakes. And if she doesn't learn from mistakes, she may repeat them. However, when they are repeated, in her mind they will not be her fault. This can be a vicious cycle that frustrates coworkers and keeps the person with the external locus of control from moving beyond mistakes and growing as an employee.

Research on these four variables together (higher esteem, self-efficacy, emotional stability, internal locus of control) suggests that those with a more positive core self-evaluation are more satisfied with their jobs (Judge & Bono, 2001), a finding that has been replicated across cultures (Judge, van Vianen, & De Pater, 2004). According to Judge and Hurst (2007), those with more positive core self-evaluations view events in their workplace in more positive ways. For example, they may view obstacles as less substantial and imposing, and therefore experience less stress from them, and be more likely to believe that they can overcome them. This may happen in part because these individuals choose to pursue goals that are more personally meaningful to them. Beyond liking their jobs, having a more positive core self-evaluation is positively related to job performance (Judge & Bono, 2001), likely because individuals are more motivated to be persistent on tasks (Erez & Judge, 2001). In addition, they are more likely to respond positively to feedback they receive on their performance (Bono & Colbert, 2005). Because of this positive outlook, those with a positive core self-evaluation also are better able to recover from the loss of a job (Wanberg, Glomb, Song, & Sorenson, 2005). Over time, the benefits of having a positive core self-evaluation may continue to grow. Those who respond positively to their jobs may experience greater success and rewards, which in turn will increase their positive reaction to work, leading to further success, and what Fredrickson (1998) calls "upward spirals." This also means that those with less positive core evaluations could experience negative spirals in the opposite direction. Judge and Hurst (2008) found evidence for this example of the "Matthew Effect" (the rich get richer, the poor get poorer). Those with positive core self-evaluations experience early career success that led to steeper career growth over time. They pursued more education and maintained better health. Those with more negative core self-evaluations "acquired education more slowly, which affected growth in pay, occupational status, and job satisfaction. They also experienced a steep rise in health problems that interfered with work, compromising growth in pay and job satisfaction" (Judge & Hurst, 2008, p. 858). This body of research suggests the importance of having a sufficiently high self-esteem, sense of self-efficacy, emotional stability, and internal locus of control. Near the end of this chapter I will address ways we can improve some of these aspects of our outlook.

Explanatory Style and Optimism

Many jobs can be incredibly challenging and present us with daily obstacles and setbacks we have to overcome. Lawyers will lose cases. Teachers will flop in front of students. Those that interact with the public will be very frustrated by customers. Managers will have nonresponsive, ineffective, or resistant employees. Salespeople will be rejected often. Consider sales agents who have to make cold calls, often during the evening, when others do not want to be interrupted. For every one that buys from a salesperson, ten or more may hang up or say "no." The following is an account from an insurance executive:

> Selling . . . requires persistence. It's an unusual person who can do it well and stick with it. Every year we hire five thousand new agents. We select them very carefully out of the sixty thousand people who apply. We test them, we screen them, we interview them, we give them extensive training. But half of them quit anyway in the first year. Most of those who stay on produce less and less. By the end of the fourth year eighty percent are gone. It costs more than thirty thousand dollars to hire a single agent. So we lose over seventy-five million dollars every year in hiring costs alone.
>
> (Seligman, 2006, p. 97)

Beyond the costs listed above, consider the stress experienced by individual employees and, consequently, their families. So in the face of this problem, our question is, What separates those who leave from those who succeed? This was the challenge faced by Martin Seligman, a psychology researcher who had studied the characteristics of being helpless, and giving up. Interestingly, in his research he also found participants who were not helpless, but instead quite resilient in the face of adversity. He began to shift his focus from helplessness to resilience and in the process helped usher in a new school of psychology called "Positive Psychology." He worked with the insurance executive mentioned above to see if his measure of resilience could predict which insurance salespeople would overcome the adversity of their profession and succeed. He found that the ability to be resilient is based on how we label the setbacks and failures we experience, and the way we label events we encounter is known as *explanatory style*. Below I will discuss the elements of explanatory style that we can hear when listening to others. But if you find this interesting and want more information, or if you struggle to overcome adverse events in your own life, you should consult his book *Learned Optimism: How to Change Your Mind and Your Life*. It is an interesting read, but unlike many self-help books, it is based on a considerable amount of research and has a great deal of practical substance.

When we encounter setbacks, we explain them (at least to ourselves internally, if not to others). Our explanations have three different characteristics that help explain why we are or are not able to overcome adverse events: **permanence, pervasiveness,** and **personalization.** The first element is *permanence,* or the extent to which the problem is temporary or will continue for some time. Those who believe their problems are permanent are going to struggle considerably to overcome them, while those who think they are more temporary will have a greater sense that they can persevere. Below are some examples of permanence. When you read each, consider how easy it would be to overcome a setback when viewing it in these ways (see Table 2.2).

Notice the differences in attitudes in these columns. In the one on the right, there is at least a chance that the person will succeed, by having a better day tomorrow, by finding a way to figure out the problem, or by correcting mistakes. It might not be easy, but compared to the left column, it is worthwhile to keep trying. In addition to making negative events temporary, more optimistic people tend to see good events as permanent ("I always have a good day") while pessimists see good events as temporary ("I finally managed to have one good day").

The second element of explanatory style, *pervasiveness,* is concerned with the extent to which a problem in one area of our life affects that one area versus many

Table 2.2 Explanatory Style, Permanent vs. Temporary

Permanent	*Temporary*
"This is **never** going to work."	"I'm having a bad **day**."
"I'm **no good** at this."	"This is so hard to **figure out**."
"You are **always** making mistakes."	"You've made some mistakes **lately**."

Spotting permanence: Look for words like "always" or "never," or words that imply either: "I'm no good at math"–"no good" implies the person always will be this way.

other areas of our life. If we view a problem as pervasive, it affects many areas. Here are some examples.

A poor presentation at work may be just a glitch at work (specific) or an example of how we manage to screw everything up (very pervasive). According to Seligman, "People who make *universal* explanations for their failures give up on everything when a failure strikes in one area. People who make *specific* explanations may become helpless in that one part of their lives yet march stalwartly on in others" (2006, p. 46). Notice from the examples above that, even though those in the specific column may be tough to overcome, they're far better than the universal explanations in the left column.

Table 2.3 Explanatory Style, Universal vs. Specific

Universal	Specific
"I can't get **anything** right."	"I really gave **a poor presentation**."
"I have **no talent**."	"I'm no good at **presenting**."
"**People** make me miserable."	"My **coworkers** make me miserable."

Spotting pervasiveness: Look for words that suggest broad effects, rather than limiting the concern to one skill or area of a person's life: "anything" "everyone."

The final element of our explanatory style is *personalization*. According to Seligman, "When bad things happen, we can blame ourselves (internalize) or we can blame other people or circumstances (externalize)" (2006, p. 49). Here are some examples.

The goal should not be to just externalize all of our failures (and therefore avoid responsibility, while also making it less likely that we will learn from them), but rather to take a reasonable amount of responsibility for them, in an appropriate way. Specifically, it is important to not make our responsibility for setbacks both internal and permanent. For example, there is a difference between thinking "I'm no good at presenting" (internal & permanent) and "I really should have prepared better for my presentation" (internal & temporary). In both cases, the person is internalizing and taking responsibility. But the second example is much more reasonable because it is far less permanent. So when it comes to personalization, our goal

Table 2.4 Explanatory Style, Internal vs. External

Internal	External
"**I** really botched this project."	"This was a **hard project**."
"**I** don't present very well."	"**They** scheduled me for a bad time slot."
"**I** did not prepare enough for the presentation."	"**They** were a tough audience."

Spotting internalization: Look for people who are blaming themselves, even when they might reasonably point to at least some external circumstances.

should be to take a reasonable amount of responsibility, yet realize that the situation is not necessarily permanent. And to complement this focus, we should be willing to acknowledge reasonable elements of the situation that made it challenging. In other words, we should work to understand what we can and cannot control.

Research by Seligman and others (reviewed by Seligman, 2006) has demonstrated many areas in which having an optimistic explanatory style (particularly with respect to permanence and pervasiveness) benefits people (health, school, work, politics). Interestingly though, researchers have found that those who are pessimists are more grounded and realistic when assessing events, while optimists inflate how well things worked out or how well they did (Seligman, 2006). So while optimism will benefit people in a variety of types of jobs, Seligman is quick to acknowledge that pessimism also is important at times, particularly in positions in which the risk of failure is high. In other words, during a fire we don't want firefighters merrily saying "Oh, I'm sure things will work out on the other side of this burning building." Contrast this with jobs like sales, in which the risk of failure (one person hangs up) is minimal. We still can go on and try to sell to others. But when the consequences of failure are considerable, having some pessimism will help people do their jobs better, as long as the pessimism isn't so great that it prevents them from doing a good job.

Can Our Personality Change?

Now that we have covered several individual differences, you may feel that you want to move more toward or away from certain characteristics (or you want others to move!). This raises the question of the extent to which personality can change. In the academic world they still are sorting out this issue, but in this section I will try to provide you with some of the most useful available information.

In short, personality can change somewhat, but change typically follows certain patterns. Over long periods of time we do see change. According to Roberts and Mroczek (2008), we see the greatest amount of change between the ages of 20–40. Interestingly, most of the changes we see are in a positive direction, in that people tend to become warmer, calmer, more confident, and more responsible and socially mature. People also increase in conscientiousness and decrease in openness over time (Roberts, Walton, & Viechtbauer, 2006). Roberts, Wood, and Smith (2005) suggest that we may change over time as we invest in certain social institutions (work, marriage, family), which help change our identities. In the process, these experiences shape our personality.

Another interesting part of the personality development process is the way our early adult experiences help influence later changes in our traits. The process works like this: because of our traits, we select or seek out certain experiences more than others; in the process, the traits that are most likely to be influenced and change are the ones that led us to select these experiences in the first place (Roberts & Robins, 2004). For example, someone who is proactive will take initiative at work and likely experience many positive outcomes. These outcomes will reinforce the proactive behavior and help encourage the person to be even more proactive. So while our environment can influence our personality, that influence often is shaped by the influence our personality first exerts on our environment. This process has been demonstrated both with positive and negative behaviors. Those who experience success early in their careers are more likely to experience increases in emotional stability and conscientiousness (Roberts, Caspi, & Moffitt, 2003). Those who gained higher status as young adults experienced decreases in anxiety and increases in happiness, confidence. Those who made a strong commitment to their work worked harder over time. Conversely, those involved in negative activities at work (theft, aggression, etc.) are more likely to decrease on measures of conscientiousness and emotional stability (Roberts, Walton, Bogg, & Caspi, 2006).

So what does all of this mean? Although social science research establishes what tends to happen and there may be exceptions, available evidence suggests that our traits are fairly stable (Ludtke, Trautwein, & Huseman, 2009). When there is change in our traits, it tends to be over a long period of time, and the change we do experience tends to end up amplifying our existing traits. If we started out conscientious, we are likely to become more conscientious, and not drastically change to be far less conscientious. I recognize that there may be exceptions, and that you may know someone who seems to have changed, but the research would suggest that these changes are more exceptions than norms. Based on this, at least in terms of strong personality characteristics, we should be cautious about expecting people to change considerably. A highly aggressive person, who is aggressive across types of situations, probably will not change into a far less aggressive person, any more than you or I are likely to alter our strongest predispositions. Slight change might be possible, but in general we should focus more on how to handle people as they are, rather than expecting significant changes. This is part of the reason why it is important to be versatile with our communication style. We will encounter various types of people, and although it would be nice of them to change in order to suit our needs, in reality, we often will have to adjust our communication to complement their temperament (at least if we want to communicate effectively and get through to them).

The stability of our personality also suggests that an important consideration for both job seekers and employers is the extent to which individuals are a good fit for the positions they hold and the tasks they are asked to do. For example, while the aggressive tendencies I mentioned above probably won't play well in a Hallmark store, on a football field or hockey rink they will be celebrated. Being pushy might be a turnoff in many professions, but in the field of sales, it may lead many to success. So ideally, there will be a good match between individuals and organizations and job assignments, or what researchers call a good person–organization fit (Ryan & Kristof-Brown, 2003).

I respect that you still might be wondering whether anything can be done to help ourselves or others change. To explore this possibility, it might be helpful to ditch the idea of wholesale personality change and instead focus on the idea of learning to do things differently. After all, we don't really need to turn an aggressive person into a "doormat," we just need that person to conduct himself or herself with less aggression in the workplace, or at least when dealing with us. We need the person to see that there are alternative ways to behave and then choose a better alternative. Or if we are the ones who would like to change, we can consider alternative ways we might approach situations. The trick isn't to change personality, just modify some of the negative tendencies within an individual's that may cause problems in the workplace (Hogan, 2007). The next several chapters will provide examples of the types of behaviors that are worth learning and demonstrating in order to increase your chances of success within your workplace.

References

Barrick, M. R., Mount, M. K., & Strauss, J. P. (1993). Conscientiousness and performance of sales representatives: Test of the mediating effects of goal setting. *Journal of Applied Psychology, 78*, 715–722.

Bateman, T. S., & Crant, J. M. (1993). The proactive component of organizational behavior: A measure and correlates. *Journal of Organizational Behavior, 14*, 103–118.

Beatty, M. J., McCroskey, J. C., & Heisel, A. D. (1998). Communication apprehension as temperamental expression: A communibiological paradigm. *Communication Monographs, 65*, 197–219.

Becker, J. A. H., & O'Hair, H. D. (2007). Machiavellians' motives in organizational citizenship behavior. *Journal of Applied Communication Research, 35*, 246–267.

Bono, J. E., & Colbert, A. (2005). Understanding responses to feedback: The role of core self-evaluations. *Personnel Psychology, 58*, 171–203.

Boudreau, J. W., Boswell, W. R., & Judge, T. A. (2001). Effects of personality on executive career success in the United States and Europe. *Journal of Vocational Behavior, 58*, 53–81.

Carmeli, A. (2003). The relationship between emotional intelligence and work attitudes, behavior and outcomes: An examination among senior managers. *Journal of Managerial Psychology, 18*(8), 788–813.

Christie, R., & Geis, F. (1970). *Studies in Machiavellianism.* New York, NY: Academic Press.

Crant, J. M. (1995). The proactive personality scale and objective job performance among real estate agents. *Journal of Applied Psychology, 80*, 532–537.

Dulewicz, V., & Higgs, M. J. (1998). Emotional intelligence: Can it be measured reliably and validly using competency data? *Competency, 6*, 28–37.

Erez, A., & Judge, T. A. (2001). Relationship of core self-evaluations to goal setting, motivation, and performance. *Journal of Applied Psychology, 86*, 1270–1279.

Fredrickson, B. L. (1998). What good are positive emotions? *Review of General Psychology, 2*, 300–319.

Gardner, L., & Stough, C. (2002). Examining the relationship between leadership and emotional intelligence in senior level managers. *Leadership & Organization Development Journal, 23*, 68–78.

Goleman, D. P. (1995). *Emotional intelligence: Why it can matter more than IQ for character, health and lifelong achievement.* New York, NY: Bantam Books.

Goodboy, A., & McCroskey J. C. (2008). Toward a theoretical model of the role of organizational orientations and Machiavellianism on nonverbal immediacy behavior and job satisfaction. *Human Communication, 11*(3), 287–302.

Grams, L. C., & Rogers, R. W. (1990). Power and personality: Effects of Machiavellianism, need for approval, and motivation on use of influence tactics. *Journal of General Psychology, 117*, 71–82.

Gray, J. A. (1982). *The neuropsychology of anxiety: An enquiry into the functions of the septo-hippocampal system.* Oxford, UK: Oxford University Press.

Harrell, T. W., & Alpert, B. (1989). Attributes of successful MBAs: A 20-year longitudinal study. *Human Performance, 2*, 301–322.

Hegarty, W., & Sims, H., Jr. (1978). Some determinants of unethical decision behavior: An experiment. *Journal of Applied Psychology, 63*(4), 451–457.

Hogan, R. (2007). *Personality and the fate of organizations.* Hillsdale, NJ: Erlbaum.

Judge, T. A., & Bono, J. E. (2001). Relationship of core self-evaluations traits—self-esteem, generalized self-efficacy, locus of control, and emotional stability—with job satisfaction and job performance: A meta-analysis. *Journal of Applied Psychology, 86*, 80–92.

Judge, T. A., Higgins, C., Thoresen, C. J., & Barrick, M. R. (1999). The Big Five personality traits, general mental ability, and career success across the life span. *Personnel Psychology,* 52, 621–652.

Judge, T. A., & Hurst, C. (2007). The benefits and possible costs of positive core self-evaluations: A review and agenda for future research. In D. Nelson & C. L. Cooper (Eds.), *Positive organizational behavior* (pp. 159–174). London, UK: Sage.

Judge, T. A., & Hurst, C. (2008). How the rich (and happy) get richer (and happier): Relationship of core self-evaluations to trajectories in attaining work success. *Journal of Applied Psychology,* 93, 849–863.

Judge, T. A., & Kammeyer-Mueller, J. D. (2007). Personality and career success. In M. Peiperl & H. Gunz (Eds.), *Handbook of career studies* (pp. 59–78). Thousand Oaks, CA: Sage.

Judge, T. A., Locke, E. A., & Durham, C. C. (1997). The dispositional causes of job satisfaction: A core evaluations approach. *Research in Organizational Behavior,* 19, 151–188.

Judge, T. A., van Vianen, A. E. M., & De Pater, I. E. (2004). Emotional stability, core self-evaluations, and job outcomes: A review of the evidence and an agenda for future research. *Human Performance,* 17, 325–346.

Li, N., Liang, J., & Crant, J. M. (2010). The role of proactive personality in job satisfaction and organizational citizenship behavior: a relational perspective. *Journal of Applied Psychology,* 95(2), 395–404.

Lopes, P. N., Grewal, D., Kadis, J., Gall, M., & Salovey, P. (2006). Evidence that emotional intelligence is related to job performance and affect and attitudes at work. *Psicothema,* 18, 132–138.

Ludtke, O., Trautwein, U., & Huseman, N. (2009). Goal and personality trait development in a transitional period: Assessing change and stability in personality development. *Personality and Social Psychology Bulletin,* 35, 428–441.

Luthans, F. (1998). *Organizational behavior.* New York, NY: McGraw-Hill.

Magnusson, D. (1988). *Individual development from an interactional perspective.* Hillsdale, NJ: Erlbaum.

Martin, M. M., Anderson, C. M., & Thweatt, K. S. (1998). Aggressive communication traits and their relationships with the cognitive flexibility scale and the communication flexibility scale. *Journal of Social Behavior and Personality,* 13, 531–541.

Mayer, J. D., & Salovey, P. (1997). What is emotional intelligence? In P. Salovey & D. Sluyter (Eds.), *Emotional development and emotional intelligence: Implications for educators* (pp. 3–31). New York, NY: Basic Books.

McCroskey, J. C., & McCroskey, L. L. (1988). Self-report as an approach to measuring communication competence. *Communication Research Reports,* 5(2), 108–113.

McCroskey, J. C., Richmond, V. P., Johnson, A. D., & Smith, H. T. (2004). Organizational orientations theory and measurement: Development of measures and preliminary investigations. *Communication Quarterly,* 52, 1–14.

McCroskey, L. L., McCroskey, J. C., & Richmond, V. P. (2005). Applying organizational orientations theory to employees of profit and non-profit organizations. *Communication Quarterly,* 53, 21–40.

Mudrack, P. E. (1993). An investigation into the acceptability of workplace behaviors of a dubious ethical nature. *Journal of Business Ethics,* 12, 517–524.

Oginska-Bulik, N. (2005). Emotional intelligence in the workplace: Exploring its effects on occupational stress and health outcomes in human service workers. *International Journal of Occupational Medicine & Environmental Health,* 28(2), 167–175.

Presthus, V. (1962). *The organizational society.* New York, NY: Vintage.

Pruden, H. O. (1973). The upward mobile, indifferent, and ambivalent typology of managers. *Academy of Management Journal,* 15, 454–464.

Richmond, V. P., & McCroskey, J. C. (2009). *Organizational communication for survival: Making work work* (4th ed.). Boston, MA: Allyn & Bacon.

Richmond, V. P., & Martin, M. M. (1998). Socio-communicative style and socio-communicative orientation. In J. C. McCroskey, J. A. Daly, M. M. Martin, & M. J. Beatty (Eds), *Communication and personality: Trait perspectives* (pp. 133–148). Cresskill, NJ: Hampton Press.

Roberts, B. W., Caspi, A., & Moffitt, T. (2003). Work experiences and personality development in young adulthood. *Journal of Personality and Social Psychology, 84,* 582–593.

Roberts, B. W., & Mroczek, D. (2008). Personality trait change in adulthood. *Current Directions in Psychological Science, 17,* 31–35.

Roberts, B. W., & Robins, R. W. (2004). A longitudinal study of person-environment fit and personality development. *Journal of Personality, 72,* 89–110.

Roberts, B. W., Walton, K., Bogg, T., & Caspi, A. (2006). De-investment in work and non-normative personality trait change in young adulthood. *European Journal of Personality, 20,* 461–474.

Roberts, B. W., Walton, K., & Viechtbauer, W. (2006). Patterns of mean-level change in personality traits across the life course: A meta-analysis of longitudinal studies. *Psychological Bulletin, 132,* 1–25.

Roberts, B. W., Wood, D., & Smith, J. L. (2005). Evaluating five factor theory and social investment perspectives on personality trait development. *Journal of Research in Personality, 39,* 166–184.

Ryan, A. M., & Kristof-Brown, A. L. (2003). Personality's role in person-organization fit: Unresolved issues. In M. Barrick & A. M. Ryan (Eds.), *Personality and work* (pp. 262–288). San Francisco, CA: Jossey-Bass.

Salovey, P. & Mayer, J. D. (1990). Emotional intelligence. *Imagination, Cognition, and Personality, 9,* 185–211.

Seibert, S. E., Crant, J. M., & Kraimer, M. L. (1999). Proactive personality and career success. *Journal of Applied Psychology, 84*(3), 416–427.

Seibert, S. E., Kraimer, M. L. , & Crant, J. M. (2001). What do proactive people do? A longitudinal model linking proactive personality and career success. *Personnel Psychology, 54*(4), 845–874.

Seligman, M. E. (2006). *Learned optimism: How to change your mind and your life.* New York: Random House.

Tett, R. P., & Burnett, D. D. (2003). A personality trait-based interactionist model of job performance. *Journal of Applied Psychology, 88,* 500–517.

Tosi, H. L., Mero, N. P., & Rizzo, J. R. (2000). *Managing organizational behavior.* Hoboken, NJ: Wiley.

Wanberg, C. R., Glomb, T. M., Song, Z., & Sorenson, S. (2005). Job-search persistence: A time series investigation. *Journal of Applied Psychology, 90,* 411–430.

Zeidner, M., Matthews G., & Roberts, R (2004). Emotional intelligence in the workplace: A critical review. *Applied Psychology: An International Review, 53,* 371–399.

Chapter 3

Networking

Over the years, I have learned many things from my students, and it was one of my students who taught me a great deal about the benefits of networking. One day a couple of years into my teaching career, a graduating senior (I'll call him "Tom") stopped by my office and during our discussion he mentioned how he was trying to decide between a few different job offers. This sparked my interest, because I did not think he would be the type of student to have several job offers before graduation. He was a good guy, and was outgoing and friendly, but he was not one of my strongest students. His grades consistently were in the B range. When I asked him how he set himself up with these opportunities, without hesitation he said "a lot of networking." He proceeded to discuss different people he had met, and how he had tried to make connections with different people related to his interests.

One of Tom's classmates took a different approach (I'll call her "Angie"). Angie focused on her in-class work, and in that arena she was very successful, earning grades mostly in the A range. She also was a good person, and if I had my own business and a position that fit her qualifications, I would have hired her with enthusiasm. However, she did little to network outside of class, and as graduation approached, she did not have many promising job leads. She eventually was hired after graduation, but not in an area closely related to her interests. A few years later she still was unhappy with her position, and emailed me for ideas on alternatives (she since has found a position that is a better fit for her). I would be oversimplifying the situation if I attributed the difference between these students entirely to networking. Tom was at an advantage because early on he knew of a general profession within which he wanted to work, while Angie was much less sure. He was more able to target his job search. But in spite of the many possible causes of these different outcomes, to me this was an example of the importance of **networking,** and since that time I have tried to teach students about the importance of building their personal networks. When I encounter friends and former students who are professionals, networking is one of the things they stress first and foremost. Therefore, this chapter will discuss various aspects of networks, as well as the process of networking.

What Do We Know About Networks?

Small World Experiments

Researchers have helped us learn many fascinating things about networks, and perhaps the best-known idea is the concept of six degrees of separation. Although researcher Stanley Milgram (1967) never used this term, his **"small world"** experiments helped introduce the general concept to the public. In an attempt to study just how connected we are with other strangers in the world, he asked residents of two Midwest cities (Omaha, NE, and Wichita, KS) to send a folder containing a document to a stranger in Massachusetts. Milgram purposely chose to start the chain in areas that were distant and demographically different from Massachusetts. The document the participants were asked to send contained the name of the target person, along with information about him. It also outlined the rules, which directed participants to deliver the folder by contacting a personal acquaintance whom he or she knew on a first-name basis who "is more likely than you to know the target person" (p. 64). The folder also contained a roster on which each person who helped send the letter recorded his or her name (so the researchers would know how many people it took to get the letter to its destination). The results indicated that it took between two to ten people (not counting the initial sender and the final recipient) to deliver the folder, with six being the most common number of individuals needed. This tends to be what is most remembered from Milgram's research. Less coverage is given to the additional finding that only 44 of 160 chains (27%) were completed successfully. The remaining 116 folders never reached their destination. Other studies have observed similar results: the average chain length is six to seven people, but only small percentages of chains ever are completed (Goel, Muhamad, & Watts, 2009).

From this we can conclude that in some conditions, we are separated by others by just a few degrees. Goel et al. (2009) suggest two important conditions that may influence the length and completion of chains. The first is belief about the task. If a person believes she can successfully use the network, she may be more likely to continue trying to deliver the message. In addition, some people simply may use better strategies to get a message through the network. This suggests that we should explore attitudes toward networking and the strategies people use to network. We will examine each of these in the second half of the chapter, but first there are additional aspects of networks that we should consider.

Networking and Job Hunting

On average, how are we more likely to find out about jobs that might be good for us: through employment agencies, by contacting organizations directly, or through personal contacts? You probably won't be surprised to know that we are more likely to get a job through a personal contact (Granovetter, 1995). Mark Granovetter (1995) found that the majority of applicants (55%) found out about their jobs via personal contacts, while 18% used formal approaches and 18% used direct application (the remaining were in a "miscellaneous" category). Those who found jobs through personal contacts also were more likely to be very satisfied with their jobs. Granovetter (1995) summarized the results as follows:

> Personal contacts are of paramount importance in connecting people with jobs. Better jobs are found through contacts, and the best jobs, the ones with the highest pay and prestige and affording the greatest satisfaction to those in them, are most apt to be filled in this way.
>
> (p. 22)

Given the general familiarity with the phrase, "It's not what you know, it's who you know," the above results and conclusion probably aren't very surprising. But among our personal contacts (people who are linked or "tied" to us in our network), who is most likely to provide us with new and useful information, such as that about new jobs: our closest friends and relatives (strong ties), or more distant acquaintances with whom we rarely interact (weak ties)? In the same study discussed above, Granovetter found that, of the respondents who learned of their jobs from contacts, only 16.7% gained the information from a close contact (the "often" category), while the majority were informed by weaker contacts (55.6% learned from those they saw "occasionally" and 27.8 from those they saw "rarely"). In other words, respondents were more likely to learn of a job from those they saw occasionally, or even once a year or less (*weak ties*) than they were from those closest to them (*strong ties*). In addition, the weak ties were more likely to "put in a good word" for the job-seekers. These findings suggest that, when it comes to getting a job, casual acquaintances may be more valuable to us than our closest contacts. More recent research (Brown & Konrad, 2001) also found that those who used weaker ties were more likely to obtain a job and earn higher salaries than those who used stronger ties.

Granovetter (1973) came to label this idea as the **"Strength of Weak Ties,"** and this perspective has been an important contribution to our understanding of networks and how they operate. But why might it be better to rely on weak ties than strong ones when looking for a job? First, consider the connections between all of our weak ties, and then all of our strong ties. Our strong ties (closest friends) are more likely to be connected to each other, while our weak ties are less likely to be connected to each other (Granovetter, 1973). Our friends probably know some of our other friends and some of our family members. But a person we met in passing last year is not likely to be connected to someone we met in passing last week, or to other acquaintances scattered throughout our network. Our network of close contacts (strong ties) is more dense than our network of weak ties. However, each of those distant, weak ties in our network is linked to his or her own dense network of strong ties whom we probably do not know. This means that our weak ties can help link us to people we do not know and to information we do not currently possess (such as information on jobs that might be a good fit for us). Information that comes from our weak ties is new to us, but think about the information we get from our closest ties. These people live near us, work with us, and largely have access to the same people and information as we do. Therefore, in dense networks like this, the information we gain often is redundant with what we already know. We are less likely to encounter something new from our closest contacts.

The Benefits of Weak Ties: Notice that the people in each cluster are tightly connected, and therefore they're all exposed to the same information. However, if we can connect with someone who is tapped into other networks (that connection is the dotted line below), we will be exposed to more information than we would be if we didn't have that tie.

To apply these ideas more concretely, consider two fictional people, named Beth and Stacey. Assume that Beth's network consists mainly of strong ties, and Stacey's a balance of strong and weak ties (while being equal in size). Some of Beth's strong ties include her parents, boyfriend, several best friends, and a couple of her closest coworkers. It is likely that her parents, boyfriend, and best friends all know each other. Now assume that Stacey is close to her parents, a couple of best friends, and

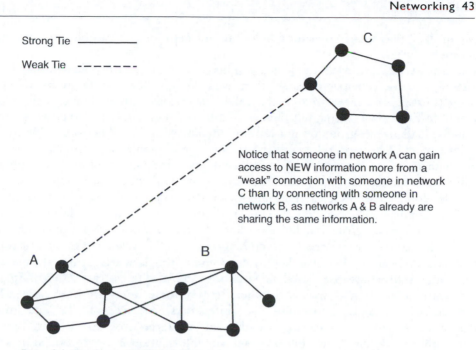

Strong Tie ——————

Weak Tie - - - - - - -

Notice that someone in network A can gain access to NEW information more from a "weak" connection with someone in network C than by connecting with someone in network B, as networks A & B already are sharing the same information.

Figure 3.1 The Strength of Weak Ties

a coworker, but also that she knows two other people who hold her job, but at different companies. She also knows three people she met at different times at the YMCA, each of whom work in different professions. Beth may benefit professionally from her close contacts, but Stacey is in a position to gain much more from her network. Each of her weak ties is tied into a network of her own, and therefore is exposed to different information. Stacey is in a better position to gain new information about different organizations and professions. To the extent that Beth and Stacey would benefit by learning about the practices of other organizations, or gaining creative ideas from other professions, Stacey would have a considerable advantage, thanks to the weak ties in her network. Furthermore, this advantage would be because of the nature of her ties, and not the size of her network. This is one way in which the nature of our network can provide us with social advantages.

Networks and Social Capital

Building on concepts like the strength of weak ties, many researchers have focused on a concept known as social capital. **Social capital** can be summarized as "the advantage created by a person's location in a structure of relationships" (Burt, 2005, p. 4). In other words, our place in a network (social structure) and the connections we possess are linked to our success in organizations and in our careers. Those who are more optimally connected to others in the network will benefit more than people whose connections are less strategically beneficial. As we've seen above, being connected to weak ties can be advantageous for us, in terms of accessing information and learning about job opportunities. Similarly, by serving as a **broker,** or "**bridge**" that spans "**structural holes**" in our network, we can benefit in several additional ways.

In a network, a structural hole is a gap between clusters of people who pay little attention to the activities of each other, even though they may be aware of each other (Burt, 2005). If we were to chart the connections among people, each group would form its own cluster, but there would be no lines connecting the two groups if individuals in one group do not talk to individuals in the other group. Structural holes may exist between different departments in an organization who have little to no contact, or between two organizations that have little to no contact. For example. within an organization, a structural hole between marketing and product research and development would mean that nobody in marketing talks to anyone in research and development. The two departments are isolated from each other. It may be even easier to recognize structural holes outside of organizations. If two organizations are not linked by any contacts, a structural hole exists. However, not every structural hole is equally important. The key to determining this is whether the information each organization possesses is redundant. For example, suppose two different Target stores are not in contact with each other. Because these stores are run in the same way and everything is uniform, these separate stores have access to the same information across stores. Therefore, if we go from one Target store to the next, we are not likely to gain much new information. The information in the second store will be redundant with the information in the first store. We will not gain new ideas on how to shelve products, on promotions we might consider running, on how to train employees, or other factors. Everything is pretty much the same. Because this information is redundant, a structural hole doesn't really exist. However, imagine that there are no connections between a local branch of Target and the local Sears. We would expect information between these two stores to be much less redundant than between the two Target stores. Sears will do several things differently than Target, so the structural hole between Target–Sears would be more valuable than the structural hole between Target–Target.

Now that we've defined structural holes, we'll consider the importance of being a "bridge" between two structural holes (see Figure 3.2). A bridge is someone who is linked to two groups, without being a member of either group. Using the examples above, a bridge between marketing and product development may herself be in human resources, or accounting, or some other department. A bridge between Target and Sears may work at Best Buy or somewhere else. Compared to people who are not bridges, bridges are likely to have more social capital because their position in the network gives them several advantages (Burt, 2005). Suppose Andrew works in the human resources department, but has at least some regular contact with acquaintances in both marketing and research and development. In contrast, Robert is a talented member of research and development who has little contact with other departments. Of these two, Andrew has access to more diverse information, as he can learn from both marketing and research and development. In addition, he will have early access to information, as he is positioned in the flow of information. He knows what is happening in human resources, marketing, and research and development. In addition, to the extent that it might be advantageous for marketing to be linked to research and development, Andrew has some control over when and how this link should be made. Also, those in marketing face different tasks and pressures

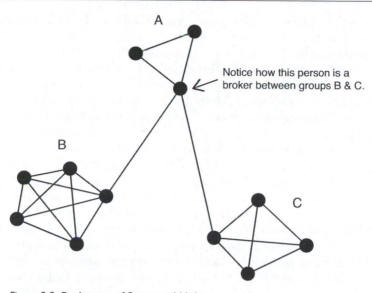

Notice how this person is a
broker between groups B & C.

Figure 3.2 Brokerage of Structural Holes

than those in research and development. And like many groups, these two likely are characterized by the use of different terminology, expressions, and so on. Andrew also is more likely to understand the different ways in which marketing and research and development operate, and the "language" they speak, enabling him to communicate effectively with each group (when others who don't speak the different "languages" might struggle to communicate with the groups). Thanks to this increased vision and access to information that bridges possess, those who bridge structural holes in networks are in a better position to have good ideas and offer creative solutions to various problems or challenges their organizations face (Burt, 2005).

As a result of these advantages, individuals whose position in a network allows them to act as bridges that span structural holes are considered to have greater social capital than those who do not span structural holes within their networks. These differences in social capital can be seen when we consider the networks of Andrew and Robert. Because he bridges a structural hole, Andrew has more social capital. He can see links between marketing and product development that others cannot see. As a result, he may develop ideas or exhibit creativity (by making connections) that otherwise would not be possible, or at least likely. In addition, Andrew will be a much more informed member of human resources than others in the department who do not bridge structural holes. His enhanced perspective can enable him to bring information and ideas to his division that may benefit his department. All of this is possible because Andrew happens to bridge a structural hole in the network by being in contact with a person in marketing and a person from product development. He has gained social capital by virtue of his place in the network.

Although the above example is hypothetical and speculative, it is supported by research conducted in organizations. Burt (2004) found **several interesting results with respect to personal networks.** First, those with more structural holes in their networks were more likely to have their ideas rated more favorably by senior managers, and less likely to have their ideas dismissed. In fact, the number of structural holes in an employee's network had a much greater impact than rank, age, and education. This points to a clear benefit of having structural holes in our network. But Burt went further. He also examined the relationship between structural holes and salary, job evaluations, and promotions. The number of structural holes was less related to salary at lower levels, but the relationship was stronger at higher levels of management (where success is more dependent on interacting with multiple groups, divisions, etc.). As one gains higher positions in an organization, his or her salary is influenced more by the extent to which his or her personal network contains structural holes. In addition, with respect to evaluations of employees, although employees in general were unlikely to be rated as "poor" for two consecutive years, those who did receive these evaluations were more likely to have networks with fewer structural holes. Employees also were unlikely to be rated as "outstanding" for two consecutive years, but those that had more structural holes in their personal networks were twice as likely to receive these positive evaluations. With respect to promotions, managers with more structural holes in their networks were much more likely to earn a promotion to a higher position (and higher salary).

To sum up, **those with more structural holes in their personal networks have several advantages over those with fewer structural holes.** Those who bridge structural holes have early access to information that others may not have, and can control the flow of that information. This information enables greater vision, and therefore our creativity and the quality of our ideas is likely to be enhanced. This translates into improved salary, employee evaluations, and likelihood of getting promoted. As we explore networking strategies later in this chapter, part of our focus will be on bridging structural holes.

With an emphasis on weak ties and staying at the boundaries of networks in order to bridge structural holes, so far this section seems to be implying that being part of a close-knit group is not very useful in professional life. However, beyond our intuitive sense that close relationships are important, they also are considered important from a network perspective. The central issue is **trust,** and the various ways in which we might earn it. The first way we can earn trust is by developing good working relationships with others, a process that will be encouraged often in this book. However, Burt (2005) outlines some disadvantages of relying on relationships as the only means of building trust in a business environment. First, the process takes time that we may not have. We have a number of exchanges with someone and over time we develop a sense of how he or she will behave. This predictability serves as a basis for our future interactions with the person. However, this process can take years (Burt, 2005), which presents a problem if we want or need to bridge the structural holes in our network. Think about how we rely on people in our network. Often, they are a shortcut that helps us save time with something. Rather than researching meticulously for a good physician, hair stylist, or other service provider, we often will ask those around us if they would recommend anyone. For example, when making their schedules, students will ask each other about different teachers. This also happens in a professional setting, but with higher stakes that require greater trust in the sources of information we gain. Therefore, it often is helpful to have a more immediate kind of trust available to us. **Close-knit closed networks** provide conditions that help develop this trust more rapidly than when we rely only on building strong relationships.

In these closed networks, we can more reliably assume that someone will behave appropriately. In more constrained, or closed networks, everyone knows everyone. As a result, if an employee misbehaves in some way, it will be evident to everyone in the close-knit group, and it will damage the person's reputation within that group. Therefore, we can be more trustful of how a person in a closed network will act than we can of someone in a more open network (where there are more holes and less scrutiny on one's actions). When a network is closed, if someone misbehaves, word will pass through the network quickly and with little cost. In a more open network (in which people are less connected and less likely to be in regular contact with each other), it is much easier for bad behavior to go undetected. Because it is less risky to trust others in densely connected groups, trust in these situations is more likely. Burt (2005) presents research evidence supporting the relationship between increased closeness in groups and increased trust between members of the groups. In addition, if we lack close connections with at least some in our network, even if we have good ideas, it may be difficult to persuade others to consider and accept them.

This brings us to the importance of striking a balance in our personal networks between close-knit closed groups and structural holes, as these network features complement each other. According to Burt (2005), bridging structural holes (what he calls **brokerage**) "provides a vision mechanism associated with achievement and rewards" while working in a relatively closed group (what he calls **closure**) "provides a reputation mechanism associated with happy and safe" (p. 127). Our close-knit groups provide us with security and enable us to develop a reputation that we cannot gain as easily when we are disconnected from a group (Burt, 2005). Bridging structural holes improves our vision of the entire network or organization, which leads to a variety of advantages. Therefore, it is in our best interest to have a personal network in which we are embedded in one or more close-knit groups, while still bridging other groups.

The importance of doing this can be understood when we consider what it would be like to have one, but not both, of these features in our network. Suppose we are an acquaintance of people in three to four different departments, but we're a relative outsider in our department (by our choice—we haven't become an outcast). Our vision of the network will be impressive, and we will be in a position to benefit from it. But who will listen to us? We have few close ties in our own department, and we're only acquaintances with the people in other departments, so there are few people to speak to our trustworthiness. We may have great suggestions, but it likely will be hard to convince others to take a chance on our ideas, because without trust in us, doing so would involve risk for others.

Conversely, consider the situation of being embedded in a close-knit group, but without having ties to outside groups. Everyone knows what everyone else is doing, so trust will come more readily (because sanctions for misbehaving would come quickly, as there is nowhere to "hide"). We will have the opportunity to build a reputation. In general, our environment will be more secure. However, we also will be more provincial or closed-off from outside groups. As a result, we will have the same information as everyone else in our group, and little more. To the extent that our goal is to display innovativeness or creativity, or to advance in the organization, we will be depriving ourselves of ways to gain these advantages elsewhere in the network.

The above issues help explain the benefit of belonging to closed groups while still bridging structural holes by connecting outside groups to each other. By being well integrated into a close-knit group, we can earn trust and develop a reputation by behaving appropriately within the group. Then as we interact with other groups and bridge structural holes between them, we will be in a position to secure valuable information and ideas. As long as we have developed a good reputation, we also will be in a position to act on them. If we have a good reputation, it will be less risky for others to follow our suggestions, adopt our ideas, and so on. Therefore, we should expect those with a balance between openness and closedness in their networks to have a professional advantage over those whose networks lack such balance.

Summary about Networks and Networking

1. It is a "small world," but connecting to just anyone requires the right strategy. Studies of degrees of separation show that people usually are not able to navigate their networks to get a letter to the right stranger. But when the right attitudes and strategies are adopted, on average, it takes six to seven contacts to reach the person (Goel et al., 2009).
2. We can benefit from having weak ties in our network, as these people are exposed to different ideas and information than we are (Granovetter, 1995).
3. In our personal networks it is in our best interest to be connected to close-knit groups but also to act as a bridge between structural holes in our network (Burt, 2005). The group will help us grow trusting relationships with others and to develop our reputation. Bridging structural holes will give us greater vision and perspective, while improving our chances of being creative by exposing us to other people, ideas, and so on.

These three claims make a strong case for the importance of strategically building our personal networks. In the final two sections of this chapter, we will explore why people often fail to take advantage of networking opportunities, and how we can build our own personal networks.

Why Don't More People Network More Often?

In my experience teaching reluctant networkers, I've encountered a few sensible reasons that people resist networking: They **don't recognize its importance, don't know how to do it,** are **uncomfortable doing it,** and/or have **personality characteristics** that don't make networking very easy for them. I briefly will cover each of these reasons.

They Don't Recognize Its Importance. It's possible that people may not know the extent to which they may benefit by networking, or they simply don't think that networking will help them. I see this all of the time with students like the one mentioned at the beginning of this chapter. Unfortunately, many people assume that it is good enough to get good grades, or to stay in their own department and diligently do good work. That is a great start, but often much more effort to build a personal network is needed. This is why much of this chapter has been devoted to providing a better understanding of how networks work. I hope by this point the benefits of building a personal network are more clear to you.

They Don't Know How. But even if we are sold on the idea of building a personal network, we may not know how to do it effectively. How do we establish weak ties, or bridge structural holes? The final section of this chapter will explore these and other issues in considerable detail.

They Feel Discomfort. We simply may be reluctant to network due to our discomfort with one or more aspects of the networking process. This might be due to negative associations with networking, such as that it involves schmoozing, or using people (perhaps we've known people who only contact us when they need something). We might not like the idea of "working a room" or making small talk with strangers just to gain some advantage. To some it may ring as "hollow" or "fake" behavior. For example, those with more positive attitudes toward workplace politics are more likely to place an emphasis on being "visible" within their organizations (Forret & Dougherty, 2004). But even if someone has little problem with the idea of networking, he may feel that he has little to offer or talk about during networking interactions. Each of these concerns will be taken into account during the discussion of networking strategies.

They Have Certain Personality Characteristics. Certain personality characteristics also may influence our comfort with networking. Recall from our discussion of willingness to communicate that some people simply are less likely to communicate in social situations, whether because of the situation, anxiety, introversion, or self-perceived communication competence. Networking situations can be intimidating because we may not know anyone else. This usually means we will have to engage in a great deal of small talk, which we may not enjoy. This process will be even worse for those who have communication apprehension or are highly introverted. This helps explain why those who are more extroverted are more likely to engage in networking behaviors than those who are more introverted (Forret & Dougherty, 2004). In addition, those with a lower self-esteem are less likely to network (Forret & Dougherty, 2004). An individual simply may not feel that he or she is very effective at small talk and networking.

De Janasz, Dowd, and Schneider (2009) identify additional reasons someone may be uncomfortable with the networking process. An individual might be reluctant to ask others for help, whether because she wants to reach a goal by herself, or because she cannot reciprocate the favor and does not want to owe the other person. And recall our discussion from Chapter 1 about the way in which our educational system emphasizes individual effort, and relying on others usually is considered cheating. Someone with this mindset would be less inclined to rely on others for help.

I will take each of the above concerns into consideration when offering networking strategies in the next section. However, at some point, individuals who are reluctant to network simply will have to work to get out of their comfort zone. Given the potential benefits we can gain from effective networking, I hope you'll agree that it can be worth the effort.

Networking Strategies

There is a lot of advice available for those wishing to improve their networking skills. Unfortunately, little in this area is supported by actual quality research. Below I've done my best to offer strategies that are grounded in what we have learned from research about networks, and that reflect the realities that may cause people to be reluctant to network.

Dimensions of Networking

In their study of networking within an organization, Forret and Dougherty (2004) identified *five* dimensions of networking. *Maintaining contact* involved things like giving business cards to contacts, and following up with contacts periodically. *Socializing* involved attending social functions, and engaging in activities like golf. *Professional activities* involved things like attending professional conferences. Another category involved *participating in community activities,* such as church or local civic groups. Finally, *internal visibility* involved accepting new work assignments that increased one's visibility, and engaging in activities like going to lunch with a supervisor. More recent research by Wolff and Moser (2009) distinguishes between building and maintaining contacts, and distinguishes between internal and external contacts (internal or external to the organization). This section will focus first on how develop contacts, giving special attention to those seeking jobs. Then we will discuss ways to maintain our contacts.

But before we explore specific strategies, it is important to discuss an **attitude** with which one might want to approach the networking process. Skills involve specific steps which can be hard to remember or to treat as a one-size-fits-all approach. Unfortunately, our educational system often emphasizes facts and specific steps over attitude. But attitude involves a way to view the process. As we discuss ways to network, I encourage you to focus more on attitude than specific strategies. Then if you're not sure what to do, you at least can stay consistent with the overall attitude.

So what kind of attitude should you develop when approaching networking? Well, consider the problematic attitudes shared by those who are reluctant to network: "It involves using people;" "it is better to achieve things on our own;" "I don't have anything to offer people." Or consider the attitude of networkers who might turn others off: "I want to meet as many people as possible," or "I will contact people who can help me when they can help me." The networking attitude I suggest is not based on research, but it is inspired by many of the things that prevent us from networking. I will keep it fairly simple, as I think the networking process can be made easier if you focus on *two* key dimensions: (1) **having an interest in meeting and learning about others**, and (2) **having an interest in helping others** out.

The first dimension of a healthy networking attitude is a genuine interest in meeting others and learning about them. This boils down to being curious about people. What interests them, what experiences have they had, what have they learned from their experiences, and so on? Think about how you behave when you are curious about something. It becomes almost effortless to pay attention and to conduct research to learn more about it. While being curious won't make networking effortless, it can transform it into a more enjoyable process. Even if we are intro-verted, it might be enjoyable to learn about others. And if we have concerns about making small talk, we've made the process easier by encouraging the others to talk about themselves. Finally, because people likely are going to appreciate your interest in them, they are likely to respond in a positive way, making the process easier on your end.

The second dimension in a healthy networking attitude is an interest in helping others out. Just focus on what you can offer others now, or on the fact that some day you might be in a position to help them out. This dimension of attitude requires some flexibility and tolerance for uncertainty. We may feel like we cannot offer anything to someone, or we may not be able to envision any way we may be able to help them weeks, months, or years later. In fact, there is no guarantee we will be able to help them. But if we maintain this attitude and focus, at least we will have avoided being the kind of opportunistic networker that turns many people off. If we use our curiosity to learn about new contacts and display an interest in help-ing them out, then at worst we've shown interest in someone and had a positive encounter with them. And if the encounter is positive, that will help alleviate our anxiety and make the networking process less stressful for us. In each of these dimensions of a healthy networking attitude, we are shifting the focus from ourselves to other people. This reframing of the process can help with those who might be reluctant to network due to concerns about their ability. Hopefully, approaching networking with a curious and helping attitude will make the remaining strategies easier to adopt.

Developing Contacts

There are several ways to develop contacts, and perhaps the easiest is to **start with our existing contacts.** However, that may not sound easy, as we may underestimate just how many contacts we have. But if we write down both our strong and weak ties (including friends, family, and acquaintances), most of us will have a good start-ing point. Even if the list doesn't feel impressive, consider the fact that each person on the list is connected to a network of his or her own. And the weak ties on our list are likely to be connected to many people we don't know. The easiest way to develop new contacts is to ask our existing contacts for help. If we tell enough con-tacts that we are interested in a certain type of opportunity, they may know someone in their network who can help us. Many people in our network might be of little help, but if one or two are helpful, then we have benefited from our network.

Even college students, who often seem to think that their networks are small, can use this strategy to great effect. Every time they walk into a classroom, they see a room of peers whom they think of as just being other students. Another way to look at it is that they usually are in a room with 20 or more weak ties, each of whom has a personal network full of people who have access to information that might benefit other classmates. And in each class session, students have a few minutes before class in which they could network. Sometimes this happens, but usually only during course scheduling "season," during which students frequently ask each other for the "dirt" on other teachers so they can decide which classes to take. Students likely would benefit professionally by building on this practice and taking advantage of each other's personal networks. Furthermore, when I've had students share their career interests with the class, I have NEVER had an occasion when no other student in the class was able to help. Even when one student expressed an interest in working as an equestrian (showing horses), at least one other student was able to offer a contact. So don't underestimate the value of those around us.

If we don't have existing contacts, and those in our network aren't able to help us, we will have to **develop contacts on our own.** There are at least a couple of ways we can do this. We can cast a wide net and get used to making connections throughout our day, and we can seek out specific people who might be in a good position to help us. Casting a wide net is about as simple and unrefined as it sounds. It involves connecting with whomever we encounter throughout our day and talking to them about their background, interests, and what they do for a living. We may have opportunities to do this while waiting in line somewhere, while at work, or traveling. With a curious attitude, we can turn these mundane run-ins with others into potentially helpful networking encounters. College students can do this in their classes, dorms, dining halls, the student union, and other places on campus. Different approaches to socializing in these types of situations will be discussed below. For now, it is worthwhile to consider the many networking opportunities we encounter every day. Remember, it only takes one potentially useful contact to make the effort worthwhile. So while most of the time the interaction may yield little more than a brief conversation, at other times it may provide a professional lead, or even lead to a friendship (or maybe even a date!).

As helpful as in might be to develop a habit of connecting randomly with people throughout our day, it also is worthwhile to **connect more strategically** with others. This can be done both with contacts we gain from others and with strangers by arranging what is known as an **informational interview,** in which you ask someone about his or her career or job. This can be valuable for those who might be interested in switching careers, such as those who are laid off or who are a few years out of college and realizing that they do not enjoy the career they chose. And it can be very useful for college students. In fact, in one of my courses, I ask students to do a few informational interviews as part of an assignment. I ask them to find people who hold a type of job that interests them and then interview them. You can find people to interview either through existing contacts or by contacting organizations that employ people in your position or career of interest. At this point, many people, and definitely students, reasonably think "Why would a person take the time to let me interview him or her?" When asked this, I respond that if the request begins with "I think what you do is really interesting and I would love to learn more about it," most people will be willing to talk about themselves. Of course, you might encounter people who are too busy, or who are burnt out (and really not interested in talking about their job), but my experience is that students usually are able to find a few people who are happy to be helpful.

During the interview, there are a variety of questions you might ask. In general, the point is to learn about whether a job or career is a fit for you and the path you should follow to get a job. With that in mind, here are some possible questions to ask:

1. Can you describe a typical day at work?
2. What do you like best about this career? Least?

3. What surprised you the most about this career?
4. Where do you see your profession heading, in terms of trends?
5. What path should someone in my shoes follow to work toward this career (keep probing on this issue to get a detailed answer)?
6. What other questions should I be asking/considering about this career?
7. Does your organization offer any internships?
8. Who else should I speak with about this career? Who are the must-contact people?

Notice that these questions are consistent with our attitude of genuine curiosity. Notice also that the last question can help you identify additional people with whom you can network. Finally, remember that within a day after the interview you should send a sincere thank you note to the interviewee, in which you specifically note what you appreciated or found helpful. Some people ask whether this thank you should be via email or a card, and the answers vary. Personally, I recommend a hand-written card, simply because so few people send these. For little cost or effort, one can stand out nicely by sending a hand-written card.

It is not necessary to ask every question listed above, but if you are a student, I strongly suggest you ask #7. Why not? It's worth a shot. The last two times I have done this assignment in one of my courses, about 10 out of 30 students in each class said they received an internship opportunity through their interviews. This may not sound like much, but I was very impressed. Just by taking initiative and conducting a fairly straightforward interview, one in three students gained an internship opportunity. But even if that's not your goal, it should be clear that you at least can expand your personal network by using informational interviews. At worst, you will have gained a weak tie in your network, who eventually may help you some day (or whom you may help).

An additional way to develop contacts is to **attend events that involve or encourage networking.** There is no one best place to find these events. They may be conventions sponsored by professional associations, or meetings by clubs or other groups, such as those that focus specifically on networking. These can be found a variety of ways, whether through your existing contacts or an Internet search. A good starting place would be to research your local chamber of commerce, as it may sponsor networking events, or at least be in a position to direct you to events. Once at these events, it will be important to seek out different people (avoid acting like it's a grade school dance, with everybody on the side of the room and nobody in the middle!). So be sure to avoid staying distant and on your own.

The above methods will help give us access to people we might want to add to our network. However, if we randomly meet people or attend a networking event, we will have to handle another phase of networking: socializing and making small talk. We will explore this process in the next section.

Socializing With Others

Ok, so what do we say to these strangers? First remember the two components of our attitude: a genuine interest in learning about others, and an interest in helping others out. These components will guide our interaction with our new contacts.

First though, it is important that we make sure we **remember each person's name.** If you are not very good at doing this, part of the trick is to actually plan in advance to remember names, so that it is on your mind as you are being introduced. Plan also on immediately repeating the name back to the person. Finally, plan on making some kind of association with the name, based on other names you know, something the person or name reminds you of, or other tricks. There is no best way to do this, but some form of association can help. The other person may have a nametag or give you a business card, but it still would be best to prepare by planning to remember names.

Now what? Remember our attitude of **being genuinely curious.** Using this attitude **to ask sincere questions** will help ensure that we have a reasonably enthusiastic nonverbal demeanor. It also will make the interaction easier by enabling you to focus on the other person. Just assume that it will be interesting and enjoyable to learn about someone else, and remember that most people enjoy talking about themselves. To help them do this, think in terms of asking open-ended questions. A closed question requires a single answer (like "yes" or "no"), while open-ended questions allow for a greater range of responses. "Do you like your job?" is closed, but "What do you like best about your job?" is open. Notice the open question is more likely to encourage conversation, in that the other person will say more, and there will be a greater chance that you can respond to something. And that is partly the key to all of this: encouraging the other person to talk enough until we can find some kind of common ground with him or her. Many people say they dislike small talk, but when we can find common ground with someone, the process becomes much easier. So when networking, we can help ourselves by encouraging others to open up, until we eventually find something we both can discuss. Comments like "I'd love to hear more about your job," "What interested you in it?" "What do you like most about it," "What's the biggest misconception people have about it?" can be helpful. They're safe in that they're free of controversy, and they encourage the other person to open up. And if we ask them with genuine curiosity, it probably won't take long for us to have a response to one of their answers. The response may be to follow up with more questions, or to share similar experiences we've had. And even if it is difficult for the conversation to get "off the ground" and you have to transition to another person, at least you've shown interest and let another person talk about herself. Beyond this, Baber and Waymon (2002) suggest additional benefits to remaining quiet and letting others talk about themselves. We can stand out positively (in a room in which most people are doing the talking), we will learn something, we will find out how to follow up, and we will be in a better position to connect people with each other (because we will listen for details about them). So while it may seem like you continually should be talking, there are many benefits to asking questions and letting others talk about themselves. Although it's important to listen and learn, we also want to be remembered, and that is where our personal story comes into play.

When meeting others, it is important to **have our own personal story developed** (de Janasz et al., 2009). What if you had someone's attention for 30 seconds and had to tell the person about yourself in that time—what would you say? To prepare for networking situations, you should think about this issue, and develop your own personal story. The goal with the story should be to (1) get attention, (2) be memorable, and (3) be brief, so that you don't overwhelm the listener. Later in the book we will discuss stories in more detail, but we can cover some basics here. When it comes to a personal story, think about what excites you the most about what you have to offer (relevant to the occasion). Why did you choose your profession or major? What do you find fascinating, challenging, perplexing, funny, about it? Think of the story as a verbal kind of cover letter—the goal is to get attention, not outline your qualifications (that can come later). Give some information, but make it interesting enough so the other person will ask follow-up questions out of genuine interest.

While we're on the subject of stories, it is worth noting that **additional stories** about experiences and events can be helpful to use throughout your interaction. Stories can help hold attention and make our points more memorable. I can state something I've learned during my teaching career, but it's often more useful and memorable to tell the story of how I learned it (as I've done on a couple of occasions in this chapter). This can be difficult to do for people who don't feel like they have any stories to tell. However, if you think of your interests, why you're pursuing a specific career, there usually is at least a brief story behind it. The story at the beginning of the chapter about how I learned the value of networking from a student was brief and not terribly dramatic, but even that simple story was far more compelling and interesting than if I had said "It is important for college students to network." Similarly, even if a story does not seem that substantial to you, when you're in a conversation, need something to say, and would like to be remembered, telling a few stories can help you accomplish important goals without much effort.

Even if you like the above suggestions for socializing, I can appreciate how you still might feel anxiety about the process. One way to overcome this is to practice the skills in what I call a **"low-consequence" environment.** A low-consequence environment is one in which the consequences of failure (even miserable failure) are minimal. This kind of environment is ideal for practicing, because we can try techniques without fearing failure. For example, if you want to work on socializing, you could start on an acquaintance or distant friend with whom you are reasonably comfortable. Obviously you wouldn't ask basic questions (you already know the answers), but it is possible to ask open-ended questions about their interests in order to get people to open up and talk about themselves, to search for areas of common ground, and to get used to sharing stories with others. If we do these things around friends, they aren't likely to notice or care when we make mistakes. They will appreciate our genuine interest in them. With little effort or risk on our part, we can use this practice strategy to refine our skills and gain confidence.

The above strategies don't come close to covering everything there is to know about socializing with others, but they will help you navigate networking situations. With the right attitude (sincerely curious about others), some good questions, and some stories, you can have a balanced interaction in which you maximize your chances of finding common ground with someone. To the extent you're able to do this, you will have developed a contact who may be able to help you some day, or who you may be able to help. Once you do develop contacts, it's important to maintain them.

Maintaining Contacts

The first step of maintaining contacts is to thank them after first meeting them, preferably with a hand-written note (as with the informational interviews), or at least a brief email. After that, there is no single best way to maintain contacts. It may be natural to contact some often, but rarely contact others. Earlier I mentioned that part of a good networking attitude is to be interested in helping others. This can be a problem if we genuinely feel we have little to offer them. But at some point after we've made a contact, we may be in a position to offer him something (making us a helpful weak tie). One way to maintain our contacts is to **reach out** to them when we have information that they may find helpful or interesting. It could be as simple as sending a link to an article with a message of "I saw this and thought you might find it interesting." Even if the person doesn't read or like the article, the point is that you were thinking of her, and offering something, rather than asking for something. If we network with individuals online, we can congratulate online contacts whenever they post good news or offer support when they post bad news. Additionally, as your network grows, you may be in a position to **introduce your contacts to each other,** again an act of good will in which you're trying to help people in your network. And if the people belong in groups that might be worth connecting, you will have bridged a structural hole in your network. In addition, as we will see in the next section, you also may be able to use LinkedIn or Twitter or both to keep in touch with contacts. Overall, the general approach to maintaining contacts is to try to think of ways in which you can periodically reach out to your contacts with something helpful. In turn, they will appreciate you and probably will be happy to help you if an opportunity to do so presents itself.

Networking Online: How Can LinkedIn and Other Sites Help?

Before I begin this section, I want to mention a couple of things worth keeping in mind. First, while it can be easier to network online than in person, it would be a mistake to think that you can accomplish all of your networking from a computer. You should not expect it to replace face-to-face networking. Instead, plan on strategically using a combination of face-to-face and online approaches. Second, innovations in how to network online likely will develop faster than can be covered in a book like this that does not have a new edition every year, and I don't want to do a new edition every year! So I encourage you to do online searches like "best practices for LinkedIn." Also remember that you probably have some experienced people in your Facebook network and that it may help to post something to your status asking for them to give advice based on their experiences. That will help you stay current when it comes to online networking and job hunting.

LinkedIn. For those who are unfamiliar, LinkedIn is a free professional networking site on which people create profiles with professional information. Profiles include a reasonably professional picture and the kind of information that belong on a resume. Members can invite anyone they know to join their network, follow companies, and join discussion groups related to their professional interests. Members can recommend other contacts and receive recommendations from their contacts. They also can "endorse" their contacts for any of the skills that their contacts have listed in their profile. Below is a collection of "best practices" advice I have compiled regarding LinkedIn. I have separated them into sections regarding your profile, your contacts, and your interactions with companies.

There are a number of things to keep in mind regarding your LinkedIn profile. First, it should not be treated like Facebook. You should have a picture that looks professional, and anything you write, post, or share on your profile should be professional. Second, you can be more detailed in your profile than you would be on your resume. You can add more detail and list relevant skills. It can be good to list skills so others can endorse you for them (though they can write in their own skills if they wish to endorse you). Once you have set up a basic profile, there are a few things you can do to make it stronger. If there are certain key words that are common to an industry or profession that interests you, be sure to add them in a relevant spot in your profile. It also is important to keep your profile up-to-date, so be sure to update it whenever you can add something. In the update section you might post enthusiastically about an internship or accomplishments in your workplace. One way to update it even if nothing is new with you professionally is to post links to blogs, articles, or events in your field in the update section that are relevant to your area of interest. This will show others that you are engaged and enthusiastic about your area of expertise. One final piece of advice about profiles: check out the profiles among some of your more successful contacts in order to get ideas on how to best represent your skills and experience.

It also is important to know how contacts work on LinkedIn. First, unlike Facebook, it is common to connect with anyone you may have interacted with professionally. If they may not know you, it helps to include a brief personal message explaining your invite. In fact, with every invite I encourage you to write something personal rather than using LinkedIn's default "I would like to connect with you" message. It's a quick and easy way to set yourself apart from others. Keeping in mind what we learned about the power of networks in a previous section, I encourage you to make a long list of possible contacts, even if they are not close. Even if they seem irrelevant to your professional interests, each person on the list will have her or his own network and may be able to refer you to someone who can be a great help to you. You also should try to connect with recruiters who may be in a position to recruit you. And once you have gained some contacts, you may want to endorse others for various skills, as they likely will be willing to reciprocate by endorsing you. The same applies to recommendations. If you write brief recommendations for others they will do the same for you (or if they don't, it will be easier to request one if you've written one first). You also can interact with groups in addition to individuals. There are many groups on LinkedIn, and it likely will be easy for you to find several that are relevant to your interests. By joining these groups and positing when you have something to offer, you will be demonstrating further initiative. Finally, I would encourage you to have the same attitude on LinkedIn as you should when networking face-to-face: when possible, try to help others or at least recognize the work they are doing. You can send them relevant links or congratulate them on accomplishments. LinkedIn actually makes it pretty easy and cost free to do these kinds of positive gestures for many people in a short period of time. Notice that if you do some of the these things, you'll appear to be ambitious and engaged in your area of interest.

In addition to interacting with individuals, you also can engage with companies on LinkedIn. If you are interested in working for certain companies, be sure to follow them. If you are following them, there is a chance someone from the company will check out your profile. And if you've done some of the things with your profile that I mentioned, once someone sees your profile it will be obvious that you are very engaged in your field.

Twitter. Twitter also presents you with an opportunity to develop your network. In this section I offer a few ideas to get you started, and after that you should dig deeper on the web for additional ideas and suggestions. As with LinkedIn, it is important to have a good picture and bio on Twitter. From there, you can connect with others by following companies and individuals who hold the types of jobs you would like. You also can show your interest in certain types of jobs in a few ways. You can directly tweet that you are looking for a certain type of job, share your LinkedIn profile, share interesting links related to your industry (as with LinkedIn), and re-tweet posts that are relevant or by people whom you hope will notice you. You also can ask thoughtful questions about an area or your field, then acknowledge the answers by adding your own answer or re-tweeting. Doing these things will not guarantee success, but they can increase your chances. For example, I received this story from a former student who used Twitter in many of these ways before she relocated to a new area:

> I got the attention of several people in town, including someone that worked at the local paper. We met for coffee one day (after I had moved but before landing a job). She had the inside scoop on a couple of marketing positions at the paper that were opening very soon. She sent me the position description before it was published, she even mentioned me to the hiring manager and to the people that worked in that department. I applied, interviewed twice and landed the job within three weeks of meeting my new Twitter friend.

Notice in the story that my former student did not succeed solely because of one strategy. She networked both online and in person. With all of this in mind, I encourage you to consider using all of these means as part of your networking approach. And if you do use some of these online methods, once you've done those things with LinkedIn and Twitter, I encourage you to periodically do web searches for best practices on using these and other websites.

Networking Within Our Organization. For anyone who is networking within an organization, there are a few things to keep in mind. First, it is important to be part of one or more close-knit groups, so that one can be part of trusting relationships. Then, to the extent that one wants to gain an advantage, it is important to bridge structural holes by being connected to groups who themselves are not connected. This will expose one to valuable information and ideas. To accomplish this, one should strive to avoid being too "local" in her workplace. One should try to meet or work with people in other departments. There are a couple of ways to do this (beyond just walking around to various departments). First, if it is possible to rotate into different jobs in different departments, this can help one develop his network. Second, if you have a choice of office location, choose a central or high-traffic area that will put you in the crossroads of information flow. Third, don't overlook the value of socializing after hours, or during lunch, if a variety of people gather in a central location. These less formal situations can provide a great opportunity to establish connections.

Overcoming Reasons to Not Network

Earlier we explored reasons people may not network. They included a lack of knowledge about how to network, concern over the possibly "sleazy" nature of networking, and general discomfort with small talk and socializing. I hope that the suggestions provided above help you overcome these concerns. First, I hope your knowledge of how to network is sufficient enough to at least get you started. Second, I hope the approach of being curious and interested in helping others helps alleviate concerns about unfairly "using" people in our network. Without asking for anything, we can show an interest in others and contact them in helpful ways. It is unlikely anyone would be turned off by an approach like this. Third, I hope this discussion has helped alleviate anxiety over networking. If we start by learning about the other person, we've made the other person the focus, and taken it off of ourselves. If we're concerned about what to say, listening to others will buy us time until we can find an area we want to talk about. And if we've thought of some stories ahead of time, we can enter into a networking situation with greater confidence. If helping people means thinking of them and contacting them when we have information or opportunities they might appreciate, it's possible to see how we all can be in a position to help others. No suggestion or list of techniques is perfect, but the above ideas should help even those with discomfort navigate networking situations more smoothly.

References

Baber, A., & Waymon, L. (2002). *Make your contacts count: Networking know how for cash, clients, and career success*. New York, NY: AMACOM.

Brown, D., & Konrad, A. (2001). Granovetter was right: The importance of weak ties to a contemporary job search. *Group and Organizational Management, 26*, 434–462.

Burt, R. S. (2004). Structural holes and good ideas. *American Journal of Sociology, 110*, 349–399.

Burt, R. S. (2005). *Brokerage and closure: An introduction to social capital*. New York, NY: Oxford University Press.

De Janasz, S. C., Dowd, K. O., & Schneider, B. (2009). *Interpersonal skills in organizations*. New York, NY: McGraw Hill.

Forret, M. L., & Dougherty, T. W. (2004). Networking behaviors and career outcomes: Differences for men and women? *Journal of Organisational Behaviour, 25*, 410–437.

Goel, S., Muhamad, R., & Watts, D. (2009, April). Social search in small-world experiments. In *Proceedings of the 18th international conference on World Wide Web* (pp. 701–710). New York, NY: ACM.

Granovetter, M. (1973). The strength of weak ties. *American Journal of Sociology, 91*, 481–510.

Granovetter, M. (1995). *Getting a job*. Chicago, IL: University of Chicago Press.

Milgram, S. (1967). The small world problem. *Psychology Today, 1*, 61–67.

Wolff, H., & Moser, K. (2009). Effects of networking on career success: A longitudinal study. *Journal of Applied Psychology, 94(1)*, 196–206.

Chapter 4

Adjusting to the Culture Shock

Why Do They Do It Like This, It Doesn't Make Sense?

When you first enter a new workplace, some of the common practices, ways of handling problems, and so on will make little sense to you, and your first instinct may be to say "You know, it would work better if you did it this way." Please suppress that instinct until you've read this chapter, because in this chapter we will explore just why members of the organization have come to behave in such peculiar ways, and why we must understand their methods before we can expect to change them. An important theme of this chapter is that things that initially make no sense to us make perfect sense once we gain a better understanding of the organization, and why members do the things they do. For example, when I first became a doctoral student, I was struck by an interesting ritual among faculty in our department. On most days, faculty who were around would gather and drive to the mall on the other side of town, and have lunch at the food court, somewhat shattering my image of the professor as someone who prefers more upscale, fine dining! From my perspective, their behavior was puzzling. The mall was about 15 traffic-filled minutes away, and there were plenty of places with good food near the department's offices. But when I asked why they did it, I received an answer that took this quirky behavior and made sense of it for me: They went to the food court so (1) everyone could eat whatever they wanted, and (2) so there would be no issues about who pays. In other words, even if it still doesn't make sense to you, and even if those in other organizations might have different solutions to the exact same problems, in this department, they had found an approach that worked for them. This chapter is about understanding that there often are very good reasons that organizational members behave in ways that are peculiar to us, and that before we criticize and or try to change their behaviors, as new employees we should work to understand the reasons behind them. We can do this by better understanding the culture within our organization.

According to Schein (2004), a **group's culture** is defined as "a pattern of shared basic assumptions that was learned by a group as it solved its problems of external adaptation and internal integration, that has worked well enough to be considered valid and, therefore, to be taught to new members as the correct way to perceive, think, and feel in relation to those problems" (p. 17). Now that is an impressive academic definition! As cumbersome as it is, I've included it because it contains many important elements of culture. First, you have a group that has had to solve problems, and as it has found approaches that worked well enough, their approaches became ingrained as patterns and ways of doing things. Over time, these patterns have become solidified to the point that they are taken for granted and taught to newcomers as the correct way of doing things. Unless we are present at the very beginning of an organization's existence, pause for a moment to consider all that happens before we arrive in an organization as a new employee. People have been hired and fired. There may have been important battles over key issues. Quite likely, mistakes have been made, and the organization had to respond to them. In other words, there is a rich history that has shaped the organization as it presently exists, and that history is bigger than any one person. It certainly is bigger than any new employee, which suggests that we need to approach an organization's culture with respect and humility. It also means that we will need to spend much of our initial time in the organization getting a feel for the culture. How can we do this? To start with, we can observe at least some of the levels of the culture (see Tables 4.1 and 4.2).

Levels of Organizational Cultures

Artifacts

According to Schein (2004), organizational cultures have three levels, which vary in terms of the ease with which we can identify them. The first and most visible level consists of *artifacts,* or anything "that one sees, hears, and feels when one encounters a new group with an unfamiliar culture" (Schein, 2004, p. 25). Because artifacts are the most visible level of an organization's culture, as new employees it will be important to pay careful attention to the artifacts you see in an organization. However, it is important to realize that we should not draw sweeping conclusions about the artifacts we notice, as there may be many ways to interpret them. According to Schein (2004), the artifact level of culture is "both easy to observe and very difficult to decipher" (p. 26). In other words, these artifacts can serve as important initial pieces of the cultural puzzle, so we will examine a few different categories of artifacts.

The first type of artifact consists of *physical things* we can see. This includes the outer and inner architecture of buildings, the layout of rooms within the building(s), decor, furniture, any technology that is present (Miller, 2003; Schein, 2004). Another

Table 4.1 Levels of Culture

Artifacts	3 Types: • Physical things (buildings, furniture, paintings) • Patterns and rituals (informal events that recur) • Things we hear (words, phrases, stories that frequently are repeated)
Espoused Beliefs and Values	Sense of the way things should be done that is expressed by employees. May not actually be how things are done.
Shared Basic Assumptions	Things that have been taken for granted as "the way we do things," though they aren't necessarily noticed or expressed by employees. They've been internalized to the point that it is stressful for employees to go against these assumptions.

type of artifact we can observe is the attire worn by employees. It may range from formal to informal, or have other distinct features. For example, I once visited an adult dentist office in which all of the staff members' uniforms had child-like designs on them, as if they were working in a pediatric dentist office (they wanted to keep things fun and lighthearted). Beyond attire, we can observe many other types of artifacts. For example, you might observe whether a floor plan encourages interaction among employees (few walls/barriers) or discourages it (offices separated by walls, cubicles). You can note who has the largest and smallest offices, and who is located closest to those in high status positions. You also can examine whether offices are arranged to facilitate communication. For example, a round table or furniture that enables people to face each other can encourage communication, while chairs which place people side by side and facing an authority figure on the other side of a desk help solidify the status of the person behind the desk. You might observe whether technology seems current and well maintained. You also may notice interesting decor. For example, at Southwest Airlines, some areas feature many pictures of employees at various functions (office parties, etc.), and enhance the sense that Southwest is an enjoyable place to work where people are like family.

If all of this discussion about the noteworthiness of artifacts seems boring, consider the ways in which some organizations have shaped their culture through the creative use of artifacts. Some advertising and marketing organizations are known for their creative use of space. They may have a Nerf basketball hoop set up or other games available. Or consider Dixon Schwabl, an advertising and public relations agency in Rochester, NY. If you were to enter Dixon Schwabl, you would notice a number of interesting artifacts. First you would notice a feature "that you just can't miss—a slide. And it's not just for show. There are scuffs down the silver cylindrical slide to prove its frequent use by employees and clients alike" (Shearing, 2010). In addition, you will see bold words like "Pizzazz" and "Vision" painted on the wall, and if you end up in the waiting area, your wait will be spent sitting on children's furniture. The office also includes a kind of soundproof "scream" room, into which people can go if they need to vent without disturbing others!

Or consider that at the SAS Institute, the staff includes two artists who are paid to create paintings and acquire artwork to place around the organization's campus. These positions exist because the CEO of SAS believes that making the campus more visually appealing will inspire his employees' creativity. Other visible artifacts on the SAS campus include a pianist in the cafeteria during lunch hours, and onsite perks like a daycare center, medical facilities, a dry cleaner, and a country club (SAS employees either are charged little for these perks or are given considerable discounts). By the way, you may find it peculiar to know that the product created at SAS is far from exciting—they create statistical software!

Google also has tried to be creative with its artifacts:

> Between the three daily catered meals, on-site massage therapist, free gym membership and game room (complete with air hockey, darts and Foosball), Google's new development center in Fremont boasts amenities that rival some resorts.
>
> Just in case there aren't enough entertainment options, kayaks are available so staffers can go for a midday paddle on the nearby Lake Washington Ship Canal. There's even a "quiet room"—complete with lava lamp, massage chair

and wonderful views of the water—where Google employees can presumably dream up the next great Internet application while their muscles relax.

(Cook, 2008)

And Google's New York office boasts features such as an impressive cafeteria with a "make your own sandwich" bar, and Razr scooters so employees can have a more entertaining ride from office to office (Zjawinski, 2008). Although examples like Dixon Schwabl, SAS, and Google probably are not typical, I've included them to point out that professional does not have to mean "stuffy," and that organizations can succeed without taking themselves too seriously (all of the organizations I've mentioned consistently have been successful).

A second type of artifact we can observe in organizations consists of *behavior patterns and rituals*. Noteworthy behavior patterns may include the way meetings are conducted, how differences of opinion are handled, the level of formality with which members conduct themselves, and the way members use their time (whether it is strictly controlled or employees have considerable flexibility and discretion). Rituals are certain types of behavior patterns that are performed on a recurring basis. In the example I used at the beginning of this chapter, the faculty members had a ritual of going to the mall for lunch. Some offices have rituals that involve going out for drinks after work. A former student once mentioned that at a small restaurant where she worked, after closing time, the chefs would make a meal and all of the employees would eat together. A different student said that in one organization, every morning employees would gather in a circle and do an enthusiastic company chant (picture a football team huddled up before kickoff)! In many organizations, employees play on various company sports teams outside of work. And continuing with our earlier examples, it is not surprising that some interesting rituals have developed at Dixon Schwabl. There are "unplugged Thursdays, where musically inclined employees perform in the lobby" (Shearing, 2010). They also have "Ice Cream Thursdays," and during lunch on Wednesdays throughout the summer months, employees can grill their lunches outside. They also receive a free vacation day on their birthday. Again, professional and successful does not have to mean "stuffy" (unless that's how the culture of your organization defines it)!

Artifacts also come in the form of *things we hear:* common words, phrases, or stories that one consistently hears throughout the organization. Sometimes, specific words or labels are noteworthy, such as labels assigned to employees or clients or customers. For example, Disneyland calls all employees "cast members" and its customers "guests," and the Disney interviewing process is known as "casting." And as employees use phrases to describe life in the organization, some may catch on and be repeated often. In college when I worked on a town road crew, the phrases "good for town work" or "good for government work" helped characterize full time the employees' approach to their job. We also might hear stories that characterize an organization's culture. These stories often will be used to reinforce certain points or lessons, and typically will contain depictions of admirable or problematic behavior. There may be a story of an employee who handled a challenging situation, or of an employee who failed because of the way he or she acted. Stories like these can serve as a less-direct way of sharing expectations and shaping employee behavior.

Although it may be harder to observe in a tangible sense, we also can get a general feel for the climate, or vibe of an organization. In fact, I suspect that as you read about SAS or Dixon Schwabl above, you may have been able to get a general sense of the atmosphere in each organization. You also can notice this idea when going from store to store in the mall. Each store may have its own unique feel. Although artifacts can tell us a great deal, it is important to avoid drawing sweeping conclusions from them. They only are a superficial indication of an organization's culture. To know the culture in greater detail, we have to better understand deeper layers of culture, beginning with an organization's espoused beliefs and values.

Espoused Beliefs and Values

How should an employee provide good customer service? How should we handle an angry customer? How should we market a product? An answer to any of these questions would reflect a **belief or value,** which is our "sense of what ought to be, as distinct from what is" (Schein, 2004, p. 28). If you say that we should handle an angry customer by giving him or her some kind of perk for his or her troubles, you are making a suggestion about the way things ought to be. That doesn't mean that an angry customer will be handled this way, it's simply what you believe should happen. In organizations, it is common to hear employees or management express their beliefs about how things should be done.

However, it is important to realize that actual behavior may not reflect these values, which is why they're called "**espoused** values." Organizations may have carefully crafted messages about how they value customer service, but that will not necessarily translate into good service. In fact, many organizations may have key proclamations of values, and even put them on banners, buttons, and T-shirts for employees to wear. But in recognition that the organization's behavior doesn't follow from these espoused values, employees may just ignore them or, worse, openly mock them (Larkin & Larkin, 1994). So when trying to spot key values, it is important to avoid assuming that espoused values are legitimate and consistent with employees' actions. It is necessary to dig deeper into the culture, and to an extent, this involves examining the next level of culture: shared basic assumptions.

Shared Basic Assumptions

According to Schein (2004), "When a solution to a problem works repeatedly, it comes to be taken for granted" (p. 30). Members of the organization's culture have found certain approaches to certain problems to work well enough for so long that these approaches no longer are discussed or debated. They simply become "the way we do things around here." In fact, because they are so taken for granted, employees may not even notice or realize that their decisions are guided by these **underlying assumptions.** For an example within our national culture, every presidential election there are at least a handful of people who are legitimately on the ballot for president. However, most of us, including the media, typically focus on two candidates, and operate with an "either-or" assumption. It's either the Republican candidate or the Democrat. Occasionally a third candidate will gain attention, but notice how hard these candidates have to work to get positive media coverage and break through the powerful "either-or" assumption. At most colleges, most teachers share some basic assumptions: (1) each course should have a textbook, (2) students should be given tests, and (3) students should be assigned grades. While there are exceptions to these assumptions, they don't seem to be too common. In the business world, there often is an assumption that a service is not credible unless it is expensive. For example, if you do a web search of advice to new consultants, you will see that they are advised that if they charge too little, they may not be taken seriously.

There are a number of important things to **keep in mind about basic assumptions.** First, because they are so ingrained and taken for granted, they are very difficult to debate or change. This explains the puzzling response new employees might receive when they make a suggestion but before any discussion of the idea takes place, they are met with responses like: "No, that's not how we do things around here" or "That won't work." It is hard for us to envision acting in ways that go against our basic assumptions. In fact, it can create considerable anxiety to change them. For example, imagine trying to talk to a staunch liberal about embracing a conservative view of the world, or asking a staunch conservative to embrace a liberal view. In a sense, you're asking someone to take a view that helps her interpret and understand the events of her world, and asking her to abandon it. As a result, we tend to feel more comfortable around those who share our basic assumptions than with those who do not (Schein, 2004). In addition, because it is psychologically easier and comforting to stick to our assumptions, our perceptions of events around us will be colored by and conform to those assumptions. For example, suppose one organization's culture contains a shared assumption that customers are annoying. If employees in this organization encounter a customer with a few questions or a complex problem, they likely will be annoyed at having to deal with the customer (even if the customer is friendly throughout the exchange). They will see the customer as needy and not able to figure things out for himself. We can contrast this with an organization in which employees share the basic assumption that it is gratifying to help customers. When confronted with the same customer used in the example above, these employees likely will see the customer's questions/issues as quite reasonable (or may not even question whether they are reasonable) and be happy to help.

Although we've identified the three levels of culture, we have not explored how a group of employees comes to develop shared assumptions that they take for granted. In the next section, we will address this issue by exploring how cultures develop.

How Cultures Form

Schein (2004) outlines the process by which a group comes to take certain things for granted. Consider a group of employees at a newly formed organization, with little shared history and without a developed culture. How do they solve common problems that come up? How should they market their product/service? What is the most efficient way to create the product or provide the service? What is the best way to train employees? Because the group has not developed norms for handling these tasks, it will have to make decisions about how to do them. At this point, the organization consists of a group of individuals, each of whom approaches these issues with his or her own assumptions that have been formed by years of learning.

At this point, either a leader will tell the group how to handle the problems, or group members will have to deliberate about how to address the various issues they collectively face. Because the initial leaders are present before a strong culture has formed, it is not uncommon for them to have more power in shaping the initial culture than leaders who later enter an already well-developed culture. But regardless of who suggests a course of action, before an idea can be considered to be effective the group will have to test it and "together observe the outcome of that action" (Schein, 2004, p. 28). According to Schein, "if the solution works, and if the group has a shared perception of that success," then the group will see the value of the solution (p. 28). Over time, as the group continues to use the solution to solve the problem, as long as the group continues to perceive it as a success, it gradually will become a shared value. And if this shared value continues to help the group solve the problem, the group eventually will come to take it for granted, as it will become a shared assumption. Or, an initial idea might prove to not work well, and others may need to be tried before the group collectively identifies something that works for them.

To get a better feel for this process, consider the example of how two different organizations might develop different approaches to customer service. In one, employees might notice that those who complete transactions with customers more quickly are free to do their own work (such as paperwork). Others may try out this approach. If they find that it "works" and allows them more time for their own work, they may stick with it. If this continues over time, it may be internalized as a belief that being quick in helping customers provides more time for personal work. Along the way, they may encounter customers who are frustrated with this approach and vent their anger at employees. This might reinforce a value that customers are a "pain," and it's best to be done with them quickly, to enable one to work individually on other projects. If this continues long enough, employees in the organization may develop the unspoken and undebatable shared assumption that customers are a pain to be avoided, or to be handled quickly, when possible. But this assumption started with individuals trying approaches until employees collectively found one that they thought "worked."

In another organization, the process might transpire differently. Employees might notice that, of all of the individual approaches being used to serve customers, those who were friendly and went above-and-beyond for customers seemed to be the happiest employees with the friendliest customers. Others who were less friendly were more miserable and often had to deal with less positive customer behavior. Also, the friendly employees tended to establish ongoing relationships with customers, in the sense that customers would come back and request them, while trying to avoid less friendly employees. To the extent that other employees might come to see the friendly approach as "working" better than the less friendly approach, they may adopt the friendly approach. If this continues over time, employees might internalize the belief that it is important to give friendly customer service. And if this behavior pattern continues among enough employees, eventually they may come to take it for granted as a basic shared assumption.

You may have noticed that the above examples did not involve identical organizations. For one group of employees, customer service had to be balanced with paperwork, and the link between customer service and outcomes like profits was not clear to them. In the other example, customer service was much more central to the mission of the organization, in that there seemed to be less pressure to complete individual paperwork in addition to serving customers. But in each case, the process was the same: individual members tried to address challenges they faced, certain approaches became recognized as more effective, and as more employees repeated those approaches over time, they became internalized as beliefs about customer service. And as employees continued to use them, they eventually came to take them for granted as the way things are done. But the cultures turned out differently in part because the organizations were responding to different kinds of constraints with respect to service. But even if the organizations had been identical, different customer service cultures could emerge, depending on what kinds of behaviors emerge and "work" for the employees.

The process above also represents a transition in the way a group handles its problems. When new problems are encountered, there is much debate about how to handle them. These debates often are informed by each individual's own personal assumptions. But as groups come to see that some ideas work, and as the ideas are internalized as values, less debate is needed. And by the time the ideas become basic assumptions, not only is debate not present, but it likely will not be welcome or tolerated. This can be a challenge for an employee who is new to an organization. The employee is informed by her own learning, and arrives with her own basic assumptions about how to solve certain problems. Unfortunately, she will encounter an organization that quite likely will not want her input on certain issues. From their perspective, they have found ways to handle these issues and no further discussion is needed. We will address some of these issues later in this chapter, but for now, it is important to realize that, as a new employee, usually you are entering into an organization with a rich history. Problems have been encountered, battles have been fought over solutions, solutions have been tested, and those that fared well have become "the way we do things around here."

From the perspective of the organization that has developed shared assumptions, it will encounter something with the potential to upset these values and assumptions: new employees who have their own ideas and who do not necessarily share the group's values and assumptions. As a result, the organization will have to devote effort to shaping new employees so that they fit the organization's culture. But how do they do this?

How Are We Socialized into a Culture?

The process of socialization is interactive, in the sense that it involves effort by the organization and by new employees. To varying degrees, organizations try to train us and to get us to share in the values and assumptions that are common among employees. And to varying degrees, new employees try to learn the job and adjust to the culture. I say "to varying degrees," because some organizations will work harder than others to socialize new employees, just like some employees will work harder than others to adapt to the organization's culture.

The socialization process occurs in different stages (Jablin, 2001). We will cover these so you can be better prepared when you encounter them in a new organization.

The first stage involves *anticipatory socialization,* which consists of the ways in which we are socialized prior to entering an organization. Some aspects of this start very early. For example, as children, we are socialized to learn about the working world, and possibly specific professions and organizations, from our parents. Our parents' experiences with work may shape our view of it. Consider the varying messages about work we might have gained from our parents. Their experiences may have been positive and fulfilling, or parents may have found work to be stressful, may have complained a lot about work, or may have been laid off or fired. In addition, our experiences may be shaped by the media, whether in news stories or fictional portrayals of work. For example, I rarely get far into a semester teaching this material before I hear comments like "Oh yeah, just like on *Office Space*," or "That's like what happened on *The Office*!" In addition, books like this largely are about socializing you to the professional working world. This anticipatory socialization continues as we lean more about specific professions of interest to us from a variety of sources. In the process we try to assess the extent to which we could make sufficient money or how well the profession would fit our interests. Finally, we learn about one or more specific organizations in our profession of interest. We may research organizations in a variety of ways, including reading their website, visiting them, or interning for them. The informational interviews I suggested in Chapter 3 are a means to better understanding different types of jobs, as well as specific organizations.

The *encounter* stage of socialization is when we first enter a new position in an organization (Jablin, 2001; Miller, 2003). When we enter, we bring our individual beliefs, expectations, and hopes with us. And if the organization does not conform to those beliefs or live up to our expectations, we can experience a considerable amount of stress. We also experience stress and anxiety because everything is new to us and we have not established routines for handing various situations (Cable & Parsons, 2001). We also cannot predict how others will behave or respond to us. In this stage we may encounter various types of attempts by the organization to socialize us. These may include orientation or training programs and formal or informal mentoring programs (Miller, 2003). In this process, to some extent we will be expected to adopt the beliefs and values that are shared by members of the organization. However, the amount can vary from little adoption of beliefs to considerable. Some organizations may not have a well-defined culture, or may not devote much effort to encouraging newcomers to adopt it. In these cases, you may have freedom to decide how many of the cultural beliefs and values you want to adopt. In other cases, there may be a strong culture or the organization may have to devote considerable effort to making sure you conform to it. For example, at Disney, new employees, or more accurately, cast members, go through a very careful training program to ensure that they adapt to the "Disney Way." Training at Southwest Airlines also is carefully focused on making sure new employees fit into the Southwest culture (Gittell, 2003). Overall, there is a great deal of variation in how employees socialize new members during the encounter phase. Employees may be given little or considerable guidance, work closely with others or be left on their own, be trained individually or with a cohort group. But overall, if you hope to succeed in an organization, during this stage you should expect that you will have to be flexible with respect to your own beliefs and values, and willing to adopt the beliefs and values that are shared by members of the organization, at least if you want to assimilate into the office culture.

The final stage of socialization is *metamorphosis,* which is when you no longer are an outsider and instead have become an "insider" in the organization (Jablin, 2001). In other words, you have adapted to the organization and its culture and have become a regular member. You feel like "one of the gang," and not a newcomer. You have come to adopt the values and beliefs shared by most employees in the organization. It is worth noting that there still is room for fluctuation in our acceptance of shared beliefs and values (Miller, 2003). We may take issue with certain practices at times, and not completely be "on-board." But by this point, much of your uncertainty about your job and the organization has been reduced, and you feel more like an insider than an outsider.

But what kinds of things do we have to learn during the encounter stage to even get to the metamorphosis stage? According to one research team who reviewed the various ways in which we are socialized, there are six areas in which we are socialized (Chao, O'Leary-Kelly, Wolf, Klein, & Gardner, 1994).

The first area is *performance proficiency,* which involves learning the tasks that are necessary for us to do our job. Regardless of how it happens (formal training, on our own, etc.), we will need to acquire the knowledge and skills that will enable us to do our job.

We also will have to get to know *people,* and develop successful working relationships with our colleagues. Organizations may facilitate this by creating activities that enable us to work with one or more members, or with a group of new employees. For example, when I arrived at Ball State University to begin my Master's degree, I had just driven to Indiana from New York and did not know anyone. The Master's program in Communication immersed myself and the other new graduate students in a kind of graduate school "boot camp," involving various orientation sessions and activities. This was very effective, and by the end of that first week, I felt like I was on the way to being good friends with a number of the other students. That experience of going through the graduate "boot camp" together helped accelerate the process of getting to know each other. But if you do not experience this kind of cohort group socialization, it is important to learn about the organization from the right people (Fischer, 1986). Think back to your high school days when a new student would enter the school. That person's experience could be shaped in various ways, depending on the students he or she befriended. Similarly, in organizations, the people who guide us will have considerable power in terms of how they frame the organization for us. If we end up listening to an employee who is a frustrated outcast (something that may be difficult to notice early on), he can frame the organization in a very negative light. So until you have a better sense of the organization, it can be beneficial to "cast a wide net" and remain open to listening to all employees, and to avoid prematurely relying on any single person to gain your perspective on the organization. This suggestion is echoed in our coverage of the next dimension of socialization.

The *politics* dimension of socialization involves learning about the formal and informal networks within the organization, as well as various power structures (Chao et al., 1994). Unlike some dimensions, this one likely will not be spelled-out for us.

Instead, we will have to carefully observe employees and departments to better understand the answers to questions such as: Who has the most/least power? Who is aligned with whom? Who is in conflict with whom? What kinds of agendas are on display? In this organization, what kinds of actions are politically correct/incorrect? Although this can be challenging, our coverage of politics in Chapter 13 will help you develop a sense for the kinds of things you might observe to better understand the political landscape of an organization.

The *language* dimension of socialization is about learning both the technical language of one's organization and profession, as well as learning key terms, slang, jargon, and acronyms that are common in the organization (Chao et al., 1994). As we discussed earlier, language is an important type of cultural artifact. Those who "speak the language" are considered to be insiders, and those that don't, outsiders.

The *organizational goals and values* dimension is about learning the values, beliefs, and basic assumptions that are shared by employees. This includes formal written goals and values, but also those that are implied or assumed without being expressed. As with politics, some of the most important values and beliefs we will need to learn will not necessarily be overtly shared with us or be obvious to us. It may take some detective work on our part to identify key values. We will discuss some ways to do this in the next section.

The final dimension of socialization is the *history* of the organization. An organization's "traditions, customs, myths, and rituals are used to transmit cultural knowledge and thereby perpetuate (i.e., socialize) a particular type of organizational member" (Chao et al., 1994, p. 732). As I said earlier, we usually will be entering organizations with rich histories, involving successes, mistakes, and battles between individuals and departments that may have been won or lost. Getting to know this history can help us better understand some of the beliefs, values, and assumptions that are held by many employees. It also can help us better understand what behaviors among employees are considered to be appropriate/inappropriate.

So precisely why do these dimensions of socialization matter? Chao et al. (1994) studied the relationship between these dimensions and four indicators of career success. They found that each of the six dimensions above was a better predictor of several types of career success than tenure in the organization or tenure in a specific position. This means that socialization made a difference, and that those who were not socialized as effectively did not simply make up for it by sticking around on the job. Even more significant, even three years after the study began, the dimensions of socialization were meaningful predictors of career success. Based on these findings, the authors offered the following conclusion: "Generally, people who are well socialized in their organizational roles have greater personal incomes, are more satisfied, more involved in their careers, more adaptable, and have better sense of their personal identity than people who are less well socialized" (Chao et al., 1994, p. 741). This suggests that as new employees, it is very much in our interest to pay careful attention to the six dimensions of socialization. Even more telling, this study found that the goals/values dimension of socialization was the strongest predictor of the career success outcomes. In other words, learning the organizational culture (shared values, beliefs, and assumptions) is integral to our success in an organization. This will be the focus of our next section.

What Can New Employees Do to Get a Feel for the Culture?

In this section we will focus on how a new employee can be a kind of organizational culture "detective" in order to carefully get a feel for one's new workplace. In doing so, we will return to Schein's levels of culture and examine how we can learn about each level. When you first encounter an organization, it will be easiest to study the available artifacts. Before you first visit the organization, the company website can serve as an artifact. The website can be interesting because it gives you a sense of how the company wishes to frame itself. You may notice key words or phrases that recur or a mission statement or other types of statements of values and goals. Once you are able to visit the organization, you can pay attention to a wider array of artifacts. Messages may be conveyed by what you see: layout of the grounds, nature of buildings, placement and layout of rooms, the way desk and office space is configured, materials on the wall and on employees' desks, the way employees are dressed, and so on. Keep in mind that these artifacts may or may not convey important meaning about the organization. Sometimes, a building is just a building, so if you don't see anything profound about a building or parking lot, it's probably for a good reason! You also may be able to notice language or behavioral artifacts, though these may be harder to spot, because it can take time for you to figure out whether language you're hearing or behaviors you're seeing are common and indicative of rituals or values, or just one-time instances. Please remember that it is important to not draw sweeping and permanent conclusions based on your inspection of artifacts, even if your assessment has been thorough. At this point, all you know is that the artifacts are present, but you do not know why they are present.

Table 4.2 Getting a Feel for Your Organization's Culture

Observe artifacts: look for meaning in the following:	*Physical Things*
	• The layout of buildings
	• How space is used within buildings
	• How space is decorated (pictures, etc.)
	• Quality and layout of furnishings within the building
	• Ways communication is encouraged/discouraged by the layout
	Patterns and Rituals
	• Routines that may seem strange to outsiders
	• Events that employees look forward to with anticipation
	• Events that repeat themselves that are not necessarily part of formally required work
	Things We Hear
	• Repeated words, phrases, stories, descriptions of work, etc.
Listen for Espoused Values	Declarations about how things should be done in the organization, but may not actually be the way things are done. These provide a clue about what people value.
Infer Shared Basic Assumptions	Harder to spot. Consider artifacts and espoused values, and try to identify assumptions that are revealed by the other information you have collected.

For example, when I visited a graduate program to which I had applied, I was struck by the dreariness of the office area. And while I was waiting in the lobby, a faculty member came out and harshly complained to a secretary. Although everyone else was fairly nice, my main memory was of the unhappy faculty member. In spite of this, when I was accepted to the program, I decided to attend the school. I quickly found that most people actually were quite respectful of the staff and each other. And the faculty member I saw yell at the secretary . . . he actually was friendly most of the time. In fact, he was one of the most easy-going and friendly faculty members. Clearly what I saw was an exception, and not the norm. My observations did not reflect the way things really were, and I am happy that I did not act on them. Because we cannot draw firm conclusions based on artifacts alone, we will have to try to identify beliefs and values that are shared among organizational members.

How can we discover the beliefs and values of our new coworkers? We can ask them, and they will give us espoused values. They may tell us nice-sounding things like "we value working together," or "we value customer service." However, just because employees say these are values does not mean their actions embody the same values. Therefore, we will have to dig deeper to identify the values and beliefs that drive behavior in the organization. To do this we simply can ask "why" questions in reference to the artifacts we're noticing. They should be asked with a curious and interested attitude, as opposed to an "I can't believe you would do something lame like that" demanding attitude. You might ask questions like "I'm curious, why did you choose to arrange the office space like this?" "Why were those particular paintings picked for the wall?" "I'm curious about why you (describe whatever ritual you've noticed)?" "I keep hearing the phrase '_____,' what inspired it?" The point of asking these questions is to understand the "why" behind the artifacts you see. They can lead you to answers that reveal employee's beliefs and values. For example, you might receive an answer like "We do (whatever ritual you mentioned) because we think it is important to (whatever is said here would be a belief that may be shared by other employees)." During this process, be sure to ask these questions of a variety of employees, so that you can assess the consistency in their answers. If there is consensus, then you may have identified a value that is shared among most employees. Or, you may find that some groups of employees share certain beliefs that are different from the ones shared in other groups. Or you may find very little consensus at all, indicating that the organization may not have developed many shared beliefs and values. In addition to learning about your coworker's values, this approach can help you learn reasons why you are expected to do your job a certain way. This can be important because it gives you a "bigger picture" about how your position fits into others. This perspective can help you do your job more effectively, make informed decisions, and, as we'll see in the next chapter, take greater initiative. In addition, your coworkers will find you to be engaged and interested in what they do, and this will help you make a good first impression. But first, it is important to see if we also can identify our coworkers' shared basic assumptions, so that we more fully can understand the culture of our new workplace.

To begin to comprehend our coworkers' shared basic assumptions, we can "check whether the espoused values that have been identified really explain all of the artifacts or whether things that have been described as going on have clearly *not* been explained or are in actual conflict with some of the values articulated" (Schein,

2004, p. 344). If you have completed the earlier steps, you will have identified a number of artifacts, and also some explanations for their existence. At this point, you can consider whether the explanations you've received really do explain the artifacts, or whether they would cause us to expect to see a very different set of artifacts. If everything adds up, in the sense that the expressed values are consistent with the artifacts, then you probably have identified key aspects of the culture. But if espoused values seem to conflict with the artifacts you've seen, there may be basic assumptions that explain the apparent contradiction.

For example, suppose you work in an office in which you notice people often debating work-related issues in each other's offices. The debates are fairly civil and issue-oriented (as opposed to featuring personal attacks). Following the steps mentioned above, you ask about this artifact: "I'm curious why people often have long debates in each other's offices?" In response you are told that "everyone's input is welcome" and "it is ok to disagree—it helps us develop stronger solutions." You can consider whether the beliefs you've been told match up with the artifacts you see. Suppose you see some of the following artifacts during meetings: People are relaxed and informal when entering, employees encourage coworkers to share their views, and even any reservations they have about something, different kinds of ideas are embraced, and so on. These artifacts are consistent with the beliefs your coworkers mentioned, so everything adds up. You probably have discovered a reliable belief that is shared by most employees, and therefore is a reliable element of the organization's culture.

But what if you uncover a very different set of artifacts in the same organization? Suppose: People are tense when they arrive at meetings, and don't make small talk before them; the group rigidly follows Robert's Rules of Order and is not tolerant of deviations from it; those who disagree usually are challenged aggressively, and sometimes on a personal level, and many employees seem reluctant to speak up. This set of artifacts is in stark contrast to the belief you heard that "everyone's input is welcome." There probably is a deeper basic assumption at work here. You may or may not be able to identify it on your own, but you can work in that direction by asking colleagues questions about the artifacts you've noticed: "Someone mentioned that input is welcome, but it hasn't seemed welcome in the meetings I've attended?" If you have this discussion with a few people, they may help you uncover a basic assumption that explains the contradiction you've noticed. You may hear something like "The real work of this place gets done one-on-one, the meetings are for show and protecting territory," or "Meeting time should not be devoted to endless debating." Or you may be told that some value disagreement, and that the people who happen to be more vocal in meetings don't value it as much. Unfortunately, when you try to uncover assumptions, what you find may be tentative and hard to decipher. As a result, your goal should not be to research it like an academic and find the one perfect answer. Instead, your focus should be on learning what you can from the culture, so that you can understand the nuances of it as well as possible, even if that understanding is imperfect. Realize that it just will take time for you to adjust and more completely understand the culture. There still is a benefit in being aware, even if you do not find answers to all of your questions. By being aware, you may not know exactly why people behave in negative ways at meetings, but you will know to not "get in the way" during them. You also will know that the espoused values are not reflective of the artifacts you see. This kind of knowledge will help ensure that you tread carefully until you have a better sense of the culture. But keep in mind that, even if you don't have perfect answers, it is worthwhile to keep working toward them. As Chao et al. (1994) found, understanding the values and goals of those within the organization was the strongest predictor of various indicators of career success.

However, what if we have been able to reliably uncover the values and basic assumptions within the organization, but feel that they are creating problems for employees or the organization? How can we change the culture in the organization?

How to Change an Organization's Culture

As a brand-new employee, how can you change the culture in your organization? It's a trick question, because as a new employee you should not be trying to change the culture. Just think of your own work experience, and how employees responded when a newcomer came in and prematurely tried to make changes. The response probably was not positive. As we've seen, we take basic assumptions for granted to the extent that we cannot imagine doing things a different way. As a result, we experience anxiety when faced with the possibility of changing (Schein, 2004). But even if anxiety isn't an issue, there is another problem: "Who is this newcomer to tell us how to do our job?" Newcomers don't know the values, history, or politics of an organization, and therefore are ignorant of why certain things are done certain ways. Because of this, seasoned employees will be suspicious of newcomers who try to make significant changes. So as a newcomer, you first have to understand the culture, before you can hope to change it. You have to keep relatively quiet and focus on paying careful attention to artifacts, values, and, if possible, basic assumptions. You need to transition from being an outsider to being considered a member of the group. Until this happens, do not expect to exert considerable influence or that you can do much to change the culture. The exception might be if you are in a position of considerable power. But even then, unless you are in an emergency situation and have to act fast, you should work to understand the culture before trying to push for sweeping changes.

But once you thoroughly understand the culture and have established yourself as a member of it, there may be a few things you can do to inspire changes to the culture. First, let's discuss what won't work: proclamations of change. These may take the form of revisions to a mission statement, a new slogan, or, senior management may roll out an entire program signifying change (it may include banners, buttons, T-shirts, etc., with some new slogan on it). These attempts to change will fail because simply changing words will not lead to meaningful changes in actual values (Larkin & Larkin, 1994). Saying it will not automatically make it happen (just consider New Year's Resolutions, for example!). In fact, trying to proclaim change with dramatic wording or slogans might result in resistance to the ideas, or employees may mock the idea. Just consider the examples provided by Larkin and Larkin (1994): "We watched as employees took Working with Pride and turned it into 'working for pricks'; Beliefs We Share into 'bullshit we share'; and Quality is Everything We Make into 'quality is everything we fake.'" Again, saying it will not automatically make it happen.

Some things will change the culture, but individual employees cannot control them. These might include major events in the organization's environment, a merger or acquisition, massive layoffs, changes in technology, a major scandal, or changes in leadership (Schein, 2004).

So what can individual employees do to change the culture? To start, remember how the culture developed in the first place: with behaviors that were tried and, over time, were found to "work" well, in terms of helping the organization address whatever issues it faced. To change the culture, you will have to get people to change existing behaviors or adopt new ones. Keep in mind that it will be difficult to change major behaviors. You should not expect to revamp an entire training program, marketing strategy, or revamp or eliminate a major ritual or tradition. This would involve too much psychological change for employees and create anxiety. As a result, you would be met with considerable resistance.

Instead, you should **focus on "smaller" behaviors** that might be changed more immediately. For example, if people in your office or department keep to themselves and you think the culture might improve if people socialized a bit more, you could do a variety of things that might change behaviors in small ways, yet lead to bigger change. You could try to create an area in the office where people can socialize, and make it the kind of place people might want to hang out. In some organizations, this might mean having comfortable furniture and some music or interesting reading materials. In a less conservative organization, it might involve having games (maybe a Nerf basketball hoop). Rather than changing the setting at work, you could try to encourage employees to get together during work (maybe by eating lunch together), or after work, whether at your place or somewhere else people would enjoy. You could try to start a company or department sports team. The trick is to make sure you are staying true enough to the existing culture, while encouraging slight changes in behavior patterns. As a result, some of the above suggestions might make sense in one organization yet be considered ridiculous in another. Also, remember that you are not trying to force attitude changes or persuade others directly. You're simply trying to encourage small changes in behavior that can lead to bigger changes. If you can get people to share enjoyable experiences with each other, they will have fun stories and memories to share, and gradually over time, they may become closer around the office. In other words, if, over time, they find that the new behaviors "work" and serve a useful purpose, they will continue to repeat them, and eventually they will be internalized as shared values. However, note that this is a gradual process. You should not expect this kind of change to happen quickly. After all, consider how long it took the culture to solidify. It would be unrealistic to expect it to change drastically in a short period of time.

There are a couple of benefits to making "small" changes like those suggested above. First, as mentioned, a small change often will cause less anxiety and resistance than a major one. Second, a small change enables you to address the root of the problem, rather than the superficial symptoms. For example, another way to change the problem in the example above would be to address the symptom: people keeping to themselves. You could be direct and tell people that they should be hanging out more, or try to force the issue in some other way. But by adjusting aspects of the office or encouraging new rituals, you're getting at the possible roots of the problem: There is no place in the office that encourages "hanging out," or there are no common activities for employees to share together. Making the small changes mentioned above involves trying to create conditions that make getting together more natural for employees.

For an example of a significant cultural change that was aided in part by relatively small changes to behavior, consider the case of crime in New York City. In 1990, there were 2,262 murders in New York City, and in 1998 there were 629 (Bratton & Kelling, 2006). What led to this drastic reduction? Were the police more aggressive and brutal? In fact, police shootings and complaints against police were reduced during these years (Bratton & Kelling, 2006). Many argue that the change is due in part to the implementation of what is called the "Broken Windows" theory. The idea of this theory is that if there is a broken window in a neighborhood and if it is not repaired, it is a signal to others that no one cares, and that it is ok to break more windows (Wilson & Kelling, 1982). And if nobody cares, it is ok to engage in more destructive activities. In response, law-abiding citizens will retreat (rather than collectively discouraging lawlessness), thereby making it easier for crime to flourish. This idea is rooted in an experiment by Zimbardo (1969). He placed an auto in two different cities, New York, and Palo Alto, CA. There were no license plates on the car and the hood was left up. The car in the Bronx was attacked almost immediately, and within about a day, the car was stripped of anything of value. After this, people proceeded to damage the car (smash windows, tear parts off, etc.). The car in Palo Alto was left alone for over a week. Then the researchers damaged part of it with a sledgehammer. It took only a few hours for that car to be destroyed. The car in New York City was left in an area that long ago had neglected to tend to its "broken windows," and the car in Palo Alto was fine until it featured a "broken window" that nobody fixed.

New York City acted on this theory by trying to address various "broken windows." The police began to address "smaller" crimes, like prostitution, aggressive panhandling, fare-jumping in subways (jumping over turnstiles without paying fares), graffiti (by painting over it within 24 hours), and other kinds of disorderly behavior. Many believe that addressing these small problems helped signal that behavior mattered, and that it helped lead to a drastic reduction in major crimes. Although some suggest that other factors were responsible for the improvement and have disputed the Broken Windows theory, a recent carefully controlled study by Braga and Bond (2008) found that neighborhoods in which police attended to small problems saw greater reductions in crime than control groups. Furthermore, when the crime was reduced in one area, it did not shift to other areas. Results like these suggest that small changes can lead to more significant cultural changes.

So how does this relate to how we can change organizational culture? On one hand, the Broken Windows idea has not been applied to organizational culture, so I don't want to overstate any suggestion that it should be applied to organizations (we don't want to lock up colleagues who forget to clean up a minor coffee spill, or who forget to pick up a piece of paper when they miss the wastebasket). However, consider the changes in New York City using the cultural concepts we've been studying. Essentially, they made small changes to certain artifacts, such as the way things appeared (graffiti) and certain behavioral rituals (aggressive panhandling, disorderly behavior, etc.), and these led to larger and lasting changes in behavioral patterns. In this sense, the Broken Windows approach is aligned with our focus on making small changes to behavior (as in the example above, when we tried to change certain office conditions to encourage people to hang out more as a group).

Beyond getting creative and finding ways to make small changes that can shape the behavior of coworkers, in some positions you may have the opportunity to simply lead by example, by demonstrating alternative ways to accomplish tasks. If you demonstrate these without trying to push others to follow, it's possible that your ways may catch on with some people, and gradually be adopted. You also can speed change by securing the support of key coworkers. We will discuss these and other approaches in much greater detail when we examine organizational politics in Chapter 13.

To close out this chapter, we can review some key things to keep in mind when it comes to the culture of our new workplace:

- We should expect to have to adjust to the culture, rather than expecting it to adjust to us.
- The organization's culture is based on what "works" for the employees, in that it has been shaped by behaviors that survived a trial-and-error process and have come to be internalized as shared values and beliefs.
- We should devote effort to learning the culture by observing artifacts and trying to identify shared values, beliefs, and basic assumptions.
- We should become an accepted member of the culture before expecting to be able to change it.
- When we do change it, we should focus on changing small artifacts and behavior patterns, in order to open the door to more significant changes.

References

Bratton, W., & Kelling, G. (2006, February 28). There are no cracks in the broken windows. *National Review Online.*

Braga, A. A., & Bond, B. J. (2008). Policing crime and disorder hot spots: A randomized controlled trial. *Criminology, 46*(3), 577–607.

Cable, D. M., & Parsons, C. K. (2001). Socialization tactics and person–organization fit. *Personnel Psychology, 54,* 1–23.

Chao, G. T., O'Leary-Kelly, A. M., Wolf, S., Klein, H. J., & Gardner, P. D. (1994). Organizational socialization: Its content and consequences. *Journal of Applied Psychology, 79,* 730–743.

Cook, J. (2008, January 16). Perks make Google office hardly feel like work. *Seattle Post Intelligencer.* Retrieved June 1, 2012, from www.seattlepi.com/default/article/Perks-make-Google-office-hardly-feel-like-work-1261652.php

Fisher, C. D. (1986). Organizational socialization: An integrative view. *Research in Personnel and Human Resources Management, 4,* 101–145.

Gittell, J. H. (2003). *The Southwest Airlines way: Using the power of relationships to achieve high performance.* New York, NY: McGraw-Hill.

Jablin, F. M. (2001). Organizational entry, assimilation, and disengagement/exit. In F. M. Jablin & L. L. Putnam (Eds.), *The new handbook of organizational communication: Advances in theory, research, and methods* (pp. 732–818). Thousand Oaks, CA: Sage.

Larkin, T., & Larkin, S. (1994). *Communicating change: How to win support for new business directions.* New York, NY: McGraw-Hill.

Miller, K. (2003). *Organizational communication: Approaches and processes* (3rd ed.). Belmont, CA: Wadsworth.

Schein, E.M. (2004). *Organizational culture and leadership* (3rd ed.). San Francisco, CA: Jossey-Bass.

Shearing, E. (2010, May 9). Dixon Schwabl focuses on having fun at its office playground. *Rochester Democrat and Chronicle.* Retrieved June 1, 2012, from www.democratandchronicle.com/article/20100509/BUSINESS/5090323/Dixon-Schwabl-focuses-having-fun-its-office-playground

Wilson, J.Q., & Kelling, G. (1982, March). Broken windows: The police and neighborhood safety. *Atlantic Monthly,* 29–38.

Zimbardo, P.G. (1969). *The cognitive control of motivation.* Glenview, IL: Scott, Foresman.

Zjawinski, S. (2008, November 13). Look! Google's New York office (blog post). Retrieved June 1, 2012, from www.apartmenttherapy.com/look-googles-new-york-office-69492

Chapter 5

Credibility

This chapter is about two important questions: (1) How do we establish ourselves in our new workplace? and (2) How can we become an influential employee within our organization?

How Do We Establish Ourselves in Our New Workplace?

Why Do First Impressions Matter So Much?

Think about the times in your work experience when new employees have made a good impression on you, and when newcomers have failed to make a good impression. What were the consequences of that impression? It's one thing to say that first impressions matter, but rather than taking that assumption at face value, let's consider the reasons first impressions matter. First, once formed, they are difficult to change. In the first chapter we discussed the concept of schemas that help us mentally arrange and categorize information. When we meet someone, we develop a schema for him or her. We will remember some characteristics and possibly make a few additional associations (he or she reminds me of _____). Once we have a rough schema for someone, psychologically, when we have follow-up interactions with the person, it will be easier to fit him or her into our existing schema than to rearrange our schema. For example, if a new coworker makes a bad initial impression on us, when we encounter that person again, in our mind we will have negative associations for him or her. Suppose the person acts in a more positive way. Rather than adjust psychologically, we may just selectively perceive his or her behavior. We may notice and remember only negative things, downplay positive things, and so on. In other words, we likely will perceive the situation in a way that conforms to our schema rather than changing it. This isn't to say that we never will change. If the person does something dramatically positive, or consistently behaves in a positive way, it will be more difficult for us to cling to our negative schema, and our thoughts about the person will change. But look at what it will take for this person to overcome an initial bad impression. If the person had made an initial impression that was good, or even fairly neutral, he or she would not have had to work so hard for our respect.

First impressions also are important because of the ways others will respond to us after they have formed their impression of us. In this sense, a good reputation will lead to more good outcomes (Pfeffer, 1993). This is due to what is known as a **self-fulfilling prophecy**. Once someone has developed a schema for us, that schema

Table 5.1 The Importance of First Impressions

They:
- Form fast.
- Influence the way people continue to see us. They will pay more attention to things that are consistent with impressions, and less attention to things that are inconsistent.
- Are slow to change once formed. It is mentally more easy to fit others' behavior into our initial impressions of them.
- Can be self-fulfilling. People will treat us based on those impressions, causing us to behave in a way that reinforces those impressions.

shapes her expectations of us. We typically will act in accordance with those expectations, which will cause the other person to exhibit the behavior we were expecting. In other words, because of the way we behaved, we helped fulfill the expectation we had by shaping the other person's behavior.

For example, if our initial impression of someone is that he or she is obnoxious, we will expect that he or she will be obnoxious in the future. We will act accordingly the next time we see the person. Because we expect an obnoxious response, we may be more reserved, distant, cautious, or possibly sarcastic. And what happens when someone acts these ways with us? Often, we will attempt to compensate by trying harder to engage them. We may move closer, use more animated gestures, speak with greater volume. In other words, we will exhibit the kind of behaviors the person likely will label as obnoxious! By expecting obnoxious behavior and acting accordingly, a person can influence someone to behave more obnoxiously.

Consider another example. Suppose one person was told he would be working with a gifted coworker, and another was told she would be working with a not-so-gifted coworker. Would both people be treated the same? According to well-known studies by Rosenthal and Jacobson (1992), they would be treated differently, in accordance with expectations that had been formed. In one study, teachers were presented with a group of students, and told that the students either were high achievers who were excellent students, or low achievers who were a challenge to teach. But actually, there were no significant differences between the students. After the teachers had the opportunity to instruct the students, the students' achievement was tested. Those whose teachers were told they had strong students actually performed better than those whose teachers were expecting lower-quality students. The conclusion from this is that the teachers acted in accordance with their expectations, and their expectations were fulfilled.

When we apply this idea to the first impressions and reputation in the workplace, we can consider how early impressions shape the way others respond to us. When we make a good impression, others will expect future interactions to be positive. Our coworkers may respond to us by being positive, supportive, and encouraging. And when opportunities for attractive positions, assignments, or development opportunities come up, coworkers may be more likely to think of us. Responses like this will help us remain positive and enable us to grow and add to the early good reputation we established. Contrast this with someone who starts off as a new employee by making a negative impression on others. This likely will evoke less positive and more distant responses, or worse, actively negative, or even aggressive, responses (ridicule, shunning, etc.). When positive new opportunities come up, coworkers will not think of this person. The person may even notice this and wonder why others are being favored. All of these factors will make it harder for this person to succeed in the organization. Yes, it is possible that he or she can overcome this, turn things around, and earn a more positive reputation, but consider how much work this will take, relative to the work it takes to start off with a good impression. Because of this, it is important for new employees to make a good first impression and earn a good reputation.

But how can we do this? What should we do or not do? There is no one answer, but there are a few sources of information on getting off to a good start. Richmond and McCroskey (2009) describe some common behaviors of **DOAs,** or those new employees whose behavior causes them to be "dead on arrival" in their new organizations. This list is not based on careful scientific study, but when reading it you will be able to tell that Richmond and McCroskey have encountered several new employees who have made bad impressions. And while it is not an exhaustive list and additional behaviors might come to mind, in my professional experience this list has captured a great many mistakes I've seen that have caused new employees to be "dead on arrival." Consider it a highlight reel of things you should do if you want to quickly get off to a poor start in your new organization!

Richmond and McCroskey argue that many DOAs *hold their supervisors responsible for their growth and motivation.* They expect the supervisor to motivate them and assume that the supervisor is responsible for providing them with opportunities. If something isn't going well, the response may be "Well, my supervisor didn't _____" rather than taking personal responsibility (notice the external locus of control at play here).

Some DOAs *think they know it all* and are likely to decline help from others. And when given good advice by more informed coworkers, they often will ignore it and do things their own way. They may even ridicule suggestions they're given and flat out state that they have a better way of doing things. When I've given advice to newcomers, it's based on past successes and mistakes others or I have made, and it often is information that I know the newcomer will need in order to do a good job or fit into the culture. In these situations, I rarely have seen others succeed by ignoring the advice and doing things their own way. Usually this behavior will help alienate a new employee from his or her coworkers.

As I mentioned in the culture chapter, some newcomers will *question how your organization does things* and remark that "that's not how we did it at my other job." This can put current employees on the defensive and may make them think to themselves that if your other organization was so good, maybe you should go back to it.

Some are DOAs because they *want all of the rewards available in the system without paying any dues or putting in time to earn them.* They may resist doing the kind of unattractive "chores" that newcomers often are asked to do, yet complain about senior members who, thanks to the time they've put in, have earned various perks (like leaving early, etc.). Again, there is a sense of entitlement here that has not been earned by the newcomer.

DOAs also may *resist following norms* that most others in the organization follow. And they may be openly critical of certain rituals or traditions (possibly in the presence of one or more employees who like or helped start those traditions!). So when everyone takes time for an office party, gets together after work, takes turn bringing food to meetings, or follows some other norm, the newcomer who does not participate quickly will make himself or herself an outcast, or at least needlessly create distance from his or her coworkers.

Often, DOAs are *nosy*. They make everything their business, even though they probably should be spending their time on more important things. They will participate in gossip yet not really know the people whose personal lives they may be discussing. They should not expect that we would enjoy hearing a stranger exchange gossip about a coworker whom we've known for some time. By trying so hard to get information, these newcomers likely will find that others lose trust in them and actually make an effort to exclude them.

Some DOAs *enjoy arguing over insignificant issues simply to get attention*. Again, rather than getting their work done, they fill their time with meaningless arguments so that they can be seen as right. They will get attention, but not good attention. And even if they do end up having some good ideas, others may steer clear of them simply so they do not get bogged down in mind-numbing arguments.

DOAs often will *cross the organization's "good old boys/girls,"* a term coined by Richmond and McCroskey (2009). An old boy/girl is an employee who has been in the organization a long time, and therefore has made connections with many people throughout the organization. While these people may not appear to have much power in the formal network, they quite likely have a great deal of informal power. They have forged alliances with many people and have learned how to get things done, as well as to keep things from getting done. As a result, they have a great deal of informal power within the organization, and it is in our best interests to recognize this power. For example, if you fail to spot these key people and start criticizing them, you may be talking to one of their many allies. And if they find out, they will know how to make life miserable for you.

Similarly, DOAs may *talk negatively about supervisors or coworkers behind their back* (p. 193). This may not happen within the workplace, but it still can be problematic even if done at informal gatherings outside of work. I once had a colleague who did this. I actually was the newcomer and she had been in the organization for a few years. She tried to form an alliance with me by criticizing other employees. First, I knew some of these employees, so her criticisms fell flat. Second, I figured that if she was willing to criticize them (and they had been in the organization longer than I had), she would have no hesitation criticizing me behind my back. Needless to say, during her brief time in the organization I never trusted her, and I doubt my reaction was unique.

Finally, DOAs may try to *deviate from normal communication channels to get what they want*. If their supervisor denies a request, they may go over that supervisor and appeal to a more senior manager. As Richmond and McCroskey say, "this is a stupid move" (p. 193). First of all, the supervisor will find out. Second, it probably won't work. The senior manager will be far more "tight" with the supervisor than the employee, and is unlikely to go against the supervisor in favor of the employee. In addition, the more senior level manager probably will not want to be bothered with the concerns of a newcomer, and will see the issue as the supervisor's responsibility. So the employee likely come across as annoying. But let's say it works and the newcomer gets his or her way. That person will have earned the resentment of the supervisor. By circumventing the chain of command, the newcomer may have alienated himself or herself at two separate levels of management, and probably not for an outcome that was worth all of the trouble.

It's possible you may see this issue differently. You may see it as someone exercising initiative, or a "can do" attitude, by not taking "no" for an answer. Indeed, when done by more informed and seasoned employees, the results may be different. But often, supervisors have a broader perspective and know more information than lower-level employees that they cannot share with them. Often there is a good reason behind their "no" answer that subordinates may not realize. By ignoring this and going above a supervisor's head with the sense that they are entitled to a "yes" answer, new employees can damage their relationship with supervisors and others.

To briefly summarize, notice some of the trends in these DOA behaviors. There is a sense of entitlement, whether it is to be motivated by others, to have the perks everyone else has, to do things their own way, or to receive "yes" answers to our questions. There also are many ways our mouths can get us into trouble, whether it's by whining and complaining, mocking the way your new organization does things, or by talking about others behind their backs. Finally, there is a lack of willingness to learn the culture and the wisdom behind the way employees in the organization handle problems and issues.

So What Should New Employees Do?

In this section we will address some of the things that new employees can do to establish themselves in their organization, by making good first impressions and developing a good reputation. In many cases, this information is based more on advice by professionals than on information generated by careful research (simply because research doesn't always capture the kind of practical issues that still are important to address).

Plan to Embrace the Organization's Culture

Before we get to specific things you can do as a new employee, it is important to address the importance of attitude. Notice that many of the issues common among DOAs center around resisting a workplace culture that is foreign to us. New employees should plan on looking forward to learning the new organization's "way" of

Table 5.2 Establishing Ourselves in a New Workplace

Plan to embrace the organization's culture.
Plan to listen and observe before talking.
Be positive with coworkers and supervisors.
Be a good follower.
Handle your concerns appropriately.
Focus on why, in addition to how.
Try to see the "big picture" or think like your supervisor or the owner.
Demonstrate Initiative.

doing things. Realize that however perplexing the culture may be, it has developed into that culture for very logical reasons. Their approach has worked for them. So at least initially, assume that things will work their way, and try to figure out how they work. There may be things you don't like, but challenging them early on probably won't do you much good (see DOAs above). Before you can expect to be able to change the culture, you first will have to accept it as it is. However, this raises the question: "What if the culture is so negative or destructive that it is unbearable to tolerate?" Or what if the culture is not destructive, but essentially requires you to act in opposition to your most important values? In this case, unless you can find a few more seasoned employees like you who would like to see the culture change and become more positive, you should respect that you alone, as a new employee, probably will not be able to do a great deal to change the culture (unless you are in a leadership position or have political influence in the informal network). In this case, you likely will find that the best option is to work somewhere else, unless you would rather put up with a considerable amount of stress during (and probably after) work each day. But if the culture is tolerable, even if peculiar, you should approach it with an open-minded attitude.

Plan to Listen and Observe Before Talking

Quite naturally, there is so much that new employees do not know, and therefore there are risks to speaking up prematurely, before first understanding the culture. To observe the culture, you can do the kinds of things we explored in the previous chapter: Take note of artifacts and try to uncover shared beliefs, values, and assumptions. In the process, you should be careful to notice any norms or rituals, how meetings are conducted, how people handle various types of challenges, and so on. It also can be important to listen for stories people tell, as those often contain lessons that guide the behavior of employees. What is the point of all of this observation? It is so that you will develop a sense of (1) how people really do their jobs (as opposed to what's in the employee manual), (2) when it is appropriate to speak up (in terms of timing and acceptable topics), and (3) how to approach employees in this organization. In other words, you need to make sure you follow the norms and avoid "putting your foot in your mouth"!

Be Positive With Coworkers and Supervisors

Some of your new coworkers may annoy you. Your supervisor may rub you the wrong way. Even if this happens, it is important to be positive with everyone, at least initially. Sounds obvious, but what does that mean in practice? First, if you don't have anything nice to say to a person, just try to be civil to him or her, and remember to not complain about him or her. Even if a coworker complains to you about the same person, you should take care to avoid joining in. Instead, you can offer something generic like "I hadn't noticed that" or "She's probably having a bad day." The point is to avoid standing out for talking behind the backs of coworkers. Instead, you should spend time getting to know everyone. If that does not come naturally to you, then just focus on learning about what each person does. You can get things started with comments like "I'd enjoy hearing about what you do," and then asking follow-up questions on aspects you find interesting. Or you can do what salespeople do, by paying attention to the artifacts each person has in his or her office or work area: posters, pictures, remnants of hobbies, and so on. When employees display things in their office, they are inviting conversation about them. You also can apply this to your own work area, and adorn it with things that might stimulate discussion. Although I didn't strategically set out to do this in my office, I found by accident that it works quite well. For example, I have a framed collection of concert ticket stubs on my wall, and there is enough variety in the shows I've seen to enable people with different interests to comment on it and begin sharing stories about their concert experiences. Happily, I've stumbled onto something that for students occasionally has made visiting and waiting in my office a slightly better experience than the "stuffy" experience they may have been expecting. Similarly, as a new employee, you can use artifacts to help you establish rapport. Just make sure your use of artifacts is consistent with how other employees use them (certain types may be common in one organization but entirely absent in another, and it is important to take notice of this).

Besides having positive interactions with everyone, remember the value of networking and making connections with everyone. Recall our discussion in Chapter 3 about the benefits of being part of and bridging networks. An additional benefit of getting to know people is that you can learn the informal network more quickly, and in the process you will more quickly learn of the good old boys/girls in your organization.

Be a Good Follower

The word "follower" has a fairly negative connotation. It suggests a weak-minded "doormat" doing whatever an employer wants. But when I refer to a good follower, I simply am thinking of an engaged employee who thoughtfully does his or her job and takes initiative. And because he or she is thoughtful, if problems or issues arise, this employee will question them. There are a few aspects to being a good follower. First, as you might have guessed from the other suggestions, it is important to tone down your ego, and focus on learning from others (Richmond & McCroskey, 2009). You may have been a great employee at another organization, or an excellent student who was loved by all of your professors, but your new coworkers do not know about any of this. They just want you to do a good job in their system. So before you can expect to lead or impress others, you first have to follow their lead.

This also means asking for help, or accepting it when it is offered. Unfortunately, asking for help sometimes is seen by new employees as a major weakness. From another perspective though, it is a way of demonstrating that you are trying to do a good job and "get it right." It only becomes a problem when you're constantly doing it, asking about the same thing over and over, asking for things that, with a little effort, you really could have figured out yourself, or if you are ignoring the answers in advice you receive.

Similarly, often people very naturally are reluctant to admit their mistakes, for fear that they can reveal incompetence. I encourage you to consider an alternative perspective on mistakes by thinking through some of the following implications. First, there are some problems that come with not admitting mistakes: (1) someone may find out and not only will we look less competent, but also less trustworthy; (2) our mistakes may unwittingly affect others' work or other departments, and therefore create significant problems; (3) if we don't receive feedback on what we did wrong, we may be likely to continue repeating the mistake (each time increasing the chance of experiencing outcome numbers 1 & 2). Conversely, there may be some benefits of mistakes that are hard to anticipate when we're concerned about being embarrassed: (1) you can learn how to avert the mistake in the future; (2) others can receive a head's up on the problem and make adjustments if needed; and (3) it often is a pleasant surprise to encounter someone who owns up to his or her mistakes (so long as the person tries to learn from the mistake and doesn't keep making the same one over and over). In my experience across different types of jobs and organizations, I've encountered a fairly consistent reaction when I have admitted mistakes to supervisors: (1) they typically weren't thrilled that I made the mistake, but (2) they sincerely appreciated that I was honest enough to share it with them. They knew they could trust I would admit to future mistakes, and they also knew that they could trust that things were going ok if I wasn't mentioning any mistakes (in other words, they weren't left with any lingering doubts about whether things were going ok). Based on these experiences, in most situations I would recommend being very forthcoming with any problems you might have created. You should bring these issues to others' attention as soon as possible, for two reasons. First, you may be able to help prevent a minor problem from becoming a major problem. Second, it is better for you to deliver the news and frame it for the supervisor than for a supervisor to hear it from someone else and form an opinion about it without your input or perspective. Again, while it is an uncomfortable situation for you, it also is an opportunity to build trust with your supervisor and coworkers.

Handle Your Concerns Appropriately

Rather than the DOA approach (whining, complaining, talking behind coworkers' backs, going above your supervisor for a "second opinion"), consider the ways in which you might use questions to make progress without alienating yourself from others. You can ask respectful questions with genuine and sincere curiosity, such as: "I'm curious why you do it that way? What is the thinking on that?" "That's different—it will be interesting to try it this way. Why do you choose to approach it this way?" One of two things will happen if you take this approach. First, the answers you receive may help you better understand why things are done a certain way. You may not agree with it, but at least you will see the logic behind it. Or, the answer will make no sense at all, and you may have to continue asking followups until things are more clear to you. And if the person cannot answer your questions, either he or she will refer you to someone who can, or the organization may have to address the issue. If this happens, by using questions, you will have helped the organization address a potential flaw in its approach, but you will have done so respectfully, as opposed to condemning your coworkers. So if something doesn't make sense to you, rather than whining or ridiculing the approach, respectfully try to question the reasons behind it, so you can better understand it or so others will realize the need to question it themselves.

Focus on Why, in Addition to How

During high school I worked in a pharmacy, and one of my jobs was to replenish the greeting card supply. The instructions I was given were simple. If there was an empty slot, go to the drawer underneath, take out two cards and envelopes, and put them in the empty spot. I did this for a while until my teenager logic helped me realize there was a better way to avoid doing all of that work, simply by taking all of the cards out of the drawer and putting them in the slot (rather than just two at a time). The slot would be more reliably filled up and I wouldn't have to come back as often to replace it. Brilliant, and to me it was yet another reason teenagers were smarter than adults! Within a week or two of my implementing my new system, one of the owners asked me if I had been doing it, and (in keeping with the advice mentioned above), I told them I had been doing it to be more efficient (notice the "more efficient" part of how I framed it). At that point, he informed me that when all of the cards were removed from the drawer, it was an indication that more needed to be ordered. In other words, my innovation of putting all of the cards in the slot at once falsely gave the sense that the cards were selling out. This caused the owners to prematurely order many more cards than they needed. I don't think they were as impressed by my brilliance as I initially was!

In this example, I knew how to do my job, but not *why* it was supposed to be done a particular way. As a newcomer, to the extent you are able, it is a good idea to try to learn why you are being expected to do your job a certain way. Ideally, your organization will train you in a way that enables you to understand the "why" of your job. If not, over time, you eventually will learn this from observation and experience. But you may be able to accelerate your learning again by using questions effectively. In fact, you can use the same questions you would use to explore areas of concern, because you're interested in why things are done certain ways. So again, you can ask questions like: "I'm curious why you do it that way? What is the thinking on that?" "That's different—it will be interesting to try it this way. What makes you approach it this way?" Doing this can help you begin to develop a perspective that your supervisors will value in you: the ability to see the "big picture."

Try to See the "Big Picture" or Think Like
Your Supervisor or the Owner

Although it is impossible to gain the perspective of a supervisor or owner without serving in those positions, you can give some thought to these perspectives (Kelley, 1999). If you are in regular contact with various levels of management, you can get a sense for what is on their mind, or you can occasionally pause every now and then and consider "what would I be focused on if I was in their position." For example, our college president frequently mentions popular business books in speeches, and I know he sometimes has his cabinet members read them. I enjoy reading them too, as it helps me be a more informed teacher. On one occasion, I encountered a book that I thought our president might like or find relevant, so I mentioned it to him in a brief email (that is ok in our culture, but in many organizations, it may be a bad idea to directly contact any members of senior management like this). I knew to do this because I had considered things from his perspective.

He has to manage a large organization, and he has certain goals. The book I noticed was relevant to one of his initiatives, and I thought I could be useful by sharing it. I should add that this was not a highly calculated move. I don't spend additional time looking for books for him, and I didn't continually follow up on this one. It struck me as relevant, so I mentioned it, as opposed to digging for a book that would give me an excuse to contact him. Without having to fake any behavior to appear to be someone I'm not, and by just paying attention and sending one additional email, I was able to help my president access new information that might have been helpful. This leads us into what may be the most important thing for you to do as a new employee: **demonstrate initiative.**

Demonstrate Initiative

The main thing you should do, once you've gained a sense of the organization, is to demonstrate initiative. This is not the same as doing your job, but rather it's finding opportunities to contribute in meaningful ways above and beyond what you're expected to do. I can share an example of when, as a newcomer, I partially demonstrated initiative, but not nearly as well as I could have. Early in my time as a professor I encountered the advisement process, which happens every semester. During this time, faculty meet with advisees for about 20 minutes to help them figure out their schedules and register for the upcoming semester. Each faculty member has 30+ advisees, so this process takes a great deal of time. Unfortunately, it takes up even more time when students are not prepared. I often encountered students who hadn't given much thought to their schedule and really weren't prepared to meet. Most of the meeting time would be spent with them looking through the course schedule, trying to find good courses to take. This is not a good use of the student's time or the advisor's time. I was not alone—other advisors were experiencing the same problem. By helping the advisees, I was doing my job. But I found a way to go beyond that and take initiative. To address the root of the problem (students not being prepared), I developed a worksheet for them to complete *before* they met with me, and indicated that we could not meet for advisement until they had completed the form. It actually worked pretty well. It helped students understand my expectations and it helped me because most students showed up having prepared more completely for our meeting. I had taken initiative and found a way to contribute. Now, all faculty in our department, and I think some others, use this system, and have for about ten years. It is taught to new faculty when they begin to serve as advisors. Not bad.

Unfortunately, someone else got credit for this initiative, even though that person repeatedly was quick to credit me for the idea. The problem is that I kept the idea to myself and didn't share it with others. I just started doing it. Another faculty member noticed and liked it, and mentioned it to everyone at a department meeting (while giving me full credit for it). For some time, when faculty would talk about it, they would credit him for the idea (and he graciously would correct them and give me credit). It was almost comical how many times that process happened, but I think that some people appreciated that he was thoughtful enough to present the idea to the department, when I wasn't so thoughtful. The point of this example is not that I feel robbed. It was just one idea, and I care more that it was useful for everyone more than I do about getting credit or some kind of medal for it! But we can learn some important lessons from this. First, I was lucky at all that anyone credited me for the idea. In a more "cutthroat" environment, I may never have been given any credit at all. Second, my initiative meant very little to my coworkers until it was shared. Not shamelessly broadcasted, just generously shared in a way that could benefit others. My colleague did this well, in that he was smart and thoughtful enough to try to help all of his colleagues. He deserved the credit he was afforded by others.

And that is an important part of taking initiative: doing things that can contribute to the betterment of the entire office, department, division, or organization. There is no roadmap to this, though the ability to take initiative follows from the things I outlined above about establishing a good reputation as new employees. If we understand the culture, gain a sense of the "why" behind our job, and give some thought to the "big picture," we will be enhancing our reputation. The goal should be to consider how we can go above and beyond and contribute in positive and meaningful ways. The way we might do this can vary considerably, and I'll do my best to share a few examples. Early on, we might demonstrate initiative simply by staying a little late or offering extra help when others seem stretched. Perhaps a large project is due and we can offer assistance. If people are stressed, we can be supportive. Sometimes initiative will require some creativity on our part. We may spot a way to make something more efficient, notice a problem others don't see and offer a way to address it, think of ways to help others do their job more effectively, or notice things that are falling through the cracks (two departments may be partially responsible for something, but neither is following up on it completely or sufficiently).

The goals of this section have been to help you avoid being a DOA and instead to make an excellent impression and establish a good reputation in your organization. In the next section, we will begin to transition away from the newcomer stage and focus how you can increase your influence as a regular employee. In the process we will examine different levels of influence, bases of power we can earn, and the dimensions of credibility that will influence the extent to which others consider us to be a believable coworker.

Levels of Influence

How much influence do you have on those around you, and how much influence do they have on you? Why do you have more influence over some than others, and why do some people have more influence over you? According to Kelman (1961), there are three distinctly different levels of influence. As we go through these, consider which levels of influence you have over others, as well as which levels of influence others have over you.

Compliance

If we influence someone at the compliance level, the person will do what we want in order to gain a reward or avoid punishment (Kelman, 1961). On the road, speeders will slow down if they think a police officer will be around (or if their radar detector alerts them to police radar). Some students will work only because they need a grade. And some employees will do things only for a paycheck, or to avoid disciplinary action or other kinds of headaches that a supervisor can arrange. If we are able to distribute a reward that someone would value or implement a punishment that would matter to someone, then we can influence others at this level. Unfortunately, once we remove the possibility of reward/punishment, the person will stop complying with us. The driver will go back to speeding, and once the supervisor has left the work area employees will speak freely and go back to doing the job their way. The short lasting effects of someone's compliance with us suggest that if we hope to have greater influence over others, we will have to use something more than rewards or punishments. When spelled out this way, it sounds pretty obvious. You may even be saying "Of course you'll need more than that." But think for a moment of how many people you have encountered who have attempted to influence others only at the compliance level. These might be teachers who too often fall back on "If you don't do this, I will deduct points," or supervisors who say "As long as I'm the manager, that's the way it's going to be." Again, these will work, but how come the very same people will work harder for a different teacher, or respond much more willingly to another manager? It has a lot to do with our next level of influence.

Identification

This level of influence is based on our relationship with the person who is asking us to do something (Kelman, 1961). We will do what a person asks because we identify with that person, in the sense that we respect the person, want to be like him or her, and care about living up to the person's expectations for us. This also can happen when we identify with a group, and want to live up to our role in the group. In each case, our identity is based on our relationship with another person or group. If a teacher influences us at the identification level, we value what he or she thinks of our work, and will want to submit good work in order to maintain a positive relationship with the teacher. Similarly, if we identify with a supervisor, we will want to do a good job so that we can continue to have a good working relationship with him or her. Notice that it is important that we do not disappoint the person. However, also notice that while behavior is much more voluntary in this situation, it still is the result of an external influence (this time a person rather than something rewarding or punishing), not a value or behavior we have internalized. Fortunately though, at this level, our influence can be longer lasting than at the compliance level. It is based on a positive relationship, and if we earn this level of influence as a supervisor, at least we know work will get done even after we leave the room! Although we've done more to explain why people would respond beyond minimal compliance, there still is a group of people we have not explained: those that will work hard for all of their teachers, or all of their supervisors/managers, regardless of how effective those people are at establishing an identification level of influence. To better understand this issue, we need to explore one additional level of influence.

Internalization

When we are influenced at this level, we have internalized a behavior, meaning that we do something because it is consistent with our value system and pleasing to us

(Kelman, 1961). It may make others happy, and it may bring us rewards or help us avoid punishments, but the main reason we are doing it is for us. Those who have internalized behaviors will work hard even for lousy teachers or supervisors (or conversely, if they have internalized negative behaviors, they may resist excellent teachers or supervisors). We may internalize something because we find it to be an approach that works well for us, or it is logical to us, so long as it is consistent with our value system.

Suppose you are in charge of at least a few employees, and consider the consequences of earning one of these three levels of influence with them. What would make your job the easiest, compliance, identification, or internalization? With compliance you continually would have to monitor employees or otherwise assure the presence of a reward or punishment. With identification you would have an employee who would work hard for you. With internalization you would have an employee who would work hard for anyone. Either of these last two would make our life easier than only earning influence at the compliance level, so for the remainder of the chapter we will explore how we can earn this influence.

Influence, Power, and Credibility

Mottet, Frymier, and Beebe (2006) proposed a model of influence in which the influence we have is based on the power bases we establish with others, and I would add to that and suggest that those power bases are rooted in the credibility we establish with others. To elaborate on this model, I will discuss the nature of power and outline key power bases that have been identified by research.

Power

French and Raven (1959) are well known for identifying power bases, or ways we might hold power over others. Before I discuss the specific power bases, it is important to stress that from this perspective, power is something we earn from others, and we only have as much power as others are willing to grant us. In other words, we only can have power over someone if they willingly grant it to us. This may not make sense, but I can offer a funny example to demonstrate it. When I was beginning as a doctoral student, early in the fall semester, another doctoral student, who was a teaching assistant with his own courses, held class outside on a day when the weather was good. The problem was that this was a large lecture course with almost 200 students in it! He and his class subsequently made the front page of the school newspaper. The department chair, probably sensitive to the fact that Communication sometimes is viewed as a "fluff" major, definitely did not like the image of one of his lecture classes being taught outside. It is an understatement to say that he made this very clear to the doctoral student. He had been a powerful chair for some time and his authority was well respected. However, power is something that we grant to others, and this doctoral student was not prepared to grant as much power to this chair as the rest of us. When the weather warmed up in the spring, and the chair was out of town at a conference, the doctoral student took a different large lecture class outside and again made the front page of the paper (to this day I suspect he arranged for the paper's photographer to take more photos of his class!). Sure, when the chair returned to town and was even more upset than the first time, the doctoral student steered clear of the office for a while. But the point of this is that, even though the chair was powerful, in this case, he had only as much power as that doctoral student was willing to grant to him.

The point of framing power like this is to emphasize the fact that **in order to have lasting power over others, we have to earn it.** For another example of the importance of earning power, just consider a time when you've encountered someone in a position of leadership who just assumed he or she could boss others around. This tactic may have worked to earn compliance, but chances are it also earned ill will and resistance. Or people may have done their jobs poorly on purpose. Contrast this with someone who treated people better and commanded respect. I suspect that people responded much more positively. With this in mind, we are going to explore some of the major power bases that have been identified by French and Raven (1959).

Power Bases

If we have the ability to administer punishment or withhold rewards, we can operate from a *coercive* **base of power.** By using this power base, we will be able to influence others at the compliance level, in the sense that if the punishment means enough to a person, the person will comply with us, as long as the punishment is present. Although this power base can help us achieve results, it is not conducive to establishing good working relationships. This may be good if as a manager you want to distance yourself from subordinates, but otherwise it can be problematic. We only should expect short-term compliance when using this power base.

If we can administer rewards or remove punishments, we can operate from a *reward* **base of power.** Although rewards are more welcome than punishment, like punishment, they are effective only at earning compliance. Once the possibility of reward is removed from a situation, compliance will end. In addition, rewards can be problematic because over time they can lose their power (Richmond & McCroskey, 2009). For example, if you were allowed to leave an hour early from work on Fridays, over time this practice will become commonplace and expected, rather than seen as a special reward. And if for some reason the practice had to end, it would seem like a punishment, rather than a return to what used to be normal. So while rewards are more positive than punishment, they also are limited to the short-term, and over time they can lose their power (Richmond & McCroskey, 2009).

Legitimate **power** is when we are assigned a certain amount of power by the organization, in the form of a title and policies that allow us to exert authority over others. Teachers can require attendance, assign grades, and so on. Supervisors can expect attendance, evaluate employees, override decisions. Someone using this power base expects others to listen and comply because "I am the boss," or "It is my job to make sure that you show up on time." This power base can be effective, but as with reward and coercive power, it will enable us to influence others only at the compliance level (Richmond & McCroskey, 2009). People will comply because we are in charge and that implies a power to administer rewards or punishments. To have more meaningful and lasting influence, we need to look to at the final two bases of power.

When we are considered to be knowledgeable in an area, we have an *expert* **power** base. People will comply because they consider us to be a knowledgeable source of information. It should be noted that perceptions of our expertise will be domain specific, meaning we may be considered to be experts about some things but not others. When we are knowledgeable of an area, others are likely to recognize our expert power base. According to Richmond & McCroskey (2009), the expert power base is one way we might influence others at the identification or internalization levels. Out of respect for our expertise, others may do what we ask (identification). For example, we often follow the recommendations of physicians because we recognize their expertise. We are able to identify with them. Over time, if we begin to internalize their recommendations, we will have been influenced at the internalization level. But it starts with our willingness to comply due to the person's expertise in a relevant area.

If others are willing to do what we ask because they like, admire, or respect us, we will have established a *referent* **power** base with them. This power base is rooted in the establishment of good working relationships with others. When a good relationship has been established, it becomes less necessary to appeal to coercive, reward, or legitimate power. According to Richmond and McCroskey (2009), this is the other power base that can lead to identification and internalization levels of influence. Others will do things for us because they like and identify with us (identification). In the process, they may find some of these things to be intrinsically rewarding and come to do them on their own (internalization). Those who have been important influences on us likely inspired us to do something at one point in our lives (identification) and we valued or enjoyed the activity so much that we continued to do it on our own (internalization). This process started when someone earned our respect and admiration.

Notice the striking difference between the use of coercive, reward, and legitimate power and the use of expert and referent power. With the first three, we have to push hard to get others to comply, and even when that works, our success is short-term. But when we use expert and referent power, we don't necessarily have to push as hard, and the results last longer. In reality, we likely rely on a combination of power bases. Even if we have expert or referent power, there may be times when we need to appeal to legitimate authority, or use rewards. But if we hope to have any long-term influence, it will be important for us to establish expert and or referent power with others. Between this and the fact that power is something that others grant us, it is critical to remember that the power to have lasting influence over others is something we have to earn. We earn it by demonstrating our expertise and earning the liking and respect of others. In other words, we earn it by being perceived as credible by others.

Credibility

Our **credibility** is how believable others perceive us to be (Richmond & McCroskey, 2009). The key word here is "perceive." You can be intelligent, but if others don't perceive you to be intelligent, your intelligence won't matter much. Others will respond to us based on the perceptions they have of us. In school, some of the most brilliant teachers are met with resistant students who dislike them, don't listen to them, and so on. This is because these teachers don't communicate their ideas very well or establish good working relationships with students. The same problem can affect all of us. We may be hard workers, do some aspects of our job well, and yet still not be perceived as credible. In the remainder of this chapter, we will explore the dimensions of credibility and explore ways to increase others' perceptions of our credibility.

To put a more human face on credibility, I can tell you what I learned about it once I served in various leadership positions. I do not know if other leaders share the same perspective, but I can say that my evaluation of those working for me can be summed up with one question: "Can I count on this person to get the job done?" The answer to this question informed my decisions on what I could delegate to various people, whom I would have to monitor more carefully, whom I thought of when opportunities for coveted assignments arose, and whom I thought deserved special recognition. Essentially, I was asking a question of who was credible. Although I wasn't thinking of the dimensions of credibility when I asked that question to myself about each employee, essentially, they were at the heart of my answer to it. So as you consider these dimensions and your own work experience, it would be worthwhile to conduct yourself as if others are asking of you: "Can I count on this person to get the job done?"

Dimensions of Credibility

Credibility is a common word and you will see different writers describe it in different ways. But most contemporary communication researchers focus on three key dimensions of credibility: *competence, character,* and *good will* toward the receiver of our message (McCroskey & Young, 1981). These are the same elements that Aristotle identified 2,400 years ago as constituting what he called *ethos* (McCroskey & Young, 1981). Each dimension is distinct from the others and plays an important role in how others perceive us. *Competence* is others' perception of our knowledge and ability with respect to a particular area. As with the expert power base, it is likely to be domain specific. We may be perceived as competent in some areas and incompetent with others. To be a credible source of information in a particular area, we have to be perceived as competent. However, it is possible for us to be perceived as competent, and still not be considered credible. *Character* matters too. We also must be perceived as trustworthy. This means that others consider us to be honest and believe that we will follow through on any statements or commitments we make. As you can imagine, in an often-competitive business environment in which many people are competent, being perceived as trustworthy can set us apart from others. Notice though that if we have character without competence, the result is someone who is appreciated on some levels, and probably well-liked, but who ultimately cannot be counted on. Both character and competence are important, for different reasons. Although a combination of competence and character often can be "good enough" in terms of enhancing our believability, an additional dimension of credibility is *good will*, or the perception that we have our receivers' best interests at heart (Richmond & McCroskey, 2009). There is a perception that we care. Although caring is important, it also needs to be accompanied by a perception of competence and character. A person who cares but who is perceived as incompetent will not be

Table 5.3 Establishing Credibility

Dimension	What It Involves	How to Earn It
Competence	Others believe we have the knowledge and ability to do something. Can be specific to one area of knowledge or skill.	• Do our job well • Deliver impressive results • Make ourselves difficult to replace • Demonstrate initiative • Refer to past experience and successes • Deliver messages with a level of breadth, depth, height, and sight to fit the expectations of listeners
Character	Others trust us and believe that we will follow through on something when we say we will.	• Follow through on commitments we make • Be tactfully honest with people • Be consistent with people • Treat others with respect and fairness
Good Will	Others believe that we have their best interests at heart.	• Take an interest in others • Praise the work others are doing • Be responsive to others and demonstrate empathy • When others are frustrated, reflect and acknowledge their feelings • Help others "save face" • Take your work seriously, but not yourself

considered to be reliable. A competent person who cares but who fails to follow through on things will be appreciated for good intentions, but also considered unreliable. So as we move forward to consider how we can earn credibility in the eyes of others, it is important to realize the contributions of each of these dimensions to the overall perception of our credibility.

Earning Credibility

It's one thing to discuss dimensions of credibility, but in this section I will attempt to translate them into some tangible things that can be done in the workplace to enhance our credibility. This can be difficult to do though, because different individuals will have different standards for what is credible. Half of the "battle" is being appropriate to your audience. Still, below I'll outline a number of things that can help enhance our credibility. Please keep in mind that it is not an exhaustive list. My goal is to identify a few major areas worth considering. And as you go though these different ideas, notice how much of the focus is on what we do, rather than what we say.

Enhancing Perceptions of Our Competence

First, it is important to only commit to tasks that we are capable of doing. It makes perfect sense that we might want to impress people by taking on multiple duties, or by tackling very challenging products. But that motivation will not be very useful if we are not capable of actually performing the tasks. If we recognize our limitations and stay within our means, we can make the most of our time and ability. This will enable us to **deliver more impressive results,** compared to doing a mediocre job on a task that is beyond our abilities. Related to this, we can enhance perceptions of our competence simply by **doing our job well.** It sounds obvious, yet all of us have worked with people who were not concerned with doing a good job. Sometimes we can stand out simply by being competent.

Beyond this, we can take initiative and **make ourselves difficult to replace.** It is important to remember that all of us are replaceable. Michael Jordan retired years ago, and the Bulls have fielded a team every year since. They might not have been as good, but the Bulls organization still is running. When Tom Brady went down a couple of years ago, another quarterback was on the field for the next play. Again, the organization survived, even though it did not do as well. But suppose you're the popular CEO of a major company who in your 15 months as CEO turned the company around, and even were named by some as "CEO of the Year" thanks to your results. I've just described Jim Cantalupo who in 2003 became the CEO of McDonald's at a time when the franchise was in trouble and actually losing money. He led a change that dramatically increased McDonald's profits and was very well respected. Clearly he was valuable. On April 19, 2004, Cantalupo unexpectedly died of a heart attack. McDonald's named a new CEO within six hours (Dye, 2005). If someone like Jim Cantalupo is replaceable, than so are you or I. Still, while keeping this in mind, we can do things that at least might increase our value and make others reluctant to replace us. This is where initiative comes into play again. **If we demonstrate initiative and earn a good reputation, we will be likely to receive opportunities to further enhance our reputation** (Pfeffer, 1993). In the process, perceptions of our competence will be enhanced.

Although much of competence is about demonstrating competence through behavior, it also is important to sound competent when we communicate. Alan Weiner (2007) has written a comprehensive book about being credible at work, and one of his most useful contributions is the idea of communicating a message at a level that is appropriate to our audience. Specifically, he outlines different aspects of a message that we can convey: the main point, *breadth, depth, height,* and *sight.* The main point involves saying exactly what we think. *Breadth* involves all of the reasons we feel the way we do about our main point (Weiner, 2007). If your main point is to advocate a particular course of action, the breadth consists of the reasons we should do it. *Depth* consists of specific information and details about the point we're making. Weiner (2007) suggests we can address issues related to depth with: "(1) an ease of manner with names, dates, and numbers; and (2) a memory for conversations with important players. If you say, 'The new technology is much faster,' you would follow that with words like, 'In successive rounds of testing, we saved three man-hours per cycle'" (p. 21). The idea is not to flood people in statistics and details, but to be able to provide some key details regarding results. The second part of details involves being able to relay discussions you've had with people that like your idea. *Height* and *sight* both have to do with elements of the "big picture." *Height* is the perspective of how the main point affects the entire organization, or maybe even profession. According to Weiner, some key phrases that convey your appreciation of height can include: "Here's what I see when I helicopter up," and "Let's get up on the balcony for a moment and look at this from the broader perspective" (p. 21). In my own experience I also have heard others use a phrase along the lines of "I'm not on the field, but when I look at this from the bleachers." *Sight* involves considering future implications related to your main point. As with height, the sight perspective has some distinct phrasing: "When I look down the road, six months from now, here's what I see. When I look out over the horizon, here's what I see" (Weiner, 2007, p. 24). As cheesy as some of these phrases may sound, notice how using them conveys an understanding of a bigger picture.

So why cover these different aspects of messages? Consider different audiences you may encounter. Many will want you to get to the point first (Weiner, 2007). But audiences may vary in how many details they want or how much height or sight they need. If you're talking to coworkers, their perspective likely will be the local work area, so you won't have to worry about the bigger picture. But as you talk with those who are in higher positions of status, keep a few things in mind about how they probably operate: They likely are busy, and their focus is on the entire organization and long-term success. So with them, you will have to get to the point and be sure to include an awareness of height and sight issues. If you do this, they will appreciate you as someone who can see the "big picture." In other words, when you're able to tailor your message to your audience's point of view, they will see you as competent (so long as you're backing up your words with quality work).

Enhancing Perceptions of Our Character

There are a number of things we can do to in our workplace to demonstrate character, and again I will focus on behaviors over words. First, **we should follow through on any commitments we make.** It sounds obvious, but sometimes people with the best of intentions will promise to do something yet fail to come through. This makes it more difficult to count on them. The key to this is to avoid promising more than you can deliver. Commit only to what you definitely know you can accomplish. Beyond simply following through, if possible it is a good idea to exceed whatever we have promised to do. This is exemplified by the phrase "under-promise and over-deliver." You don't want to lower expectations too much, you just want to make sure you don't inflate others' expectations. Delivering something under budget, ahead of schedule, or with more features can enhance perceptions both of your character and competence. And when you fail to deliver, or fail in other ways, as we've discussed already, you should admit it.

We also can demonstrate character by **being honest and consistent with people.** The honesty part is pretty straightforward, though if we have negative views of someone, respectful silence likely will be preferable to blatant honesty! Regarding consistency, I am talking about treating the same people consistently in different situations, and being consistent with different coworkers. Of course there are times when we have to treat people differently or behave differently toward the same people, but in some situations, consistency is better. For example, people damage their credibility by being nice to people when they want something from them, while otherwise treating them with indifference. And while we will be closer to some coworkers than others, we can demonstrate character by **treating everyone with respect and fairness.** This can be hard to do when some of your coworkers are "difficult" people, but if you can rise above these issues and treat everyone well, you will be demonstrating excellent character. Finally, we can demonstrate character by exhibiting good will toward our coworkers.

Enhancing Perceptions of Our Good Will

There are a variety of ways we can demonstrate that we care about others. First, we can **take interest in others.** If they mention something about family, a hobby, or other interests, ask for more information, preferably with a detailed question. For example, if a coworker has a son or daughter who is starting college, you could ask a general question, "How is it going?" This will work and demonstrate your interest. But you can go even further by being specific "How is he or she adjusting, and how are you adjusting?" or "What courses is he or she taking?" This will show that you are engaged in the conversation and that interest is more than generic. Asking follow-up questions like this has benefits beyond demonstrating good will. You will get to know a coworker better and build good rapport with him or her. You also may learn something or uncover interesting connections between you and the coworker. Above all, it can feel good to listen to others talk about their interests and personal sources of pride. As has been mentioned in earlier chapters, it starts with a curious attitude.

We also can demonstrate good will by **praising the work others are doing.** How would it make you feel if a coworker said something like: "I noticed how you handled that situation, and I think you did a great job with it." I suspect that anyone would appreciate hearing that kind of comment from a coworker at any level. Now consider how often you hear those kinds of things. You may hear them from a supervisor, but aside from supervisors, we typically don't expect to hear those kinds of things from coworkers. Imagine how positively you would stand out if you started praising the work of others. In the teaching world, we call this "catching them doing something good." When done by parents or teachers, it produces an amazing look of pride on a child or student's face. Similarly, as long as you are being sincere and you are specific in pointing out what the person did, your coworker likely will appreciate your thoughtfulness. When doing this, just be sure to focus on behavior (what they did) rather than labeling them personally. In other words, saying "you did great on this," is better than saying "you are great at this."

We also can demonstrate good will when things do not go so well for our coworkers, by **being responsive and demonstrating empathy** for them. By empathy, I mean considering things from the perspective of your coworker, in order to appreciate the tough times he or she is experiencing. This is an easy concept to understand, but how do we apply it in practice? There is not any one way to do this, but one approach is to actually demonstrate empathy by **reflecting and acknowledging the feelings** of our coworkers when they have encountered a frustrating situation (Ginott, 2003). The amount of acknowledgment needed may vary. In my experience, some people would like the focus to quickly turn to possible solutions for the problem. In other cases, more time and effort is needed to address feelings. The point of acknowledging feelings in this manner is to convey the message that we recognize a person is frustrated and can understand why the person would feel that way (in other words, validating the person's feelings). We could do this by offering comments like: "It must be disappointing to not get the promotion, I can see why you would be frustrated," and "I know you put a lot of work into the project, I'm sorry it didn't work out as you hoped, and I can understand why you would be miserable." In each case, we are acknowledging a colleague's feelings and their legitimacy. We don't have to agree with the colleague's feelings, just acknowledge them in a supportive tone. There will be time to focus on solutions and the next steps to take soon enough. But while the coworker is experiencing a negative emotion with some intensity, we should not expect to make a lot of progress until the emotion has been addressed (for reasons we will see more clearly in the chapter on conflict).

We also can help demonstrate good will by **helping others "save face,"** even when we may not feel like it. We will discuss the concept of saving face more in the chapter on conflict, but the idea of allowing others to save face is about helping them avoid unnecessary damage to their public self-image (Goffman, 1967). When employees enter the public arena in an organization, there are times when they may encounter a threat to their face. They may make a prediction and be wrong, get angry with someone only to find out the person was trying to help them, fail miserably at something, or other scenarios. In these situations, it is easy to think of ways to enable a person to save face: "The predication actually made a lot of sense"; "I would have predicted the same thing"; "Ha, no problem, I would have gotten angry too"; "Don't worry, it was just a misunderstanding"; "Nobody could have seen that problem coming"; "It may look like a failure, but it also creates a great opportunity."

But what happens when we have less motivation to help another person save face? What if they just insulted us at a meeting, only to have "egg on their face" later in the same meeting? Or what if they ridiculed our advice, and their way failed, setting up a perfect "I told you so" situation? It can be hard to resist temptation in these situations, but these moments present a great opportunity to take the "high road" and demonstrate good will by enabling others to save face. It might not feel as good as an "I told you so," but consider what is more impressive in these types of situations: giving the obvious face-damaging retaliation, or rising above it and still enabling the person to save face? Sure, sometimes you may just have to retaliate, but to the extent you can resist that urge and help others save face, you will be accomplishing an impressive feat of good will.

One final act of good will toward others can be summed up with a well-known phrase: **Take your work seriously, but not yourself.** It is ok to show some weakness, admit a mistake, and have some fun, so long as you're also doing a good job. In fact, it not only is ok, it's refreshing. In contrast, think of the person who holds onto his or her image with a stern, white-knuckle grip. They build themselves up by putting others down, pointing out the flaws in others, and in refusing to admit any mistakes or shortcomings. Unfortunately, while they may get their way at times, they also will alienate others and in the process, damage their credibility. So remember that most coworkers will not expect perfection (in fact, it would make them uneasy), and that people enjoy a good laugh every now and then, especially at work!

Credibility and Electronic Communication

Although I've finished addressing the dimensions of credibility, I have to address the realm of electronic communication, because I've seen people (including myself) damage their credibility by failing to realize some important things about electronic communication. Below I will cover some things to keep in mind regarding email, web browsing, social networking sites, and texting. Failure to adhere to these guidelines can help you undo the credibility you've worked hard to establish using all of the methods outlined above.

Email. First, before you send an email, assume the whole world will see it, and consider whether you still want to send it. Once it is sent, it can be forwarded or cut and pasted. This warning is especially true of sending emails when you are angry about someone or something, or sending it to someone with whom you are experiencing conflict. In these situations, emails are easy. You don't have to face the person, and you can make sure you get to say everything you want to say. But you then may agonize over the equally angry response you're expecting, to the point that it may be stressful to even open your email. I rarely have seen any good come of using email in this way in the workplace. So what should you do? First, don't send the email in the heat of the moment. Either go talk to the person or, if you have composed the email, at least save it as a draft, "sleep on it," and come back and read it the next day. If you wait until the next day, there will be many times when you realize you don't want to send the email, at least not with its original wording. So remember, once it's sent, it belongs to the rest of the world.

Second, treat emails less like texts and more like traditional letters. When composing a message, put the recipient's name ("Hi Bill,") and when done, include your name. This sounds minor, but many emails are impersonal. And unless you're writing to someone who typically does not respond to you in a timely manner, do NOT tell the person to hurry up and get back to you ("let me know," "please get back to me ASAP," "I need to hear back from you soon"), unless you want the recipient to feel like he or she is working in a McDonald's drive-thru window. Your message likely implies or states elsewhere that you want a response, so adding these additional directives is at best redundant, and likely will be perceived as annoying or rude. Now if you really do need an immediate response, then use a more appropriate communication medium and call rather than emailing.

Web Browsing. In short, assume that your employer is looking over your shoulder at every website you are viewing, as they may be. If you don't want them viewing a site with you, do not view that site at work.

Social Networking (Facebook, etc.). Not to be redundant, but assume the whole world, including current and prospective employers, can view every single word, picture, and video on your Facebook page (including your posts on others' walls), every tweet, and so on. And even if you've done a good job controlling access with your own privacy settings, realize that your friends may have not. So when a coworker and Facebook friend posts "Sarah I can't believe how hammered we got, and that you still were hung over when you came to work," and your friend has not made his or her settings private, your employer (or a prospective one) may be able to see the comment. And if your drinking buddy tagged any photos of you from the party, those may be widely visible too. There are ways to control many of these settings, but it does take some effort to carefully cover your bases. At the time I'm writing this, the website www.reclaimprivacy.org/ enables you to scan various Facebook settings so that you can be more aware of your privacy. I recommend taking the time to ensure that your profile and related information are sufficiently private. And if you don't wish to make your setting private, then I recommend treating your profile as your own personal brand, and shaping it so that you will be attractive to prospective employers.

Texting. I have loving but serious advice for anyone who may be addicted to texting (if you're a person who feels a compulsion to check every few minutes for texts), primarily the younger generation: unless the culture of your organization is very texting friendly, you will be damaging your credibility by constantly texting during social gatherings, meetings, conversations. To those who do not text (and that may be the majority of your coworkers), it may be seen as rude, or as an indication that you lack the self-control to discipline yourself. It also may suggest that you are lacking face-to-face communication skills.

Notice the ways in which earning credibility is conducive to earning expert and referent power, and therefore likely to increase your chances of influencing others at the identification and internalization levels. If you think about those who have influenced you at these more lasting levels, I suspect you will see that lasting influence ultimately is rooted in credibility, as determined by competence, character, and good will.

References

Dye, C. F. (2005, February 1). Is anyone next in line? Succession plans are critical to ensuring a smooth transition when an organization faces an unexpected or an expected leadership vacancy. *Healthcare Financial Management.* Retrieved June 1, 2012, from http://findarticles.com/p/articles/mi_m3257/is_2_59/ai_n9772397/?tag=content;col1

French, J. R. P., & Raven, B. (1959).The bases of social power. In D. Cartwright & A. Zander (Eds.), *Group dynamics* (pp. 259–269). New York, NY: Harper & Row.

Ginott, H. G. (2003). *Between parent and child* (2nd ed.). New York, NY: Three Rivers Press.

Goffman, E. (1967). *Interaction ritual.* New York, NY: Pantheon.

Kelley, R. E. (1999). *How to be a star at work. 9 breakthrough strategies you need to succeed.* New York, NY: Crown Business.

Kelman, H. C. (1961). Processes of opinion change. *Public Opinion Quarterly, 25,* 57–78.

McCroskey, J. C., & Young, T. J. (1981). Ethos and credibility: The construct and its measurement after three decades. *Central States Speech Journal, 32,* 24–34.

Mottet, T. P., Frymier, A. B., & Beebe, S. A. (2006). Theorizing about instructional communication. In T. P. Mottet, V. P. Richmond, & J. C. McCroskey (Eds.), *Handbook of instructional communication: Rhetorical and relational perspectives* (pp. 255–282). Boston, MA: Allyn & Bacon.

Pfeffer, J. (1993). *Managing with power.* Boston, MA: Harvard Business Press.

Richmond, V. P., & McCroskey, J. C. (2009). *Organizational communication for survival: Making work work* (4th ed.). Boston, MA: Allyn & Bacon.

Rosenthal, R., & Jacobson, L. (1992). *Pygmalion in the classroom: Teacher expectation and pupils' intellectual development* (2nd ed.). New York, NY: Ardent Media.

Weiner, A. N. (2007). *So smart but . . . : How intelligent people lose credibility—and how they can get it back.* San Francisco, CA: Jossey-Bass.

Chapter 6

Workplace Relationships

The previous chapter was about credibility and earning influence and power from others. You may have noticed that good relationships are at the center of the most positive and lasting kinds of power and influence. The first half of this chapter will explore a general cluster of questions. What does it take to establish good relationships in the workplace? Why do some do this better than others? And even if most of us can make a few friends in the workplace, a select few become well liked and respected by almost everyone. What are these people doing when communicating with coworkers that the rest of us aren't doing? The second half of the chapter will focus on these same kinds of questions within the context of superior–subordinate relationships.

Investment Model of Relationships

To answer these questions, first I will discuss why we decide to stay in relationships with some people yet distance ourselves from others. This question was answered well by Carol Rusbult and colleagues, who offered an **Investment Model** of commitment in relationships (Bui, Peplau, & Hill, 1996). The model was focused on romantic relationships, but the ideas themselves can be applied to workplace relationships without much difficulty. According to the investment model our **commitment** to a relationship depends on **three factors**: our **satisfaction** with the relationship, the amount we've **invested** in the relationship, and our **perceived alternatives** to the relationship.

Satisfaction. According to the investment model, we are more likely to stay committed to relationships that we find to be satisfying. Our satisfaction with a relationships is based on what we perceive to be the **rewards** and **costs** in the relationship. A reward is anything that is a positive benefit, and could include attention, feelings of belonging, any boost to our esteem, support, financial gains, status, among others. Costs might include time, stress, frustration, or financial costs. However, satisfaction does not come down to simply deciding whether rewards outweigh costs. Instead, our perception of rewards and costs is filtered through our **comparison level,** which is based on all similar relationships we've been in or observed. In other words, through our relationships and those we observe, we develop expectations for what it takes to have a good relationship. Those who have had very good relational experiences will expected subsequent relationships to be very rewarding (the rewards far outweigh the costs), but those with less positive relational histories may have vastly lowered expectations (rewards and costs may be even, or the costs even may outweigh the rewards). Chances are that at least one time we've all observed a relationship and said to ourselves or others "I don't know what he or she sees in her or him." When we've done this it's because we have a different comparison level than our friend and therefore have higher expectations for what is possible in relationships. This explains why some may be satisfied with a relationship while others would feel that the relationship is too costly.

Investment. According to the investment model, our commitment to relationships increases the more we invest in them. Investments into relationships might include spending time, spending financial resources, defending the person and the relationship to others, sticking up for another person, mentoring a person, relocating with and/or for a person or company. The idea is that the more we invest in the relationship, the harder it is to walk away from it. If you think about it, you can appreciate that it is easier to walk away from a relationship with a likeable acquaintance you haven't known very long than it is to dissolve a friendship.

Perceived Alternatives. According to the investment model, commitment also is increased when we perceive ourselves to have few viable alternatives to a relationship. All other things being equal (satisfaction and investments), the opposite is true too. The more alternatives we have, the less committed we will be. This explains why we might be in an unsatisfactory job and have little invested in it, and yet stay. We may see it as our only option. Similarly, if we're forced to work with certain coworkers, we may be stuck with them if there are no other options, even if our satisfaction and investments are low.

So when we look at all three of elements, we are most likely to pursue workplace relationships that are satisfying, based on previous workplace relationships and relative to our alternatives. And then our commitment to the relationship will increase to the extent that we invest in it and it remains satisfying (compared with previous relationships) relative to the alternatives. This helps explains why we actively try to get to know some coworkers but not others, and also why we might start to distance ourselves from certain people in our workplace.

It also provides a blueprint for what we need to do if we want others to have any interest in developing professional relationships with us. When first meeting others **we will need to signal that the relationship will be sufficiently satisfying for them relative to their alternatives, so that they will want to invest their time and other resources in us. And then we need to maintain good working relationships so that others will continue to want to invest their time with us.** Notice how this is consistent with the ideas for establishing credibility and the opposite of the DOA behaviors from the previous chapter. In this next section we will explore how to do this even more specifically, by looking at a model for what it takes to communicate successfully with others so that they will find relationships with us to be satisfying.

A Model for Successful Communication Interactions

The point of this model is to capture what it takes to handle workplace communication interactions effectively. How the model is applied may change based on the nature of the interaction (for example, some interactions need us to assert ourselves, while others require us to back off). It is not a blueprint for how to have flawless interactions, but instead attempts to capture all of the things we need to do well in order to have successful interactions. The model involves several elements, each of which is discussed below.

Cognitive Complexity. Our cognitive complexity is about how many elements we see when perceiving a person, situation, event. It also is about the relationship we see among those events. The best way to understand high versus low complexity is to think of the way children and adults view situations differently. If a child is in conflict with someone, he or she likely only will see a few elements to that situation: "He is a jerk" and "He made me mad." Adults might think this too, but they're likely to see additional elements: "He always pulls this on me," "He is being very manipulative," "He doesn't listen very well when I try to explain myself." A highly cognitively complex adult may see the situation with ever greater sophistication: "He gets angry because he is frustrated with things that have nothing to do with me," "He actually means well and we do agree on some things," "We both want things to work out well—we just approach things differently." At least a couple of things are likely to happen when we are able to see situations with greater complexity. First, notice how our emotions might change as we view situations with greater complexity. As we're able to notice more aspects of the situation, we may be more "level-headed" in our approach to the situation. Second, in addition to viewing the situation with greater complexity, we also can vary in the complexity with which we respond to situations. We can have simple, child-like responses (yelling back at someone or saying something hurtful vs. listening and asking questions to calm the person down before resolving the dispute). In other words, to become better communicators with more options for thoughtfully handling challenging communication situations, we need to become more cognitively complex. A major goal of this book has been to improve your cognitive complexity with respect to communication, so that you will communicate in a way that enhances your stature in your workplace. So far, that's been attempted in different areas, including networking, organizational culture, and credibility. The present model is aimed at helping you see individual communication interactions with greater complexity. The model will be overviewed here, but some elements are reviewed and some will be discussed in greater detail in future chapters.

In order to communicate effectively, we should have the cognitive complexity to do the following in any interaction: handle our personality, adjust to the context and situation, be responsive to our relationship with the other person, handle our emotions and theirs.

Handle Our Personality. As I discussed in Chapter 2, our personality is relatively enduring. However, if we can have the cognitive complexity to know our personality strengths and weaknesses, we can put ourselves in positions to enhance our success and avoid positions or situations that might be problematic. Someone who is aggressive can make sure he or she temporarily exits conflict situations until calming down. Someone with social anxiety can focus on asking questions so others will talk about themselves, so and he or she is less "on the spot." This will be discussed more later on in this chapter, but in general, the idea is to put ourselves in a position to maximize our strengths and minimize our weaknesses. While it is not absolutely necessary for us to do this in order to have a successful interaction, it helps.

Adjust to the Context and Situation. It also helps to be very sensitive to the context we are in, as well as the current situation. Recall from Chapter 1 that the context is the general setting, whether it be an office, church, or bar. Most adults adjust automatically to these different contexts, so you likely won't need to exercise much skill to do this. More specific than the context, the situation is the specific set of circumstances going on within the context. So what is happening in the office? What is the mood? What events are taking place? What kind of approach is needed to appropriately fit the mood of the people and the events that are taking place? Chances are we all have some experience at communicating in ways that have been a poor match for the situation. But as we learn from those experiences, our cognitive complexity improves, and as it does improve, we will become more sensitive to the importance of communicating in ways that fit the situation.

Be Responsive to Our Relationship With the Other Person. It also helps for us to communicate in ways that are a good fit for the nature of our relationship with the other person. So when we are just meeting someone, this means being somewhat formal and not overly disclosing too much personal information. This likely is obvious to most readers, but then again we all can think of examples of times when someone communicated in ways that didn't fit the relationship. A coworker on our level may have acted with too much sense of authority over us, or a new manager may have conveyed more power than had been earned. Because of possible missteps like this, this kind of responsiveness to relationships should be another element of our cognitive complexity.

So far, the elements of complexity I've mentioned have been fairly straightforward, and possibly obvious. They also don't seem to involve much skill. However, the final element, handling emotions, probably is the most important element, and it definitely takes more effort.

Handle Our Emotions. If we are going to communicate successfully, we often have to overcome emotions we are feeling that are very natural yet can interfere with effective communication. We will learn more about emotions in the next chapter, but we can consider some problematic emotions. Anxiety may prevent us from communicating effectively with someone and we may struggle to say the right thing, or to say anything. If we doubt ourselves we may have trouble projecting confidence. We may be angry with someone. There is no one best way to handle each specific emotion. We can't just decide to become confident or that we're no longer angry or anxious. In general though, we can change our emotions by changing our perspective on whatever is triggering the emotions. There is no one way to do this, but there are different ways of doing it for different emotions. The trick is to understand what thoughts are driving the emotions and then adjust those thoughts in realistic ways. I will cover a few examples below.

If we are experiencing anxiety, we are worried that something will go wrong and that a situation will not work out well. There are a couple of things we can do. First, rather than building up the event in our mind, we should remind ourselves that even if things don't work out, we will be able to make more choices. If we embarrass ourselves by saying something stupid, we later can explain ourselves, clarify, and so on. Even if it costs us, it will not remove all of the options we have. We still will get to make more decisions. Second, to the extent that we have time in advance, we can address the problematic "what if" questions we have in our mind. "What if she doesn't like my idea?" "What if I make a fool of myself?" "What if I'm not able to persuade everyone?" In each of these situations, we can "game plan" for how we will handle the situation if it doesn't go well. We likely won't eliminate anxiety, but if we can prepare for situations and have answers to some of our "what if" questions and can avoid building situations up too much, then we have a shot at minimizing our anxiety. And if we can do that, it will be less likely to interfere when we're communicating.

Anger is another emotion that can cause problems in our workplace. Whether it's an angry conflict situation or just having to work closely with someone who profoundly annoys us, anger often can interfere with our efforts to communicate effectively. This anger is driven by our **attribution** of the other person's behaviors, or our explanation for why they are behaving that way. When we attribute their behavior to internal causes (they're a jerk, they're intentionally trying to be disrespectful) becoming angry at them is effortless! But if we can have a more benign attribution (they're having a bad day, they're just passionate about the issue and don't mean to be disrespectful), then it is easier to approach them with more level-headedness. In addition, most times it would be fair to say that people aren't trying to annoy us on purpose, they're just not using optimal strategies for pursuing their goals. In other words, they're not cognitively complex enough to see that they have more options for how to handle the situation. If you can view their behavior in this light (without excusing it), it will be easier to handle these situations without being angry at them. Much more on this will be discussed in Chapter 11.

Handle Their Emotions. Perhaps the most important thing we need to do when communicating with others is to handle their emotions effectively. If we fail to do this, they will attend to and retain little of what we say, and anything they do remember likely will be distorted. I don't have numbers to support this, but in my experience I would say that the failure to handle the other person's emotions probably is at the root of a significant percentage of our communication failures. In Chapter 5 I covered the two most potent ways we can manage others' emotions in positive ways: **using face-saving strategies** and by **reflecting and acknowledging others' feelings**. Although I covered the reflecting and acknowledging others' feelings enough in Chapter 5, I want to add to the discussion of face saving by going into greater detail in this section.

Face Saving. I would argue that a central goal of communicating with others should be to make sure that we sufficiently are preserving their "face," at least if we want the interaction to be constructive. Remember that our "face" is the way we want to present ourselves and be seen by others. Another element of face is our autonomy, or freedom to do what we want to do. So in the workplace that usually means that people want to be seen as competent people who do a good job and can be trusted, and that they want to be free to do their job as they please. When that face is threatened by public comments or challenges it can cause a lot of resentment. This might sound obvious but it presents us with a serious challenge, because often in the workplace we will need to convey messages that easily could threaten someone's face. We are at risk for threatening autonomy by ordering coworkers to do something, to not do something, or to do something in a different way. And we are at risk for threatening the way people want to present themselves when we have to disagree with them, side with others, correct them, and in general if we are critical of them.

The answer to this dilemma cannot be to just tell everyone what they want to hear and let them do whatever they want. Instead, we have to tactfully accomplish our goals while minimizing the threat to others' face. How might we do this? There is no one best way or master list, but below I've offered some ideas for how these situations can be handled tactfully (see Table 6.1).

The above are just a few examples, but notice the sensitivity to others' face in each of them. They may seem like "weak" responses to these situations, but because they are so respectful of others, using them on a daily basis will help us build good working relationships with our coworkers. You'll notice that I used questions in some of these. Honestly, the use of questions is probably one of the most powerful communication tools that we're not really taught to use. I will elaborate more on this in Chapter 8.

There is another workplace situation that involves the need to save face, and that is when others end up in face-threatening situations that may cause embarrassment or frustration for them. We can be supportive in these situations by framing the situation in ways that help them save face. You've probably done this with friends who failed a test (by telling them it was a hard test), didn't get a job ("There was an insane amount of competition for it"), or did something to embarrass themselves ("Nobody even noticed"). So overall, we can be good at saving face. But what about when a coworker we dislike is in one of these situations and we have a chance to

Table 6.1 Facework Strategies for Different Workplace Situations

Situation	Possible Face-Saving Strategies (all delivered in a constructive nonverbal tone)
Telling someone "no"	• I can't do it because I wouldn't be able to give it the full attention it deserves. (This is affirming the importance of what they're asking.)
	• I'm sorry that I won't be able to help you out this time. (It at least expresses some regret, rather than indifference.)
Disagreeing with someone	• I like several of the points you're making but could I share some of my concerns? (This gives deference to their opinion, yet without giving in to it.)
	• I see what you're saying but what about (insert some concern with their idea/proposal). (This acknowledges their point and rather than arguing with them, you're getting them to answer to you. Keep doing this and either you will be convinced or you will expose flaws in their thinking.)
Asking someone to do something	• I know you're busy, but I think you'd do a great job with this, what do you think? (It's flattery and acknowledging that they're busy. Don't underestimate this one—I got talked into becoming a department chair by a secretary who repeatedly used this strategy!)
	• I'll understand if you say no, but would you consider _____? (This reduces resistance by inviting a "no" answer. We will learn more about this in the negotiation section in Chapter 10.)
Directing to do something in a different way	• I notice that you're doing this a certain way, what is your thinking on that? (First understand why they're doing it, and then use the questioning strategy above. Either they will convince you that it's the right way, or they will come to see flaws in their approach. Either way, you're inviting dialogue rather than shutting them down.)

capitalize on it by saying something like "I told you so," "So how did that work out for you?" or some other comment that probably would feel great to say. I have a suggestion for those situations: Please try to resist the urge to further damage the other person's face. I know this is hard, and I've had to resist the urge myself a few times, but in the long run, it is a better way to conduct ourselves. If we do give in, the person (and possibly others who are present) likely will resent us. But if we resist the urge, the "target" person actually may be grateful to us for not attacking him or her. And even if he or she doesn't get it, others likely will respect that we took the high road. I've regretted saying things that damaged others' face, but I've never regretted holding back and taking that high road.

Ok, so to review the model I've proposed, communication is very easy. We just need to have enough cognitive complexity to make the most of our personality strengths while minimizing our weaknesses, be appropriate to the context and situation, along with our relationship with the other person, all while managing our emotions and being responsive to the emotions of the other person. And we just have to do this on-the-fly, as we're trying to think of what we want to say in the situation. That might sound like a lot, but I suspect we've all managed to do this well a number of times. The trick is just to do it consistently in our workplace, even around people we may or may not find likeable.

So how can we improve our cognitive complexity and develop a broader array of options for how to handle communication situations. I've mentioned this in other chapters, but the key is **deliberate practice**. When communication situations do or do not go well for you, stop and consider how well you executed the various elements of the model outlined above. Chances are you'll see areas for improvement. You also can do this when observing others who communicate well or poorly. It is especially fun to watch great communicators to try to capture what they're doing to make their communication so "great." If you repeat this process until you've internalized it as a habit, your communication likely will improve in meaningful ways.

What About Charisma?

What role can charisma play in helping us become valued by many other people in our workplace? I tend to not give much attention to charisma because I think it gets too much attention already when there should be more focus on substance over style. But recently I came across a news story (Haden, 2012). I wouldn't call it highly credible from an academic perspective (it was one of those cheap "10 Habits of Charismatic People" lists that online writers come up with to fill space). However, some of the recommendations actually were pretty solid, and are very consistent with different things I've written in other chapters. Therefore, I'll present a few. Even if you have no interest in being charismatic, I think these behaviors can help you develop better relationships in the workplace and beyond. So what do these charismatic people supposedly do? First, **they listen way more than talk**. Think of the last time you were with someone who tended to ask questions and let you talk about yourself. They speak when they have something worth saying, but otherwise, they put you first. I don't think it happens often, but I suspect you have viewed these people positively. Second, **they put their stuff away**. In other words, they didn't look at their phone or iPad, or stare at a computer screen. You had their full attention. Third, **they don't act self-important,** and instead would rather learn something from you than continuously talk about themselves. Fourth, **they shine their spotlight on others.** This involves catching others doing something well. This is an easy one to try. Just give credit (sincerely) to someone in your workplace for doing something well and watch how the person responds. I suspect the outcome will be very positive. Fifth, **they don't discuss the failings of others.** This is very relevant to the workplace because we often will be aware of how those we dislike have experienced some amount of failure. We will have a lot of chances to enjoy the failure of others, but these situations also present additional opportunities to take the high road. Now these are only five things from a list of ten, but consider how much impact you could have on others if you did just these five things with some consistency. Or consider the impact of doing the exact opposite of each. Regardless of outcomes related to charisma, I think you will agree that these behaviors can do a great job helping us develop positive relationships in our workplace.

In this next section we will move from specific things we can do when communicating with others and focus on some more general qualities of good relationships. There are just a few, but they make a big difference.

Relational Coordination

Although research on these relational characteristics is aimed at what organizations can do to increase the chances that employees will work well together, this information can give us a sense of some aspects of optimal working relationships.

Consider the challenge of working at an airline and, shortly after a plane lands, moving as quickly and efficiently as possible to turn the plane around so it can take off as soon as possible. This kind of turnaround time can be critical for airlines. And yet think of all that needs to be done. Passengers and luggage have to be moved off of the plane, the plane has to be cleaned and refueled, and new passengers and luggage have to be loaded. This requires a team of interdependent employees to work quite closely together. If one makes a mistake, it could throw others off, create delays, and cost the airline money. This is the process that Jody Gittell (2003) began studying in the early 1990s, in order to determine the characteristics of effective flight departure teams. As she studied airlines like American, Continental, and United, she kept hearing about Southwest Airlines. When she finally turned her attention to Southwest, she noticed that it had the fastest turnaround times in the airline industry. She eventually identified a few aspects of employee relationships that she felt set Southwest apart from the other airlines. So she measured these factors and compared the airlines. She found that Southwest rated higher than the other airlines on these factors, and she found that these factors were correlated with stronger performance. She then measured these same relationship aspects in a completely different setting, by examining the patient discharge process in several hospitals. This is another process that involves the interdependent coordination of people in several different roles. She found the same factors to be related to a more efficient discharge process, and that patients who were discharged by these high-performing groups of employees felt as if they recovered more quickly from their surgeries (Gittell, 2003). Consider this point again:

Table 6.2 Relational Coordination

Relationships that involve:	Communication that is:
• Shared Goals	• Frequent
• Shared Knowledge	• Timely
• Mutual Respect	• Accurate
	• Focused on Problem Solving (not blaming)

She found that communication among employees at the time of discharge mattered to the extent that it was related to how patients felt they were recovering, even though they no longer were in the hospital.

These are impressive outcomes of what Gittell labeled *relational coordination,* which is "coordination that occurs through frequent, high-quality communication supported by relationships of shared goals, shared knowledge, and mutual respect" (Gittell, 2009, p. 25). So what aspects of high-quality communication and relationships made such a difference? High-quality **communication was** *frequent, timely, accurate,* and **focused on** *problem solving,* while relationships were characterized by *shared goals, shared knowledge,* and *mutual respect.* Employees who are highly coordinated communicate with each other fairly *frequently* about some aspect of the job or their clients. This helps them respond more efficiently to changes that may come up. This also helps employees establish strong ties with each other. Quality communication also is *timely* in the sense that coworkers speak with each other at optimal times (as opposed to discussing something when it is too late to do so). Being timely can prevent delays or errors. It also is important that communication is *accurate* so that errors and delays are prevented. The most interesting aspect of quality communication may be that it is focused on *problem solving* rather than blaming. In any process involving a coordinated effort among multiple employees, things will go wrong. Someone will make a mistake. When this happens, the group either can focus on figuring out who is to blame or it can focus on solving the problem. Focusing on problem solving is a sign of stronger relational coordination. Besides the way blaming or searching for those to blame can add to the stress already created by the mistake or problem, consider the long-term effect on employees. If blame is a central focus of the group's culture, employees may avoid taking chances so that mistakes don't happen. Or instead, they may try to cover up mistakes or avoid responsibility for them. In such cases, while all of this is happening, two things are NOT happening: (1) the problem is not being solved, and (2) the group is not really learning how to alleviate the problem in the future. The outcomes outlined in this paragraph help demonstrate the benefit of frequent, timely, accurate, and problem-solving communication.

Beyond communication, there are important characteristics of relationships that are effectively coordinated. First, there are *shared goals,* in that participants have a sense that they are working toward the same outcome. This can be a challenge to achieve when people serve different functions or work in different departments. So if the organization does not make it easy for employees in different areas to visualize the goals they may unknowingly share, it can be worthwhile for employees to try to work to identify the goals they may share. Effective relationships also are characterized by *shared knowledge,* in the sense that coworkers understand the tasks that each other performs. This knowledge can be important, because it can enable us to better understand the ways in which we can most effectively support our coworkers (and how they can support us). With a high degree of shared knowledge, we can know what coworkers need to know and when they need to know it. As with shared goals, this knowledge can be hard to grasp, without actually holding the jobs that our coworkers hold. We often are in our own "worlds" when we work in different positions or departments. Therefore, it can be worth our efforts to try to learn as much as possible about the jobs of the coworkers with whom we are the most interdependent. We can ask them what kinds of things they do and, more important, why they have to do certain things a certain way. In turn, we can share this information with them in regard to our positions. Doing this legwork can help us gain a more complete picture of what key coworkers do. In the process, we are likely to notice ways that we can work together more effectively, thanks to an increase in shared knowledge. The final dimension of good relationships is *mutual respect,* which we can work toward using many of the behaviors that have been discussed throughout this book.

Beyond understanding the various elements of relational coordination, it is worthwhile to notice the ways in which the elements relate to each other. The elements of high-quality communication can help increase shared goals and knowledge (frequent, timely, and accurate communication), and foster mutual respect (problem solving rather than blaming). And having shared goals, shared knowledge, and mutual respect can help ensure more frequent, timely, accurate, and problem-solving communication. Or for a more vivid picture of relational coordination, consider a group of employees who do not have good relational coordination. They don't communicate enough, or at key times. Communication may be inaccurate. When things go wrong, the focus is on finding who is to blame. Each person is focused on his or her own goal, rather than group goals. Because people don't have knowledge of what others are doing, it can be easy to get frustrated with others, which can undermine mutual respect. In an environment like this, employees will experience more mistakes, and by handling them poorly, they will only make their stress worse.

So regardless of whether we are working in the kind of job that has the coordination demands of the organizations Hoffer Gittell has studied, it is not a stretch to see the potential benefits of working toward the above characteristics in our daily relationships at work. Notice also how much of the activity that contributes to relational coordination involves positive social exchanges. When we communicate with others frequently in timely, accurate, and problem-solving ways, we maximize opportunities to enhance rewards and minimize costs. And over time, both parties can help make the working relationship more mutually rewarding.

Subordinate–Superior Relationships

Researchers have focused more attention on superior–subordinate relationships than on coworker relationships. Before we talk about these relationships though, it is important to consider some different assumptions that leaders make that, in turn, influence their approach to leadership. The approach you take to establishing a good working relationship with your leaders will depend on the approach they take, so to help you tailor your approach to your leader's approach, we first will identify a few ways to classify leaders.

First we will consider the question: "What type of leader do I have?" (or "What type of leader am I?"). Considering this issue will help you better understand how to approach the various leaders you will encounter, or how to improve your own leadership. Researchers have made a virtual sport of finding different ways to classify leaders, so to keep this book shorter than ten volumes, I will narrow things down and talk about a few different models which have been influential. The first, by Blake and Mouton (1964), is known as the **managerial grid.** It classifies leaders based on two dimensions: concern for production and tasks, and concern for people. When combining these concerns, we can consider several different styles of leadership. A low concern for task and for people amounts to phoning it in, or doing as little as possible to support the organization. These types do not want to be bothered, and if you work with one, you will have to take care of things yourself, rather than counting on your supervisor (Richmond & McCroskey, 2009). Leaders with a high concern for production and a low concern for people will be **task masters** who are focused on the bottom line. If you work for one, you should expect that he or she will not want to be bothered by your personal concerns, and that your messages to him or her should be framed in terms of how your concerns or ideas relate to accomplishing the tasks that concern him or her (Richmond & McCroskey, 2009). At the other end of the spectrum are leaders with a high concern for people, and a low concern for tasks. These types will be very focused on the happiness and well-being of their staff, even when it is at the expense of getting work done. Blake and Mouton (1964) aptly labeled them as **"country club leaders."** If you need to communicate with these leaders, frame your concerns in terms of how worker happiness, morale, and well-being might be affected. Otherwise, keep things social and superficial (Richmond & McCroskey, 2009). Blake and Mouton (1964) identified **"team leaders"** as those who have a very high concern for tasks and people. These leaders work hard to accomplish tasks, yet also devote time to employee concerns. As good as this may sound, Richmond and McCroskey (2009) suggest that these types are at risk for being workaholics and for burning out quickly. These types may be effective, but they also may have to accomplish this by arriving early, staying late, and in general making the kind of sacrifices that could adversely impact their life outside of work. A more sustainable approach is to have a moderate concern for tasks and for people. Given the challenge of trying to balance a concern for both task and people, Richmond and McCroskey (2009) suggest that it is more realistic to hope for a moderate leader than a team leader. They may not be as impressive, but because they can balance different concerns, work will get done and employees will be taken into consideration.

Another classic perspective is McGregor's (1960) **Theory X** and **Theory Y** approaches to management. These represent different sets of assumptions managers may have about employees. Some assumptions of what McGregor labeled "Theory X" managers include: the average person dislikes work; people will be motivated to get out of work when possible; to get work done, employees must be controlled heavily, and possibly even punished. Theory Y assumptions include: work is just as natural as play; people have the capacity to be creative if allowed; anyone (not just managers) can make good decisions. Rather than treating these as either-or categories, realize that while a manager may lean toward one group of assumptions, it is likely that managers have assumptions that are in both groups.

Richmond and McCroskey (2009) provide another way to classify managers, based on whether they lean more toward having an **administrative** or **supervisory** role. Those who focus on administration are focused more on operations, paperwork, budgeting, communicating with their superiors or those outside of the organization, planning, and other tasks. In contrast, supervisors focus more on having contact with their subordinates. They may engage in mentoring, oversight, answering employee questions, and are seen as more employee-oriented than those who gravitate toward an administrative role. Leaders may gravitate more toward one of these orientations, or may switch back and forth between them (Richmond & McCroskey, 2009). Therefore, it can be important to recognize the orientation your leader has, so that you can have a sense of whether he or she wants to be approached, and the kinds of things that concerns him or her most.

Kaplan and Kaiser Leadership Model

Now that I've sampled three different ways of classifying leaders, you may have noticed some overlap among the approaches. In recognition of the various approaches in the literature, **Kaplan and Kaiser** (2003) examined various leadership models and proposed a model that tries to capture elements that are common among many models. Their model has two dimensions, but rather than combining them and examining various resulting combinations, they emphasize the importance of achieving a balance between two extremes. For example, one continuum they offer **ranges from *enabling leadership* to *forceful leadership*.** They suggest that at their extremes, there are problems with being either too forceful or too enabling. But they suggest that when applied in moderation and at the right time, there are virtuous elements to both forceful and enabling leadership. To illustrate more clearly, I'll follow the continuum that Kaplan and Kaiser offer. At the extreme end of enabling leadership, we have highly enabling leaders who fail to hold others accountable, avoid taking clear stands, and are too accommodating of employees. Moving toward moderation, we have more virtuous aspects of enabling leadership, which can include being able to empower subordinates by delegating, considering others' ideas, and being responsive to employees' ideas and feelings. Moving more toward forceful leadership, yet still in moderation, we can see some of the virtues of moderately forceful leadership: holding others accountable, making tough decisions, and taking charge when necessary. But if we take forceful leadership too far, we end up with problematic leader characteristics, such as being too dominant, failing to consider others' opinions, being insensitive toward others, and being too rigid. In this example, the extreme of either approach is problematic, while the more moderate application of each is beneficial.

Kaplan and Kaiser's (2003) second dimension of leadership style **ranges from *strategic leadership* to *operational leadership*.** Strategic leadership involves having long-term vision (where is the organization headed?), while operational leadership

The Virtues and Vices of Leadership Styles

Taking one leadership approach to the extreme while giving its complement short shrift leads to imbalance and ineffectiveness. The versatile, and therefore effective, leader can draw upon the virtuous aspects of each approach to suit the circumstances at hand. Below is a partial list of the virtues and vices associated with each of leadership's dominant dualities – forceful/enabling and strategic/operational.

FORCEFUL LEADERSHIP		ENABLING LEADERSHIP	
Vice	**Virtue**	**Virtue**	**Vice**
Dominant to the point of eclipsing subordinates	Takes charge; in control	Empowers subordinates; able to delegate	Abdicates responsibility for oversight
Doesn't hear and value others' opinions	Takes stands and articulates them clearly	Listens to others' opinions and ideas	Takes no clear stands
Insensitive; callous	Makes tough calls, including those that have adverse effects on people	Compassionate; responsive to others' needs and feelings	Overly accommodating
Rigid; demoralizes others	Holds others accountable	Understanding	Doesn't hold others accountable

STRATEGIC LEADERSHIP		OPERATIONAL LEADERSHIP	
Vice	**Virtue**	**Virtue**	**Vice**
Looks down the road too much	Focused on setting long-term strategy	Focused on getting short-term results	Myopic; has tunnel vision
Hopelessly conceptual	Thinks broadly; focused on big picture	Knows the specifics of how things work	Bogged down in detail
Too ambitious	Expansive; aggressive about growing the business	Respects the limits of the organization's capacity	Too conservative and limiting

Figure 6.1   The Virtues and Vices of Leadership Styles

Source: From Kaplan & Kaiser (2003), p. 22.

involves a focus on accomplishing short-term operational goals (where is this task or project headed?). Each side of this dimension also has positive and negative elements. At the extremes, operational leading can be problematic in that a leader can get overwhelmed by details, have tunnel vision (an inability to see a bigger picture), and fail to consider longer-term implications. A more positive application of operational leadership involves having an understanding of the organization's limits, being focused on accomplishing short-term results, and so on. Moving along the continuum, we have a positive application of more strategic leadership, which involves being able to set long-term strategy and understanding the big picture. But if we take this too far, we have negative aspects of strategic leadership, such as being too conceptual and not able to offer tangible ideas, having plans that are too ambitious, and looking too far into the future than is practical.

So far, when covering all of these categories, I've resisted the question of "Which approach is best?" The answer is "It depends." Sometimes force is needed, while sometimes encouragement is needed. Sometimes planning is needed, while at others short-term execution is more important. Sometimes paperwork needs to come first, and at others, issues involving employees need to be addressed. As a result, the ideal characteristic for leaders is **versatility,** or the ability to shift one's approach to meet the demands of the situation (Hogan, 2007; Kaplan & Kaiser, 2003; Richmond &

McCroskey, 2009). To appreciate the value of versatility, consider Hogan's (2007) discussion of what it takes to be an effective leader:

> Effective leaders tend to be resilient and handle stress well, they promote a vision and develop strategies to translate the vision into reality, they solve tactical and strategic problems, they set high goals and work hard to achieve them, they project a sense of self-confidence, they build relationships, they build teams, they follow through on their commitments and treat people fairly, and they plan and organize work. These attributes are no guarantee of success, but they improve the odds of a person being able to build a high-performing team that achieves results.
>
> (p. 36)

Notice how leaders are pulled in different directions and need to be different things to different people, at different times. This explains why versatility is highly correlated with leadership effectiveness (Hogan, 2007). Solving problems involves moderate operational leadership, while planning involves moderately strategic leadership. Setting high goals and projecting confidence is moderately forceful leadership, while building relationships and teams is moderately enabling leadership. Effective leaders need to recognize when a situation demands a certain approach, and then be able to shift their approach accordingly. Kaplan and Kasier (2003) suggest that versatility is preferable to being lopsided, or leaning only toward one end of the spectrums we've outlined above. Beyond versatility, Richmond and McCroskey (2009) also suggest that **consistency** is needed in addition to versatility, in the sense that leaders need to be reliable and predictable in their decisions, so that there is sufficient continuity. This is evidenced in the above comments by Hogan, with respect to treating people fairly and following through on commitments.

Beyond versatility and consistency, and the characteristics outlined above in Hogan's comments, is there anything else worth keeping in mind about effective leadership? I have a couple of additional characteristics to mention, but before I do, I want to make some observations about leadership, based on personal experience. In Chapter 1 I discussed problems with the way teams are handled in college settings, in that students are grouped only temporarily and usually are not able to develop as a team. Between this, and the fact that undergraduate students typically are not taught leadership skills in a formal and effective way (beyond memorizing ideas from a book), I sometimes see students making problematic assumptions about what leadership is and is not. Often, leadership seems to be equated with who is the most vocal and powerful member of a group. Along these lines, I have a colleague who says that the person who emerges as student leader of these groups is the most vocal person who has the least amount of trust for everyone in the group (and therefore wants to direct the project so his or her overall individual grade won't suffer). In fairness, in the context of the way these groups typically form and work, this actually is reasonable behavior. The groups usually are short on time and there usually isn't time for leaders to emerge in more nuanced ways. But because things can operate differently in organizations, I want to address these assumptions about leadership by briefly discussing the work of Jim Collins. In his book *Good to Great* (2001), he carefully studied organizations that fit certain criteria. On a variety of performance indicators, the organizations had to have transitioned from a 10-year period of moderate productivity to at least 15 years of sustained profits. Unlike many business books, his was supported by sustained research. And by requiring a company to have 15 years of profits in order to be considered, his standards clearly were very high. He and his team identified 11 companies that fit the criteria, and then tried to isolate factors that they all had in common. Some of the factors were related to leadership and are worth mentioning here. Each company had a **CEO who actually was fairly humble personally,** yet who had considerable will power when it came to **pushing the company to meet its goals.** This suggests that they put the welfare of the company before their own egos. This runs counter to the assumptions mentioned above, and to a lot of popular business literature that suggests that charisma is a must for any leader. These companies also hired carefully, were willing to get rid of weak performers, and were open to criticism and information about their shortcomings (which they used to drive improvement). Beyond the humility of the leaders mentioned above, another concept that we have not yet mentioned is implied above in the discussion of great companies: **accountability.** This process starts with leaders who are humble and possess considerable will power to help the company succeed, and who are willing to remove poor performers. It also involves a willingness to acknowledge weaknesses in order to address them and increase strengths. The great companies studied by Collins were driven in part by a sense of accountability, and ambition to perform effectively. And this started with a humble yet determined leader.

Leader Member Exchange Relationships

Beyond specific leader characteristics, it also is useful to ask: What are the different types of relationships supervisors have with their subordinates, why do they develop that way, and what difference does all of this make for subordinates? These are questions that have been addressed by a perspective known as *leader member exchange* theory, which involves an application of social exchange ideas to the leader–subordinate relationship. Sounds interesting, I know. To help make this idea more vivid, I will begin our discussion from the perspective of a leader.

Put yourself in the situation of the following supervisor. You didn't sleep well last night. When you checked your email at 9 p.m., you had been copied in on a heated email argument between two coworkers about how to handle an upcoming decision. You didn't reply, but you were distracted about it the rest of the night, and when you woke up early (4 a.m.), you couldn't get back to sleep. When you get to the office you notice you have about 15 unread emails that, when combined with other emails that haven't been addressed, means that you have about ten different things you need to work on. Some are related to the budget, others to personnel decisions, and others are less important, but you still need to respond. You also are trying to prepare for two meetings today, but as your employees arrive, they have additional questions and issues for you, so you will have to follow up with some of them. You have a couple of employees to whom you relate most easily. They stay away when you are busy and are helpful and willing to pitch in when you need the help. They also share your frustration about the brewing issue that was the subject of last night's emails (you also will need to deal with this issue throughout the day). There are a couple of employees who do a decent job, but are high maintenance in the sense that they need you to attend to concerns that are important to them but, in your opinion, could wait, as they are less urgent than other matters. Then you have a couple of people who are slackers, and you have to keep after them, as well as listen to others' complaints about them. And don't forget the mini "war" brewing between the two employees who sent those emails last night. With this in mind, what will your interactions with various employees today be like?

Clearly you are busy. It would be ideal if you could spend a considerable amount of time attending to all employees with a "my door is always open" or "management by wandering around" policy. But you cannot. You have too much to do, and you have to make choices about how you will handle each subordinate. This is where the leader member exchange perspective begins to make predictions. According to this perspective, you will communicate differently and establish different relationships with different employees (Graen & Uhl-Bien, 1995). With some, you will have a *supervisory relationship*. This relationship will be fairly by-the-book, in the sense that you will do what you are required to do as a supervisor, and the employees with whom you have this type of relationship will do what they are required to do (Graen & Uhl-Bien, 1995). But it will be a fairly formal relationship, and the two of you will not get to know each other beyond what is required to do your jobs. Your influence over this person primarily will come from your authority (akin to having a compliance level of influence and reward, coercive, and legitimate bases of power). But with employees who stand out because you consider them to be excellent performers, loyal, likeable, or promising, you probably will have a *leadership relationship*. These relationships develop when leaders invest more resources in an employee (support, attention, informal rewards) and also are more flexible in letting them develop their roles within the organization (Graen & Uhl-Bien, 1995). In these relationships, influence is more reciprocal and relationally based (identification and internalization levels of influence; referent and expert bases of power). As a leader you will have a greater influence over these employees, and they will have a greater influence over you (Waldron, 1991). They are the ones who you most likely will consult about various matters. In other words, you will have stronger exchange relationships with these employees.

At this point we will consider how leader member relationships evolve to become like one of the two above relationships. Graen and Uhl-Bien (1995) outlined a model involving three leadership relationship stages. Not all employees will pass through each stage with their supervisor. Some will remain at the first stage, and others will

Table 6.3 Leader–Member Exchange Relationships

Supervisory Relationship	Leadership Relationship
• Fairly formal	• Less formal
• Both parties do what is required	• Leaders invest more resources in employee
• Individuals don't get to know each other well	• Individuals get to know each other well
• Task focused	• Employee is afforded greater flexibility
	• Task and personally focused
	• Both members influence each other

progress through the second and third stages. At the *stranger* level, the leader and subordinate first meet. Interactions are formal and both individuals stick to their roles. The leader acts formally like a leader, and the subordinate acts like a subordinate. This stage is representative of the *supervisory* relationship I outlined above. It is possible that the leader and member will remain in this stage permanently. However, either person may take the initiative to exchange greater resources (time, attention, effort, etc.) with the other person. If this happens, the relationship may move to the *acquaintance* stage. In this stage, there is a greater exchange of resources between the leader and member, and they are not necessarily the types that are required by the organization. Interaction also is less formal than in the stranger stage, though both individuals still are getting a feel for each other. If things do not go smoothly at this stage, the relationship may regress to the stranger stage. If things do go smoothly, the pair may progress to the next stage: *mature partnership*. Relationships that reach this stage are characterized by mutual respect and trust, in addition to reciprocal influence (both the leader and member influence each other). The two act more as partners than superior–subordinate. This is representative of the *leadership* type relationship outlined above. This also is representative of what is known as transformational leadership, or leadership in which both leaders and followers work together to push each other to higher levels of motivation and productivity (Burns, 1978).

But what difference does all of this make for employees? To what extent is it to our advantage to establish a mature partnership with our supervisor? Research suggests that the benefits are considerable. Employees that establish stronger exchange relationships with their supervisors are more satisfied with their job (Gagnon & Michael, 2004) and their communication with their supervisor (Mueller & Lee, 2002), perceive their leaders to be more person-centered (Fix & Sias, 2006), and are more committed to their organization (Gagnon & Michael, 2004). In terms of tangible outcomes, greater leader member exchange is related to employee creativity (Tierney, Farmer, & Graen, 1999), organizational citizenship behavior (Konovsky & Pugh, 1994), and performance ratings and actual positive performance outcomes (Sias, 2009).

On the flip side, what are the consequences of not establishing a good exchange relationship with a leader? Manzoni and Barsoux (2003) have examined outcomes of less positive leader member exchanges, and have identified the "Set up to fail" syndrome to explain the ways in which reasonable managers unwittingly encourage some employees to perform poorly. Here is how this negative exchange process works. First, in the stranger stage, an employee makes a less-than-ideal impression on the leader, and the outcome is that the leader has less faith in this employee than in others. In other words, the new employee has become, in the leader's eyes, a "Perceived Weaker Performer (PWP)" (Manzoni & Barsoux, 2003, p. 26). According to Manzoni and Barsoux, leaders will approach PWPs in similar ways. As we go through this section, be sure to remember everything I discussed in Chapter 5 about the power of first impressions. When giving directions for a task to PWPs, leaders will be much more precise about how it should be done, and they will spend more time monitoring these employees, in case problems might come up. In other words, they will be more hands-on than they would with an employee who seems to be a stronger performer. This makes perfect sense. The leader means well and is trying to offer additional support. However, Manzoni and Barsoux suggest that in response to more controlling leaders, employees often will react negatively to all of the monitoring, and performance will suffer as a result. Even if they didn't get so frustrated, notice how it would be more difficult to impress a leader with your performance under these conditions. You're being monitored, so even if you do a great job, it may be attributed more to the monitoring than to your efforts. So as their performance deteriorates, things continue to spiral. The leader increases supervision and critical feedback, making the employee even more tentative, leading to worse performance, and so on. This is a tough situation, because in fairness, some people will perform poorly without any influence from their leader. But to the extent that this might happen, we should consider what leaders can do to establish positive exchange relationships with their employees.

What Can Leaders Do to Enhance Leader Member Exchange?

Helpful advice for leaders comes from a study in which managers were taught to establish quality exchange relationships with all of their employees (Graen, Novak, & Sommerkamp, 1982). Specifically, they were told to do things like spending more time with employees to consider their concerns and perspectives; listen carefully to what members had to say, recognizing members' perspectives as legitimate; sharing the leader's expectations about his or her job, the member's job, and the leader member relationship. When leaders implemented these strategies, employee satisfaction and performance improved considerably, which both affirms the leader member exchange concept and suggests that supervisors can do a number of things to improve exchange relationships with subordinates, and in turn improve employee satisfaction and productivity.

Now What Can Employees Do to Enhance Leader Member Exchange?

But what can you do if your supervisor does not do much to initiate positive exchange relationships? There are two reasons to think that you can work on your end to establish a quality exchange relationship with your leader. First, in much of the research, when we say that something is correlated (leader member exchange and organizational citizenship), it simply means that there is a relationship between them. It does not mean that one thing causes the other. In other words, using the exchange–citizenship relationship, a positive exchange relationship may lead to an increase in employee citizenship behavior, but it is just as reasonable to think that increases in employee citizenship behavior would make a leader more likely to establish a quality exchange relationship with that employee. Second, a number of factors contribute to strong leader member exchange relationships, and employees can control many of these factors. Those who rated as performing better enjoy better leader member exchange relationships with their leaders (Sias, 2009). In addition, those whose attitudes toward work-related issues are similar to their leader are likely to enjoy higher-quality exchange relationships with their leaders (Engle & Lord, 1997). In addition, those with a higher internal locus of control are more likely to develop stronger exchange relationships with their leaders.

So what does all of this mean? First, it echoes what has been said throughout this book about performing one's job effectively, taking initiative, and going above and beyond when possible. When this happens, employees are noticed in positive ways, and this opens the door to the development of a stronger relationship with one's supervisor. With regard to the similarity factor, it is not necessary to change who you are to be perceived as more similar to your employer. First, you simply can get a feel for the categories of manager (discussed earlier in this chapter) into which your supervisor may fit. This will enable you to tailor your communication to better fit your supervisor's perspective. We will learn in Chapter 9 on listening how you can tailor your language to the linguistic style of others. And in the networking chapter (Chapter 3) we discussed ways to find areas of common ground. You don't have to be like your supervisor, but when you can find legitimate areas of common ground, why not discuss them? Through a combination of hard work and astute communication, you can increase your chances of establishing a quality exchange relationship with your supervisor.

Concluding Summary Points

We have covered a lot of ground in this chapter, in terms of various models and categories, so below I will try to offer some concluding points.

- We develop good working relationships by making it worthwhile and satisfying for others to invest their time in us.
- If we develop greater cognitive complexity, we will increase the number of strategies we have for dealing with challenging communication situations in our workplace.
- As both followers and leaders, you will encounter a variety of types of people, so it is important to understand different styles and to be versatile enough to adapt to them.
- There is no one best way to lead all of the time. Versatility is much more important, at least if we hope to be able to adapt to the variety of situations we will face as a leader.
- Our personalities present us with good and bad tendencies, and it is important to minimize bad tendencies while we use good tendencies in moderation.
- As leaders, you should try to establish good exchange relationships with all employees.
- As followers, it is important to make a good first impression and to do what you can to establish a quality exchange relationship with your leader.

References

Blake, R., & Mouton, J. (1964). *The managerial grid: The key to leadership excellence.* Houston, TX: Gulf.

Bui, K. T, Peplau, L. A., & Hill, C. T. (1996). Testing the Rusbult model of relationship commitment and stability in a 15-year study of heterosexual couples. *Personality and Social Psychology Bulletin, 22,* 1244–1258.

Burns, J. M. (1978). *Leadership.* New York, NY: Harper & Row.

Collins, J. C., & Collins, J. (2001). *Good to great: Why some companies make the leap . . . and others don't*. New York, NY: Random House.

Engle, E. M., & Lord, R. G. (1997). Implicit theories, self-schemas, and leader-member exchange. *Academy of Management Journal, 40*(4), 988–1010.

Fix, B., & Sias, P. M. (2006). Person-centered communication, leader-member exchange, and job satisfaction. *Communication Research Reports, 23*, 35–44.

Gagnon, M. A., & Michael, J. H. (2004). Outcomes of perceived supervisor support for wood production employees. *Forest Products Journal, 54*, 172–177.

Gittell, J. H. (2009). *High performance healthcare: Using the power of relationships to achieve quality, efficiency and resilience*. New York, NY: McGraw-Hill.

Gittell, J. H. (2003). *The Southwest Airlines way: Using the power of relationships to achieve high performance*. New York, NY: McGraw-Hill.

Graen, G. B., Novak, M., & Sommerkamp, O. (1982). The effects of leader–member exchange and job design on productivity and satisfaction: Testing a dual attachment model. *Organizational Behavior and Human Performance, 30*, 109–131.

Graen, G. B., & Uhl-Bien, M. (1995). Relationship-based approach to leadership development of leader–member exchange theory of leadership over 25 years applying a multi-level multi-domain perspective. *Leadership Quarterly, 6*, 219–247.

Haden, J. (2012, July 10). 10 habits of remarkably charismatic people. *Inc.* Retrieved January 15, 2013, from www.inc.com/jeff-haden/10-habits-of-remarkably-charismatic-people.html

Hogan, R. (2007). *Personality and the fate of organizations*. Hillsdale, NJ: Erlbaum.

Kaplan, R. E., & Kaiser, R. B. (2003). Developing versatile leadership. *MIT Sloan Management Review, 44*(4), 19–26.

Konovsky, M. A., & Pugh, S. D. (1994). Citizenship behavior and social exchange. *Academy of Management Journal, 37*, 656–669.

Manzoni, J. F., & Barsoux, J. L. (2003). The set-up-to-fail syndrome. *Harvard Business Review, 76*(2), 101–113.

McGregor, D. (1960). *The human side of enterprise*. New York, NY: McGraw-Hill.

Mueller, B. H., & Lee, J. (2002). Leader–member exchange and organizational communication satisfaction in multiple context. *Journal of Business Communication, 39*, 220–244.

Richmond, V. P., & McCroskey, J. C. (2009). *Organizational communication for survival: Making work work* (4th ed.). Boston, MA: Allyn & Bacon.

Sias, P. M. (2009). *Organizing relationships: Traditional and emerging perspectives on workplace relationships*. Thousand Oaks, CA: Sage.

Tierney, P., Farmer, S. M., & Graen, G. B. (1999). An examination of leadership and employee creativity: The relevance of traits and relationships. *Personnel Psychology, 52*(3), 591–620.

Waldron, V. R. (1991). Achieving communication goals in superior–subordinate relationships: The multi-functionality of upward maintenance tactics. *Communication Monographs, 58*, 289–306.

Chapter 7

Nonverbal Communication

In this chapter we will explore the ways in which our nonverbal communication represents an intersection between our basic and primitive emotions and the social expectations placed upon us to display those emotions in ways that are appropriate to the culture we are in. In other words, we will explore the ways in which emotional systems that are better suited for our cave-dwelling days function in the modern workplace, the problems this creates, and how we might address them. We also will use this information to consider ways in which you can improve your nonverbal communication at work.

One of the primary functions of nonverbal messages is to communicate our emotions and, in doing so, to serve as a **relational message** that complements the verbal message we are sending. Given the important emotional component in nonverbal messages, we will explore the nature of emotions in some detail, so we can better understand how our expression of emotions sometimes can get us into trouble in the workplace (and sometimes get us out of trouble!). We will look at the ways in which our emotional expression is shaped by both evolutionary and more contemporary social forces. It is important to examine both of these influences to gain a sufficiently complete understanding of emotions and our communication of them.

Evolution and Emotional Experience and Expression

Our nonverbal messages are strongly linked to our emotions (Anderson & Guerrero, 1998). And these emotions are thought to exist because they have contributed to our survival as a species. Fear has helped us avoid dangers, expressing anger helps us ward off threats, and expressing positive emotions helps us bond with others. From an evolutionary perspective, an emotion is a kind of "program" that, when elicited, directs many of our activities (including attention, perception, memory, movement, expressions, etc.) (Cosmides & Tooby, 2000). For example, fear makes us very attentive, narrows our perceptual focus to threatening stimuli, will cause us either to address a situation head on (fight) or avoid it (flight), and may cause us to remember an experience more acutely (so that we avoid the threat in the future).

Regardless of the specific ways in which they activate our systems, the specific emotions we possess are thought to exist because they have helped us (as a species) survive challenges within our environment long ago. If they had not helped us adapt and survive, they would not have evolved with us (Anderson & Guerrero, 1998).

In support of this idea, researchers have noted that the displays of basic emotions are largely universal, and not bound to a specific culture or geographic region (Ekman, 1993). In other words, regardless of where they live on the planet, humans all share the same basic emotion displays. However, to the extent that the evolutionary perspective is accurate, it raises a very interesting question: What kinds of problems are our emotional "programs" designed to handle? In answering this question, we will begin to see the ways our emotional makeup presents challenges for us in the modern workplace. First, evolution moves at a much slower pace than culture. Think of how much culture has changed in just the last 25 years versus how much people fundamentally have changed biologically or psychologically. Twenty years ago, mainstream email, texting, Facebook, and use of the Internet did not even exist. In just this one area, culture has changed considerably. But people fundamentally have not. Infants today are born with the same emotions that infants 25 years ago (and much longer ago) possessed at birth. This is because it takes a considerable number of generations for us to see major evolutionary changes (like the widespread occurrence of a brand new emotion, or a major change to an existing one).

This means that the emotional system that we possess today and bring into the modern workplace is designed to address problems that existed a long time ago, when civilization was much different. And while some of the same problems exist in the present day, some challenges in our environment are likely to be different. For example, "being ostracized or abandoned by one's group had dire survival consequences for those individuals and their potential offspring" (Anderson & Guerrero, 1998, p. 51). They do not have the same consequences today, but we certainly feel a pressure to belong to groups. It might seem counterintuitive, but even an emotion like jealousy has been explained by this strong need to be part of a group (Anderson & Guerrero, 1998; Cosmides & Tooby, 2000). Although it can be problematic in relationships, jealousy is a way of demonstrating a strong attachment. This example helps us to see how emotions that might have helped us also can create problems. Just consider the unique environment of the modern workplace, and how it is different from the environment in which our emotional capacity developed. The concept of survival in business differs considerably from survival in the natural world. Our emotional capacity is well suited to ward off physical attack from predators, to minimize rejection from others (promoting group membership), among other things (Anderson & Guerrero, 1998). But in an organizational environment, we often need to display emotions very differently. Often we have to minimize emotions (both positive and negative), project composure, or even mask negative emotions (Kramer & Hess, 2002). In a sense, our emotions are quite outdated, and better suited for a different, and more primitive world. As a result, as we develop, we encounter many socialization efforts designed to make our emotional expression more appropriate for today's social world.

Socialization and Emotional Experience and Expression

Our expression of emotion is socialized in the sense that "the innate propensity to express emotions nonverbally and verbally is modified in each culture and each family by interpersonal forces that dictate norms and rules of emotional communication" (Anderson & Guerrero, 1998, p. 52). In other words, the ways we express our basic emotions will be shaped by our culture and those around us (family, etc.). We gradually learn how our culture expects us to display the emotions we are feeling. To get a sense of what would happen without this socialization, just think of the ways in which young children display their emotions. In a sense, children are great examples of pure unfiltered emotional expression. If they see someone fall in public, they will laugh. They will invade our personal space. If they are mad, they will pout or throw a tantrum. And even if onlookers flash looks of disapproval, it won't deter the child from acting out. This reality places parents in the position of being on the front lines of socializing children to display their emotions appropriately (though they are not alone, as teachers, family members, peers, television, and other forces can contribute to socialization).

According to Anderson and Guerrero (1998), parents and others **socialize their children's emotional expression** in a variety of ways. The first is *modeling,* which involves children learning how to behave by following the example of their parents and others. Of course, children don't always follow examples (or they may emulate examples of bad behavior) so additional socialization methods are needed. The second is *directives,* in which parents and others specifically tell a child how to express emotion. This may include comments like "calm down," "don't yell," and so on. Parents and others also socialize through their *reinforcement* of certain behaviors. Behavior is reinforced when it is followed by a consequence that encourages it to be repeated in the future. If a parent reacts positively to a behavior, it is thought to be a reinforcing consequence, in that it will encourage the behavior to be repeated again in the future. Although the above examples involve parents and children, the socialization process continues to refine our behavior well beyond our childhood. College freshmen undergo socialization for how to behave in their courses. In fact, many sections of this book are an attempt to socialize your expression by advising you how to behave in certain professional situations. And new employees encounter additional socialization when entering an organization. All of these socialization efforts provide us with display rules for how to express our emotions.

Anderson and Guerrero (1998) identify different types of **display rules** we develop as we are socialized to express our emotions in certain ways; *simulation, inhibition, intensification, deintensification,* and *masking.* In discussing each, I will give examples of how we might follow these rules in an organization. *Simulation* involves displaying an emotion when we are not feeling it. This might happen if we were to pretend to be surprised when we hear information that we already knew (but weren't supposed to know). Or it might be when we pretend to be happy for someone, even if we're not feeling much of anything for them. *Inhibition* is when we try to give an impression that we are not feeling anything, even when we are experiencing an emotion. We might do this by keeping a "poker face" during a meeting, so that we do not give away our feelings. *Intensification* is when we try to give the appearance that we have stronger feelings than we actually have. It is different from simulation in that we already are feeling an emotion, just not as strongly as we are displaying it. This happens whenever an employee exaggerates his or her laughter at a joke told by someone of higher status. More intense liking and appreciation also is likely to be directed at those of higher status. *Deintensification* is minimizing the display of an emotion we already are feeling, though we still are displaying some of that feeling. This might happen when we try to minimize our anger at a coworker or customer, or even we try to minimize our excitement so that we appear composed in front of coworkers. Finally, *masking* involves displaying an emotion that is completely different from the one we are experiencing. For example, a skilled political operator may smile when in the presence of a disliked opponent. Or we may mask disappointment with happiness if we do not want others to sense our frustration.

As I said before, organizations socialize us on how to display our emotions in the workplace. In a recent study, Kramer and Hess (2002) surveyed employees from a variety of professions about appropriate and inappropriate displays of emotion in the workplace. In doing so, they identified a number of "rules" that may informally govern nonverbal behavior in the modern American workplace (they did not survey people in other cultures). The most common rule concerned expressing emotions professionally. This rule suggested that we should be neutral or even positive when feeling negative emotions in the workplace, while avoiding excessive or poor-timed displays of positive emotions. Those who were too negative or too positive were considered to be less professional. A second rule was that people should express emotions to improve situations by preventing or correcting problems, creating a good climate in the workplace, and avoiding emotional displays that lead to negative outcomes. This suggests an implicit view that our emotions can contribute to others' emotions and well-being, which is an idea we will explore later in this chapter. A third rule was concerned with expressing emotions at the appropriate people, which involves praising and giving credit to the right people and not reprimanding the wrong people. Another rule suggested that certain expressions always are inappropriate. Specifically, it focused on expressions that were too warm or intimate, and those that were too aggressive. Although we should be careful about drawing sweeping conclusions from one study that may or may not capture the unique display rules within individual organizational cultures, this sampling of rules is evidence that when we enter organizations we encounter a variety of display rules to which most organizational members will expect us to conform.

Later in the chapter we will explore the question of how we can modify our nonverbal behavior to follow certain display rules and convey the right emotion at the right time in the workplace. But before we do that, we need to examine nonverbal messages we will use to communicate various emotions. First we will focus on various types of nonverbal cues. Once we've explored the various cues, we will examine some of the main functions of our nonverbal behavior in the workplace. Finally, we will examine both good and bad ways to improve our nonverbal behavior at work.

Nonverbal Cues

In this section we will examine various nonverbal cues, but we will not go into considerable detail on what is communicated by each individual cue, aside from highlighting some key implications of using the cue in the workplace. This is because it can be problematic to focus on individual cues (Burgoon & Bacue, 2003). An individual cue (like eye contact) may have multiple meanings, depending on the context and what is happening with other cues (like gestures, posture, facial expression, etc.). As a result Burgoon & Bacue recommend focusing instead on constellations of cues and the context in which they are displayed. So while we will focus briefly on specific cues, we will go into greater detail on a few important functions that are achieved when we group various nonverbal cues together in specific ways. In this brief review, we will examine the following nonverbal cues: gestures and body movements, face and eye behavior, touch, vocal behavior, silence, personal space, time, and dress and artifacts.

In examining **gestures and body movements,** we are focusing on the movement of our hands, arms, torso, and our posture, head movement, and the extent to which we are facing toward or away from others. We often use our arms, hands, and possibly fingers as illustrators that help complement and accentuate what we are saying verbally. Sometimes this is most evident when we see politicians doing it poorly, such as when they raise their hand or point in a way that seems calculated and timed (later in the chapter we'll discuss ways to avoid doing this while still using nonverbal behavior effectively). We also may use gestures and movements to regulate interaction, such as when we hold up a finger or hand to signal that we want to have a conversational turn. In addition, by leaning forward or nodding our head, we signal that we are interested and want the other person to keep talking. And when talking we can look at another person if we want them to take a turn (or turn away from them if we don't want them to talk). This is not an exhaustive review of gestures, but it does give a sense of some of the ways in which we use them in everyday conversation.

The use of **touch** in the workplace is interesting, because it can be both beneficial and very costly. Unlike the other cues, it is the only one that involves actual physical contact with others, so it can communicate closeness more potently. Given the norms in most workplaces, it can be problematic to communicate too much closeness. If you try a keyword search of "touch in the workplace," you quickly will be led to articles on sexual harassment. And yet some people argue that touch is an effective nonverbal behavior, even in the workplace. For example, researchers have identified a positive relationship between higher tips and very briefly touching customers on the shoulder or arm (Crusco & Wetzel, 1984; Guéguen & Jacob, 2005; Hornik, 1992).

In order to reconcile the fact that touch can be perceived negatively, yet also have a variety of benefits, it is important to note two very important aspects of touching that can make the difference between touch being perceived as helpful or harassing. The first is location, or where we touch. Depending on the context, the hands, shoulders, and arms can be "safe" areas, but that depends heavily on the second important aspect of touch: duration, or how long the touch lasts. In the studies on tips given to waitresses, the touch was to the forearm or shoulder, and very brief (just a glancing touch, which the recipient probably didn't even notice). Even when touch has been to a "safer" area, such as the shoulder, I've seen people be very annoyed when someone has kept patting them on the shoulder from behind (almost like a parent might). This underscores the importance of duration. Beyond these concerns, it also is worth noting that some people are touch avoidant, and therefore may be very inclined to dislike any kind of touch in the workplace (Richmond & McCroskey, 2009). So based on the pros and cons, when it comes to touch in the workplace, we can conclude that in some organizations, those with certain roles may be able to benefit from very brief touching to the appropriate location if it is appropriate for the context and the individual. But you should note from all of the qualifying I've done in the above sentence that touch in the workplace is best done with great care.

The use of **face and eye behavior** is concerned with facial expressions (involving the mouth, cheeks, eyebrows, forehead, chin, etc.) and eye movement and contact. For the most comprehensive understanding of face and eye behavior, one should read the work of Paul Ekman (2003), who painstakingly mapped all of the facial and eye movements humans are capable of making. In doing so, he has demonstrated in detail the expressions we use (worldwide) to demonstrate basic emotions like anger, happiness, sadness, disgust, fear, and surprise. In addition, he has identified what are known as micro expressions, which are very fast and fleeting (lasting less than one-fifth of a second) expressions that briefly pass across our face. They only pass briefly because they actually are a form of emotional leakage that we are trying to conceal (Ekman, 2003). Ekman has studied micro expressions and deception in detail. In addition, he provides web-based training on how to detect them and even is a consultant on the TV show *Lie to Me*. Beyond Ekman's work, additional research suggests the ways in which our faces communicate a great deal about ourselves. Rule and Ambady (2008, 2009) had participants look at photographs of male and female CEOs from Fortune 500 companies and, using nothing more than the photo of their face, rate the CEOs likely level of competence. When controlling for variables like attractiveness, in both studies Rule and Ambady observed a moderately strong correlation between facial pictures and ratings of competence. This means that participants were able to rate a CEOs success (at a level better than chance) using nothing more than a picture of his or her face. Using a similar approach, the same team found that when shown facial pictures of senatorial candidates, or even other college students, participants often could accurately guess whether the person in the photo was a Democrat or Republican (Rule & Ambady, 2010). Even more impressive than guessing behaviors, research by Ambady, Koo, Rosenthal, and Winograd (2002) revealed a link between the positivity of physical therapists' facial expressions and the short- and long-term improvements in functioning of their patients. This means that patients who had therapists who had more positive and expressive faces were more likely to demonstrate improved functioning both when they were discharged, and even three months after they were discharged. Although this only is a brief review, it is clear that we communicate a great deal with our faces.

Beyond the words we use, characteristics of our **voice** (like tone, pitch, pacing, fluency) also can communicate a great deal. We can add emphasis by raising or lowering the volume of our voice, or by altering our pacing. The tone of our voice also can send powerful messages for others. For example, Ambady, LaPlante, Nguyen, Rosenthal, Chaumeton, and Levinson (2002) found that surgeons who were "judged to be more dominant and less concerned/anxious on the basis of their tone of voice were more likely to be sued than surgeons who were less dominant and more concerned/anxious" (p. 7). This finding was independent of other ratings of the surgeons' actual effectiveness. That nothing more than tone of voice was required to enable this kind of prediction points to the potential for our voice to have an important impact on our interactions with others.

Although the way we use our voice is important, it also is worthwhile to consider various ways in which we use **silence**. To learn about the power of silence, I will discuss Steve Kroft's experience with it. Kroft is a correspondent for *60 Minutes*. He has interviewed all kinds of powerful people, and an important part of his job is asking tough questions. Of all of those people he has interviewed, "Clint Eastwood intimidated him as no one ever has" (Beck & Jenel Smith, 1997). Kroft is referring to a portion of the interview in which his questions were met with a long silence (with a little digging, video of the interview can be found online by searching "Kroft and Eastwood," and is worth checking out!):

> Things went fine until he entered the area of Eastwood's private life—specifically the fact that, as Steve worded it, "You've had seven kids with five women, not all of whom you were married to." The subject, says Kroft, "brought the temperature in the room down to about 40 degrees. He just stared at me for about 30 seconds. He's got a very complicated family—all these kids with all these women. And when I said it was an unconventional lifestyle, there was another long pause. Then I asked if he had a relationship with all of his children, and there was another glare with his steel blue eyes. I told him, 'That's a pretty awesome expression—no one has ever shot me in all the years I've been doing interviews. You're certainly letting me know I better approach with caution.' "

The point of this example is not to encourage intimidation using silence, but rather to demonstrate just how much Eastwood communicated with silence and a particular facial expression. Although there hasn't been a great amount of research on the communicative uses of silence, a few functions of silence have been identified by Bruneau (2008). We may use silence to *increase our distance* from others or signal mistrust. For example, we may shun others with silence. We also can use it to *conceal information* from others. It also may be used to *show deference* to others, particularly authority figures. Silence also helps *aid turn-taking* during conversation, by letting listeners know it is their turn to talk. Silence also can be used to *exert control,* such as when we pause to gain the attention of listeners (Bruneau, 1973). Another form of silent control is when we *refuse to answer or reply* when one is expected. This signals our decision to not cooperate with others. This partial listing of functions of silence is quite varied, and it is important to realize that both context and other nonverbal cues can play a role in shaping the way silence is interpreted by others and functions for us. But even with this caveat about using silence, it is important to not overlook the ways in which silence sometimes might enable us to communicate more profoundly or effectively than we could by talking.

Personal space also is an aspect of our nonverbal communication with others. This becomes noticeable when others invade our space. When this happens, we will attempt to restore distance in a variety of ways (Andersen, 1999). We may move away, change our body orientation (face away), avoid eye contact, or use some kind of buffer between ourselves and others (some object that can act as a barrier, folded arms, etc.). This helps explain the scene we encounter in elevators, in which occupants are trying to increase their space from others in ways other than actually moving farther apart.

Space and the way we arrange objects within it also can serve communicative functions in the workplace. Larger spaces can suggest greater authority. Table or desk arrangements can encourage or discourage greater amounts of communication. Arrangements of tables, chairs, and desks also can communicate greater or lesser amounts of authority and power. For example, one can arrange her office so that visitors are on the other side of her desk, thereby enhancing her authority. Or, she could have an area where she could talk with visitors without being separated by the desk. This would reduce the amount of authority being communicated. These are just some of the ways space and object layout can be used to communicate to others.

Time also can be an aspect of nonverbal communication. In America, we may see this most clearly with respect to the act of waiting. Lower-status people are expected to be on time, and not make others wait (Burgoon, Buller, & Woodall, 1996). Those with higher status actually may reinforce their status by making others wait for them (Andersen, 1999). However, attempting to do this when one does not have sufficient status can work to enhance perceptions of status, but it also may annoy coworkers. Time also is something we "donate" whenever we choose to spend time with others. This can be important in an office setting, in terms of whether we "make time" for others and they "make time" for us. At least while we're lower in status, when we want to talk to others it is important to be sensitive to their availability and make sure that they have time to speak with us. By doing this, we will avoid encroaching on their time.

Our use of **attire and artifacts** also can communicate a great deal in the workplace. Both our clothing and artifacts (rings, necklaces, watches, earrings, etc.) should fit the formal and informal norms of our organization (Richmond & McCroskey, 2009). Although typical expectations for male attire in business settings are fairly consistent and well-known, the norms for female attire in these environment are less clear-cut (Kaiser, 1997). The closest we have to a norm for women is the skirted business suit, at least early in one's career. Once establishing herself, there is greater freedom to deviate from this norm (Saunders & Stead, 1986). Beyond this, Richmond and McCroskey (2009) offer a few suggestions related to dress in the workplace, with the understanding that the norms of a specific workplace may suggest alternative approaches. They recommend to only use a few accessories (watches, earrings, etc.). Specifically, they suggest not more than two for men, and five for women. They also suggest wearing darker colors, and keeping fabrics wrinkle-free. When it comes to norms and deviations (like casual or dress-down days), they suggest checking with more experienced employees to find out what is appropriate. Finally, a good rule of thumb is for people "to dress similar to the person who is one level above them, unless that person's dress is completely inappropriate for the organization" (p. 37).

Functions of Nonverbal Messages

Although each of the above cues communicates specific messages on their own, it is important to note that to interpret what many of them mean, we have to consider several cues at once (for example, it is hard to interpret silence without facial expression, body orientation, etc.). With this in mind, we will review some key functions of nonverbal messages as they apply to the workplace. In the process, we will see some important ways in which several nonverbal cues cluster together to convey important meanings. We will focus specifically on the ways in which nonverbal messages serve the following functions: (1) **increasing rapport and liking**; (2) **managing conversations**; and (3) **conveying appropriate competence via dominance and composure**. Although some might include "influencing others" as another function, I see influence embedded in each of the above three functions.

Increasing Rapport and Liking

In professional situations we frequently need to establish at least some level of closeness with others. We need to establish rapport with interviewers, new coworkers, customers, and potential clients. We need to maintain good working relationships throughout our time in an organization. Nonverbal behaviors are an important part of this process, and a cluster of behaviors known as *nonverbal immediacy* behaviors (see Table 7.1) are particularly important. Immediacy is "the degree of perceived physical or psychological closeness between people" (Richmond & McCroskey, 2009, p. 42). Notice that it can involve both physical and psychological closeness. We may increase others' perceptions of our immediacy to them by actually moving closer or, as we reviewed above, briefly touching them in an appropriate way. However, additional nonverbal behaviors can increase feelings of closeness, even if physical closeness is not present or possible (we're on the phone, giving a presentation to a large group, on the opposite side of the room from someone in a meeting, etc.).

There are a variety of nonverbal immediacy behaviors which when we perform them in moderation (rather than too little, or with too much intensity) help increase perceptions of closeness (Burgoon & Bacue, 2003). These include smiling, leaning forward, facing someone (as opposed to having our shoulders facing away from them), head nodding while others are talking, having vocal variety (not remaining monotonous), making direct eye contact, and having a relaxed posture. Removing barriers between our listeners and us also can increase perceptions of immediacy. Regarding all of these immediacy behaviors, picture someone doing at least a few of these, and contrast that image with one of someone who does not exhibit them: little smiling, eye contact, or facial expressiveness, a monotonous voice, little nodding while we are talking, and so on. Alternatively, think of a few teachers you've

---

Table 7.1 Nonverbal Immediacy Behaviors

Nonverbal Immediacy involves a constellation of at least some of the following NV cues in moderation:
- smiling
- eye contact
- vocal variety (voice is not monotone)
- shoulders facing the listener
- expressive gestures
- facial expressiveness
- head nodding when listening
- actual physical closeness
- brief and appropriate touching

---

liked and a few you liked less, and you may see that the ones you liked exhibited more of the immediacy behaviors than the ones you liked less. However, it is important to understand that it is not necessary to display all of the above behaviors to be perceived as immediate. A highly immediate person may display some but not all of these. The idea is to demonstrate a sufficient cluster of these behaviors to convey a sense of closeness. Later in the chapter we will explore how to improve our nonverbal behavior to enhance perceptions of immediacy, along with other perceptions.

Research on nonverbal immediacy consistently points to a variety of advantages of displaying immediacy. Students like immediate teachers more and believe that they learn more from immediate teachers (Chesebro & McCroskey, 1998), though they do not necessarily learn more (Chesebro, 2003). Richmond and McCroskey (2009) suggest additional advantages of being nonverbally immediate. They suggest that it gives us a more approachable communication style, helps reduce anxiety and tension between people, decreases perceived status differences, and increases closeness between people. Given these outcomes, it becomes easy to see the importance of being immediate. It can help us establish rapport with others, and if we are in a position of authority, it can help reduce the anxiety of those below us, as well as reducing the status differences those below us perceive. Given all of these advantages, Richmond and McCroskey (2009) offered the following principle of immediacy: "The more often communicators employ immediate behaviors, the more others will like, evaluate highly, and prefer such communicators; and the less often communicators employ immediate behaviors, the more others will dislike, evaluate negatively, and reject them" (p. 42).

In spite of the advantages of being nonverbally immediate, it is important to consider some possible disadvantages of immediacy that have been outlined by Richmond and McCroskey (2009). First, because immediacy promotes closeness, it might be possible for someone to get the wrong message by interpreting immediacy behaviors as more forward intimacy behaviors. Second, for people who are communication apprehensive, introverted, or prefer to not communicate, being immediate in their presence may decrease their comfort and increase their anxiety. It is with these first two disadvantages in mind that above I mentioned that it is important to display immediacy behaviors in moderation (so we don't come across as being too intense). It also is important to develop the ability to recognize when it can be helpful to further moderate immediacy behaviors in order to bring greater distance to the interaction. A third drawback also can be a strength of immediacy, depending on your perspective: Immediacy invites more communication from people. This often is good, but if you are busy or short on time, this additional communication may be problematic. Again, this suggests the importance of developing the ability to create distance in interactions, whether by reversing certain immediacy behaviors, or by verbal means.

Managing Interactions

In addition to becoming closer to others, we also often use nonverbal behaviors (along with verbal messages) to regulate the flow of our conversations with others. In meetings we may want to "get a word in." We may be pressed for time and need to shorten an interaction. We may be saying something important and want to keep the "floor" without yielding to others. Much of this likely comes naturally to us and probably goes unnoticed. However, beyond using nonverbal behaviors to manage conversations, it's also important to recognize when others are trying to direct conversations, so that we can respond appropriately. As we've just seen, immediacy behaviors can invite conversation, and a lack of immediacy behaviors can discourage it. We also can encourage a person to talk more by some combination of remaining silent, nodding our head, having an encouraging facial expression, gesturing for the person to continue, and using vocal back-channel cues. These cues are when we vocally affirm what the person is saying, without attempting to take a speaking turn (Andersen, 1999). This might include an affirmative "uh-huh" or other similar vocalizations that encourage interaction.

At times, we may want to take a turn in an interaction. The other person may yield this turn to us with a long pause, eye contact, an expression that conveys that it's our turn. But at other times we may wish to take a turn before it is yielded. This might be done simply by interrupting, but often we will try to "earn" our turn using nonverbal cues. We may raise our hand slightly (not as if we were in a classroom), change our position (shift in our chair), use an abbreviated vocalization in which we don't intend to continue with an interruption, but hope it will cause the other person to yield a turn to us. It might be as simple as saying something like "but" or beginning to say any other word or two that will overtly signal our wish to speak. Or we may want someone to wrap up their turn because we want to end the conversation. We may look at our watch, turn our body away, begin collecting our things (for example, if we have to leave the area), or nod our head more vigorously to hurry the other person up. Unfortunately, when we do this, we are using the same type of behavior that is used to encourage people to speak longer (our nod likely will be seen as an affirmation of what the person is saying, and as encouragement to keep speaking). The alternative is to not nod, and to remain fairly expressionless (as expressions also will signal interest and encourage the person to continue). However, it is hard to remain expressionless and avoid nodding. In addition, it temporarily may make the other person talk more. So while it can work to encourage someone to wrap up what they are saying, this stoic and expressionless approach may be difficult to actually use. Unfortunately, if the other person does not pick up on our other cues, we may just have to interject and tell him or her that we have other things to do.

Finally, we may want to keep our speaking turn, even when others want to talk. For example, we may have a colleague who interrupts frequently. In addition to using cues to suggest we want to keep speaking (few pauses, little eye contact, no other messages that suggest it is another person's turn), if our message is important, we may have to go as far as to keep talking until the other person stops interrupting us. By doing this we are choosing to not yield the turn to the other person. I hope this will be a last resort that you don't have to use often in your professional careers! Although much of what I've just outlined probably strikes many of you as obvious, notice that a theme in the above strategies is how to handle people who do not pick up on the cues we are giving (that we would like to have a turn, keep a turn, end the conversation, etc.). Chances are that you've experienced times when others did not pick up on some of these cues you've used. For this reason, when communicating, it is important to remain attentive to the cues of others. Doing this will help you know when you do or do not have an attentive audience, and therefore whether you are reaching an audience or wasting your breath!

Demonstrating Competence: Dominance and Composure

In addition to enhancing closeness and regulating the flow of our interactions, in organizations it also is important for us to be able to display our competence in ways beyond what we say and the work we do. A combination of dominance and composure helps us do this. We will begin with dominance, which may surprise you by its inclusion, due to the negative connotation it often carries. But we will examine dominance in a more balanced and positive light, as opposed to one which involves oppressing others. Burgoon, Johnson, and Koch (1998) distinguish dominance from power:

> Power refers to the ability and potential to influence others and may be exercised through a variety of resources, such as offering rewards, controlling information, using ingratiation, or appeasement. Dominance consists of expressive, relationally-based strategies and is one set of communicative acts by which power is exerted and influence exercised.
>
> (p. 315)

Rather than treating dominance as ominous and oppressive, Burgoon et al. (1998) stress the ways in which we might achieve dominance in an interaction by being expressive, dynamic, and energetic, while acknowledging that it still may involve negative qualities, such as being demanding. Burgoon and Le Poire (1999) identified a number of behaviors exhibited by those who are considered to be interpersonally dominant, including vocal relaxation, being moderately expressive, and using moderate and relaxed gestures. Additional dominance cues include backward leaning, infrequent head nodding, speaking faster and with greater fluency, taking longer speaking turns, adhering to schedules without being noticeably early or late, and so on (Burgoon & Hoobler, 2002). When we consider how these cues might cluster together in various ways, we get a picture of someone who is poised and in command, but not necessarily highly aggressive. This serves as an example of how we might be dominant

Table 7.2 Interpersonal Dominance Behaviors

Interpersonal Dominance involves a constellation of at least some of the following NV cues:
- vocal relaxation
- being moderately expressive
- moderate and relaxed gestures
- leaning backward
- infrequent head nodding
- taking longer speaking turns
- speaking slightly faster and with greater fluency
- adhere to schedules without being noticeably early or late

in positive ways that help us exert power and influence, yet without damaging our relationships with our coworkers.

In addition to exerting some level of power and influence using our nonverbal behaviors, we also may find ourselves in stressful situations in which we need to demonstrate composure. It is an extreme example, but regardless of political affiliation, most people seem to agree that during the very chaotic first hours when the events of September 11, 2001, were unfolding, New York City's mayor Rudy Guiliani conducted himself with a considerable amount of composure. Again, an extreme example, but it gives us a sense of the value of being composed in stressful situations, and the way in which that composure can enhance perceptions of our competence. Cues associated with composure include a relaxed body, a relaxed and pleasant voice, smiling, more expressive gestures, fewer adaptors (nervous gestures like fidgeting, running fingers through one's hair, etc.), shorter turn lengths, and more smiling (Burgoon & Hoobler, 2002; Burgoon & Le Poire, 1999).

In this section we have examined three ways in which nonverbal cues cluster together to serve various functions, including increasing our closeness to others, managing conversations, and increasing perceptions of competence by being composed or appropriately dominant. Each of these areas has offered specific behaviors we can enact in order to give a desired impression. We now are left with two questions to address: (1) When should we display certain nonverbal cues and not others? and (2) What are the most effective ways to demonstrate skillful nonverbal behavior?

Adapting to Others' Nonverbal Behaviors

We've already explored some of the ways in which communicators mutually influence each other. This mutual influence is particularly strong when it comes to our nonverbal behaviors. In fact, even in routine conversation two communicators continually are adapting to each other. And how well they adapt to each other can influence their perceptions of each other. For example, if your supervisor is talking faster than you, should you speed up or slow down? Or if your supervisor becomes less expressive and animated during a discussion, should you become less or more animated? Burgoon, Stern, and Dillman (1995) have studied this **adaptation process** in detail. The first aspect of adaptation is that we can adapt in a couple of general ways, either by **converging** toward or **diverging** away from what the other person is doing. When we converge, our behavior **reciprocates,** or is similar to the behavior of the other person. They talk more loudly, we talk more loudly. They talk more softly, we talk more softly. On the other hand, divergence is when our behavior differs or is in the opposite direction of the other person's behavior. They talk more loudly, we talk more softly. They talk more softly, we talk more loudly. Whether we converge or diverge depends on several factors that constitute what I call our *comfort zone* (Burgoon et al. call it our interaction position). Our conversational comfort zone is based on what nonverbal behaviors we *require, expect,* and *desire* from the other person during a conversation. *Requirements* are based on basic biological needs of which we often are not conscious. Things like fatigue, hunger, anxiety (or other emotions) may influence our capabilities during an interaction. For example, if we are tired and therefore have trouble paying attention, we will need our conversational partner to adjust and not overwhelm us. *Expectations* are the behaviors we think we will see from the other person, based on our prior experiences with the person, or people in general. When we first meet someone, we expect him to follow some basic "getting-to-know-you" rituals, and we expect him to maintain a certain distance. If we know someone well, our expectations for how she will behave will be more refined. It is important to note that we won't necessarily like the behaviors we're expecting the other person to exhibit. If our relationship with the other person is not in very good standing, we may expect very negative behavior from her. Still, even if our expectations are negative, expectations serve us by helping make interactions more predictable, and therefore easier to approach and navigate. Finally, we approach interactions with desires with how we *hope* the other person will behave. We may hope a supervisor will be attentive to our concerns, or that the person we don't like will refrain from negative behaviors (even if we expect that the person probably will be negative). These three factors, requirements, expectations, and desires, help inform a general comfort zone for our interaction, and help explain how we will act in response to the other person's behavior (whether we will converge or diverge in response to certain behaviors). This interaction adaptation theory predicts that when a person's behavior is more positive than what is represented by our comfort zone, we will reciprocate and converge toward their behavior. And when the person's behavior is more negative than what is represented by our comfort zone, we will diverge or move away from whatever behaviors the person is exhibiting. In other words, we always are moving toward our comfort zone. The central idea is that we adapt in interactions in ways that meet or exceed our comfort requirements, expectations, and desires.

To get a better idea of this process, we can consider a few examples of how we try to move interactions toward our "comfort zone." Suppose we encounter an acquaintance whom we hope will be friendly. If the person is reasonably friendly (thereby exceeding our "comfort zone"), we are likely to reciprocate. And if the person is more distant, at least initially we will diverge from that distant behavior and display warmer cues in an attempt to "bring" the acquaintance toward our comfort zone. I mention that this is our initial move, because our subsequent behaviors in the interaction will be based on how the person responds to our initial moves. Now suppose we are in a situation in which we would like to remain distant from others (maybe an acquaintance or coworker we don't like very much, or strangers on an elevator). Again, we will try to move the interaction toward our comfort zone (which involves being distant from the other person). If the person is fairly distant (what we had hoped for), we will reciprocate that distance by displaying nonverbal cues that promote distance (little eye contact, facing away, backing away, etc.). And if the person is too warm and friendly for our liking, we will diverge by displaying cues that try to increase distance (using the same cues mentioned above). In each of the situations above, we are trying to move an interaction toward our comfort zone, either by converging toward or diverging away from what the other person is doing nonverbally.

There are a few implications of the adaptation process that give us lessons we can apply to the workplace. First, whenever we are interacting, all parties are **interdependent** and are adapting to each other, trying to move toward their comfort zones. Second, there is no guarantee that the process will go smoothly. When comfort zones are incompatible (as in the teaching example above), it may be difficult to reconcile different preferences. Third, and most important, knowing about adaptation helps us better understand how to be responsive to others, so that we can keep them in their comfort zones (and therefore less frustrated, uncomfortable, anxious, etc.). Think of a situation in which you are interviewing for a job. If you watch the interviewer carefully, you will gain a lot of important information. She may be friendly, attentive, leaning forward, which means you should move toward that comfort zone, by being friendly and engaged yourself. Perhaps if you are giving a longer answer, you will notice the person nod less or back away slightly. This may be a cue for you to wrap up your answer (the listener's comfort zone no longer involves you continuing to answer that question). Perceptiveness of adaptation can be helpful in a variety of other situations: It can help you avoid talking too much at meetings, greet coworkers with an appropriate level of warmth and enthusiasm (different coworkers may prefer different levels), among others. Although the theory focuses on how we automatically adapt to others, notice how we can take these ideas and use them in order to keep others in their comfort zones, thereby enhancing their experience with us.

Beyond the kind of general approach/avoid behaviors we discussed with the adaptation process, there may be many times at work when we need to convey something specific with our nonverbal behavior. In some situations we may need to project confidence, in others, calmness or composure. We may need to project calmness in the face of an angry customer, caring with a patient, or authority with someone working under us. In situations like this we have a few choices. We could display whatever behavior we want, and just "be ourselves." However, because doing this sometimes can get us fired (we can't yell back at customers, even those who might deserve it!), we often will have to carefully modify our expression. Below we will discuss a couple of ways this might be done, and why one way is much better than the other.

Manipulating Our Expressions: Surface Acting Versus Deep Acting

What do you do if you're a DJ with a shift coming up, but you've had a rough few days at home, and are in no mood to be "on"? Or what if a customer is "pushing your buttons" and you don't want to be nice? What if you're in a committee meeting with a coworker you dislike, but you have to work together, and need each other's support? In her study of flight attendants, Hochschild (1983) brought attention to this kind of emotional challenge we often face in the workplace. She found that much of a attendant's job involved dealing with passengers' emotions. This involved their own emotions (for example, if they were tired, or annoyed with a passenger or coworker), and passengers' emotions (often negative ones, such as bad moods, anger, etc.). The emotions that the attendants had to display were shaped by the expectations of their employer. This initial research led others to examine what became known as emotion work, or the "effort planning, and control needed to express organizationally desired emotions during interpersonal interaction" (Morris & Feldman, 1997, p. 987). According to Zapf (2002), emotion work has three characteristics: "(a) emotion work occurs in face-to-face or voice-to-voice interactions with clients; (b) emotions are displayed to influence other people's emotions, attitudes and behaviors; and (c) the display of emotions has to follow certain rules" (p. 239).

This perspective recognizes that we try to use emotions to influence others, and that our employer formally or informally outlines the expectations for how we display emotions in our workplace. In addition, societal norms may help shape our behaviors (Zapf, 2002).

Emotion work, and following our organization's rules for emotional display, can become problematic when we are required to display an emotion that is quite different from the emotion we actually are feeling (such as when a customer has insulted us). For example, when I worked at an amusement park while in college, I sometimes worked rides that required me to turn away kids who were not tall enough. This inevitably required me to turn away adorable kids, which often angered their parents. Sometimes they would appeal to my supervisor, and at times when my supervisor would overrule me and let the child go on the ride, parents sometimes were quick to give me a look or comment that said something like "I told you so," "Ha, you were wrong," "What do you think about that?" or some other arrogant comment or smirk. During these moments I had to do emotion work. These were face-to-face encounters, my employer expected me to display emotions in certain ways (and avoid negative displays), and I needed to assure that our guests had a positive experience.

The above situation is an example of emotional dissonance, which is the difference between the emotions we genuinely are feeling and the emotions we are required by our organization to display (Middleton, 1989). My real emotions were in sharp contrast to the positive expressions I was required to display to customers. Dissonance is important, because when these emotional mismatches exist, we will have to devote more attention and effort to emotion work (Morris & Feldman, 1997). At the other end of the continuum, there is so little dissonance that we naturally and spontaneously may feel the emotion we are expected to display. A daycare worker may feel genuine compassion when a child is injured, so it requires no thought or effort to display the appropriate emotion. But for those situations in which an emotion does not come to us naturally, we often will have to do emotion work and modify our expression, and we may do this either by what is known as surface acting or deep acting.

Surface Acting and Deep Acting

Surface acting is when we try to use masking to manipulate the outer visible aspects of our emotion so that we are in-line with the emotion that the organization expects us to be displaying (Hochschild, 1983). This is represented by the expression "put on a happy face." The emotion we display is not consistent with the one we are feeling. Our expressions are empty of emotional content, and we're just trying to look the way we are supposed to look. In contrast, *deep acting* is when we change the way we are feeling internally in order to display the appropriate emotion (Hochschild, 1983). We are manipulating how we feel in order to manipulate our nonverbal display. When faced with a hostile customer, we can just express supportive understanding without changing our emotion (surface acting) or we can think of ways the customer's anger is legitimate (without excusing the behavior), so that we naturally display supportive understanding (deep acting).

Although we have these two ways to manipulate our expression, research suggests that surface acting is problematic in a number of ways. First, a superficial display

Table 7.3 Deep Acting in Different Situations

When we're nervous:	• Think of past times you were nervous and the successes you had in that situation. • Think of what could go wrong but also consider what you can do about it. Repeat until you've planned for realistic contingencies.
When we need to be calm around someone who is making us angry:	• Think of legitimate reasons they may be angry. Without agreeing with them or excusing the anger, understand why they're angry that don't involve personal characteristics or issues they personally have with you.
When we need to appear confident:	• Think about past successes you've had. • Think about what you do well that can apply to the situation. • Plan and prepare so well that you're ready.
When we need to be nonverbally dynamic:	• Find what excites you about whatever you're talking about. • Consider why you're excited about that particular occasion. • If you're not excited, try to find tangible reasons to be more enthusiastic.
When we need to establish rapport with someone:	• Think about what you like about the person with whom you're speaking (or talk until you find something you like). • Try to be naturally curious about the person so that you'll show greater interest.

of emotion might not be enough, particularly if we are in professions that require us to have a strong emotional display (for example, nurses). In addition, we may fail to completely conceal our real emotion, or to successfully display the desired emotion. Grandey (2003) identified some additional key differences between those that used surface versus deep acting. Although each type of acting was negatively related to job satisfaction (the more acting one did, the less he or she was satisfied), the relationship was stronger for those who tended to use surface acting. Surface acting was related to emotional exhaustion, but deep acting was not. Furthermore, those who used deep acting had more positive interactions with customers. In other words, deep acting was less linked to job dissatisfaction, less emotionally exhausting, and more effective than surface acting. This led Grandey to conclude that "the payoffs of deep acting—reduced emotional dissonance and positive reactions from customers—may restore an employee's emotional resources in a way that surface acting cannot" (p. 93). In contrast, surface acting is more emotionally taxing to us and yet less effective. These findings suggest that it is important for us to consider how we might engage in deep acting in the workplace.

Improving Our Deep Acting

This section will not attempt to substitute for a method acting course or a theatre degree, but it will identify a couple of ways in which you might be able to use deep acting when the need presents itself. I suggest trying to find something in a situation that allows you to naturally display the necessary emotions. Frequently this will involve adjusting our attitude toward other people. For example, if you know you have to get along with someone you dislike, try to find areas of common ground, noble aspects of their intentions, or other things. The goal is not to become best friends or for you to love everything about the person—just to see him in a more balanced light that leaves room for some positive qualities. This may not be fun, but the alternative of doing poorly on a project, or not having a job, likely is worse. Over the years, when encountering classes who were distant and not engaged or responsive, I found that my attitude toward students would improve when I would stop and see the situation from their point of view. This helped me improve my demeanor with those classes, and it even helped give me ideas for how I could do different things to improve their engagement and enthusiasm. Beyond changing our attitudes toward people, we may need to adjust them toward situations. For example, as a teacher, whenever I teach a subject, one of the first things I do is to find one or more angles in the topic that I find very interesting. If I do this, I won't have to fake enthusiasm in class—my enthusiasm will be real and effortless.

What we can learn from this is that, when we want to modify our nonverbal behaviors, rather than worrying about gestures, how our voice sounds, or whether we are saying "um" too much, we should focus first and foremost on our attitudes toward our listeners and toward whatever we are saying. This will work better than just displaying the emotion without feeling it, and it will take much less of a toll on us emotionally. We can apply this approach to some of the nonverbal messages we discussed earlier: immediacy, dominance, and composure. If we want to increase our immediacy naturally (and not try to remember the entire list of immediacy behaviors), we should think of our listener in a way that makes him more likeable to us, so that we naturally will be more expressive and dynamic with him. When you need to project confidence, think of similar situations in the past when you have had doubts, and how you overcame those doubts. That will help give you a more natural confidence. Like any new application of a skill, this will not necessarily come easily to you, but given the benefits of deep acting (vs. surface acting), it is worthwhile to try to use this approach to improve your nonverbal skills.

References

Ambady, N., Koo, J., Rosenthal, R., & Winograd, C. (2002). Physical therapists' nonverbal communication predicts geriatric patients' health outcomes. *Psychology and Aging, 17,* 443–452.

Ambady, N., LaPlante, D., Nguyen, T., Rosenthal, R., Chaumeton, N., & Levinson, W. (2002). Surgeon's tone of voice: A clue to malpractice history. *Surgery, 132,* 5–9.

Andersen, P. A. (1999). *Nonverbal communication: Forms and functions.* Mountain View, CA: Mayfield.

Anderson, P. A., & Guerrero, L. K. (1998). Principles of communication and emotion in social interaction. In P. A. Anderson & L. K. Guerrero (Eds.), *Handbook of communication and emotion: Research, theory, applications, and contexts* (pp. 49–96). San Diego, CA: Academic Press.

Beck, M., & Jenel Smith, S. (1997, November 14). Kroft questions don't make Eastwood's day. Retrieved June 6, 2012, from www.highbeam.com/doc/1G1–83892053.html

Bruneau, T. J. (1973). Communicative silences: Forms and functions. *Journal of Communication, 23,* 17–24.

Bruneau, T. J. (2008). How Americans use silence and silences to communicate. *China Media Research, 4,* 77–85.

Burgoon, J. K., & Bacue, A. (2003). Nonverbal communication skills. In B. R. Burleson & J. O. Greene (Eds.), *Handbook of communication and social interaction skills* (pp. 179–219). Mahwah, NJ: Erlbaum.

Burgoon, J. K., Buller, D. B., & Woodall, W. G. (1996). *Nonverbal communication: The unspoken dialogue.* New York, NY: HarperCollins/Greyden Press.

Burgoon, J. K., & Hoobler, G. (2002). Nonverbal signals. In M. L. Knapp & J. Daly (Eds.), *Handbook of interpersonal communication* (pp. 240–299). Thousand Oaks, CA: Sage.

Burgoon, J. K., Johnson, M. L., & Koch, P. T. (1998). The nature and measurement of interpersonal dominance. *Communication Monographs, 65,* 309–335.

Burgoon, J. K., & Le Poire, B. A. (1999). Nonverbal cues and interpersonal judgments: Participant and observer perceptions of intimacy, dominance, composure, and formality. *Communication Monographs, 66,* 105–124.

Burgoon, J. K., Stern, L. A., & Dillman, L. (1995). *Interpersonal adaptation: Dyadic interaction patterns.* New York, NY: Cambridge University Press.

Chesebro, J. L. (2003). The effects of teacher clarity and immediacy on student learning, receiver apprehension, and affect. *Communication Education, 52,* 135–147.

Chesebro, J. L., & McCroskey, J. C. (1998). The relationship between teacher clarity and immediacy and students' experiences of state receiver apprehension when listening to teachers. *Communication Quarterly, 46,* 446–455.

Cosmides, L., & Tooby, J. (2000). Evolutionary psychology and the emotions. In M. Lewis & J. M. Haviland-Jones (Eds.), *Handbook of emotions* (2nd ed., pp. 91–115). New York, NY: Guilford Press.

Crusco, A., & Wetzel, C. (1984). The Midas touch: The effects of interpersonal touch on restaurant tipping. *Personality and Social Psychology Bulletin, 10,* 512–517.

Ekman, P. (1993). Facial expression of emotion. *American Psychologist, 48,* 384–392.

Ekman, P. (2003). *Emotions revealed: Recognizing faces and feelings to improve communication and emotional life* (2nd ed.). New York, NY: Holt Paperbacks.

Grandey, A. (2003). When "the show must go on": Surface and deep acting as determinants of emotional exhaustion and peer-rated service delivery. *Academy of Management Journal, 46*(1), 86–96.

Guéguen, N., & Jacob, C. (2005). The effect of touch on tipping: An evaluation in a French bar. *International Journal of Hospitality Management, 24,* 295–299.

Hochschild, A. (1983). *The managed heart: Commercialization of human feeling.* Berkeley: University of California Press.

Hornik, J. (1992). Time estimation and orientation mediated by transient mood. *Journal of Socio-Economics, 21*(3), 209–227.

Kaiser, S. (1997). Women's appearance and clothing within organizations. In L. K. Guerrero & M. L. Hecht (Eds.), *The nonverbal communication reader* (pp. 74–81). Long Grove, IL: Waveland Press.

Kramer, M. W., & Hess, J. A. (2002). Communication rules for the display of emotions in organizational settings. *Management Communication Quarterly, 16,* 66–80.

Middleton, D. R. (1989). Emotional style: The cultural ordering of emotions. *Ethos, 17,* 187–201.

Morris, J., & Feldman, D. (1997). Managing emotions in the workplace. *Journal of Managerial Issues, 9,* 257–274.

Richmond, V. P., & McCroskey, J. C. (2009). *Organizational communication for survival: Making work work* (4th ed.). Boston, MA: Allyn & Bacon.

Rule, N. O., & Ambady, N. (2008). The face of success: Inferences from chief executive officers' appearance predict company profits. *Psychological Science, 19,* 109–111.

Rule, N., & Ambady, N. (2009). She's got the look: Inferences from female chief executive officers' faces predict their success. *Sex Roles, 61,* 644–652.

Rule, N. O., & Ambady, N. (2010). First impressions of the face: Predicting success. *Social and Personality Psychology Compass, 4*(8), 506–516.

Saunders, C. S., & Stead, B. A. (1986). Women's adoption of a business uniform: A content analysis of magazine advertisements. *Sex Roles, 13,* 197–205.

Zapf, D. (2002). Emotion work and psychological well-being. A review of the literature and some conceptual considerations. *Human Resource Management Review, 12,* 237–268.

Chapter 8

Using Words Skillfully

Early in my professional career, I would not have thought to write a chapter focused on the specific language skills that are featured in this chapter. Surprisingly, they usually don't get much coverage in communication textbooks, so for years they were not on my "radar." But as I have gained experience as both a leader and follower, and as I've been in many situations in which one person or group is trying to persuade others, I've been struck by the impressive power of using language to enhance framing, tell persuasive or informative stories, and effectively use questions. So in this chapter I will cover each in detail, guided by the general question "How can this skill help us in the workplace?"

Think of people you know who are tactful communicators. This type of person usually has the right thing to say at the right time. They word things quite well, when others may struggle. How do these people pull it off? Essentially, when presented with a social situation, they are aware of many options for how to express something, and they choose options that fit the situation appropriately and effectively. The appropriate and effective part comes from careful observation, listening, and by learning from our experiences (as opposed to not paying careful attention to the lessons our experiences teach). We note how people react to different kinds of messages and adjust our future messages accordingly. Being aware of options means that we have a well-developed schema for how to communicate messages in different ways. More tactful people have a more sophisticated set of communication strategies. This chapter will help you work toward being more tactful by focusing on three different strategies for using words in order to be successful in a variety of communication situations. We begin with a discussion of framing, and then move on to stories and questions.

Message Framing

Suppose you work in health care and are tasked with persuading women over 40 to get a mammography (a test that can provide early detection for breast cancer). Which of the following messages would work better: "It is your responsibility to get a mammography," or "Doctors recommend that you get a mammography"? Essentially, the message is the same: It is important to get a mammography. But in the first case, the responsibility is the patient's, while in the second, it is the doctor's. Rothman, Salovey, Turvey, and Fishkin (1993) studied this question by having women view a presentation of health facts about mammography. Although everyone received the same general information, in a few spots, the message was framed in one of the above ways (it is your responsibility vs. doctors say it is important), and the researchers followed up with the women at 6 and 12 months to see who had obtained a mammography. Within 12 months, 57% of those in the external condition (it is the doctor's responsibility) had obtained a mammogram. However, 66% of those in the internal condition (it is your responsibility) had chosen to have the test. In other words, a slight change in how the message was framed (to emphasize a person's responsibility) resulted in meaningful gains in persuasion that in some cases may have saved lives. Not bad for a few words.

Shifting to a less dramatic example, Pfeffer (1992) describes a case in which an executive solicited feedback from other senior executives on an idea. As the discussion moved from executive to executive, each executive expressed concerns with the idea and suggested why it would not work. According to Pfeffer, the senior executive then said: "The objections that you raised were good ones. However, I decided to go ahead. So, the question now becomes, how do you solve the problems you described so articulately" (p. 204)? According to Pfeffer:

> A funny thing happened. With the issue now framed not as, should we do this? but rather, we're going to do it, so let's solve the problems, the same vice presidents, sitting at the table, quickly began to come up with solutions for the problems they themselves had articulated. . . . Once the question was reframed, the discussion and attitude changed accordingly.
>
> (p. 204)

Although this example unfortunately highlights a practice of soliciting opinions only to ignore them, it also demonstrates something I have seen often in my professional experience. The way an idea is framed can have considerable influence on the subsequent discussion of that idea. In this section, we will explore this issue of framing and discuss some ideas for how to effectively frame messages.

A **frame** involves the language we use to describe an object, person, or situation. According to Goffman (1974), the frames we use when discussing an issue help define situations and aid in the interpretation of situations. When we frame information, we are deciding how to present it. We decide what to **include and exclude,** and what to **emphasize.** Suppose I'm about to introduce you to someone who many find to be intimidating. I can shape your interpretation of this person in a variety of ways. I could just say that he or she is intimidating. Or, I could say that he or she is passionate about his or her job. These different frames will lead you to have different interpretations of the person's intense behavior during your meeting. A more comprehensive definition of framing suggests that "to frame is to select some aspects of a perceived reality and make them more salient in a communicating text, in such a way as to promote a particular problem definition, causal interpretation, moral evaluation, and/or treatment recommendation" (Entman, 1993, p. 52). In other words, when we frame messages, we are selecting and emphasizing some things and omitting and deemphasizing others. What we choose to select/omit can shape our message in different ways.

So if framing is selecting and emphasizing some things, we need to explore how framing can work to our advantage when we communicate. According to Burtis and Turman (2010), the frames we choose set the agenda for the conversation. This concept of **agenda setting** comes from research by McCombs and Shaw (1972) on the media. They suggest that by choosing what stories to cover and how to cover them, the media helps determine what we are talking about with those around us (what is on our "agenda"). Later research pointed to a **second level** of agenda setting, which involves ways in which media may also shape opinions about the stories, by selecting/omitting some aspects of stories, and characterizing some things more positively or negatively (McCombs, 2005). For example, some aspects of stories may not even get coverage. And those that are covered may emphasize some aspects and minimize others. Similarly, when we frame something in conversation, we are setting the agenda for our listeners. In Pfeffer's example above, the executive framed the situation in a way that focused his listeners on strategies needed to move forward (when they otherwise might have become bogged down in debate on whether to even move forward). In the mammography example, the frames emphasized who is responsible for an individual's health (the patients or physicians). In each case, the listeners' agendas were shaped by the ways in which information was framed. In addition, we shape frames by characterizing information within them as positive, negative, or neutral (Coleman, McCombs, Shaw, & Weaver, 2009).

Suppose you were in a meeting and about to discuss whether your department should create and staff a new position to help serve current functions and expand some. If you are introducing the topic for discussion, you could shape the discussion in a variety of ways by framing the issue differently. You could say something like "Next up is the new position, and one issue on my mind is whether we can afford it." This frame likely will lead to a long discussion in which supporters of the position will have to defend it by arguing that it can be covered in the budget. Or you could go in a different direction when introducing the issue: "Next up is the new position, and specifically what kind of tasks we want the person to do." This moves the group forward by assuming the position will happen. Those against the position now will have to back up the discussion and, contrary to the first frame, will have to work much harder to convince the group that you cannot afford the position. Or you could begin: "Next up is the new position, and the kind of person we want to hire for it." Like the second frame, this one is forward-looking and contains an assumption that the position will be created. This frame would lead to a discussion about desired types of employees. If you are a manager of this group, this discussion would let you put a spotlight on desired behaviors. Regardless of the frame used, there are a couple of things that are consistent in each of these scenarios. First, the way we frame an issue shapes the subsequent discussion of that issue by setting the agenda for the discussion. Second, a frame can create extra "work" for those opposed to the way the issue is framed, or less work for supporters. A frame just sets the agenda and shapes the discussion, it does not guarantee that others won't try to reframe the discussion. In the second frame above (what kind of tasks do we want the new person to do), someone concerned about the budget could change the frame by saying "Wait a minute, first we need to discuss whether we can afford this position." Their efforts might work and the discussion may shift based on this reframing. Still, if you're not favorable to their position, you've created more work for people who hold it. They still have to fight against the momentum you've created with your initial frame. With your initial frame you have given yourself an initial edge in the conversation.

In my experiences of leading meetings, I have observed some interesting things about the use of frames. I offer them as examples and observations, not facts that are supported by research. First, people rarely take note of the role that framing plays in shaping discussions. Like the executives in Pfeffer's example, people often do not question a frame, but instead proceed in accordance with it. And if the initial frame was not conducive to pointing the group in a productive direction, it could get bogged down in details without even focusing on the main part of the issue. In the example above, the first frame easily could get the group mired in a long discussion of budget issues, and they might have to meet at another time to even discuss the substance of the position (if it survives the budget discussion). Members might be frustrated about the unproductive meeting, and not even know why the discussion moved in the budget-focused direction. And because I have not found people to be sensitive to frames, they may inadvertently introduce alternative frames before a legitimate one has been explored sufficiently. In the example above, suppose it was important to discuss whether you could afford the position. Then in that discussion someone else could add "and what do we want the person to do?" A few minutes later, another person could add "and what kind of person do we want in this position?" Thanks to these additional frames, in the span of a minute your group could go from discussing one issue (budget) to three (budget, type of position, type of person), without really recognizing what has happened or making meaningful progress on any of the issues. Frustrating productivity-threatening experiences like these led me to see the importance of frames, and to sometimes see discussions as a kind of "war of frames" in which the frames used shaped subsequent discussion. I came to see my job during meetings as offering up the most useful frames, and monitoring when problematic frames potentially could derail the discussion. Because frame shifts can be difficult to spot while participating in discussions, it was a challenging task! So as you find yourself in meetings on your own, or any conversations in which decisions have to be made and people are trying to persuade each other, I encourage you to pay greater attention to the frames people are using and the implications of the frames that have been chosen. Below I will offer some suggestions on how you might improve your ability to recognize frames and use framing to your advantage when communicating.

Although I've discussed framing, we haven't explored the different types of frames we might use. Different researchers have come up with different categories of frames. Rather than covering all of them, I will attempt to identify a few types of frames that apply well to a professional environment. First, we can frame something (an individual, object, situation, issue) by *naming or labeling* it a certain way (Burtis & Turman, 2010). For example, we may frame the same obstacle to a goal as a "problem" or "challenge," and these different frames will evoke different meanings for the same obstacle. When characterizing some initiative in the workplace, we can enhance positive perceptions of it with labels such as "exciting opportunity," "great idea," "a step forward," or we can create more negative perceptions of it by characterizing it as "a drain on resources," "problematic," "unrealistic," and so on. Perhaps the late comedian George Carlin summarized the power of labeling succinctly when he noted that "rainforests and wetlands came into existence because nobody would devote money to saving jungles and swamps" (Carlin, 1999). There are many more possible ways naming might be important, but regardless of the specific words used in these examples, the common theme among them is that the words we choose to name or label something can shape others' perceptions of what we label.

We also can frame the *causes of a situation or event,* whether the causes are people or other circumstances (Hallahan, 1999). When we label causes, we are making an **attribution** (Heider, 1958) about why something happened. We may attribute what happened to **external or internal** causes. If we make an external attribution, we are saying that some circumstance beyond an individual is responsible for whatever happened. We might say that a person did not finish a work assignment on time because: her committee members did not submit their work to her on time, she was asked to do several additional tasks first, she had a personal issue at home that was beyond her control. In each case, some external cause influenced the person's ability to submit her work on time. We also might attribute the outcome to internal causes, possibly by saying that her work was not finished because she: was lazy, didn't care about the assignment, chose to do other things first. In each of these cases the cause is something internal, or within the person in question. In many situations, an outcome is influenced by a variety of internal and external factors. In that first batch of external attributions, it is fair to say that she could have worked harder to get her committee members to submit their work, or that she could have chosen to say "no" to the tasks she was asked to do. And in the second batch of internal factors, there could be a number of external forces that explain why the work wasn't done. Therefore, the frames we use when discussing situations like these can lead us to characterize others in a variety of ways, some much more flattering than others. This is another example of the power of framing.

Third, we can *include and exclude* information to shape perception of something (Hallahan, 1999). We may emphasize the benefits or drawbacks of something depending on our position on it. Or when giving feedback to others, we can emphasize what they are doing well, rather than focusing too much on what they are doing wrong. We can emphasize things we like about an initiative or our concerns to varying degrees. This area of framing also can create ethical issues, for example, if we are withholding valuable information that the receiver should have in order to make an informed decision. For example, drug representatives sometimes have been trained to minimize information about risks and to focus on benefits (Lyon & Mirivel, 2011). Therefore, it is important to keep in mind that some information should not be omitted if it is unethical to do so. But even in situations that do not involve these types of ethical choices, we rarely can include all information on a topic, and therefore we will have to make choices about what to include or exclude. It is important to realize that these choices can alter the frame of our message in significant ways.

Having covered three different types of frames, we briefly can address how to develop skill in framing messages. I don't know of any agreed-upon steps for improving framing skills, so I will do my best to offer a few thoughts on the matter that you may find helpful. First, realize that most situations can be framed in a variety of ways. Second, consider what some of these frames might be. Third, pick a frame that portrays the situation in the way you want to portray it. Fourth, practice the above steps on your own in regard to various people, events, or issues until you start to notice that you are becoming more sensitive to the ways we might use different types of frames. I will walk through these steps with an example. Suppose your company has an online newsletter, but people aren't really using it. First, realize that we could frame this situation in a variety of ways, and that we can consider different ways to frame it. Maybe it's a bad idea because (1) employees rarely use online newsletters, (2) the content doesn't interest employees, or (3) the layout makes it difficult to access information. Or maybe it's a good idea that isn't working because (1) employees are too lazy to use it, (2) employees haven't been properly trained to use it, or (3) employees just haven't been given enough time to use it. Notice that the six examples above each approach the situation from a slightly different angle. We encounter situations like this every day, in which we can use a variety of frames to describe the issue. Notice how the frames we use could lead to several completely different discussions of the same problem. Therefore, in an organization, it is in our best interest to be sensitive to the frames that are being used and to be able to frame issues effectively.

The above discussion has focused on how we frame people, issues, and situations in a fairly direct manner. However, we also can frame using questions or stories. In the next section we will discuss stories in detail, and in the section that follows, we will discuss the use of questions.

Stories

Several years ago when I taught Organizational Communication for the first time, I had an ambitious plan to have the class act as a consulting organization, in which we would analyze the communication of an organization on-campus, and provide recommendations on how the members might improve their communication. I placed students in self-directed groups, so that the class would feel more professional and "grown-up" than typical college classes. Teams were selected and each team elected members to serve various roles within the team. I outlined the assignment and placed relevant readings on reserve in the library for the students to consult as needed. When we worked on the project, I acted as a facilitator. Rather than telling students what they had to do for each step, I expected them to use the reserve readings to learn how to do parts of the project (with me available for as much help as they wanted, once they had taken some initiative to consult the available sources). I quickly became frustrated with students because they were not being proactive and doing what was needed to work on the project. Instead, they waited for me to tell them what to do every step of the way. As we neared the end of the semester, I found myself taking over the project well beyond the bounds of my facilitator role. Things worked out ok in the end, but not smoothly. I had taken too much control, and the students and I were frustrated with each other. The next time I taught the course I took a much more traditional approach. And for a couple of years I was left with frustrating questions about the course. Why did students not take initiative? Why did they wait for me to spell everything out to them? Eventually, it hit me that my students were doing exactly what always had worked well for them in the school system: They were being passive and waiting for me to tell them what to do. They weren't taking chances. From the perspective of students, and considering how the educational system works, this is very reasonable behavior. The problem was that I

Table 8.1 Benefits of Stories

- They are interesting, so they can help us hold our listeners' attention longer.
- Listeners process them less critically so they can help us be more persuasive.
- They can help us make our message more memorable to listeners.
- They can help others learn better, and can be great for coaching others and sharing our intuition with them.

---

was asking them to instantly change and to abandon much of what had worked for them in their school career. I don't blame them for resisting me. Once I realized this, I began to think about some of the negative ways in which our schools may be shaping students, and in subsequent courses I've tried to more modestly and gently encourage students to alter their approach to one that will prepare them better for a professional workplace that will expect them to behave differently than they do in school.

I've included the above story to make a point about the value of stories (see Table 8.1). Instead of going through all of that, I could have just covered a few key highlights and main points. I could have argued that our school system encourages students to be passive and to wait for directions, rather than being proactive and taking initiative. Or if I wanted to make a different type of point, I could have said that it is important to reflect on our failures. Or I could have said that some of our best lessons come from failures. All of these are reasonable points, but if I had started the chapter by just stating them directly, you probably would have been less persuaded, and you would be more likely to forget my points. In this section of the chapter, I will explain why this is the case by discussing the ways in which using stories can help us be more memorable, informative, and more persuasive. In the process, I hope the association you may have with stories (that they're only for fun) will change, and that you will see stories in a new light.

When I discuss stories or **narratives,** I mean something far broader than a fictional account we might read or tell someone. One sense of stories is straightforward and will sound familiar. Stories or narratives are of events that involve one or more characters, and may be true or fictional. According to Green and Brock (2000), a story "raises unanswered questions, presents unresolved conflicts, or depicts not yet completed activity; characters may encounter and then resolve a crisis or crises. A story line, with a beginning, middle, and end, is identifiable" (p. 701).

Beyond this familiar perspective on stories, some argue that storytelling is much broader, and that most human communication actually is storytelling (Fisher, 1984, 1987). For example, your resume tells a kind of story about you; this book is my story of how interpersonal communication in organizations operates; when you make a suggestion at work, it is your story of how things should be done. Fisher's point is that, rather than being highly rational when making decisions and evaluating ideas, we often decide based on how well a story rings true with our own experiences. For example, when teaching something counterintuitive, I can present students with a great deal of research-based evidence, but if it doesn't line up with their own experience, they will not believe it. My "story" doesn't fudge with their story. The point is that rather than using logic (such as the research-based evidence) to evaluate my claims, students will evaluate the "story" I tell, based on their own experiences.

So even if I am "armed" with excellent research evidence, much of my success in convincing students will depend on my ability to deliver the information in the form of a "story" that rings true for students. If you think of recent times when you failed to persuade something (even if you had good logic, good reasons, etc.), you may find that the "story" you were telling simply didn't ring true to your listener(s).

As interesting as this "stories are everything" idea is, if we consider everything to be a story, it can be hard to grasp ways to use stories effectively in professional situations. Therefore, we will focus more narrowly on actually telling stories (sequences of events, with characters), beginning with a discussion of how some of the different functions of stories might serve for us in a professional setting.

First, stories can help us be **more persuasive,** thanks to the way we process them. For three decades, persuasion researchers have focused on how we process persuasion in two different ways (Chaiken, 1980; Petty & Cacioppo, 1981). Sometimes we process information *centrally,* by carefully considering the points or arguments others are using. When processing this way, we are devoting a lot of effort to evaluating arguments. At other times, we process persuasive messages more *peripherally,* in that we are not really thinking about arguments carefully. When processing this way we are more persuaded by less tangible cues or mental shortcuts. For example, we may associate a product with a fun or catchy commercial, like or admire a product spokesperson, or just do or buy something because it feels right, even if we don't elaborate on any arguments or even know why we're buying it. This two-route perspective has helped us understand a great deal about how we are persuaded in different ways.

More recently, Green and Brock (2000) have made a compelling argument that we may process narrative messages in yet a third way that is not related to central or peripheral routes. They suggest that we actually are "transported" into stories, and defined transportation as "a convergent process, where all mental systems and capacities become focused on events occurring in the narrative" (p. 701). In other words, transportation is when we become absorbed in a story. *Transportation* is thought to be different from peripheral processing because we are very mentally involved in processing the message, so our engagement is far more than peripheral. However, it is not central either, as we are focused more on following the story line than we are on evaluating the merit of arguments that may be contained within the story.

Green and Brock's (2000) study revealed a number of interesting things about how stories work to persuade us. They had participants read a narrative and measured the extent to which participants experienced transportation. They also told some participants that the story was true, while telling others it was fictional. They measured how participants processed the message, and participants' attitudes on issues related to the story. They found that the narrative was equally persuasive whether it was real or fictional. Those who experienced greater transportation had beliefs that were more consistent with the story than participants who experienced less transportation. From this we can conclude that stories can shape our beliefs. But the researchers identified another very interesting finding. In one of the studies, they asked participants to go back and identify logical flaws with the story (arguments that didn't make sense). Those who experienced greater transportation tended to spot fewer flaws than those who were less transported. In other words, those who were more transported into the story were less likely to find reasoning flaws within the story. This finding is important, because often when we try to persuade someone, we are met with defensiveness or resistance (Brehm & Brehm, 1981). But as Dal Cin, Zanna, and Fong (2004) suggest, "narratives may indeed be useful in overcoming resistance by reducing negative thoughts associated with the persuasive message" (p. 179). This is an advantage of narratives that enable listeners to experience transportation, but not for messages that are processed centrally or peripherally. Those who process messages centrally can be very resistant to arguments (and if TV political roundtables are any indication, it is possible to be very defensive and ignore even good arguments!). Those who process messages peripherally are not likely to be resistant (they're not giving it enough thought to resist anything), but persuasion that occurs through the peripheral route does not last as long as persuasion through the central route. So while peripheral persuasion may work, it is not a long-term solution. However, to the extent that stories (whether true or fictional) can transport listeners, they can overcome defensiveness and influence beliefs. So if you've not been having luck with straightforward arguments, you may want to consider using a story to persuade your audience. We will discuss aspects of successful storytelling later in this section, but first we turn to another benefit of stories.

Stories and Learning. In addition to helping us persuade others, stories may be able to **help make our ideas more memorable to others.** In their influential book *Made to Stick,* Chip and Dan Heath (2007) suggest that stories are one of six key factors that can make messages more memorable. They argue that stories are powerful because they help us simulate situations, so we can understand those situations more completely. Stories enable us to follow a storyline and visualize what is happening, and this act of imagining involves the same areas of our brain that are involved when we actually are doing the activities we are imagining. In fact, a recent review of studies on mental simulation (of activities such as sports or playing an instrument) found that doing nothing more than imagining performance produced about two-thirds as much improvement as actually performing a skill (Driskell, Copper, & Moran, 1994). These are impressive gains for not even performing an activity. Heath and Heath (2007) argue that good stories are like simulations that provide a kind of context that we cannot gain from information delivered in non-narrative form. They use what they call the *"Velcro theory of memory"* to explain why stories make information stick. According to this idea, like Velcro, which works because of the many hooks that latch onto fabric, "the more hooks we put into our ideas, the better they'll stick" (p. 214). Stories provide more "hooks" to enhance memory, because beyond the basic information they convey, they also associate this information with characters, events, emotions, and so on. Each of these links we make serve as additional "hooks" to make information more memorable to us. According to Zwaan, Langston, and Graesser (1995), when processing narratives, we focus on many elements in the situations they depict: time, space, the protagonist, intentionality, and causality. We focus on the time frame in which the event occurs, as well as the space in which it occurs. We focus on the protagonist of the story, and what causes events in the story to happen. Finally, we focus on the protagonist's goals. And this is just our cognitive focus, and says nothing of the extent to which we might react emotionally to a story. This perspective has been confirmed by neurological researchers who study brain scans. According to Mar (2004), "a number of brain structures are consistently activated during particular story processes. Furthermore, these brain areas appear to be unique to narrative-processing, separate from those identified for word and even sentence level operations" (p. 1429). In other words, we use more of our brain when processing narratives (more "hooks"), beyond what we use to process nonnarratives. When we consider this evidence, compared to how we process information that is not in narrative form, our processing of stories is much richer and multidimensional, which helps explain why stories may help us learn information more effectively and remember learned information longer.

Stories work for a number of additional reasons. In Chapter 1 we discussed **schemas,** or our **mental models** for information. Stories are useful because they can help us build richer mental models (Busselle & Bilandzic, 2008). And in some situations, even if information is not in narrative form, we will try to put it into narrative form in order to make sense of it. Pennington and Hastie (1988) had research participants watch a realistic reenactment of a trial and serve as jurors. Their finding was that "jurors spontaneously, without the prompting of interview questions, construct a story structure summary of the evidence" (p. 527). The researchers then examined the impact of putting evidence into story form (or not doing so), and found that "story coherence as determined by the presentation order of evidence affects perceptions of evidence strength, verdict decisions, and confidence in decisions. Subjects were more than twice as likely to find the defendant guilty of murder in our stimulus case when prosecution evidence was ordered in story form and defense evidence was not, compared to when defense evidence was presented in story form and prosecution evidence was not" (p. 529). This is another example of the important role narratives play in helping us establish rich mental models.

To illustrate this, we can use an example of learning from information in narrative and nonnarrative form. Suppose we were trying to educate medical students about not overrelying on technology, and about the importance of asserting oneself when necessary. We could outline different ways technology may lead us to false diagnoses, and talk about how asserting ourselves is the right thing to do, when it comes to the safety of the patient. Or, we could use a story, like the one relayed by Gary Klein (1999), which is based on research in which nurses are asked to discuss critical incidents they have faced on the job:

> A nurse in a neonatal intensive care unit has been providing primary care for a baby in the isolette next to the baby described here. She has noticed this other baby having subtle color changes over a period of several hours. He fades out a bit, then comes back to a healthy pink on his own. She remarks on it to his primary nurse, who has noticed these variations too. Then in a matter of seconds, the baby turns deep blue-black. The monitor shows that his blood pressure has bottomed out completely; his hear rate drops but then levels out and holds steady at eighty beats per minute.
>
> She knows immediately that he has suffered a pneumopericardium. Air has filled the sac that surrounds the heart and turned it into a balloon; the air pressure around the heart prevents it from moving blood through the heart into the baby's body. His heart is essentially paralyzed. She knows he will die within minutes if the air around his heart is not released. She knows this because she

has seen it happen once before, to a baby who was her patient. The baby had died.

Meanwhile, the baby's primary nurse is yelling for the X-ray, and a doctor to come and puncture the baby's chest wall. She figures that the baby's lung has collapsed, a common event for babies who are on ventilators, and besides, the heart monitor continues to show a steady eighty beats per minute. The nurse who first spotted the problems tries to correct her—"It's the heart, there's no heartbeat"—while the team around her continues to point to the heart monitor. She pushes their hands away from the baby and screams for quiet as she listens through her stethoscope for a heartbeat. There is none, and she begins doing compressions on the baby's chest. The chief neonatologist appears, and she turns to him, slaps a syringe in his hand and says, "It's a pneumopericardium. I know it. Stick the heart." The X-ray technician calls from across the room that she is right: the baby's pericardium is filled with air. The physician releases the air, and the baby's life is saved.

Afterward, the team talks about why the monitor had fooled them. They realize that the monitor is designed to record electrical events, and it continued to pick up the electrical impulses generated by the heart. The monitor can record the electrical impulse but cannot show whether the heart is actually beating to circulate blood through the body.

(p. 178)

Using a story like this to illustrate a point and help others remember information works for a number of reasons. First, it would be hard for even an excellent outline of information to be as interesting and memorable as a story like this. Second, the story provides context that an outline cannot, because when we process it, we are focused on many dimensions. Time is running out, the protagonist has to overcome resistance that is reasonable (based on the heart monitor reading). We can picture the room in which this would take place, and probably even the emotions and facial expressions of those involved (even though the story did not focus on these elements). Beyond these details, the context and detail in the story helps us build a rich mental model of the condition the baby faced. We now know how symptoms contradict each other, some mistaken diagnoses that may be made, and how the problem should be addressed. It would be hard to cover all of this information, weave it together, and make it this memorable without using a story.

Finally, notice how the nurse knew to make the diagnosis that others missed. Unfortunately, she already had a mental model, based on a previous experience in which a baby in a similar situation died. That experience gave the nurse a powerful mental model. The story has given us a powerful mental model. And that may be the key aspect of stories: They help give us experience without us having to actually accumulate years worth of experiences. This issue will be discussed in greater detail in the coaching chapter (Chapter 12), but for now, it is clear that stories have persuasive and explanatory power, and that they may serve a variety of uses for those trying to communicate more effectively with others.

This leads us to the final part of this section: how to tell good stories effectively. According to Green and Donahue (2009), **transportation** into stories can be influenced by story quality, familiarity with the world depicted in the narrative, and individual differences in how "transportable" a person is (some become transported into stories more readily than others). Since we can't change a person's transportability, we can focus on the other two factors. We can address familiarity by telling stories to which others can relate, and avoiding stories that "stretch" listeners' ability to envision what is happening. And finally, we can tell good stories. In the remainder of this section on stories, we will focus on what it takes to tell a good story.

Green and Donahue (2009) suggest that good stories are **well structured.** Klein (1999) suggests three features of good stories: they are dramatic, we can identify with one or more of the characters, and they reveal wisdom (lessons that encourage us to pass the story on to others). Klein (1999) suggests a few additional features stories should possess: *plausibility, consistency,* and *economy.* Stories should be *plausible* in that the events in the story are believable. They should be *consistent* in that the elements in the story should fit together. And they should be *economical* by having enough, but not too many details.

That is a long list of suggestions, so to help focus this discussion, we will consider the perspective of Heath and Heath (2007), who suggest that many stories can be boiled down to one of three basic types of plots. More important, they suggest that you should try to conform to one of these plots when telling your stories. In their research, they found that stories that conformed to one of the basic three plots were more likely to be rated as inspiring than stories that did not conform to one of the plots. They also found that the different plots evoke different feelings. The three plots are the **Challenge Plot, Connection Plot,** and **Creativity Plot.**

The Challenge Plot involves facing an intimidating challenge and overcoming it to succeed. These are the plots in movies like *Rocky, Miracle, Hoosiers,* and *Karate Kid.* According to Heath and Heath (2007), these plots appeal to our courage and willingness to persevere. The Connection Plot is about two or more people who form a relationship by bridging some kind of gap (they may be in different demographic groups, live in different geographical areas, or otherwise are in positions that would make it improbable for them to connect). It may be a story about how two people met, how they developed a relationship, how they didn't like each other at first, but came to like each other. Often the focus is on having tolerance for others or helping others. Finally, the Creativity Plot involves someone "making a mental breakthrough, solving a long-standing puzzle, or attacking a problem in an innovative way" (Heath & Heath, 2007, p. 229). These types of stories can be very relevant to the workplace, because often coworkers will tell work stories about how they figured out how to solve a challenging problem (Heath & Heath, 2007; Klein, 1999). The story at the beginning of this section is an example of the creativity plot. This kind of storytelling is key to helping coworkers informally pass along what is called tacit knowledge to others. Tacit knowledge consists of things we know that are hard to explain to others. If you can think of a time that you just *knew* something, but had difficulty explaining it to others, it may have been tacit knowledge. In organizations this knowledge, which we gain from experience, is valuable and it would be ideal if we could communicate it to others. This is why work stories can be important, as they can help us pass along tacit knowledge to others. The neonatal nurse in the example above had tacit knowledge that enabled her to make a quick diagnosis of the baby's condition. Her knowledge was formed by her prior experience. Imagine if some time before the event depicted in the story, she had shared the story during informal discussions with coworkers. They may have approached the situation with a more informed perspective. At the very least, they would have a better understanding of the situation than if they did not hear the story. We will discuss this value of stories in greater detail in the chapter on coaching in the workplace.

Regarding the ways in which these plots influence others, Heath and Heath (2007) report that in one study:

> Challenge plots made people want to set higher goals, to take on new challenges, to work harder and persist longer. Connection plots made people want to work with others, to reach out and help them, and to be more tolerant. Creativity plots made people want to do something different, to be creative, to experiment with new approaches. Notably, none of these stories was more likely to drive "feel good" activity. People weren't more likely to do something to enjoy themselves—to listen to good music, watch television, or eat a good meal; instead, they wanted to go out and accomplish something. Thus these stories drive productive action, not passive self-involvement.
>
> (p. 307)

These plots also help us to conform to some of the characteristics of good stories mentioned above. They give us a coherent plot line and we can identify with the characters in these types of plots. These results suggest that when we tell stories at work, it would be a good idea to stick close to one of these three plots, as they may be more likely to resonate with people than other types of plots.

So we know stories are important, and that it would be worthwhile to conform to certain types of plots, but we haven't addressed the important questions of "How do we identify stories worth telling?" and "What if we can't think of any stories to tell?" The trick is to get into the habit of spotting potentially helpful stories. To start, think about some memorable moments you've experienced: **frustrating moments, failures, times when you met key people, times when you had major successes, your proudest accomplishments, moments that were unexpected to you at the time, times when you overcame obstacles, key lessons you've learned,** and so on. Each of these types of moments may lead you to a variety of stories that may come in handy for you some day. And then for each of these categories, you can think of stories you've encountered, either by reading or hearing of them, or by watching others experience them. Even if you only have a story or two for each of these types of experience, that would leave you with a good collection of stories. The next step involves linking a story to a point you wish to make to someone. If you have a point you want to make, consider whether any stories come to mind that could help you make that point. Rather than trying to spontaneously do this while on the job with little time to think "on-your-feet," it may be helpful to start by reflecting on past situations in which you might have used stories. Think of recent times you tried to inform or persuade someone but wish you would have been more effective. Consider whether any of the stories you've collected could have helped you make the kind of point you wish to make, and then consider how you might have used it. Please realize that this process may be awkward at first, like driving a car for the first time. Don't expect instant fluency. Like any skill, it takes time to develop. Once you feel like you made a couple of links between stories and past situations, you may find it helpful to practice using stories in low-risk situations, such as hanging out with friends, or when the consequences of failure are minimal. If you do these kinds of things, over time, you should find yourself more readily thinking of and spotting potentially good stories, and also recognizing the "story potential" in situations. If you devote enough attention to using stories, you may be surprised at just how often you find yourself using stories in various situations.

Once you've found stories, you may wonder what you can do to tell stories effectively. Gordon (2006) offers several ideas on how to make stories more dramatic. He suggests having an interesting structure, what he calls **the three acts**: "*Act I—get your man up in the tree,*" "*Act II—throw stones at him to the point where by the end of Act II you wonder if he ever is getting down from the tree,*" and "*Act III— get your man down from the tree*" (p. 49). In the first act we introduce the problem facing the main character, and describe the main character sympathetically. We also need to present a realistic challenge or conflict. In the second act we make sure the conflict is sufficiently dramatic and that it sets up a need for resolution. In the final act the story should be resolved in a way that helps you make any points you want to make. Although you don't necessarily have to use this arrangement for every story (other structures may be better suited for less dramatic stories), this structure can help you when you need a dramatic story and conclusion (notice that the nursing story above fits this structure).

Another type of structure that can be helpful when you need to hold someone else's attention is suggested by Cialdini (2005). His focus was on using stories to keep students interested, but the same ideas can be applied to whenever we need to hold someone's interest. How did he arrive at this approach, and what is this approach? He examined the work of others who had written about complex academic material, separating what he thought were captivating examples and also ones he thought were very boring. In addition to the expected things like good writing, clear structure, and examples, he found that writers captivated readers by beginning with some type of mystery that engaged them, just like I did a few sentences ago in this paragraph. If we can engage others with some type of mystery, they will be interested in reaching the ending. But more important, in the process, they can develop memorable explanations of how something works (rather than just memorizing answers). So if you need to draw others in, rather than assuming that you or your material is interesting, you may want to **try posing some type of question** that will make others want to "follow" you to your conclusion.

Gordon (2006) also suggests **considering where dull words can be replaced** with more vivid words, such as sensory words ("see," "feel," "hear," "touch," etc.) that evoke more vivid imagery for listeners. For additional tricks of storytelling, just watch others who are good at it: friends, coworkers, teachers, TV personalities (some comedians are quite good at telling stories). As with any skill, doing all of this may feel awkward at first, but with practice it will become more fluent, so avoid expecting perfection at the very beginning. For the final section of this chapter we will discuss one final language skill: asking good questions.

Questions

I've been fortunate to have worked for many great managers and supervisors, and I've learned many lessons from each. Some of my most valuable lessons came from Frank Short, who was my dean (immediate supervisor) when I was a department chair. Before becoming a dean he was a highly successful women's volleyball coach (read: many championships!) and he used his coaching skills to great effect when managing his department chairs. The skills he demonstrated helped inspire the chapter on workplace coaching in this book (few workplace communication books give attention to coaching), and he also is part of the inspiration for this section on questions. Below I'll explain why (of course with a story!).

Being a department chair is the hardest job I've ever held, as one has to balance concerns about faculty, students, budgets, courses, and all kinds of internal paper-work. When problems arise they often are complex. When I would consult with Frank Short about problems, I frequently went in with long, convoluted descriptions of the problem, in which I outlined all of the key variables. For example, I might say something (remember, this is about one singular problem) like "Students are concerned about _____, but from the faculty member's perspective the problem is _____, but I hear informally that the problem is rooted in _____. I think _____ and _____ are problematic, but I'm not sure what to do about _____ and _____." Clearly I was confused, and it must have been confusing for Frank. But time after time when faced with my convoluted problems, he had the ability to ask one or two questions that immediately helped me get to the heart of the issue, and to sort through all of the variables, so I could focus on what was most important. I still don't exactly know how he did it, but to this day it blows my mind. It took him one or two respectfully worded questions to crystallize com-plex issues for me. In approaching my problems this way, he avoided the trap of trying to just give advice or answer all of the questions I posed, even though it would have been far easier (at least in the short term) to just give me advice. Instead, he used the right questions to help me draw my own conclusions about problems, and in the process I learned much more about handling problems than if he would have just given me advice (he also used stories very well too). I also noticed some-thing else about his use of questions. Often when I posed a more clear-cut question to him ("What should I do about _____?"), rather than answering it he would explore the problem with questions, often by asking "What would happen if we did this: _____?" or "How would people react if we _____?" In this case, he was using questions more to help me figure out solutions, and possibly to convince me what to do by using an indirect approach. From these experiences I started noticing the power of questions in other contexts (the classroom, during conflict situations, etc.). Although there isn't a great deal of scholarly research on asking questions effectively, it is fair to say that questions can be useful, so they deserve some attention here (and I will discuss them in other chapters, such as the ones on disagreements (Chapter 10), conflict (Chapter 11), and coaching (Chapter 12)). I will focus on types of questions and some of the useful functions served by questions.

Types of Questions

So what are some different general types of questions we might ask? I'm going to cover three: *closed, leading,* and *open-ended. Closed* **questions** limit the choice of answers one may give (usually one word is enough to answer them), and typically only require a brief response. Examples include: "Do you agree with me?" "Which plan do you think we should choose?" and "Have you ever _____?" They are simple and direct, and are perfectly useful and necessary in a variety of situations. However, if your goal is to get people to talk, to elaborate on a response, to explain themselves, or to become engaged in a conversation, you generally should avoid closed questions. They encourage quick answers, not elaborate responses. *Leading* questions (which also may be closed) are those that suggest the answer we are expecting to receive. Examples include "Do you *really* think we should do that?" "It's a bad idea, don't you agree?" "Don't you agree that it's a bad idea?" and "Do you want to disappoint everyone in the office?" If you are an attorney cross examining someone, or if your goal is to encourage defensiveness or resistance, or to pressure someone and have the person resent agreeing with you, then these may excellent questions to use. Otherwise, if you want an open exchange of ideas, it would be good to avoid questions like these. So if we want to encourage conversation, to get another person to elaborate, or to avoid a defensive reaction, that leaves *open-ended* questions. These are questions that allow people to freely respond, without the restrictions imposed by the other two types of questions. To contrast open-ended questions with the other types, for examples I'll redo some of the above examples in open-ended format: "What do you think about this idea?" "What do you think we should do?" "To what extent do you agree with me?" "What are you hoping to accomplish with this?" "Why would you like to _____?" "How do you think others will react?" Notice that each of these questions invites a more elaborate response. This makes them more versatile for us to use, as we can gain more information and accomplish more goals than we can with the other types of questions. Most of this section will focus on open-ended questions, as my experience has shown me that people struggle with these types of questions more than the others (it must be easier to ask closed and leading questions!). To help address this possible challenge, we briefly will explore two different questioning mindsets.

Table 8.2 Open vs. Closed Questions

Closed	Open
• Encourage one word answers: "yes," "no," etc., so they often do little to further a conversation	• Encourage longer responses
	• Enable you to learn more from the other person
• Begin with leading words, like "should," "do," "will," "are," etc.	• Give you more time to listen and formulate your own thoughts
• More likely to lead to a conversational "dead end"	• When done with sincere curiosity and without interrogating others (in other words, with a learning mindset), others likely will appreciate your interest in them
• More likely to put others on the defensive	
	• Begin with terms like "what," "how," "why," etc.
• "Do you think we should go with plan A?"	• "What are your thoughts on Plan A?"
• "Should he have done that?"	• "Why do you think he did that?"
• "Am I doing anything wrong?"	• "How do you think I might be able to improve?"

Questioning Mindsets

One of the tricks to asking any type of question is to ask it the right way, in terms of emphasis, tone of voice, and so on. Think of various ways you could ask a coworker "What happened?" You could be patient and understanding, demanding, in a hurry, frustrated, or angry. In keeping with the approach discussed in the nonverbal communication chapter (Chapter 7), rather than focusing on specific nonverbal behaviors you should demonstrate when asking questions, I will focus on a couple of questioning attitudes or mindsets: *judging* and *learning* (Marquardt, 2005). A judgment mindset is oriented in the past, and is focused on who is to blame for the current situation. The focus is on pointing out causes, rather than looking forward toward solutions. While this approach may be necessary at times, if you recall times when you've been questioned by someone in this mindset, you probably realize that there is a better way to accomplish the goals of questions than to accuse. In contrast, a learning mindset is one of genuinely seeking information that can be used to improve a situation while moving forward. The trick to this mindset is to genuinely want to hear answers from others with a goal of moving forward, rather than wanting to assign blame or remain rooted in the past. If we are genuine, then it will be more natural for us to have an appropriate nonverbal demeanor when answering questions. As we cover the advantages using questions below, consider how the examples convey a genuine interest in learning.

Advantages of Asking Questions

Help Us Listen Better. Rather than going through a conversation thinking what you want to say next, think of what question you want to ask next (an appropriate, reasonable question that follows naturally from what the person is saying). You will find that it requires you to listen more carefully to what the other person is saying. If you get into the habit of asking questions at least a little more often, it should help you become a more disciplined listener.

Encourage Others to Open Up. Asking open-ended questions with a learning mindset can get others to open up. As opposed to "Are you upset?" or "Is something bothering you?" questions like "What's on your mind?" or "What's bothering you?" encourage a greater range of responses. This can come in handy when you're trying to make small talk with others. Rather than saying "Do you _____?" or "Do you like _____?" you will invite broader responses with questions like "What kinds of things does your job involve?" or "What kinds of things do you enjoy most about your job?" Again, a learning mindset is important here. If you aren't curious to want to hear the answer, you may be better off not asking questions.

Control an Interaction. Questions probably don't seem controlling on the surface, but if you think about it, they functionally serve as requests for another person to respond to us, and there is a fairly powerful social norm that says we have to respond when someone asks us a question. This means that a person who is asking questions is in control of an interaction. This can be particularly beneficial when dealing with those of higher status, particularly when they are not being sufficiently clear with us. This can happen with physicians who don't explain themselves clearly, managers, and others. And in my line of work, students get frustrated when teachers sometimes do not explain themselves clearly enough. Over the years, I've informally coached students to use certain types of questions to get helpful answers from instructors. Usually by the time they reach me they are frustrated or intimidated by an instructor, and often have written off the instructor, assuming that the person will not be helpful. I encourage students to ask simple and straightforward questions like: "Can you help me understand what I might be doing wrong?" or "I'm still unclear about _____, could you please explain it to me?" Although these technically are closed questions (requiring only a "yes" or "no" answer), they imply the need for more elaborate explanation. Still, the student usually remains concerned that the instructor won't be helpful. I then suggest that the student think of a question or two that he or she can keep asking until receiving a helpful answer, even if it feels repetitious (repetition may be necessary when someone has failed to listen or answer our question). This approach addresses that feeling we have in our gut when a more powerful person is ushering us out the door, and we are complying, even though we don't feel we've been sufficiently helped. I tell students that they always can use questions like "Thank you for explaining that, but _____ still is unclear to me, could you please explain _____?" or "A couple of things still don't make sense to me, could you please explain _____?" These questions can be used repeatedly until you get the answers you're seeking. And they can be used even when we are frustrated. The last sample question can be helpful when we think something is unfair, but don't feel comfortable directly challenging it. Even if the respondent is of higher status, the expectation usually is that she or he will respond to the question. For those of us who frequently communicate with higher-status individuals, or have trouble asserting ourselves, respectful questions like those mentioned in this section can help us stand firm until we receive helpful answers.

Stimulate Thinking and Enhance Understanding. Questions also can be used to help both others and us better understand a situation we are facing (as with the Frank Short example from the beginning of this section). For example, at some point in my teaching career, I learned that if students do not answer a question correctly, rather than saying "No, that's not it" and moving on, it can be helpful to say something like "What makes you think that's the answer?" or "What makes you think that?" (in a sincere and curious tone, not a condescending one). These questions help me learn a great deal about how students are understanding the course material (assumptions they are making, biases in their thinking, misunderstandings, etc.), and therefore I am better able to offer useful explanations to them. Similarly, we can use them in workplace conversations to better understand why a person is thinking a certain way. This can help us see how an opinion might make sense from another person's perspective. Suppose you're annoyed with how a colleague views an issue. You can stay annoyed and befuddled that a person would think that way, or you can ask "What's your thinking on why we would be better off doing _____?" or "I'm wondering why you're thinking that _____?" (again in a sincere, nonthreatening tone). If you can better understand the other person's perspective, you may be able to respect his or her position, you might agree with it, or you might have a better sense of how to voice your opposition to it. Questions can help understanding in other ways. Sometimes when another person or an entire group gets bogged down with an issue, we can ask "why" questions to help them reframe the issue. These questions might begin with "Why can't we just . . . ?" or "Why are we assuming that we can only do _____ when other options might be possible?" As we will learn in the coaching chapter (Chapter 12), questions can also help us learn from others' mental models or help others develop mental models. If you're trying to learn from others, you can ask questions about how they handled specific challenging incidents: "What were you thinking when that happened?" "Why did you do _____?" "Why did you not _____?" "What would you have done if _____ had happened?" "How would a beginner have handled this differently?" These questions will help us understand the judgment calls the person made in the situation (Klein, 1999). Or you can help others envision things that might happen by walking through a hypothetical future situation: "What do you think would happen if we _____?" In each of these situations, using a question may be more helpful than stating an opinion or making an assumption and moving on. In each case, we can gain valuable information, or help others better understand their situation.

Reveal Opinions, Persuade, or Explore Alternatives Without Breeding Defensiveness

This may be the most fascinating use of questions that we will discuss. How often have you had verbal "sparring matches" with others, in which you try hard to convince them of something? There probably have been times when you've made great points and counterarguments, only to be amazed that the person would not budge on her position. It is pretty natural for people to defend a position that we are attacking, or for them to be resistant to persuasion attempts (Brehm & Brehm, 1981). Like stories, questions may be able to help us bypass this natural defensiveness. One of the smartest and most persuasive questions I ever asked a colleague was "What do you think about this?" (again, with sincerity). A question like this will help you understand another person's perspective. But thanks to reciprocity, it also may lead the other person to ask you (sincerely) what you think of the issue. Without even having to push, you've been invited to share your perspective. The other person may not agree with you, but at least you were able to state your case without encountering initial defensiveness.

Calm others during conflict situations. Still, there may be many times when the person will disagree with you. And as we will see when we discuss conflict, this can introduce a lot of frustration, and sometimes anger, into the situation. So beyond the suggestion above, there are some ways we can use questions to gently "argue" without seeming to argue. We can use some of the following types of questions to do this: "What do you think would happen if we (insert whatever course of action you're advocating)?" "What do you think about the idea of (insert whatever course of action you're advocating)?" or "To what extent would it make sense if we (insert whatever course of action you're advocating)?" These types of questions could be used repeatedly. Suppose you ask one and get a response of "We can't do that because. . . . " You could use the same type of question as a follow-up: "That's a good point, but what would happen if, in response we (insert your idea for how to handle the objection)?" There is no guarantee that this will work perfectly (you should be suspicious of any approach that offers such a guarantee!), but if you're in a climate in which people are hostile, defensive, or easily irritated by disagreement, this use of questions can help you make points without leading to such a negative reaction.

Conclusions

As I said above in reference to questions, the verbal skills in this chapter won't guarantee success, but in my professional career I've noticed many ways in which others have succeeded by using them (many of my current and former graduate students who also are full-time working professionals have agreed about the importance of these skills in their workplaces). I encourage you to try to pay greater attention to the use of framing, stories, and questions around you, and to try practicing them in low-risk situations (realizing that it takes time to develop a new skill you haven't practiced before). I think you will find that they can come in handy.

We will continue to discuss additional aspects of verbal messages in the next chapter, by focusing on listening, and other types of verbal messages that can play an important role in our interactions with others.

References

Brehm, S.S., & Brehm, J.W. (1981). *Psychological reactance: A theory of freedom and control.* New York, NY: Academic Press.

Burtis, J.O., & Turman, P.D. (2010). *Leadership communication as citizenship.* Los Angeles, CA: Sage.

Busselle, R., & Bilandzic, H. (2008). Fictionality and perceived realism in experiencing stories: A model of narrative comprehension and engagement. *Communication Theory, 18,* 255–280.

Carlin, G. (1999, May 13). Brain droppings. Presentation to the National Press Club Luncheon, aired on PBS.

Chaiken, S. (1980). Heuristic versus systematic information processing and the use of source versus message cues in persuasion. *Journal of Personality and Social Psychology, 39,* 752–766.

Cialdini, R.B. (2005). What's the best secret device for engaging student interest? The answer is in the title. *Journal of Social and Clinical Psychology, 24,* 22–29.

Coleman, R., McCombs, M., Shaw, D., & Weaver, M. (2009). Agenda setting. In K. Wahl-Jorgensen & T. Hanitzsch (Eds.), *The handbook of journalism studies* (pp. 147–160). New York, NY: Routledge.

Dal Cin, S., Zanna, M.P., & Fong, G.T. (2004). Narrative persuasion and overcoming resistance. In E.S. Knowles & J.A. Linn (Eds.), *Resistance and persuasion* (pp. 175–191). Mahwah, NJ: Erlbaum.

Driskell, J.E., Copper, C., & Moran, A. (1994). Does mental practice enhance performance? *Journal of Applied Psychology, 79,* 481–492.

Entman, R.M. (1993). Framing: Toward clarification of a fractured paradigm. *Journal of Communication, 43,* 51–58.

Fisher, W.R. (1984). Narration as a human communication paradigm: The case of public moral argument. *Communication Monographs, 51,* 1–22.

Fisher, W.R. (1987). *Human communication as narration: Toward a philosophy of reason, value, and action.* Columbia: University of South Carolina Press.

Goffman, E. (1974). *Frame analysis: An essay on the organization of experience.* New York, NY: Harper & Row.

Gordon, J. (2006). *Presentations that change minds: Strategies to persuade, convince, and get results.* New York, NY: McGraw Hill.

Green, M. C., & Brock, T. C. (2000). The role of transportation in the persuasiveness of public narratives. *Journal of Personality and Social Psychology, 79,* 701–721.

Green, M. C., & Donahue, J. K. (2009). Transportation into narratives. In K. D. Markman, W. M. P. Klein, & J. A. Suhr (Eds.), *Handbook of imagination and mental stimulation* (pp. 241–255). New York, NY: Psychology Press.

Hallahan, K. (1999). Seven models of framing: Implications for public relations. *Journal of Public Relations Research, 11,* 205–242.

Heath, C., & Heath, D. (2007). *Made to stick: Why some ideas survive and others die.* New York, NY: Random House.

Heider, F. (1958). *The psychology of interpersonal relations.* New York, NY: Wiley.

Klein, G. (1999). *Sources of power: How people make decisions.* Cambridge, MA: MIT Press.

Lyon, A., & Mirivel, J. (2011). Reconstructing Merck's practical theory of communication: The ethics of pharmaceutical sales representative–physician encounters. *Communication Monographs, 78,* 53–72.

Mar, R. A. (2004). The neuropsychology of narrative: Story comprehension, story production, and their interrelation. *Neuropsychologia, 42,* 1414–1434.

Marquardt, M. J. (2005). *Leading with questions: How leaders find the right solutions by knowing what to ask.* San Francisco, CA: Jossey Bass.

McCombs, M. (2005). A look at agenda-setting: Past, present and future. *Journalism Studies, 6,* 543–557.

McCombs, M. E., & Shaw, D. L. (1972). The agenda-setting function of mass media. *Public Opinion Quarterly, 36,* 176–187.

Pennington, N., & Hastie, R. (1988). Explanation-based decision making: Effects of memory structure on judgment. *Journal of Experimental Psychology: Learning, Memory, and Cognition, 14,* 521–533.

Petty, R. E., & Cacioppo, J. T. (1981). *Attitudes and persuasion: Classic and contemporary approaches.* Dubuque, IA: William C. Brown.

Pfeffer, J. (1992). *Managing with power.* Boston, MA: Harvard Business Press.

Rothman, A. J., Salovey, P., Turvey, C., & Fishkin, S. A. (1993). Attributions of responsibility and persuasion: Increasing mammography utilization among women over 40 with an internally oriented message. *Health Psychology, 12,* 39–47.

Zwaan, R. A., Langston, M. C., & Graesser, A. C. (1995). The construction of situation models in narrative comprehension: An event indexing model. *Psychological Science, 6,* 292–297.

Chapter 9

Listening Carefully to Verbal and Nonverbal Messages

In this chapter we will examine listening in the workplace, and answer two general questions: (1) Why do people often listen poorly? and (2) How can we get people to listen to us? In the process of considering these questions, we will encounter a number of interesting aspects of language in order to help you see what others miss when communicating.

Why Do People Often Listen Poorly?

If you encounter a list of professional skills that managers desire, there is a good chance that "listening" will be on that list. And I suspect you've encountered situations in which a failure to listen effectively caused problems. As a result, if you do a quick Google search, you will find many programs that offer listening skills training. In addition, many communication textbooks offer chapters on listening. However, as a teacher who has wanted to provide good instruction on listening, I rarely have found any of these available materials helpful. They may cover barriers to listening, which is legitimate, as there are many, and they may cover different listening styles, which also is legitimate. However, I have not found this information useful in helping my students improve their listening skills. For example, I have taught about listening barriers such as other information that competes for our attention (like texting), focusing on the wrong parts of the message (the speaker's appearance more than his message), being biased when hearing the information, and so on. Addressing these problems was only somewhat helpful. As I struggled with this issue, I was reminded of when I approached one of my doctoral instructors, Jim McCroskey, and told him I was interested in studying listening. He said something like "People listen just fine. If you tell them how to save money, what's going to be on the test, etc., they will listen quite well. You should focus on how to get people want to listen." I was so set on studying listening that it took a few years for his comments to really sink in, but as I struggled to teach listening effectively, I started to come around to this point of view.

If you consider this perspective, it does make some sense, at lease for people who do not experience any kind of sensory impairment (Attention Deficit Disorder, Autism, or Asperger's syndrome, etc.). Think of a time when you were attracted to someone but you weren't quite sure whether he or she was attracted to you. You probably were a model listener, carefully paying attention to every word, and also noticing facial expressions, tone of voice, and other things. In other words, there was no deficiency in your listening skill. We see the same level of mastery when students are told that "this is on the test." In other words, most people listen quite well—when they want to listen. And although listening research might suggest that people are not very good listeners, Roberts and Vinson (1998) suggest that it may because the research was conducted in situations in which participants were not very motivated to listen. So rather than focus on why people listen poorly, we will focus on why people don't choose to use their naturally good listening ability.

There may be a few reasons we don't choose to listen. There is not much research in this area, so I'll do my best to offers some possibilities. First, **listening takes effort,** and probably more than talking. We are at the mercy of another person, have to follow what the person says, and then try to extract meaning from it. In other words, we have to concentrate, and this is not easy to do for long periods of time. For example, occasionally when teaching a night course, I have to listen to presentations for three hours. Even though these are well done and enjoyable presentations, it is very hard to focus for the entire three hours of presentations—much harder than teaching for three hours. So one factor in our unwillingness to listen is simply that we can't always devote the necessary effort to it. Second, **with so much information competing for our attention, we have to be choosy.** We simply cannot pay attention to everything. We have to make choices, and we will choose messages that are novel, unexpected, interesting, dramatic, or confirming of our existing beliefs. Although the first two reasons we choose to not listen are substantial, there still are many times when we overcome them and listen quite intently. We do this because in these situations we recognize the possible rewards we might gain from listening. **Compared to listening, the rewards for speaking typically are more immediate and more obvious.** We get an instant nonverbal reaction, and often a verbal reaction. Thanks to this instant and clear feedback, we receive greater reinforcement for speaking than we do for listening. When we listen, there rarely is a response that functions to say "I notice and appreciate that you're listening," and while we often are rewarded for listening, it is less obvious. Something we pick up on may benefit us in hours or weeks, but it is not as consistently clear and immediate as our reinforcement for speaking. But when the rewards are clear to us, good listening naturally follows. Therefore, the focus of much of this chapter will be to draw your attention to many rewards of good listening in the workplace that you might not otherwise recognize, so that you might more naturally use your listening skills at key times in your own workplace. To do this, I will focus on many fascinating things we can notice when we listen carefully to others—things that we otherwise might miss.

What Kinds of Things Can We "Catch" When We Listen Carefully?

In this section we will explore a variety of aspects of language and nonverbal behavior that we might "catch" while listening perceptively to others. It is not a complete list, but it will give you a sense of the interesting kinds of meanings that might be embedded in many messages that we might take for granted. I will describe each and then address the question: "Why might it be worthwhile to notice this in the workplace?" My goal is to draw your attention to the ways in which we might benefit from more careful listening within our workplace.

Everything From the Past Two Chapters

Before moving onto new territory, it is worth noting that you already are aware of many things you can observe when listening carefully. Recall from the nonverbal chapter (Chapter 7) that you can observe immediacy cues (or an absence of them) to note when someone is trying to encourage or discourage you to be closer and more immediate with them. In the process, we can notice others' comfort levels during conversation, or the ways in which someone is trying to control an interaction using turn-taking cues. It can be helpful to notice these things so that we can adjust our nonverbal behavior so that it is within others' comfort zones. And based on the previous chapter on using words skillfully, it is possible to take note of how people are framing discussions, and using stories and questions. If you can notice frames others use, you may be able to spot problematic assumptions, and you may be in a better position to reframe discussions. And by noticing the questions others ask, you may be able to identify troubling closed or leading questions, or to offer questions that would be more helpful. Thanks to perceptive listening, your eyes will be more open and important messages will be less likely to pass you by.

Confirmation and Disconfirmation

Suppose you are in a discussion at work about how to spend part of your budget and you suggest simply that more money should be spent on marketing your organization's services to new demographic groups, and you present a few ideas for how to do this. Consider some of the responses you might receive:

1. No response. People just sit silently and avoid eye contact.
2. The next speaker simply may change the subject.
3. "There seem to be some problematic issues with some of the suggestions we're getting."
4. "How could you think of that?"
5. "You can't really think that."
6. "So you want us to throw money down the drain?"
7. "Oh great, again with these suggestions!"
8. "I don't think that's the best use of our resources."

It is to be hoped you'd receive a more positive and encouraging response. But often we don't, and all of the above examples, except the last one, are examples of different types of *disconfirming responses* (Cissna & Sieburg, 1981). When we *confirm* others, we are acknowledging them, their self-worth, and our relationship with them. When we *disconfirm* others we are failing to acknowledge one or all of these things. Notice from the examples above the variety of ways in which we might disconfirm others. We can be indifferent by ignoring others or being impersonal: using silence, changing the topic (a rejection of the speaker's message), employing nonverbal distancing behaviors, and generically not referring to the speaker when responding to the message (example 3 from above). We also can be impervious by denying or distorting a person's message (examples 4–6). This might happen even when our intentions are positive, as the following example from Laing (1969) suggests regarding a conversation between a mother and daughter:

MOTHER: You are evil.
DAUGHTER: No, I'm not.
MOTHER: Yes you are.
DAUGHTER: Uncle Jack doesn't think so.
MOTHER: He doesn't love you as I do. Only a mother really knows the truth about her daughter.

Now consider the following example:

MOTHER: You are pretty.
DAUGHTER: No, I'm not.
MOTHER: Yes you are.
DAUGHTER: Uncle Jack doesn't think so.
MOTHER: He doesn't love you as I do. Only a mother really knows the truth about her daughter.

(pp. 47–48)

In each example, the structure of the interaction reveals disconfirmation, regardless of the content of the specific messages. Each is an example of one person denying the perspective of another, and the frustration that the person experiences when her perspective is denied. This is an example of how careful listening can reveal something that is beneath the surface of otherwise positive language.

We also can disconfirm by disqualifying others, so that we can avoid saying "no" to them or avoid disagreeing with them (Cissna & Sieburg, 1981). This might involve disqualifying the speaker (example 7), or by distorting the speaker's message (example 6). However, straightforward disagreement (example 8) is not disconfirming, as we can acknowledge another person and her message without having to agree with it.

In contrast to disconfirmation, we can confirm others through recognition, acknowledgment, and endorsement (Cissna & Sieburg, 1981). We can recognize others through nonverbal involvement (eye contact, etc.). We acknowledge others by responding in ways that are relevant to their comments. We don't change the subject or get lost on a tangent. We accept others' feelings, even if we don't agree with or understand them. When we combine these aspects of confirmation, we get the picture of a communicator who is accepting of others and acknowledging of what they have to say, even if they don't agree with it.

So what might be some advantages of noticing confirmation/disconfirmation in the workplace? First, we can notice a variety of messages that may be enhancing or threatening relationships at work. And if we are on the receiving end of disconfirming messages, we may be better able to respond to them. We also can notice our own confirmation and disconfirmation patterns, and possibly improve our confirmation of others.

Equivocation

Using the same situation we used for confirmation, suppose you received the following responses to your suggestion for how to spend the budget:

1. "When people make suggestions like this, I have my doubts."
2. "Some people might say that the idea is problematic for a number of reasons."
3. "That's interesting. Budgets always present peculiar problems and challenges for how to solve them."
4. "Did you hear about the new travel policy management is contemplating?"

Each of these are equivocal responses. **Equivocal messages** are systematically ambiguous in one or more ways (Chovil, 1994). Chovil suggests that equivocal messages are used in what are known as avoidance-avoidance situations, when someone is in a kind of no-win situation in which being directly honest or directly dishonest is problematic. To be completely honest may hurt someone's feelings or embarrass others. Being ambiguous is seen as a way to give an acceptable response that is less-than-direct, or as Bavelas, Black, Chovil, and Mullett (1990) suggest, a way of "saying nothing while saying something" (p. 57). There are a few types of equivocal responses that are worth noticing when listening to others. Specifically, a message can be equivocal in terms of the *sender, receiver, meaning,* or *context.* Being equivocal with respect to the *sender* means being vague about who is sending the message. Notice in example 2 above that the person is distancing himself from the message, enabling him to make a point, without being held directly responsible for it. Messages that are equivocal with respect to the *receiver* are vague about the target of the message, such as with example 1 above. This enables the communicator to make a point, implicitly about a specific person, but without singling the person out directly. This is another way of allowing the speaker to deny responsibility for a message. Equivocal *meaning* is when someone says something that is vague, ambiguous, or unclear. Notice in example 3 above that the person is giving a long answer that in effect says nothing. Finally, messages that exhibit a *context* type equivocation simply involve changing the subject. They are unrelated to the context that was created by whatever the previous speaker said, as in example 4 above. Although I have identified four types of equivocation, keep in mind that a message can be equivocal in more than one way. Regardless of the specific type(s) of equivocation used, a consistent theme among these equivocal messages is that they avoid directly responding and therefore the person being equivocal is less accountable than he would be if he were to speak directly.

By being a sharp listener and picking up on equivocal messages, we can notice when others are being evasive and place ourselves in a position to hold them accountable, or at least proceed with greater awareness. We also can notice when others are uncomfortable being direct and when we are not getting straight answers. At times equivocal responses may be fairly inconsequential and not worth confronting, but when the stakes are higher, those who can recognize these messages may benefit considerably from their listening efforts.

Powerful/Powerless Language

Again using the same situation we used for confirmation, suppose you received the following responses to your suggestion for how to spend the budget (remember that you suggest simply that more money should be spent on marketing your organization's services to new demographic groups, and you present a few ideas for how to do this):

1. "I guess I kind of think it might be good idea."
2. "The idea has a lot of advantages, don't you think?"
3. "I am ok trying it out, but I have some concerns with it."
4. "I um . . . guess I'm uncertain about how effectively marketing will . . . uh . . . act on it."
5. "I know I'm not an expert on marketing, but I think it would be a good idea."
6. "Others probably know more about this than me, but I um . . . sort of think that we might be able to possibly make it work, right?"

When listening carefully, we also can pick up on others' powerful/powerless language. Language is considered to be powerless when it has some or all of elements 1, 2, 4, 5, and 6 above (3 is an example of a message without any powerless elements). A message is powerful when it does not contain these "powerless" elements (Areni & Sparks, 2005; Bradac & Mulac, 1984). We briefly will explore the main three dimensions of language that are the strongest indicators of powerlessness. *Hesitations* (example 4) involve awkward, and often vocalized pauses, and are quite good at conveying powerlessness. In research by Bradac and Mulac (1984), hesitations were the strongest indicators of lacking power. *Tag questions* (example 2) involve literally tagging a question at the end of what is supposed to be a declarative statement. Placing a question at the end of a statement serves to undermine the statement. *Hedges* (example 1) are when we qualify the message we are sending, by subtly using expressions like "sort of," "kind of," "seems," "might," "I guess" "maybe," and so on. Inserting words like this serves to soften or discredit the message we are sending (Grob, Meyers, & Schuh, 1997). Beyond these three dimensions of powerlessness, researchers have added the dimension of *disclaimers,* such as the one in example 5 (Carli, 1990; Grob et al., 1997). Disclaimers are when we preface a message by clarifying that we are not an authority on the subject, or that we don't have much of an answer. In one sense, a response like this may exhibit humility and clarify that we shouldn't be held responsible for our answer. But in another sense, it is a way of saying something while simultaneously saying "don't bother listening to me." When we use disclaimers we are undermining whatever message we are trying to convey. I see my students do this a lot and in fairness, I remember that I would use them often when I was a student. One day when I was giving some convoluted disclaimer (along the lines of "I'm no expert on this and I know that there are many points of view, etc."), one of my graduate instructors interrupted me and bluntly said, "Joe, stop tap dancing and get to your point." He had a point, and I "tap danced" a lot less after that. I am glad he was listening!

As with equivocal messages, we can send messages that contain more than one dimension of powerlessness, and possibly all dimensions. You probably noticed that example 6 is a marvelous example of complete and utter powerlessness. If you revisit it you will notice all of the four dimensions we discussed. Research consistently has demonstrated that those who use powerless language are perceived less positively than those who use powerful language. Powerless speakers are perceived as less dynamic (Bradac & Street, 1989; Haleta, 1996; Johnson & Vinson, 1990), less competent and credible (Haleta, 1996; Johnson & Vinson, 1990), less persuasive (Holtgraves & Lasky, 1999), and less favorably or positively overall (Erickson, Lind, Johnson, & O'Barr, 1978; Holtgraves & Lasky, 1999). And although some have explored sex differences in powerful language (whether one sex tends to use more powerful language), the research has not yielded any consistent findings in favor of a difference, suggesting that the sexes are more similar than different when it comes to powerless language (Grob et al., 1997).

By listening carefully, we can pay greater attention to powerless language. We might not gain a specific and tangible reward, but if nothing else, we may be in a better position to help others speak more powerfully when they need to assert themselves.

Sensory Language

Consider the following responses we might receive when suggesting an idea to someone:

1. "I see what you mean."
2. "I'm having trouble picturing how that would work."
3. "Sounds good to me."
4. "I hear what you're saying, but I need to think about it."
5. "I'm trying to get a handle on how it would work."
6. "It feels like the right thing to do."

These statements vary in their emphasis on different senses. Examples 1 and 2 stress sight, 3 and 4 hearing, and 5 and 6 touch. Haden-Elgin (1999) offers three important points about sensory modes. First, most people tend to have a preferred sensory mode. As she puts it:

> We all know people who understand and remember best when they can look at a picture or a diagram or a film. We know others who have to hear information if they are to do their best work. . . . The sensory system that allows you to function most satisfactorily will be your preferred—and sometimes your dominant—sensory system. And this preference will be reflected in your language, as your preferred sensory mode.
>
> (p. 80)

Second, she suggests that although during most situations we can **switch between sensory modes without** too much trouble, she argues that during tense situations in which people are stressed, "they tend to become locked into their preferred sensory mode" (p. 81). So if there is conflict or stress in a professional situation, coworkers and clients may strongly prefer one sensory mode to others. Haden-Elgin's third point is that, in order to adapt to others and "speak their language," we should

Table 9.1 Differences Between Sensory Modes in Our Language

Visual	Auditory	Kinesic
• I see what you mean. • I'm having trouble picturing how this will work. • My view of things is complex.	• That sounds good to me. • I'm not sure I hear what you're saying. • This sounds complex to me.	• This feels right to me. • I'm having trouble grasping your idea. • That sounds like a lot to handle.

match their sensory mode. And if that is not possible, we should avoid using sensory vocabulary. She suggests that matching others' sensory modes helps build trust and rapport (see Table 9.1).

I'll provide some examples of how we might follow her advice. We could respond to a comment of "I'm having trouble picturing how that would work" with "What kinds of options would look better to you?" or "I see what you are saying, do other options look better to you?" For a sound-oriented comment like "This sounds problematic to me," we might respond "I hear your concerns, but . . . ," or "It still sounds like we might be able to find areas of compromise." With a touch-oriented comment like "Something about this feels off to me," we might say "Let's see if we can put our finger on the problem," or "If we can better grasp the problem, maybe we can address your concerns." More neutral responses to the above comments might include "I still think we might be able to make it work," "What are your specific concerns?" or "I understand your concerns." If matching another person's sensory language is awkward for us in a given situation, neutral responses like these can help us avoid a mismatch of sensory terms that might undermine rapport.

I get that this advice on sensory language might seem like a stretch, and I do think it would be a mistake to assume that matching sensory language alone will enable us to succeed in an interaction, or that failing to match sensory language will guarantee failure. However, if we are looking for something that might help make a tense situation easier, or enable us to better establish rapport with someone like a new client or an interviewer, then it can't hurt to try to match others' sensory terms in order to better speak their "language." But doing this relies on careful listening, and your ability to first notice the sensory terms others are using.

Persuasion Cues

After reading this section, you will better understand how some of the following things influence us to agree to something, buy something, and do other things, even though we're not sure why we're doing it. You will understand:

1. Why it is easier to speak up about something once others have done so, and why it can be difficult to stick with a position when others in a group all favor a different position.
2. Why it can be difficult to say "no" to those we like and respect, or those who flatter us.

3. Why we might disclose too much to someone, or agree to do something for another person that we actually don't want to do.
4. Why doing a small favor for someone might lead to much greater involvement than we initially envisioned, or why those who suggest ideas often are tasked with following up on them or implementing them.
5. Why others can get us to say "yes" to something sometimes just by limiting the amount of time we have to decide, or by trying to prevent us from doing it.

You may notice a consistent pattern across these examples. They involve our doing things that we may not really want to do, because of an unseen "pull" that we feel, or emotion that we experience. There are cues in the situation or in someone's language that are creating this pull. It is the kind of pull that may make us say "yes" to a telemarketer or salesperson, even though inside we feel like saying "no." These are examples of persuasion that takes place through the peripheral route that we first addressed in the previous chapter. If we are persuaded through the **central route,** we are thinking carefully and considering the quality of arguments that are being made. If we are being persuaded **peripherally,** we are not thinking carefully. We are on a kind of mental "autopilot." Or as a colleague of mine once put it, the central route is the Lisa Simpson route (because she always thinks carefully about things) to persuasion and the peripheral route is the Homer Simpson route (because he doesn't think very carefully). Although some of us may lean more toward one particular route, we all use both routes, as it would be very mentally taxing for us to carefully consider arguments or weigh the pros and cons of every decision (imagine trying to intellectually decide whether Pepsi is better than Coke, whether beer is less filling or tastes great, etc.). So often, it is perfectly reasonable to allow peripheral influence to happen. But it may be problematic to allow peripheral cues to take over when we are doing things that matter in the workplace. With that in mind, we will examine six cues that Robert Cialdini amassed from available scholarly research and outlined in his book *Influence: The Psychology of Persuasion* (1993). For those who have or will have careers that involve influence (sales, marketing), or want to learn more about influencing and resisting others' influence attempts, his book is a must read. In the remainder of this section I will introduce some of the influence cues Cialdini identified and focus on why it can be good to listen for them in the workplace. Because these are not strictly verbal cues, by "listening" to these cues, I mean being more perceptive of them in general. To better remember these, think of them as the CLARCCS cues (Booth-Butterfield, 2009).

Comparison (Social Proof). The principle of comparison (example 1 above) is that "one means we use to determine what is correct is to find out what other people think is correct" (Cialdini, 1993, p. 116). In other words, when we have some doubt, we will look to others for cues on how to behave. Often this makes perfect sense, and it probably helps us avoid embarrassing ourselves in certain situations. But in the workplace, this tendency also can be problematic for us. In a meeting, we may not speak up until others go first. It can be hard to resist. If we are told that others are "on board" with something, or if others seem to be in agreement, it can be harder to disagree. When listening, we can spot the comparison cue in operation when someone references what others are doing in an attempt to persuade us. Once we spot this cue in "action," according to Cialdini, the best way to say "no" to the

Table 9.2 Cialdini's CLARCCS Persuasion Cues

Comparison	• We are more likely to do something if we see others doing it.
	• Examples: soccer riots; failure of bystanders in groups to help those in need
Liking	• We are more persuaded by those we like.
	• Examples: Tupperware and similar friendship-based marketing efforts; sending thank you cards after interviews; business meetings at strip clubs (yes really, keep reading …)
Authority	• We are more likely to comply when someone is in a position of authority.
	• Examples: shock experiments; advertisements that use expert endorsements
Reciprocity	• When someone does something for us (good or bad) we are inclined to reciprocate.
	• Examples: free samples of food in stores; disclosing something to someone to get them to disclose something to us
Commitment/Consistency	• When we commit to something, we feel pressure to stay consistent with that commitment.
	• Examples: Sticking with a bad boy/girl friend we have defended to our parents; why coworkers may start with small requests and continue to pile on once they have us saying "yes"
Scarcity	• We will value something more if something is limited in supply or our access to it is threatened.
	• Examples: "supplies limited," "offer expires soon," why ads sometimes preface something as a message "that others tried to keep secret." Why mundane information can become fascinating office gossip.

comparison cue is to be more aware of when the comparison cue is based on faulty or inaccurate information. For example, it is possible that others are not on board with an initiative. The silent behavior of others in a meeting does not necessarily mean that they are in agreement. The trick is to notice the signs of this cue in action and consider how it might be flawed.

Liking. This principle is simple: We are more likely to be influenced by those we like than those we don't like. But the interesting aspect of this is the number and variety of ways others may use this principle to get us to comply with them. Possible tactics include manipulating attire to enhance attractiveness, enhancing perceptions of similarity (whether by manipulating attire, discussing areas of common interest, or maybe even using the same sensory language as you!), or just by trying to increase contact with you or to get to know you better. Another powerful liking tactic is to give us compliments. Liking also can work via conditioning, as we know from countless commercials with attractive or famous endorsers (and from seeing famous people lose endorsement contracts after exhibiting behaviors with which companies do not want to be associated). A workplace-related liking tactic that involves conditioning is to try to persuade people over lunch (provided the persuasion "target" likes the food!). The idea behind this is that whatever we are advocating becomes attached by conditioning to the pleasant feelings we are experiencing from the food. Not satisfied with lunch alone, some businesses even try to capitalize on conditioning by conducting sales meetings at strip clubs. In other words, there are a lot of creative ways others will use liking to get us to comply with them. This presents a challenge if we are to be perceptive and keep the cue from working. We cannot just reject people we like, reject every compliment, or become afraid of having lunch with colleagues. Cialdini suggests that, more than looking for any possible sign that the liking cue is operating, we should be aware of situations in which "we have come to like the practitioner more quickly or more deeply than we would have expected" (p. 204). If we can catch ourselves having this reaction, we can slow down and consider whether it is in our best interests to comply with the person.

Authority. As a person, I did not change much from April 1999 to August 1999. However, one circumstance did change. In May 1999, I defended my dissertation, earned my doctorate, and was now able to add three letters to the end of my name (EdD). But fundamentally, I was still me. And yet when I taught my first classes after earning my doctorate, I was surprised at the ways in which students were more deferential to me. In small, subtle ways, they were affording me more respect than I was used to receiving from students. I had to work just a little less hard to earn it. And although I may have gained some confidence from earning my degree, I had not changed my approach to teaching, so this response surprised me. This is a small example of the ways in which we respond to authority figures. In one sense, it is natural to comply with authority figures, as we've done it most of our lives and they often are in a position to make requests that will be in our best interests.

However, obeying authority can become problematic when we do it uncritically. Consider the following experiment conducted by Hofling, Brotzman, Dalrymple, Graves, and Pierce (1966). On several different wards within hospitals, researchers posing as physicians telephoned 22 different nurses and instructed them to give a dose of medication to a particular patient. However, they ordered them to administer a drug that was not approved (it was fake), and in an amount that was very unsafe (labels on the bottles clearly indicated the levels for safe dosage). How many of the 22 nurses do you think proceeded to administer the medication? Although the researchers had people in place to stop the medications from actually being administered (before they could reach the rooms), 21 (95%) of the nurses proceeded to go to the rooms to give the medication, even though they had never met the physicians who gave the problematic orders. In experiments like this and many others (the famous Milgram "shock" studies), people consistently overestimate the extent to which they would defy authority when asked to do various things. Interestingly though, Rank and Jacobson (1977) found that if nurses actually were familiar with the medication and had an opportunity to consult with others at or above their level, they would be less likely to administer the medication (only 2 of 18 administered the drug in their study). In other words, when nurses were able to think more critically (they knew the drug and they could speak with others), the results changed.

Rather than suggesting we resist all authority, Cialdini suggests we recognize the power of authority and ask ourselves two questions when a person in a position of authority is asking us to comply with a request. First, is the authority figure a legitimate expert with respect to that which he or she is requesting? We may notice red flags in response to this question when a supervisor or manager asks us to do something in a particular way, even though she does not have the expertise to know how to do it. In cases like this, it may be important to resist the request. And if the person is an expert, the second question Cialdini recommends is "How truthful can we expect the expert to be here?" (p. 231). In other words, we should consider the person's possible motives. If the person does not seem to have our interests at heart (maybe the person is asking us to do his or her work or has some other angle), that may be another red flag worth noticing. Of course, it's easy for me to say "You should resist," but for those who are not very assertive or comfortable saying "no," it can be difficult to overcome the pressure you feel to say "yes." I don't have fool-proof advice on this, but I do have one suggestion that you can implement in a couple of ways: buy time. You can buy time most efficiently by asking for time: "Can I have some time to think about this?" or "I don't have time right now to give this the thought it deserves, but if you can give me a little time I can get back to you." With this time, you can think about whether you should comply with the request, and possibly consult with others (like the less obedient nurses did in the second experiment above). If plan A doesn't work and you can't get away to think through the request, you still can buy time by asking questions. You can ask for details about a project (What is required? Who else will be involved? Why was I chosen for it?) that may give you clues about the motives of the person making the request, and enable you to more easily say "no." Regardless of how you choose to proceed, the first step in all of this is an awareness of the power of authority, and how to "listen" for the authority cue.

Reciprocity. The reciprocity cue is that "we should try to repay, in kind, what another person has provided for us" (Cialdini, 1993, p. 17). I mention the power of reciprocity in many chapters in this book, as it plays an important role in many communication interactions. In the workplace we may see others trying to use this cue in a couple different ways. First, it may be in the form of someone trying to do us a favor, so we then will do something for them. Cialdini also discusses what he calls "reject-then-retreat" approach (also known as "door-in-the-face"), in which others may make concessions to us in order to get us to make concessions to them. Telemarketers sometimes begin with "So, can I put you down for a $50 donation" knowing that we will say no. This forces them to make a concession followed by a second request, "Ok, I understand, would you be willing to donate $20?" Thanks to the power of reciprocity, we feel like it is our turn to make a concession. As long as the initial request is within a reasonable range, this process can make us more likely to comply with a request than we otherwise would have been. In the workplace, we can spot this when others ask us to do a considerable amount of work, accept when we cannot do it, and then ask us to do a smaller amount of work. According to this perspective on reciprocity, we often will say "yes" to this request when we otherwise might have said "no" in the absence of the first request.

So how can we spot the reciprocity cue at work, and distinguish it from a sincere gesture, favor, concession? Cialdini suggests that unless we know a person is trying to use reciprocity as a tactic, initially we should accept what others are offering, though with an awareness that there could be strings attached. And then if we notice that there are strings attached, we can avoid the powerful need to reciprocate by reframing the initial offering from the other person. If we reframe it in our minds to be some kind of strategic offering, we will be less likely to feel pressure to comply, as we will more clearly see it for what it is. Again, it comes down to having an ability to spot the cue in action.

Commitment/Consistency. When we voluntarily commit to an idea or course of action, we feel compelled to remain consistent with our commitment. If we sign a petition in support of something and later are asked to donate to that cause, it will be harder to resist, because we have committed ourselves to the cause by signing the petition. Those lame, nonscientific polls that are on more and more TV programs? If we participate in them, we are making a small commitment to that show, and are more likely to continue watching it. This commitment/consistency process can create some interesting pressures in the workplace. We may agree to help out with a project only to find that we end up taking on more and more work. This can be made worse if someone attaches our identity to our initial modest efforts (the small amount we initially agreed to do): "Thank you Joe, I really appreciate what a helpful person you are. I thought you wouldn't mind pitching in on this second part of the project too?" The commitment/consistently cue works when we internally process the request as: "I'm a helpful person, so how can I possibly say 'no' now, and leave him hanging?" We simultaneously feel resistance in our gut, and yet once we have committed ourselves to helping, it can be hard to back out. Another way this cue operates is if we speak publicly in favor of some position, we can feel a pressure to defend that position, even in the face of considerable evidence that challenges it. Chances are we all have been frustrated with having to argue with a person who stubbornly stuck to a position simply because of an initial commitment to it (notice how this is encouraged by the way in which those who change their minds in our culture are labeled as "flip-floppers"). So how do we resist the power of this cue? Cialdini suggests that we listen to our gut to help us distinguish between good consistency and being mindlessly consistent for the sake of being consistent. If we have "that feeling" that we don't want to be doing something, then we should listen to it. This can be challenging, but the good news is that if we say "yes" too many times in situations like these, we may tire of giving in and become more resistant to mindlessly saying "yes" in the future.

Scarcity. This cue explains why messages such as "hurry, offer expires soon," or "supplies are limited" can be effective. According to this cue, when something is scarce or our access to something is threatened, we will value it more. This is why Disney puts movies in a "vault" and says they won't be available for a long time. We value things more when they are scarce. This cue also may be at work when others try to limit our behavior or our access to something. A new policy at work that is designed to limit behavior may encourage people to value that behavior even more. For example, even those who don't listen to music at work may be angered if a new policy against listening to music at work is implemented. In these situations, it is good to slow down to get a sense of whether we value something because it is being restricted, or because we would value it regardless.

These aren't all of the ways we may be persuaded peripherally, but they do help us address the importance of "being on our toes" and listening carefully in the workplace. So far most of our discussions have been about listening to spot things that can help us avoid being manipulated. The next section changes the pace by focusing on some things we can listen for that might enable us to be more helpful coworkers or leaders in our organizations.

Table 9.3 Combating the CLARCCS Cues

Comparison	• Look out for others persuading us by referring to others that have said yes: "Everyone else is on board." • Consider the accuracy of these statements before assuming they're true.
Liking	• Catch ourselves when we find ourselves liking someone more deeply or quickly than normally would be expected. It may be a sign of this cue at work.
Authority	• Consider whether the authority figure really is an expert, and consider how truthful you expect the authority figure to be.
Reciprocity	• Accept the offer initially, but realize there may be strings attached. • If there are strings attached, reframe the original offer as something less than generous and it will be easier to resist.
Commitment/ Consistency	• Recognize the difference between good consistency, and being mindlessly consistent just for the sake of it.
Scarcity	• Catch our emotional reaction to the scarcity. • Focus on whether we want something just to have it, or whether it has real value for us. If we based decisions on actual value, scarcity should matter less—we either will want it or we won't, regardless of how much is available.
For most of these (at least in the workplace)	• Buy time ("Can I get back to you on that?") so you can think more clearly and at least try to better resist various cues. • If you have to decide now, buy time by asking questions for details about the project. It can help you decide if it's something you really want to do and you can then base your decision on something more tangible.

Summary on Listening

As you read the following passage, take note of all of the aspects of language you now are able to recognize. Suppose this discussion takes place at a meeting to work out the details of an upcoming fund-raising event:

CHRIS: Eric, with your organizational skills, I think you would do great at handling PR and coordinating media for the event.

ERIC: I think that some would say that would be a bad choice.

CHRIS: I'm not sure why.

ERIC: I think our main concern is going to be securing volunteers.

PAT: Maybe Eric could do that, don't you think?

DONNA: Are you serious, I don't even know why you'd suggest that.

PAT: I don't know, I guess I sort of, um, thought it would be a good way to go.

ERIC: It's tough to get anything done when some people continue to be rude to coworkers.

Even though I've given you only a brief and admittedly mundane conversation, notice all of the things you now can catch when listening. One person is confirming, another disconfirming, another equivocal, another pessimistic, and another uses powerless language. You also can see how quickly the discussion can get off track, thanks to an equivocal response that changed the subject. If it is possible to notice this much during a passage like this, consider just how much we can catch when listening more carefully to those around us when it matters more. And that is the trick. Rather than worrying about your listening skill, just appreciate how much there is for us to notice, and use the natural listening skill you already have.

Getting Others to Listen to Us

For the remainder of this chapter, we will transition and discuss what we can do to get others to listen to us. Because people often can be distracted or don't necessarily recognize the need to listen when you have something important to say, you should assume that people will *not* be listening to you, and do things to make sure you have their attention. When I walk into the classroom, I assume my students are thinking about anything but my course, and that before I can expect to teach them much, I first have to get them to pay attention to me. Similarly, in organizations we are competing with other people, our listener's internal distractions, and numerous electronic devices for our listener's attention. We should be surprised that we ever are able to get through to anyone!

The first thing we need to do to make sure others are listening is to **make sure we are catching them at a good time,** when they are willing and able to listen. It sounds simple and obvious, but people commonly overlook the importance of timing. We should look for readiness cues, like the person's complete attention—facing us, and not texting, typing, or attending to anything else. If you're not sure whether someone is ready to listen to you, just ask if it's a good time, or if not, if you can set up a good time to talk to the person. And then while you are talking with the person, try to notice cues that indicate faltering attention, or a wish to end the conversation: looking away, looking a watch or clock, beginning to do other things (typing, texting), or starting to move around, whether gathering his or her things or trying to usher you out of the office. Again, it sounds obvious, but it isn't to everyone. If you spot any of these, you can return to "Is this an ok time, or would it be better to find another time to set aside?" In fairness, you could just keep talking, as that may work too, but you won't necessarily have the person's attention, and you will be more appreciated if you are responsive to the person's cues.

This still leaves us with two issues that need to be addressed: (1) What if we need a person to listen now and can't just go away and return another time? and (2) What do we do to keep a person's attention and make our points memorable to them? We simultaneously can address both of these questions by returning to the recent book by Chip and Dan Heath (2007), entitled *Made to Stick: Why Some Ideas Survive and Others Die*. In it they identify several factors that help make messages memorable (it is a great book for anyone interested in crafting memorable messages, whether for public relations, advertising, journalism, public speaking, etc.). Although their focus is on messages we can carefully craft (like advertisements, press releases, speeches) and not the everyday conversational messages we deliver on-the-fly, it still is worthwhile to consider what they have to offer, so we can better understand why people remember some messages and forget others. Heath and Heath identified six SUCCES factors that help make messages sticky: *simple, unexpected, concrete, credible, emotional,* and *stories*. We briefly will consider each of these (except stories, which were covered in the previous chapter) in an effort to answer the two questions I've posed above. Keep in mind that the goal is to be able to carefully craft important messages when it counts, not to incorporate these ideas into all daily conversations (though some of these things may start to come naturally in conversation as you practice them).

Simple. Simplicity means getting to the point, and summarizing your ideas succinctly. When we go to talk to someone about something that is relatively important, we likely will have given it some thought, to the extent that we've considered the various complexities of the issue. This is good, but when we go to talk with someone about the issue and run through all of the details, it will be very easy to lose our listener. According to Heath and Heath, there are a few things we can do to simplify our message. One tactic: Think about what we would cover if we were forced to get to the point with 30 seconds. What are the main one or two points that absolutely need to be mentioned? We typically won't be forced into this time frame, but if we approach our task with this kind of attitude, we can get to the core of our message and start there. We also can simplify complex messages by using analogies to link complex ideas to ones that are more simple and easy for our audience to grasp. For example, in interviews I've heard famous musicians describe the spontaneity of performing live as being like falling down stairs and landing on your feet. We don't need to be a famous rock star to grasp the concept. Some other examples: The brain is like a computer (there are flaws to this analogy, but it is memorable), organizations are like pyramid schemes, life is like a box of chocolates, and so on. Although these examples are dramatic, we can simplify everyday messages by trying to find how they connect to something that already is familiar to the audience. Once you have the core of your message, you'll be ready to apply the other elements of making ideas stick.

Unexpected. Earlier, in the networking chapter, I relayed a phrase used by Burt (2005) to describe the benefits of having structural holes in our networks: He said those with structural holes in their network are at a greater risk for having good ideas. That one phrase caught my attention the first time I read it, and I haven't forgotten it. Burt made his point more memorable by delivering it in an unexpected way, using the phrase "at risk" in conjunction with something positive. Consider the "haze" of messages we encounter on a daily basis, and how few we remember. Making our messages unexpected, as Burt did, is one way to break through this haze so that others pay attention and remember what we have to say. There are a few ways we can make messages unexpected. First, recall our discussion from the last chapter about beginning stories with a mystery. If you want someone to listen and can find a way to begin with an intriguing question, you will have a better chance of holding the person's attention (for examples, notice that I've tried to do this in several places in this book). Second, we can take advantage of our listeners' natural curiosity by exploiting what Heath and Heath call "gaps" in listeners' knowledge. Gaps exist when we know many things, but not everything about a topic. To understand the power of gaps, consider gossip. Gossip can be powerful because the information being discussed fills gaps in our knowledge, and we often are eager to fill our knowledge gaps. Take even mundane things: What spider is most poisonous to humans? What famous politician did Tommy Lee Jones room with at Harvard? What two famous actors from the same acting class were voted least likely to succeed in that acting class? What music group almost ended up with Chevy Chase as its drummer? Irritating to not know, isn't it? If we can use questions to exploit our listeners' knowledge gaps, we can increase our chances of holding their attention and making our points more memorable. Now speaking of attention, I will lose yours to Google searches if I don't give answers to my questions: (1) daddy long-legs (don't worry, they're not able to actually bite us); (2) Al Gore; (3) Gene Hackman and Dustin Hoffman; (4) Steely Dan. Now, if you happened to know the answer to any of these answers, think about that. They are meaningless questions, yet because your knowledge gap already had been exploited before I was able to, you remembered the answers! And if you didn't know the answers, I suspect there was some relief as you learned them (and filled in the gaps).

Concrete. I must confess that unlike many in my profession, I'm not much of a fan of mission statements, even though organizations seem to spend a lot of time crafting them. Maybe it's because I'm from Generation X and we're supposed to be cynical. But I like to think that it's grounded in the fact that, while they sound nice, they're so abstract that they mean very little. In addition, they're not very memorable, partly because they are not concrete. They lack detail and it is hard to picture them "in action." When we're trying to explain concepts, issues, and problems to others, we face a similar problem, as we often are dealing with abstract ideas. The trick to making our ideas more concrete is to use various techniques, such as detailed examples and stories to make our information much more vivid and tangible for listeners by involving a variety of their senses. In the previous chapter I discussed in detail how stories help us do this. But we also can use vivid examples to make information more concrete. For example, how much is one billion dollars? If we stacked one billion dollars' worth of hundred dollar bills one on top of the other, the stack would be as tall as the Sears Tower in Chicago. With a vivid example, I have involved more senses (you now can visualize one billion dollars). Although it sometimes can be challenging to come up with brief examples, stories can help us make ideas and issues three-dimensional, and therefore more concrete.

Credible. In an earlier chapter we explored what we can do as individuals to enhance our credibility and make our messages more believable. However, we also can do a few things with our messages to make them more believable. In addition to using vivid details and making statistics more concrete (things we discussed above), we can improve credibility with examples of others who have endorsed our message or proposal, as well as offering messages that are testable. If we offer an idea and are able to add something like "It worked for _____," or "It's been adopted by _____" and we fill the blanks with names of people or organizations who will impress our listener, we will have enhanced the credibility of our message. We also can do this by offering ideas that our listeners can test for themselves. For example, if you want to see comparison (social proof) in action, stop on a sidewalk some day when others are around and start looking up in the air. Even if you're not looking at anything specific, fix your eyes on something. Then wait. Thanks to the comparison cue, it probably won't be long before others are looking up, even if briefly. In this example, rather than saying, "Trust me, comparison works," I've probably made my message more believable by inviting you to test it for yourself. Similarly, I've invited you to try different techniques elsewhere in this book. Offering testable messages is yet another way we can make our ideas more memorable.

Emotional. While the elements I've described above can help people pay attention to us, understand us, and agree with us, this element is particularly challenging, because it is about making people care. In this day and age, how can we make people care about what we have to say? Suppose we were coworkers and I wanted to convince you that our organization should do community outreach in the schools to address bullying. How can I get you to care enough to want to devote time to this issue? According to Heath and Heath (2007), there are a few different ways. First, rather than citing statistics about how bullying is on the rise (I don't actually know if it is, but it seems to be getting more media attention than it did in the past), I would be better off focusing on an individual case or two in order to dramatically personalize the issue. So, I might go into detail about the case of Phoebe Prince. To draw you in, I probably would start by saying "Think of what you would do if you had a loved one in the following situation." Phoebe grew up in Ireland and in 2009, at the age of 14, moved to Massachusetts, where she began attending high school at South Hadley High School. Shortly after that she was in a brief relationship with a popular football player. Shortly after the relationship ended, Phoebe was targeted by a group of female students, who began bullying her both in person and online. The bullying continued for months, often in front of school officials, who did nothing to act on it, even though her mother twice complained to school officials (Drew, 2010). On January 14, 2010, Phoebe was harassed in the library, again in front of school officials, and on her way home, in a passing car one of the girls from the group of bullies threw a can of Red Bull at her from the car (Kennedy, 2010). Later that day, Phoebe went home and hung herself in a stairwell, where she was found by her 12-year-old sister. Shortly afterward, one of the members of the bully group posted the word "accomplished" and other such comments on Phoebe's Facebook page. Nine teenagers were charged with various crimes related to the case (Kennedy, 2010).

It is hard to not care about an incident like this. But it is possible to care and yet not be persuaded to act on it. So if I expect you to join my project, I probably will have to do more. Heath and Heath (2007) suggest that another way to make people care is to appeal to their self-interest, as in "What's in it for me?" However, they encourage us to appeal to something more than just ordinary self-interest (in other words, something bigger than money or fame), and instead to appeal to more ambitious goals that might align with a person's self-interest. How we do this will vary from person to person, as different things interest different people (notice again the importance of knowing your audience). So for a general approach, I might appeal to your sense of wanting to help or to make a positive difference, which I might do in the following way: "Imagine the school as it is now, and then imagine how those bullied students would feel after we've implemented our program. Imagine them being thankful for our efforts, not having to tense up every morning before school, and throughout the day when they are about to see classmates." And I could continue like this, helping you envision the difference we could make. Finally, I could use a third strategy recommended by Heath and Heath (2007), and appeal to your identity. Again, this may vary from person to person, but one approach might be for me to say, "Let's make it so that nobody gets bullied on our watch." To the extent that you have a protective ego, a phrase like this, in conjunction with the personal case and appeal to your self-interest, might be enough to encourage you to act. For added impact, I would make sure I outlined my plan in a simple and concrete way, so that it would be easier for you to envision the program in action. The point of this example isn't that it's perfect—it still may not work. But by using personal and compelling examples, and appealing to ambitious self-interest and identity, we can at least increase our chances of making others care about our messages.

So to review, to make others listen to us and make our ideas stick, Heath and Heath (2007) encourage us to be simple, unexpected, concrete, credible, emotional, and involve stories. In fairness, the point is not to cram every one of these devices into every sentence, but rather to realize how different devices can help us when we are facing certain obstacles in reaching our listener. Being unexpected can help get others' attention, and being concrete can help others better understand us. Being credible can help others believe us. Appealing to emotions can make people care, and stories can help make people act. As you find yourself in different low-risk situations, I encourage you to try some of these strategies. The good news is that they probably won't hurt anything, so it's worthwhile to see if they can help improve your ability to get through to others and be remembered.

References

Areni, C.S., & Sparks, J.R. (2005). Language power and persuasion. *Psychology and Marketing, 22*(6), 507–525.

Bavelas, J.B., Black, A., Chovil, N., & Mullett, J. (1990). Truths, lies, and equivocations: The effects of conflicting goals on discourse. *Journal of Language and Social Psychology, 9,* 129–155.

Booth-Butterfield, S. (2009). *The complete idiot's guide to persuasion.* New York, NY: Alpha.

Bradac, J.J., & Mulac, A. (1984). A molecular view of powerful and powerless speech styles: Attributional consequences of specific language features and communicator intentions. *Communication Monographs, 51,* 307–319.

Bradac, J.J., & Street, R.L. Jr. (1989). Powerful and powerless styles of talk: A theoretical analysis of language and impression formation. *Research on Language and Social Interaction, 23,* 195–242.

Burt, R.S. (2005). *Brokerage and closure: An introduction to social capital.* New York, NY: Oxford University Press.

Carli, L.L. 1990. Gender, language, and influence. *Journal of Personality and Social Psychology, 59,* 941–951.

Chovil, N. (1994). Equivocation as an interactional event. In W.R. Cupach & B.H. Spitzberg (Eds.), *The dark side of interpersonal communication* (pp. 105–123). Hillsdale, NJ: Lawrence Erlbaum.

Cialdini, R.B. (1993). *Influence: The psychology of persuasion.* New York, NY: Morrow.

Cissna, K.N.L., & Sieburg, E. (1981). Patterns of interactional confirmation and disconfirmation. In C. Wilder-Mott & J.H. Weakland (Eds.), *Rigor and imagination: Essays from the legacy of Gregory Bateson* (pp. 253–282). New York, NY: Praeger.

Drew, A. (2010, April 2). Bully writes "accomplished" on Phoebe Prince's Facebook page on day of death. *Irish Voice Reporter.* Retrieved June 6, 2012, from www.irishcentral.com/news/Bully-writes-accomplished-on-Phoebe-Princes-Facebook-page-on-day-of-death-89764722.html

Erickson, B., Lind, E.A., Johnson, B.C., & O'Barr, W.M. (1978). Speech style and impression formation in a court setting: The effects of "powerful" and "powerless" speech. *Journal of Experimental Social Psychology, 14,* 266–279.

Grob, L. M., Meyers, R. A., & Schuh, R. (1997). Powerful/powerless language use in group interactions: Sex differences or similarities? *Communication Quarterly, 45,* 282–303.

Haden-Elgin, S. (1999). *The gentle art of verbal self-defense.* Upper Saddle River, NJ: Prentice Hall.

Haleta, L. L. (1996). Student perceptions of teachers' use of language: The effects of powerful and powerless language on impression formation and uncertainty. *Communication Education, 45,* 16–28.

Heath, C., & Heath, D. (2007). *Made to stick: Why some ideas survive and others die.* New York, NY: Random House.

Hofling, C. K., Brotzman, E., Dalrymple, S., Graves, N., & Pierce, C. (1966). An experimental study of nurse–physician relations. *Journal of Nervous and Mental Disease, 143,* 171–180.

Holtgraves, T. M., & Lasky, B. (1999). Linguistic power and persuasion. *Journal of Language and Social Psychology, 18*(2), 196–205.

Johnson, C., & Vinson, L. (1990). Placement and frequency of powerless talk and impression formation. *Communication Quarterly, 38,* 325–333.

Kennedy, H. (2010, March 29). Phoebe Prince, South Hadley High School's "new girl," driven to suicide by teenage cyber bullies. *New York Daily News.* Retrieved June 6, 2012, from http://articles.nydailynews.com/2010–03–29/news/27060348_1_facebook-town-hall-meetings-school-library

Laing, R. D. (1969). *The politics of the family.* Berkley, CA: Publisher's Group West.

Rank, S., & Jacobson, C. (1977). Hospital nurses' compliance with medication overdose orders: A failure to replicate. *Journal of Health and Social Behavior, 18,* 188–193.

Roberts, C. V., & Vinson, L. (1998). Relationship among willingness to listen, receiver apprehension, communication apprehension, communication competence, and dogmatism. *International Journal of Listening, 12,* 40–56.

Chapter 10

Handling Disagreements

I wish people would agree with me more often. If I have an opinion, it will be based on thoughtful consideration, and from my point of view, it makes perfect sense. In spite of this, I frequently encounter people in the workplace who have a different opinion. What gives? Why can't these people just see the issue the way I see it and agree with me?

When I put it this way, it seems silly that we would expect others to see everything the way we see it. But think of the last few times someone disagreed with you at work. Chances are that it at least caught you off guard, or possibly worse, it may have annoyed or angered you. How could someone see the issue any differently? However, in a workplace full of different people, personalities, perspectives, and ideas, it makes perfect sense that we will encounter disagreement often. After all, a **disagreement** is nothing more than a difference in opinion (Richmond & McCroskey, 2009). And it is natural to expect that we frequently would experience differences of opinion with others. In fact, there is so much opportunity for disagreement that we should be surprised when we do *not* encounter it. This chapter is about handling these encounters in which we experience differences of opinions with others. They can be handled in a variety of ways, some of which are less constructive and productive than others. Using a continuum suggested by Richmond & McCroskey (2009), we will explore three different ways differences of opinions in our workplace might be handled: conflict, disagreement, and groupthink (see Table 10.1).

Table 10.1 Groupthink, Disagreement, and Conflict

	How differences of opinion are handled
Groupthink	• Pressure to agree and avoid disagreement • Getting along is more important than getting something right or carefully discussing it • Different opinions may be suppressed or kept from being discussed
Disagreement	• Focus is on an issue and different perspectives are encouraged and expected • Discussions may be vocal and sound like a conflict, but the participants are just engaged and arguing with energy, as opposed to being angry—their focus still is on the issue
Conflict	• The focus is on the person/people annoying us, not an issue • Anger, defensiveness, frustration, resentment • There may be a lot of verbal activity, but little of substance is being accomplished

Conflict

Conflict is when we have a difference of opinion with others that is personal and evokes our anger for one or more people (Richmond & McCroskey, 2009). We are less focused on the issue on which we differ, and more on how angry we are at the other person. In more practical workplace terms, this might translate in some of the following ways: being distracted from our work by thinking about how angry we are at someone; thinking of ways to retaliate or "tell the person off"; complaining to coworkers or to supervisors about the person; avoiding the person, or avoiding communication with him or her; spending an hour or more on a carefully worded angry email to the person; spending about a minute on a hastily worded angry email to the person, sending the angry email, and dealing with the fallout; being distracted while at home because you're still thinking about the coworker(s); experiencing stress when checking email or receiving texts, as they may be related to the stressful incident; and so on. In other words, as a way of handling differences of opinion, conflict certainly takes a toll on us and our ability to work effectively. As a result, we will devote all of Chapter 11 to better understanding conflict, and how to handle it when we encounter it in the workplace.

Groupthink

So far so good: Avoid conflict when possible. This is a fairly natural reaction, but if we take it too far in the workplace, we will be at risk for going too far toward the other end of the spectrum, and we may experience groupthink. **Groupthink** happens when members of a group favor morale, getting along, and cohesiveness above consideration of alternative solutions, debate, and disagreement (Janis, 1971). To appreciate the power of groupthink, consider a time when you were in a group of strangers and reluctant to "rock the boat" by disagreeing with anyone. This may have led you to work hard to agree with ideas that were proposed. Or if you didn't agree, you simply may have remained silent. Or you may have been in a group in which you wanted to make a decision quickly (possibly because a quick decision was needed, or possibly because everyone simply wanted to be somewhere else and were motivated to end the meeting quickly). In this case, members may have kept quiet about any reservations, and you may have noticed impatience with those who expressed concerns. Or you may have been in a group where there was a pressure to adopt a certain position, in which alternative perspectives were barely explored or tolerated. In each of these cases, we can see a pressure to agree and go along with the group, even if one or more members might have had reservations about what was being proposed.

Or consider a fairly recent historical example that has been attributed to groupthink. You may not know this, but the night before the Space Shuttle *Challenger* was set to launch in 1986, engineers from the company that made the booster rockets were on the phone with their superiors, urging them to recommend against launching the next morning. They said that the weather was far too cold for the rockets' O-rings to perform properly during the launch. They were right—investigators later found that an O-ring failure led to the fatal explosion. As the engineers pleaded their case, their superiors argued against them, as if they already had made up their minds and were trying to defend their decision (Moorhead, Ference, and Neck, 1991). They were not very tolerant of opinions that were not in agreement with their own. Ultimately, the decision makers agreed to proceed with the launch. Now we have the luxury of saying "Those superiors were reckless, should have listened to the engineers, and so on." But why didn't they? After all, I'm sure they weren't very different from you or I. They probably had families, loved their kids, and were good people. There probably was nothing that made them especially more evil or less sensible than any of us. So why did they behave that way? We do have some clues. First, they were under considerable pressure. That particular launch had been delayed a number of times, and NASA was growing impatient. Second, the president was going to be speaking to the country the next night and wanted to mention the launch in his speech. Remember that it was the first launch in which the Teacher In Space program was being inaugurated, and the program was the president's idea. So although the group wasn't being ordered to launch, it was under considerable pressure to decide to launch. Second, because it was the night before the scheduled launch, a decision needed to be made fairly quickly. There was not a great deal of time available to the decision makers (Moorehead et al., 1991). Under conditions like these, people who likely were no different than you or I behaved in ways that had deadly consequences. This suggests that you or I are no less vulnerable to this kind of flawed decision making than these individuals. So to better give you a sense of how to spot problematic decision making, we will examine some of the key symptoms of groupthink.

Janis developed the idea of groupthink by studying several famous cases of poor or effective decision making. Cases involving poor decision making have included the Bay of Pigs invasion and the escalation of the Vietnam War. These were contrasted with examples of more solid decision making, such as during the Cuban Missile Crisis. In examining various cases, Janis (1971) identified a number of symptoms of groupthink. Rather than assuming groups must have all of these symptoms to experience groupthink, it would be better to treat each as a potential warning sign, even if other symptoms are not present.

Symptoms of Groupthink

A first group of symptoms is centered around the **flawed perceptions** of group members. According to Janis (1971), members who experiencing groupthink are likely to have an illusion that they are *invulnerable,* that they are *morally* **right,** while having *negative stereotypes* of those outside of the group who oppose them. In addition, the group is under the **illusion that they are in agreement** (unanimity). First, group members feel that they are invulnerable, and therefore they dismiss possible warning signs and dangers ("That's ridiculous, there's no way that would happen"). It is hard to imagine that anything bad could happen—an entire group could not be wrong. In addition group members see themselves as being morally right, while they simultaneously stereotype outsiders negatively (in the case of the *Challenger* incident, superiors may have thought "Engineers are so uptight that you never can satisfy them 100%"). These problems are helped by the flawed assumption of unanimity, or the sense that all group members are in agreement. We probably all have been in groups in which we have had some reservations, yet did not speak up because we assumed that the other silent group members were in agreement. Silence often may be mistaken for agreement.

A second group of symptoms of groupthink centers around the actions of group members. Specifically, group members will shield the group from outside information that may suggest alternative courses of action (*mindguarding*). When this is not possible, they may *rationalize* in ways that lead them to dismiss any warnings or signs of problems with their preferred course of action. In addition they will *pressure members* to agree with the group, and therefore, members who do have doubts may *censor themselves* and not speak up. First, members may actively work to make sure that certain information does not even reach the group. And when they fail and the group is confronted with warnings, or challenges to a preferred course of action, group members may dismiss them (as the rocket engineers were dismissed in the *Challenger* example). In addition, vocal members may pressure reluctant group members to agree with the "rest of the group." It should be no surprise that in the face of all of this pressure, members may engage in self-censorship and keep their concerns to themselves.

Notice how this all becomes a cycle. When members who have concerns censor themselves (due to a pressure they feel, even if it is unspoken), it enhances the illusion that everyone in the group is in agreement, which enhances the illusions that everyone is right and the group is moral, invulnerable, and not like outsiders. So of course, we would block information from outsiders or dismiss any information we do receive from them. And since we are so right and everyone is on board, we would be less tolerant of one or two people who speak up with concerns. This in turn may make others less likely to speak up. Again, it may not take all of these symptoms to cause a group to experience groupthink, but it is easy to see how they might work together to feed the problem.

As a result of the above symptoms of groupthink, there are a number of consequences that accompany groupthink (Janis, 1971). First, groups tend to **narrow their focus** to a small number of options (likely just two). So rather than considering a broad array of alternatives, they often get locked into "either-or" thinking ("Either we do this, or we do that"). Alternatives are not explored or considered very extensively. Second, when new problems or concerns are presented, groups **fail to go back and reconsider** the preferred course of action with the newly mentioned concerns in mind. Third, **little is done to develop contingency plans**, in the event that problems are encountered after following the preferred course of action.

Preventing/Minimizing Groupthink

In light of the above symptoms and consequences of groupthink, Janis (1971) offered a number of recommendations for actions groups can take to prevent groupthink. First, the leader of the group should instruct each member of the group to act as a **critical evaluator,** and to raise questions, concerns, and doubts about proposed courses of action, even if doing so involves criticizing ideas proposed by the leader. Of course, the leader then has to be tolerant and encouraging when members disagree with him or her. For a variation on the idea of encouraging dissent, at each meeting, a different member should be assigned the role of a "**devil's advocate,**" who will constructively challenge ideas that are raised. The advantage of this approach is that it reframes disagreement within the group. When the role is assigned to someone, she is disagreeing simply because she is playing a role, and it's not a personal attack on someone's idea. This reframing frees the person playing the "devil's advocate" role to be very vocal in raising concerns, making it harder for some of the symptoms of groupthink to take hold. Another suggestion is for **key leaders to remove themselves from deliberations** (so others aren't saying what they think the leader wants to hear), or to at least refrain from stating their preferences until others have had a chance to weigh in on the discussion with their own opinions and alternatives. This reduces pressure on group members to agree with their leaders. This is important, as a lack of impartial leadership has been linked to groupthink (Esser, 1998).

In addition, the group should **welcome the input of outsiders** who have sufficient expertise and who can offer a fresh perspective. This may not always be possible (there may not be time), but doing this can help keep the group from being insulated and sheltered from outside opinion. If a group is big enough, it can do **breakout meetings of smaller subgroups,** with each having its own chair. This can make it easier for everyone to express an opinion, while making it harder for the group to have a sense that everyone is in agreement and everyone should go along with the group. In addition, leaders can **hold group members accountable as individuals,** making it difficult for them to just "hide" as a member of the group. Holding members accountable as individuals leads to greater difficulty in reaching consensus, but it makes individuals more active in trying to influence the group, and leads to better and less-risky decisions (Kroon, Hart, & van Kreveld, 1991). Finally, Janis suggests that when a group has identified a suitable course of action, **members should be invited to raise any questions or concerns** about it. When leading meetings, I have done this by asking questions like: "What concerns do you have about this?" "What concerns should we have about this?" "What are we not considering?" or "What are we leaving out?" and pausing long enough to allow others to answer.

Disagreement

Notice that many of the solutions to groupthink involve alleviating pressures against disagreement and creating conditions that encourage greater disagreement. Disagreement is more productive than conflict or groupthink, and there are several advantages to engaging in disagreement in our workplace. Richmond and McCroskey (2009) argue that by engaging in and encouraging others to engage in disagreement, we can better develop and clarify our own views and give people the feeling that they are able to have a "say" in their workplace. As a result, we may identify solutions that otherwise would not have been considered, and we likely will experience higher-quality decision making.

In order to gain the above benefits, though, we must be able to engage in productive disagreement that does not lead into conflict. Of course, if two people are offering their opinions, and allowing the other person to disagree, there is a great deal of room for give-and-take in the interaction. Rather than one person bullying the other, or both people shouting at each other, they will have to carefully navigate this give-and-take. In other words, they must negotiate with each other.

Negotiation

According to Thompson (1990), negotiation is the process in which individuals attempt to come to an agreement about what each party will provide, give and take, and receive. We may negotiate about where to go to lunch and who will pay, our salary, whether our committee should take a particular course of action, whether certain tasks are our job or someone else's, the details of an agreement or contract with someone, whether someone will hire us or accept us into a program, among other things. Negotiations involve the perception that the parties have conflicting interests, that communication between the parties is possible, solutions are possible, parties can make offers and counteroffers, and offers are not final until accepted by both parties (Thompson, 1990, p. 516). These characteristics, particularly of conflicting interests and views, and the fact that the negotiation is not final until the outcomes are endorsed by all parties, suggests the challenging nature of negotiations. Negotiating probably is one of the greatest communication challenges a person could undertake. Think about all that is happening during a negotiation: We have a goal and we have to work toward it, the other person has a goal and also is working toward it, we have to monitor the other person and adjust to each "move" she makes, all while managing distractions, disruptions, changes of topic, our own emotions, and questions about whether we are achieving a fair and desired outcome for ourselves. Therefore, we should not be surprised with the following assessment: "There is overwhelming evidence that people are ineffective negotiators (see Bazerman, Curhan, Moore, & Valley, 2000; Neale & Bazerman, 1991; Thompson, 1990 for reviews). Negotiators often fail to discover mutually beneficial settlements and thus reach suboptimal settlements leaving 'money on the table' unclaimed" (van Boven & Thompson, 2003, p. 387). In other words, their outcomes are not as good as if the participants had worked to find ways to mutually benefit each other. In this section I will discuss some aspects of negotiation, identify characteristics of successful negotiators, and offer ideas on how to negotiate effectively.

How might negotiations be approached in different ways? Some may try to win at all costs and maximize outcomes for themselves. These individuals are taking a *distributive* approach, which assumes that for one party to win or gain something, the other party must lose that amount (Walton & McKersie, 1965). Those who are focused less on win-lose, and instead focus on how both parties can gain, without one side necessarily having to lose, are taking an *integrative* approach (Walton & McKersie, 1965). You may recognize this as the win-win approach that is espoused far and wide. Although this distinction between types of negotiation is widely applied by those who study negotiation, there are a couple of problems with it. First, it implies that opposing parties in a negotiation are using the same approach (both are using a distributive approach, or both are using an integrative approach). In fact, one party may be using a distributive approach, while another may be using an integrative approach. Second, negotiators may not stay in one mode throughout an entire negotiation.

For example, using a slightly different framework, Lytle, Brett, and Shapiro (1999) found that negotiators move between different negotiation approaches during the span of a single negotiation. Either party may be focused on *interests, rights,* or *power. Interests* consist of each party's preferences, concerns, priorities. For example, in a salary negotiation, an increased salary or other benefits would be the interests. A focus on *rights* involves emphasizing policies, contracts, law, or some other standard of what is fair and right. Comments involving legal action, violation of contracts or policies, or other similar appeals have a focus on rights. In a salary negotiation, one may focus on how it is not fair to be paid less than others, or one may focus on how it is not right that his salary is so low. In these cases, the focus is on rights. A focus on *power* is meant to pressure or coerce an opponent into submission. It may come in the form of threats ("We will tell your competitors about your business practices"; "If you don't go along, we will quit doing business with you"). In the salary negotiation example, a focus on power might involve suggestions that one will quit the organization if his salary is not increased. In negotiations they studied, Lytle et al. (1999) found that each party used various approaches within a single negotiation, and sometimes within a single statement. For example, the following statement focuses on rights and interests: "There is no policy that you can hold us to, but clearly we both would be better off if we found a way to work this out." This finding underscores the complexity of negotiations.

Because negotiations are so complex, it can be helpful to examine differences between skilled and novice negotiators, to gain a sense of what separates the two groups and distinguishes effective negotiators. How do highly effective negotiators differ from less effective negotiators? Rackham and Carlisle (1978a, 1978b) compared the behaviors of effective and less effective negotiators both during negotiations and when preparing for negotiations, and their findings can help us gain a sense of effective negotiation preparation and behavior.

Skilled negotiators prepare for negotiations in different ways than less skilled negotiators (Rackham & Carlisle, 1978b). First, they try to **consider areas of potential common ground** that they may share with their opponents. Second, they are more flexible with respect to their goals. Rather than having a fixed and inflexible goal (as do less skilled negotiators), they have a goal, but also a range of what is short of the goal, yet still acceptable. Skilled negotiators also **consider a greater number of alternative proposals** they might encounter. This level of planning helps them also

Table 10.2 Behaviors of Skilled Negotiators

While Preparing for Negotiations, They

- Consider areas of potential common ground
- Develop a greater number of alternative proposals
- Focus more on issues they will encounter

During Negotiations, They

- Are less likely to use phrases that annoy their opponents
- Offer summaries
- Check to make sure everyone is on the same page
- Don't give a heads-up when they're about to disagree
- Ask a lot of questions
- Offer only their strongest reasons (not all reasons)
- Don't immediately offer counterproposals
- Don't participate in attack-defend spirals

consider how they will respond to proposals they may encounter. Finally, while less skilled negotiators plan for a negotiation to follow a specific sequence of events, more skilled negotiators **focus more on the issues they will encounter,** various positions that might be held on those issues, and other factors. They realize that negotiations can be unpredictable, and try to be prepared for whatever they might encounter. As a result, it is not hard to imagine how skilled negotiators might be more flexible in handling abrupt changes or events during the negotiation. Those who expect a specific sequence of events will be thrown off much more easily if the negotiation does not follow their "script."

Skilled negotiators also exhibit key differences from less skilled negotiators during negotiations (Rackham & Carlisle, 1978a). Some differences related to language and communication are apparent. First, skilled negotiators are **less likely to use the kind of phrases that may annoy opponents** ("This is a generous offer," "I'm offering a fair price"). They let their offers speak for themselves, without editorializing about them. During the negotiation, they are more likely to **check to make sure everyone is on the same page,** and to **offer summaries.** Interestingly, they often would **highlight the kind of comment they were about to make:** "Can I ask you a question?" "Can I offer you an idea on how you might want to do this differently?" The exception was when they were about to disagree. They **did not give a head's-up about disagreement** ("I'm going to have to disagree with you here"), though less skilled negotiators did preface their disagreements with these kinds of comments. In addition, skilled negotiators were more likely to **use questions** and attempt to seek information from their opponents. And when making arguments, skilled negotiators **offered only their strongest reasons** as support, while less skilled negotiators offered a greater number of reasons, some of which were strong, and some that were weaker. As a result, their opponents focused on attacking the weak reasons, and it was harder to progress through the negotiation. It was more difficult to do this against skilled negotiators, who offered strong reasons and avoided mentioning weak ones.

Skilled negotiators also responded to the flow of the interaction differently during negotiations. First, when they encounter a proposal, they **don't immediately respond** with a counterproposal. Instead, they consider the proposal and offer any counterproposals at a more appropriate and less abrupt time. Second, skilled negotiators are **less likely to find themselves caught in what are known as defend-attack spirals.** In other words, when attacked, they don't immediately defend themselves or counterattack and get engaged in a reciprocal back-and-forth. This finding was supported by other research that found that negotiators who get locked into spirals are less effective (Lytle et al., 1999). More skilled negotiators either refused to reciprocate or began to reciprocate, but quickly shifted the discussion away from an aggressive stance and refocused it on a key issue (Lytle et al., 1999). This is important, because being more aggressive may cause a threat to the opponent's "face," and when negotiators experience a face threat, they become more competitive and less cooperative (White, Tynan, Galinsky, & Thompson, 2004).

When it comes to identifying other effective negotiation behaviors, it is hard to avoid an answer of "It depends." Research often is divided into what is effective during distributive (win-lose) negotiations versus integrative negotiations (win-win). For example, Roloff, Putnam, and Anastasiou (2003) outline effective characteristics of each type of negotiator. On one hand, this is problematic, because as I already mentioned, there may be distributive and integrative elements within the same situation (Putnam, 1990; Roloff & Jordan, 1991). Therefore, we will examine characteristics that are common among the different types of negotiators, with the understanding that it may be important to be able to call on a full range of skills, some of which are distributive, and some of which are integrative.

According to Roloff et al. (2003), skilled distributive negotiators are tough in that they typically make bold opening offers while giving few or small concessions. They also are argumentative, in that they are willing to attack others' positions (without making personal attacks). Third, they sometimes succeed by making it clear that they have alternatives should the negotiation fall through. This practice enables them to appear less dependent, and increases the likelihood that their opponent will feel compelled to make concessions (Roloff et al., 2003). Roloff et al. also indicate that skilled distributive negotiators may sometimes mislead their opposition by bluffing. For example, they may appear to disagree when they really are in agreement, in order to gain greater concessions from their opponents. Skilled distributive negotiators also act in good faith, in the sense that they sincerely are trying to reach an agreement with their opponent.

Although some things on the above list likely are not surprising, some, such as bold opening offers, giving few concessions, or misleading their opponents, may be troubling. In fact, each can backfire. An extreme opening offer may cause an opponent to become more resistant and less likely to cooperate. And if opponents find they have been mislead, they are likely to retaliate (Shapiro & Bies, 1994). Overall, the distributive approach can make for a contentious negotiation. Research also suggest that a win-lose approach like this can prevent parties from gaining as much in negotiations as when parties find ways to work together to maximize joint outcomes (Roloff et al., 2003). This integrative approach, which focuses on how both can gain from the negotiation, can serve as an alternative way to engage in negotiation.

Roloff et al. (2003) suggest that skilled integrative negotiators "set specific and reasonably high goals" for their negotiations, and that these goals help motivate negotiators to analyze the situation completely and find ways that both parties can gain (p. 815). In addition, skilled integrative negotiators are reluctant to lower their goals. Skilled negotiators also recognize that issues differ in importance, and are willing to make concessions on issues that are of lower priority for them, in order to gain something that is more important. This approach is called *logrolling* (Roloff et al., 2003). For example, what is a low priority for one negotiator may be a high priority for another. Skilled negotiators can recognize these differing priorities and give in on a lower priority matter in order to gain what one wants with a higher priority issue (that is of lower priority to the opponent). Notice that this strategy requires that one is very knowledgeable about an opponent's priorities (this goes back to the research habits that are common among highly successful negotiators). In addition, skilled integrative negotiators are aware of possible biases, such as assuming that their priorities are in the same order as their opponents' priorities, and that their priorities will clash with their opponents' priorities. As a result, skilled integrative negotiators are in a better position to see opportunities created when they share priorities with opponents, or when their priorities are in a different order than their opponents' priorities. Skilled integrative negotiators also are "selectively contentious" in several different ways (p. 817). They are more tactful in how they phrase contentious remarks (they are more matter-of-fact than aggressive). They also are likely to couple contentious comments with integrative comments (as with the earlier example of starting contentious), and then moving the focus back to the issue at hand. They also avoid getting embroiled in the kinds of conflict spirals that were discussed earlier. Finally, skilled integrative negotiators "signal that they are concerned about their opponent's needs and interests" (p. 818). By demonstrating an awareness of an opponent's needs, a negotiator can help keep a negotiation from becoming contentious. As we will see in the next section, there are many additional benefits from being very tuned in to an opponent's "world."

Although I have outlined strengths of two types of negotiators, as you probably notice, we might reasonably see behaviors from each category within a single negotiation, or even within a single response. In order to better capture negotiations more completely, and the ways in which they include both distributive and integrative elements, I will outline a system that is advocated by a successful professional negotiation coach.

The "Camp" System

In concluding this section on negotiation advice, I will outline a particular system of negotiation. You may or may not find this system to be useful, and it may or may not fit the way you prefer to approach others. If it doesn't fit you, at least you will be aware of it, and you're always free to examine other systems. And if it does fit you and work for you, good. The system is offered by Jim Camp (2003), a professional negotiation coach whose ideas are informed by considerable experience. In many ways, he "flies in the face" of conventional negotiation wisdom, but he gives a fairly broad coverage to negotiations, and much of what he advises reflects a good understanding of how people really operate (in other words, it is consistent with research outcomes from a variety of areas of communication and psychology). You may not find this system useful, but at least you will gain another potential perspective on the negotiation process.

Camp is highly critical of popular win-win approaches to negotiations, for a number of reasons. First, he suggests that they cause people to compromise far too willingly, and therefore fail to reach a settlement that is fair to them. Second, he suggests that win-win negotiators often are taken advantage of by more shrewd negotiators who will exploit the win-win negotiator's willingness to compromise. Third, he suggests that, in the long run, solutions thought to be win-win often are lose-lose. For example, if a company agrees to deliver goods at a price that keeps them from making a sufficient profit, they will not be able to survive as a company, and the customer with whom they negotiated the deal eventually will not receive the goods, unless a new price is negotiated (meaning that a lot of time may have been wasted on a settlement that could not realistically be implemented by the company).

In support of these criticisms, Camp makes several points. First, **it is a mistake to worry about preserving a relationship with the opponent or "adversary."** One should respect an opponent as an adversary, and not seek to damage a relationship, but one should not compromise against one's interests to preserve a relationship.

He suggests that if you negotiate a deal for what you deserve and deliver on that deal, you will have a good business relationship with your adversary, and you will not be preyed upon by the many people in the business world who are eager to take advantage of negotiators who are concerned about relationships. This may seem like a harsh stance to take, but his point is not that we should be aggressive and seek to have poor relationships, but rather that we worry more about negotiating a fair deal for ourselves than becoming friends with someone.

Regarding the heightened level of emotion we likely experience during negotiations, Camp stresses that it is rooted in **neediness,** in that when we are needy, we are more likely to lose control and make poor decisions. He suggests that we often confuse things we *want* (money, a deal to be closed, to land a lucrative client, a sale, attention, recognition, a raise, a revised grade on an assignment, etc.) with things we truly *need* (air, water, food, shelter, love, companionship), which is a much shorter list. When we treat wants as needs, we become needy, and this creates problems for us during negotiations. Neediness during negotiation may show itself in a number of ways: when we talk too much or when we should be listening (*needing* to be noticed or to feel important), when we feel pressure to accept an offer (*needing* to come away with something, or needing to be liked by the other party), pressuring others to agree (*needing* to be accepted and avoid rejection), and so on. Camp argues that when we view the above things as wants, our perspective changes and we are able to think more clearly, and to be less needy. We may want to be liked, to be considered important, to close a deal, but even if these things don't happen, we still will move forward, able to take advantage of other opportunities. We always can make another decision. Therefore, when you're in situations in which you're feeling the kind of emotion and pressure that accompanies neediness, it is important to reframe your *needs* into *wants* so that you will have a more reasonable perspective during the negotiation. This may be easier said than done, but if you practice this idea the next time you feel like you need something (a book, shirt, DVD, certain food, etc.), you likely will notice a difference in how you feel if you reframe it as a want.

But why this emphasis on avoiding neediness? It is so we can implement the most prominent aspect of Camp's system: giving your "adversary" every opportunity to **say "no" to you.** This flies in the face of the idea of working toward a "yes" answer or closing a deal. To better understand why "no" is preferred, we can consider the alternatives: "yes" and "maybe." Camp suggests that a "yes" early on in the negotiation (at least a formal one that involves a number of issues) means little, and certainly not "yes." After all, if it was that easy to get to a "yes," there likely would not have been a dispute in the first place. In addition, an early "yes" can be problematic for us because we can lose our focus in the possibility of reaching an agreement, which increases our neediness. At this point, if someone were to add a condition ("but first, I need . . . ") we will be off balance and lacking the focus we need to negotiate thoughtfully. Camp suggests that "maybe" is even worse, because it means little. The adversary may be uncomfortable with saying "no," and I suspect that all of us can recall when we've used a "maybe" to delay having to say "no" or give a straight answer to others. If we hear it in a negotiation, it is vague, means little, and therefore is of little use to us.

As a result, Camp suggests that we should **be willing to say "no"** early on and that we should give our adversary ample opportunity to say "no" to us. He argues that hearing or saying "no" forces more focused thought about the essential issues of the negotiation than a "yes" or "maybe," and that it's more of a real decision than either of the alternative answers. His point is that if we cannot deliver on what others are asking, we should politely (anger would suggest neediness) say "no." At this point, the adversary may revise what he is asking. But what if he doesn't? What if he says "We can't do any better than that?" Fine. Remember, this is a want, not a need. If the agreement will not work for you, then it is not worthwhile to agree. It is better to spend our time moving on to another opportunity rather than finding out that we cannot hold up our end of an agreement. Think of the time that is wasted when people agree to do jobs they cannot do, take on contracts they cannot deliver, and so on. Had they just moved on to a better fit or arrangement, a lot of time and stress would have been avoided.

But how do we **invite others to say no**? We do it by politely saying things such as "I'm not sure if this idea will work for you, and if it doesn't let me know, no hard feelings. And if you think it might work, I'm happy to tell you more about it," or "I have something you may or may not find useful to you, I don't know. If you'd like to discuss it, I'm happy to, but if you're not interested, just tell me, and I'll take it up with others." Another example might be "These are the things we need, if you cannot provide them, please just let us know, and we will move elsewhere with this and still try to do business with you again in the future." These examples may sound absurd, but think of how people usually approach these situations. Typically they push hard for our acceptance or agreement, and we often resist. By inviting others to say "no," we take away their need to be resistant and enable them to focus on our ideas, and demonstrate that we are not needy. For example, how did you react a couple of pages ago when I first began discussing the Camp system? Notice that rather than trying to sell you on it, I gave you multiple opportunities to reject it, and acknowledged that it might not be a good fit for you. This does not mean that you will love the system, but I suspect you were open to at least considering it after I invited you to reject it. Now what if an adversary takes you up on your offer and says "no?" If you've made the best offer you can make, then move on, as it will not be in your best interests to compromise. And if there are aspects of the arrangement you can negotiate (such as engaging in logrolling), you can work them out.

You may have noticed that in the examples above, the person was almost bending over backward to be nice in inviting the person to say "no." The point is to eliminate any need for our adversary to be unnecessarily resistant (resistant to our approach, as opposed to being resistant to our proposal). Camp argues that this approach will get us much farther than pressuring others to say "yes," which either will cause them to resist or to say "yes" but regret it. We can afford to approach negotiations this way when we are not needy.

Another advantage of remaining composed and avoiding neediness is that it enables us to weather emotional shifts during the negotiation. For example, if someone becomes aggressive, or changes the terms of an offer, because we are not needy, we can politely respond. If we find the demands or changes to be acceptable, we can agree, and if we do not, we can say "no," and we can redirect aggressive responses and focus our adversary back on the issue. This also helps us prevent our adversary from becoming too positive or negative about an issue. If he is too emotional in either direction, he will be prone to rebounding in the other direction (for example, shifting from highly positive and enthusiastic to being dejected or deflated). But if we can keep him in a moderate range emotionally, we can keep him focused and avoid distracting emotional tangents. To do this, we may have to deflate some of his excitement, or if he is not being positive about our offer, we may have to point out its positive aspects.

Camp also gives a considerable amount of advice on preparing for negotiations. He suggests having a "**mission and purpose**" before entering into a negotiation (Camp, 2003, p. 69). This mission should be focused on behaviors, not outcomes (in other words, on what you hope to do, not what you hope to get from it). Behaviors are within our control, while we will be more needy if we are preoccupied with what we will get. In addition, this mission should be located in what Camp calls our "**adversary's world**," meaning that it should be framed in terms of our adversary's point of view, not our own. For example, rather than having "to get a raise" as our mission and purpose (needy, self-centered, and outcome-focused), it would be better to frame our goal as "to help my supervisor recognize what I bring to the organization and decide that the organization would benefit by increasing its investment in me." This might sound awkward, but it's more thorough and focused on things you can control, less needy, and framed in your adversary's world. There's no guarantee you would get a raise, but you will help your chances by helping your supervisor recognize your value to the organization. Even without worrying about articulating a perfect mission and purpose, it is important to recognize the value of focusing on what you can control, and on operating from your adversary's frame of mind.

Not surprisingly, Camp suggests that it is very important to carefully research our adversary. Knowing as much as possible can help us anticipate the positions they may take, and better spot any bluffs they may make. And if we talk to others who have negotiated with our adversary, we may get a sense of tactics she may use. There is an additional reason to study our adversary. Camp argues that once we are in the negotiation, much of what we have to do involves what he calls **painting the adversary's "pain"** for him (p. 159). According to Camp, "pain is whatever the negotiator sees as *the current or future problem*. People make decisions in order to alleviate and take away this current or future problem—this pain" (p. 160). Notice again that the focus is in what the adversary needs and how we can address that need, as opposed to being centered around what we want. Notice in the example above about getting a raise that the point is to demonstrate how the adversary's "pain" can be reduced by investing in a raise for you. The point is not to create pain for the adversary, but to help him visualize what already exists and how you can alleviate it. This can be done with research, and with one additional technique that Camp stresses throughout his system.

Camp again offers counterintuitive advice by saying that we should **talk as little as possible** during negotiations. When we talk, our adversaries can learn information they can use against us. When we talk we suggest neediness. According to Camp, "The single most important fuel that you have, the most important behavioral goal and *habit* you can develop, is your ability to **ask questions**" (p. 101, my emphasis). He suggests: "The adversary's answers to our questions build the vision that he needs to make decisions" (p. 103). In other words, questions help us paint our adversary's pain. In addition, they keep us in control, as our adversary will be answering to us. They also place our adversary in a position of being reactive, while affording us more time to think through our responses. Consistent with what I've discussed elsewhere in this book, Camp advises that we avoid leading questions and instead ask short, open-ended questions that begin with the classic interrogative terms: who, what, where, when, why, and how. We can find a lot about our adversary's pain by asking short, simple questions:

- What are your greatest concerns moving forward?
- What do you look for in an employee?
- How important is this issue for you?
- When do you need us to act on this?
- What would you like me to do?
- How can I help you address this challenge?
- How do you think we can work this out?
- What would you like me to do in response to this concern?

Think of times when you've been left wondering where you stand with someone, or what another person wanted from you. Notice how using simple questions like these could yield very helpful answers. In my own experience, I've been surprised at the power of questions like these. They have helped me better understand others, bring calm to tense situations, and figure out how to proceed through situations when at first I wasn't sure what to do. And in negotiations, they can help you understand your adversary much more completely, and determine whether you can relieve her "pain."

Ok, so you've had a viable mission, prepared for the negotiation, given your adversary opportunities to say "no" throughout the negotiation, painted her pain, used questions very effectively, avoided being needy, all while being very polite without pressuring her. But if "yes" is such a problem, how do you close things out and actually finish successfully? For this, Camp suggests what he calls a 3+ rule, meaning that you need to make sure your adversary agrees to the final terms of the negotiation more than once (he suggests three times, if not more). So how might this work? It can be done by asking questions such as "Before we proceed, I want to make sure this works for you?" "Are you sure you're ok with this?" "Are you sure this is how you want to proceed, because I'm reluctant to unless you are sure?" "Have we addressed all of your concerns?" Regardless of whether you think doing this 3+ times is excessive, the point is to avoid pressuring your adversary, and instead give her a chance to express concerns or say "no." Notice that when I began this section inviting you to say "no" to this system, I was redundant and worded that invitation in three different ways.

I'll continue along those lines and reiterate that I respect that this system may not work for you. On one hand, it is based on the writings of one person and has not been researched systematically. On the other hand, the source is a successful negotiation coach, and many of the system's ideas are consistent with research we reviewed earlier: careful preparation, being polite, refraining from being aggressive, not getting caught up in conflict spirals, asking questions, and so on. This brief overview doesn't capture the system entirely, but if you feel you would benefit from learning more about negotiation, it can help you decide whether you want to check out Camp's work in greater detail.

However, it is important to notice that one aspect has been consistent throughout this chapter: When we veer from disagreement into areas of conflict (aggression, reciprocation of aggression, conflict spirals, etc.), we sacrifice productivity and increase problems and stress. Because people are people, and are far from perfect, this is inevitable. Therefore it is in our interests to consider more fully what happens when we experience conflict, and to develop a sense of what we can do about it. I cover all of this in the next chapter.

References

Bazerman, M.H., Curhan, J.R., Moore, D.A., & Valley, K.L. (2000). Negotiation. *Annual Review of Psychology, 51*, 279–314.

Camp, J. (2003). *Start with no: The negotiating tools that the pros don't want you to know.* New York, NY: Crown Business.

Esser, J.K. (1998). Alive and well after 25 years: A review of groupthink research. *Organizational Behavior and Human Decision Processes, 73*(2/3), 116–141.

Janis, I.L. (1971). Groupthink. *Psychology Today, 5*, 43–46, 74–76.

Kroon, M.B.R., 't Hart, P., & van Kreveld, D. (1991). Managing group decision making processes: Individual versus collective accountability and groupthink. *International Journal of Conflict Management, 2*, 91–115.

Lytle, A.L., Brett, J.M., & Shapiro, D.L. (1999). The strategic use of interests, rights, and power to resolve disputes. *Negotiation Journal, 15*, 31–51.

Moorhead, G., Ference, R., & Neck, C.P. (1991). Group decision fiascoes continue: Space shuttle *Challenger* and a revised groupthink framework. *Human Relations, 44*, 539–550.

Neale, M.A., & Bazerman, M.H. (1991). *Cognition and rationality in negotiation.* New York, NY: Free Press.

Putnam, L.L. (1990). Reframing integrative and distributive bargaining: A process perspective. In B.H. Sheppard, M.H. Bazerman, & R.J. Lewicki (Eds.), *Research on negotiation in organizations* (Vol. 2, pp. 3–30). Greenwich, CT: JAI Press.

Rackham, N., & Carlisle, J. (1978a). The effective negotiator—Part I: The behaviour of successful negotiators. *Journal of European Industrial Training, 2*(6), 6–10.

Rackham, N., & Carlisle, J. (1978b). The effective negotiator—Part II: Planning for negotiations. *Journal of European Industrial Training, 2*(7), 3–5.

Richmond, V.P., & McCroskey, J.C. (2009). *Organizational communication for survival: Making work work* (4th ed.). Boston, MA: Allyn & Bacon.

Roloff, M.E., & Jordan, J.M. (1991). The influence of effort, experience and persistence on the elements of bargaining plans. *Communication Research, 18*, 306–332.

Roloff, M.E., Putnam, L.L., & Anastasiou, L. (2003). Negotiation skills. In J.O. Greene & B.R. Burleson (Eds.), *Handbook of communication and social interaction skill* (pp. 801–833). Mahway, NJ: Lawrence Erlbaum Associates.

Shapiro, D.L., & Bies, R.J. (1994). Threats, bluffs, and disclaimers in negotiations. *Organizational Behavior and Human Decision Processes, 60*, 14–35.

Thompson, L. (1990). An examination of naive and experienced negotiators. *Journal of Personality and Social Psychology, 59*, 82–90.

Van Boven, L., & Thompson, L. (2003). A look into the mind of the negotiator: Mental models in negotiation. *Group Processes and Interpersonal Relations, 6*, 387–404.

Walton, R.E., & McKersie, R.B. (1965). *A behavioral theory of labor negotiations: An analysis of a social interaction system.* New York, NY: McGraw-Hill.

White, J.B., Tynan, R.O., Galinsky, A., & Thompson, L. (2004). Face threat sensitivity in negotiations: Roadblock to agreement and joint gain. *Organizational Behavior and Human Decision Processes, 94*, 102–124.

Chapter 11

Skillful Navigation of Conflict Situations

The problems: Why is it so hard to reason with people during conflict and how can we successfully navigate conflict situations?

Ideally, we will be able to make the most of the disagreements we have at work and avoid finding ourselves in conflict situations. However, just as it is realistic to expect to encounter disagreements with others, when we consider the stress of the workplace, the variety of personalities we encounter, the different motives people have for their actions at work, the hierarchy of the organization, and the resources at stake (salary, status, reputation), we should expect that we will encounter our fair share of conflict during our professional lives. This is significant when we think of the toll that conflict takes. Think of the last conflict you had at work, and how it might have affected your life at work (and at home): stress, productivity lost due to the distraction (and time spent huddling with coworkers to discuss the situation), embarrassment, skipped meals, stress at home in the form of difficulty focusing on friends and family, lost sleep, among other things. And then there is the possible fallout from the conflict: loss of status, tarnished reputation, fractured relationships, and so on. The fact that most of us probably have witnessed many of these outcomes in the workplace suggests that it is worthwhile to learn about conflict and how we can handle it more effectively. This chapter examines what happens to us when we experience conflict (see Table 11.1) and uses this information to discuss some things we might do to prevent conflict or at least handle it more effectively.

Table 11.1 All of the Things That Happen to Us When We Perceive Conflict

- We feel our "face" is threatened.
- So we have a fight-or-flight response.
- The resulting emotional arousal impairs clear thinking (and thoughtful talking). We are "under the influence" of emotions.
- The attention we do have is focused on "threats"—negative looks, comments, expressions, etc. If others say something positive/constructive, we may miss it because of this attentional bias. We also likely will assume the worst of the other person, in terms of why the person is acting this way.
- If we don't calm down or if we keep thinking about what provoked us, we may experience anger flooding.
- Others can catch our highly negative and charged emotions (and we can catch theirs).
- If this happens, we may get caught in certain conflict patterns (demand-withdrawal, etc.).

What Happens When We Experience Conflict?

In the previous chapter, we learned that conflict is a difference of opinion plus negative emotion. This is important, because in my experience, those who write about conflict often neglect to appreciate the important role played by emotion. Instead, they overemphasize how rational we are during conflict situations. However, conflict situations are highly emotional because we essentially are responding to a social threat. Although it may lead to physical threat, most of the conflict we experience in the workplace likely will involve threats that are social in nature: to our reputation, status, and so on. In this section we will explore this threat and our reaction to it, beginning with a discussion of the concept of "face."

Conflict as a Threat to Our Face

A major potential threat we encounter in workplace conflict is a threat to our **face**. Our face is the identity we present publicly that we want to be accepted by others (Cupach & Canary, 2000). Our public face is important to us, and we desire and expect that it will be validated or confirmed by others (Cissna & Sieburg, 1995). We "lose face" when we perceive that our identity is being challenged or ignored (Folger, Scott Poole, & Stutman, 2005). According to Goffman (1955), there are several consequences of losing face in public, including shame and embarrassment, and feelings of diminished power. In response to this loss of face, we are motivated to save face, even if we have to be aggressive to do so (Folger et al., 2005). According to Folger et al. (2005), "face saving is an attempt to protect or repair relational images in response to threats, real or imagined, potential or actual" (p. 148). If you think about a time you were embarrassed by someone in public, you'll recognize that saving face is a kind of social "damage control," in which we try to address the threat to our face. Once we are in this "damage control" mode, our focus is narrowed to our face concerns, as our primary conversational goal now is about saving face. If we had been disagreeing about some issue, the interaction now has become personal, and likely emotionally charged. We no longer care about the original issue. Now the issue is about the person who crossed us. With our focus now on saving our face (and possibly on attacking another person's face), we have become less flexible in the range of conversational choices we are likely to make (Folger et al., 2005). And this presents one of the major challenges of conflict situations: working toward a constructive outcome with someone we believe has attacked our face. It is hard to want to work things out when someone has threatened our face. This is partly because we process the other person's actions as a social threat and physiologically we begin to become aroused. The nature and effects of this arousal are discussed below.

Physiological Arousal and Diminished Cognitive Processing

When we face a threat to our welfare, we are likely to respond in a **fight-or-flight** manner (Zillman, 1988). Whether we choose to attack or defend, when faced with a threat, our system will mobilize us to address the threat with heightened excitedness, thanks to increased activity in our sympathetic nervous system (Zillman, 1988).

This activity manifests itself in the form of several symptoms, including increased heart rate and blood pressure; blood flow to the digestive system (which is nonessential for helping us address the threat) decreases while flow to our arms and legs increases (so we can act vigorously); breathing is deeper and faster (allows more oxygen to muscles); blood vessels in the skin constrict (to reduce blood flow), while sweat glands open (producing the sweating that comes with this feeling) (Cannon, 1929). These are involuntary responses that prepare us for intense action. While this response may have been critical to help our distant ancestors face the challenges of their day, such an excited response often is less helpful in the modern workplace, when our "threat" might just be an annoying coworker in the next cubicle. However, these "response tendencies exert their influence nonetheless, and people do get excited when staying calm and collected would service them better" (Zillman, 1988, p. 53). This helps explain why our responses to conflict situations often make little sense, and suggests how fragile our self-control is in these situations.

During this time our system is mobilizing us to respond to the threat in our environment, **much of our capacity to process information cognitively and to think clearly is impaired.** Our capacity to perform cognitively is most efficient when our level of physiological arousal is moderate (Zilmann, 1988). If we have too little arousal, we may lack the motivation to think clearly (think of someone who is bored at his or her job and "going though the motions"). And when there is too much arousal, as there often is in conflict situations, "cognition is presumed to fail us" (Zillman, 1988, p. 59). In a condition such as this, our behaviors are impulsive, and we likely will follow established habits (more likely yelling and impulsive comments as opposed to interrupting with compassion). Even worse, all of this intense excitedness may make us feel invulnerable, which may further inspire aggressive action (Zillman, 1979). Based on a need to ensure survival, our system favors swift action toward the threat, not careful deliberation of theories regarding why that person across the room just ridiculed our idea!

Thanks to all of this physiological arousal we experience during conflict, the "thinking" part of our brain takes a backseat to the emotional part. We are in the grips of emotion and are not thinking as clearly as we are in most situations. Or as Thompson (2004) puts it, we are **"under the influence"** of our emotions. This means our ability to carefully consider how we want to respond to the target of our anger is compromised. Unfortunately, this comes at a time when we very much have something we want to say, and in fact we may say it more loudly than usual. This may help explain some regrettable things we've said in moments like these, as well as things others have said to us and lived to regret. They are unfortunate consequences of being under the influence of emotion.

Focus on Threats

But we have not lost all of our cognitive ability. We still are able to monitor threatening stimuli in our environment and, thanks to our emotional arousal, we're very motivated to do so. When we are in a threatening environment, our survival is enhanced by our ability to spot anything that could threaten our "safety." Cosmides and Tooby (2000) outline what happens when we perceive a threat in our environment. Our attention sharpens to focus specifically on anything in our environment that is threatening. Our goals shift to focus on our safety. We scan our environment for cues that might be related to our safety. Unfortunately, in conflict situations, these responses cause us to focus on other people as threats, to focus on the most negative and threatening things people say (and not notice positive things they might say), and often adopt either a defensive or aggressive stance and approach to address the threat. We might be waiting defensively for additional comments directed at us. Or now that we're emotionally aroused, even comments that express mild disagreement might be seen as threats and further annoy us. Or suppose the interaction involves a long discussion in which the person who has angered us actually says a handful of sincerely complementary things to us, while also offering constructively critical opinions. Thanks to our focus on threatening stimuli, we may notice and remember only the negative comments, making it more difficult to work toward a constructive outcome. You may be able to recall a time when someone was angry at you and you surprised them by not arguing back. The person might have continued to argue a couple of points before he or she realized that you weren't arguing back. He or she likely was so fixated on the "battle" that it was only with some surprise that he or she snapped out of it with a somewhat stunned reaction. This is an example of how we focus intensely on the threats we encounter.

Anger Flooding

Adding to the above ways our system mobilizes us to face threats, Zillman (1990) explains an additional danger that may be involved in this process. The **emotional excitation** involved in mobilizing us to face the threat arrives quickly, but takes some time to subside. If we are provoked a second time before we have calmed down from the first incident, the excitation we experience will combine with the first for a more powerful effect. If we are provoked a third time, those effects will combine with earlier reactions. This means that when someone or something provokes us, we need time for the effect to dissipate. If we are provoked again before it does, our emotions will build even more, possibly to the point at which we experience something Gottman (1993) calls anger "**flooding.**" Anger flooding represents arousal levels that are severely elevated, to the point that our ability to think clearly, speak rationally, or make good choices is compromised. This helps explain situations we've been in or witnessed when a "final straw" sent someone "over the edge" and the person "blew up" at another person. It is not a stretch to think that the words and actions of employees who were experiencing anger flooding have caused significant problems at work, and have likely cost many people their jobs. This is another aspect of emotion we will need to consider when trying to identify ways to handle conflict situations.

Rumination

The effects of conflict can be felt even long after the triggering event, when we are not in the presence of those with whom we are experiencing conflict, at least if we let it happen. Often we do, by **ruminating,** or dwelling on the conflict situation, and by contemplating retaliation (Zillman, 1988). We may retrace the episode over in our minds, think about what we wish we had said to the person, or think about what we will say to the person next time. While some consideration may be healthy and help us learn how to handle these challenging situations more effectively, too much rumination can be problematic. First, it can distract us from our work. Second, it can distract us when we are at home with family. Third, continuing to think about the episode can be unhealthy because it will cause us to maintain the emotional excitation we first experienced in response to the event (Zillman, 1988). In other words, our system will continue to keep us mobilized toward the threat and the excitement will not be able to dissipate as quickly as it normally should. According to a perspective on emotion provided by Schachter and Singer (1962), there are two components to emotions: (1) physiological arousal and (2) cognitive labeling. So in the case of anger elicited by conflict, we have the arousal described above (tension, increased heart rate, etc.), and we cognitively label that as anger. To understand the importance of labels, consider two people riding a roller-coaster. Both are going to feel some physiological arousal. However, that arousal can be labeled differently. One person might label it as anticipation and excitement, while the other may label it as fear or terror. The label given to the arousal will play an important role in shaping the experience of each person on the coaster. How does all of this relate to rumination? We can think about rumination as a way of persistently continuing to label a feeling, even if we're now well removed from the event that elicited the initial feeling. In other words, we may have had a conflict with someone yesterday at work. We were angry at that moment, but we also might have thought about it on the drive home, during dinner, after waking up in the middle of the night, during the drive into work today. But when we continue to ruminate about the event, we're actually prolonging the emotion we experienced with that event, and that can be stressful and damaging to our system (Seligman, 2006). As we consider how to handle conflict situations, we will need to address the possible damage caused by rumination.

Attributions

To the extent that we can reason about the conflict we are in, there is a good chance that our thoughts will be guided by the assumption that the other person meant to hurt us (Stone, Patton, & Heen, 2000). When we attempt to identify why someone did something, we are making an *attribution* about his or her behavior. Fincham, Bradbury, and Scott (1990) outline several dimensions to the attributions we make: **globality, stability, locus, intent, blameworthiness,** and **selfishness.** Globality is the extent to which the cause of the event explains just this event or several events. Stability is concerned with the extent to which the cause of the event is a consistent cause (as opposed to a temporary one). Locus is about whether the cause of the problem is internal (within the person) or external (due to the situation). Intent is the extent to which the person acted that way on purpose. Blameworthiness is the extent to which the person is responsible for the event. Selfishness is the extent to which the other person's behavior is self-serving.

To apply these dimensions, consider the attribution we might make in a conflict situation. Suppose you are working on a stressful project involving a few coworkers, and one of your team members is late delivering his or her contribution to it. We can make a variety of attributions for this. Suppose we think something as simple as "He or she is lazy and careless." This attribution would be global (if he or she is lazy, other areas of his or her work will suffer), stable (laziness is a permanent characteristic), internal (laziness is an internal characteristic), and blameworthy. Or suppose we think that the person failed to balance his or her time effectively. This is less global or stable, though still is internal and blameworthy. Or we could think that something must have come up to prevent the person from getting the work done. This is not global, stable, blameworthy, intentional, or selfish, and it is external. It is important to realize that when we initially are confronted with a situation like this, any of the above attributions could be plausible. There is no guarantee that one is more correct than the others. However, most of us make attributions with a level of confidence that does not reflect this reality. To consider the consequences of the attributions we make, review the three attributions for your coworker's behavior outlined above and consider how you might respond to the coworker based on each. The idea that different attributions would matter is supported by research on married couples by Fincham and his colleagues, who have found considerable support for something known as the attribution hypothesis in close relationships:

> The attribution hypothesis in close relationships research posits an association between attributions and relationship quality: Specifically, attributions that accentuate the impact of negative relationship events and minimize the impact of positive relationship events are associated with lower relationship satisfaction. Thus, for example, locating the cause of negative relationship events in the partner, viewing the cause as more stable and global, and seeing the partner's behavior as intentional, blameworthy and reflecting selfish motivation are more likely among distressed partners than among their nondistressed counterparts.
> (Fincham, Harold, & Gano-Phillips, 2000, p. 268)

Although this hypothesis is not applied to workplace relationships, we would expect the general differences between the types of attributions we make to play a similar positive or negative role in the workplace. The attributions we make during a conflict situation matter because they can influence how we will respond to the other person (Heider, 1958). When we discuss ways to handle conflict situations, one of our challenges will be to avoid instantly making highly negative attributions that will undermine our willingness or ability to navigate the conflict.

Mutual Influence

Consider the consequences of perceiving conflict that we've addressed so far. Thanks to a threat to our face, our focus shifts from an issue to the people involved in the situation. We now see those people as a threat, and therefore focus on the ways in which they are threatening and may continue to pose a threat. As this continues to happen and our emotional reaction intensifies, our ability to think, speak, and act thoughtfully becomes diminished. And even after we leave the situation, if we continue to ruminate about it, we will continue to relive the experience. As challenging as all of this might be, so far we only have been discussing how one individual in a conflict is affected. However, as we already have learned about communication, communicators are interdependent in that they mutually influence each other. In other words, our actions during conflict situations are not independent of the actions of the other person. We are influenced by our "opponent" and we influence him or her. One of the ways we influence each other is via emotional contagion.

Emotional Contagion. **Emotions are contagious** in the sense that it is possible to "catch" others' emotions (and possible for them to "catch" ours) (Hatfield, Cacioppo, & Rapson, 1994). During conflict, this can make a bad situation even worse, as people can feed off of each other in ways that lead to an escalation of a conflict situation. This helps explain how people who start off mildly annoyed with each other can end up shouting at each other. One person raises his or her voice, causing the other to do the same, which in turn leads the first person to raise his or her voice even more, and so on. The possibility of contagious emotions adds yet another obstacle to smoothly handling conflict situations.

Response Patterns. Conflicts also involve mutual influence through various response patterns that are common. We may **reciprocate,** or respond in a similar way to the other person. Reciprocation may involve negative or positive behaviors. Conflicts involving reciprocation of negative behaviors can be especially problematic. Imagine an interaction in which one person raises his or her voice, then we reciprocate by raising ours. If we continue to reciprocate each other's behavior, the conflict will grow in intensity and possibly spiral out of control (Cupach & Canary, 2000). Our response also might be **complementary,** in that we might exhibit behaviors that are opposite to each other. This can be good, such as when we respond with calmness to the other person's anger. However, there are some problematic complementary patterns. An attack-defend pattern is when one person is attacking and the other continually is defensive (Cupach & Canary, 2000). A demand-withdrawal pattern is when one person confronts and the other avoids (Canary, 2003). This also can spiral problematically, with one person pushing harder and harder to confront, and the other working more and more vigorously to withdraw from the situation.

The possibility of emotional contagion or certain response patterns suggests that when addressing conflict situations, we will have to both withstand the potentially negative influence of the other person, while simultaneously influencing the person in ways that help diminish the conflict, rather than to perpetuate it.

A Complete Picture of the Conflict Experience

We now have a more complete picture of what happens when we perceive conflict with another person. Someone says or does something that annoys us, we become aroused in response to this threat. As tension increases, we focus on negative cues and have difficulty seeing positive cues. Therefore, we are at risk for making a negative attribution of the other person's behavior (global, stable, internal, blameworthy, intentional). It is difficult to think and speak clearly, as our system is mobilizing to address the threat with vigorous action. We may be focused on how other people are reacting, the expression on the face of the person that annoyed us, on how we had better respond soon in order to save embarrassment. We also may be "catching" others' negative emotions. Tact and fluent communication do not come easy at this point. And if earlier events have agitated us, we may be at risk for flooding, and doing/saying things we definitely will regret. Finally, we may relive all of this angst by thinking about it later at work, on the drive home (where other drivers may increase our risk of flooding), that evening (when friends or family may unfortunately encounter our flooding), or during the next day or subsequent days. It is in this context that we will have to consider what kinds of things we might be able to do to handle conflict situations effectively. We will start by considering some of the different ways people respond when they are perceiving conflict.

What All of This Means

Now that we have a sense of how conflict affects us, we can consider a number of important implications, all of which are worth keeping in mind when we consider how we might handle problematic conflict situations.

First, the stronger a person's emotional reaction is to conflict, the less we should expect to be able to reason with him or her (or to be able to think rationally ourselves). If highly emotional, the person will not hear the specifics of what we are trying to say, and his or her responses will be informed more by emotion than thought. The person is focused on a threat (us) and saving face (minimizing the threat), not on thoughtfully sorting out the issue. At this point, the issue is far overshadowed by the personal issues between the people involved in the conflict. This suggests that, until the person calms down enough to participate in some kind of discussion, it is useless to try to reason with him or her.

Second, even when we might be able to reason with the person, there is another potential problem: the **assumptions** we are making about each other, and each other's intentions. More specifically, we are at risk for making damaging attributions of each other's behavior. Negative attributions can be an important barrier to making progress, because they lead us to assume that others intentionally are trying to make our lives miserable. They may be doing just that, but if we think of times when we've been in conflict with others, there likely are many times when someone was angry with us even though we had no intention of upsetting them. Conversely, there will be many times when we are angry at others who had no intention of upsetting us. However, all of this is hard to remember when perceiving conflict, thanks to our reduced capacity to think clearly and carefully, and our intense focus on the threat posed by our conflict "opponent." Therefore, this attribution pattern is an additional hurdle we must overcome when trying to handle conflict situations.

Third, people respond differently when perceiving conflict, and it is quite likely that each of us has a typical response or "**script**" we follow in these situations (Abelson, 1981). Scripts are patterns of behavior that we are likely to follow in different situations. For example, most people follow a similar script when greeting someone, when ordering at a restaurant, or when we accidentally bump into someone. As we begin to explore ways of constructively navigating conflict situations, it is worth considering the strengths and weaknesses of our current conflict scripts. The ideas presented later in this chapter may be able to help us improve our scripts.

Fourth, our actions during a conflict episode are **not independent,** they are influenced by the actions of the other people in the episode. In turn, we affect their behavior. In other words, participants in conflicts are interdependent, and mutually influence each other. Although it might be discomforting to realize that we can be influenced by the other participants, it is helpful to know that we also can influence their behavior. Below we will examine a number of things we might be able to do in conflict situations to move them toward constructive outcomes.

Handling Conflict Situations More Effectively: Prevent, Depart, Distract, or Defuse

In this section I outline some things we might be able to do to handle conflict situations more effectively. But please note that these are things that *might* be helpful. It is impossible to create a one-size-fits-all approach that will work in every conflict situation. Situations will vary in a number of ways, and, therefore may require different approaches. The symptoms of conflict outlined above may vary in their intensity and in the scripts a person follows in response to them. Our relationship with the person who angered us may vary. The person may be a friend, someone we dislike, or a stranger such as a customer. Our probable future relationship with the person may vary. We may be with the person long-term, or never again. The people who anger us may differ in personality. The settings in which we experience conflict may vary in a number of ways, in terms of whether it's formal/informal, the amount of people around, our relationship with the people who are around, whether we have to stay put, or whether we can leave the area. Because differences in these areas will inform our judgment, it is difficult to outline one approach that will work perfectly. Instead, it is far more important to capture the attitude with which these ideas are offered. If we *adopt an attitude of learning the other person's perspective and of problem solving (rather than winning or blaming), then we will be in a better position to navigate the conflict constructively,* without necessarily having to memorize a one-size-fits-all set of steps. As the following ideas are discussed, the importance of these learning and problem-solving attitudes will be emphasized.

Below are some general ideas that can be applied to situations in which we want to have a positive outcome, yet without sacrificing our own needs. These ideas are offered with the assumption that we want to have a reasonably constructive outcome to our conflict. In situations in which a constructive outcome is not desired or necessary, many additional options would be available to us.

Table 11.2 Handling Conflict Situations

Prevent	• Establish good relationships with others.
	• Address problems early on before they grow and cause anger and resentment.
Depart	• Constructively leave the scene.
	• "I know we need to talk about this, but now is not the best time. I will be available _____."
Distract	• Disrupt the anger process by shifting others' attention elsewhere.
	• "Do you smell something burning?" "Do you hear a baby crying?" (These may sound crazy, but they sometimes really are taught to law enforcement officials to use when handling domestic dispute situations.)
Defuse	• Stay calm, listen, let them talk, acknowledge their legitimate points or perspective, etc., until they have calmed down and you have learned what is bothering them. Then once they are able to actually process what you are saying, respond.

Prevent

Before we explore how we can respond to the conflict symptoms mentioned above, it would be in our best interests to consider how we might **prevent** these situations from happening, or at least to prevent them from happening with such intensity. This is not to suggest that we can avoid all conflict, but rather that it is in our best interest to do what we can to minimize conflict in our workplace.

One solution is to **establish good working relationships** with our colleagues. This sounds obvious, yet workplaces are full of poor relationships. Relationships are discussed more completely in Chapter 6 and are at the core of many of the concepts being discussed in additional chapters, but in this chapter we will focus on the role that good working relationships can play when it comes to conflict in the workplace. Korsgaard, Brodt, and Whitener (2002) found that when employees trust their managers, they are less likely to make an attribution that those managers are personally responsible for problems. In addition, when a likeable coworker does something that bothers coworkers, coworkers are more likely to forgive the person and less likely to seek revenge (Bradfield & Aquino, 1999). And according to Richmond and McCroskey (2009), the amount of liking we have for another person helps determine how much we can disagree with that person before perceiving ourselves to be in conflict with the person. Collectively, the research points to a number of ways in which good working relationships can help us minimize the occurrence, severity, and damage of conflicts in our workplace. However, there will be times when we have to disagree with or confront people we like, and these confrontations (or avoidance of them) can lead us to conflict, in spite of our best intentions.

Given the emotional reaction we have to conflict, and the ways in which it makes it difficult for us to have a thoughtful conversation about a legitimate problem, whenever possible, it would be ideal for us to **address problems with others before** they reach a conflict stage. This is easier said than done, because people often are resistant to confronting others (Stone et al., 2000). Still, it is worthwhile to consider the process of confronting others we explored in the previous chapter.

Unfortunately, there are many times when we cannot prevent or avoid conflict. In this section we will examine three ways to handle conflict situations once they erupt. They represent a variety of approaches that should enable us to be flexible in handling conflicts.

Depart

If we have not been able to avoid a conflict situation, then we either have to calm the person down or revisit the issue at a time when the involved parties are calm enough to discuss the issue. There are a number of benefits to leaving the scene. First, it gives us time to reduce our physiological arousal levels (as long as we don't keep the experience going by ruminating), so that we can discuss an issue more thoughtfully after we've calmed down (Gottman, 1993). Second, it reduces the likelihood that we will say something we will regret, which would make it much more difficult to handle the situation. Third, it buys time for us to think about how we want to approach the issue. If we are caught off guard with the conflict situation, leaving the scene will enable us to think through what happened once we calm down.

It also is important to consider how we should (and should not) leave a scene, as there could be some important disadvantages to leaving the scene in problematic ways. If we are abrupt or communicate indifference, apathy, or anger or frustration, we may make the other person much more angry. Instead, we should depart with comments that demonstrate our interest in addressing the issue and help the other person save face, such as: "This is important and we need to discuss it, but first I think it would be good for us to take some time on our own to cool down." "Right now I'm upset, so I'd like to take some time to cool off so that I can give you my complete attention." "I'm not able to discuss this now, but can we set aside some time to talk about this?" "This clearly is important and deserves more time than I'm able to give it right now. Can we set aside a time to talk about it?" The specifics of these comments are less important than the attitude of sincerely wanting to hear the other person out when the time is right.

Although leaving the scene has its advantages, many times it simply will not be possible to do this. We usually cannot just leave a meeting, or leave work. We usually can't just walk away from a customer. A flight attendant is stuck at the scene. While leaving the scene is good for many situations, at many other times we will have to remain at the scene and deal with a situation. For those situations, we have two additional types of choices: distract or defuse.

Distract

Earlier we discussed the way in which a threat causes emotional excitation, which then takes time to dissipate. We also examined the ways in which rumination can prevent that dissipation of excitation. However, if we can be sufficiently distracted, this excitation will subside more quickly (Zillman, 1988). For this to happen, it is important that the messages we encounter that might distract us are not related in any way to the event that provoked us or the emotion we are experiencing. According to Zillman (1988), there are important practical implications of this: "If experiences of annoyance and anger, and along with them the propensity for hostile and violent behaviors, are to be defused by reducing their intensity and by keeping them short, the cognitive looping that perpetuates such experiences needs to be disrupted" (p. 58). If someone can be distracted from ruminating on the event that triggered his or her anger, the anger will dissipate more quickly. Notice also that this will help reduce the likelihood of flooding. If we are the angry person, this means that we should distract ourselves with stimuli or tasks that do not remind us of our anger or of the event that provoked it.

However, distracting a person who is angry at us can be more complicated, because if we respond in a distracting way, we may be perceived as ignoring the issue and therefore run the risk of triggering greater amounts of anger. Therefore, the following ideas for using distraction are presented with some caution. It is clear that they can work, but they have not been studied systematically, so they should be considered interesting possibilities rather than reliable methods worth following.

Many ideas on distraction come from anecdotal cases. Thompson (2004) shared an interesting example of distraction that he witnessed while working as a police officer. His partner was very adept at handling conflict situations. One night the two responded to a domestic dispute in the middle of the night. When they arrived a couple was screaming at each other. While Thompson began speaking with them, his partner calmly walked by them, sat on their sofa, opened the classified section of their newspaper, and began to call someone who had placed an ad for a motorcycle. By the time he was dialing the phone, the couple had stopped yelling and were looking at him with some confusion. When his phone call ended abruptly (it was the middle of the night), he sounded puzzled about why the person on the phone was rude to him. Then, in possession of the husband and wife's full attention, he proceeded to explain to them that he hoped everyone could work through their issues in a civil way. The husband and wife calmly agreed to work things out, and the officers left without incident. The officer had successfully used distraction to break the conflict cycle.

Thompson (2004) suggests that we can use brief phrases in conflict situations to create enough distraction to disrupt someone's anger responses. He provides examples such as saying "Whoa" in a surprised manner, in order to break up the flow of the interaction. Recently after I taught about using distraction during conflict situations, a student returned to class with a story of how he used distraction to change the dynamic of a tense situation. After his roommate was highly angry following a phone call with his girlfriend, my student asked perfectly reasonable questions, but he whispered them! In a soft voice he asked "What's wrong?" and similar questions. After briefly doing this, his roommate actually began talking to him in a soft voice, whispering something like "I'm angry at my girlfriend." By whispering, my student used distraction to bring calm to the situation. All of these examples suggest that there may be merit to carefully using distraction as a strategy during conflict. However, these are anecdotal at best, and until systematic studies examine the use of distraction during conflict situations, strategies like these should be used with caution.

Given the potential problems associated with leaving the scene and using distraction during conflict, it is important that we consider ways we might be able to more completely defuse conflict.

Defuse

If we can or should not leave the scene or use distraction, we can do some of the following things to defuse the conflict situation. These suggestions are presented in an important order, and unless the situation prohibits it, it is ideal to do the first two steps before the rest, for reasons that are explained below. The goal of these steps is to bring the tone and intensity of the interaction to a point at which the disagreement and negotiation skills discussed in the previous chapter again will be useful to us. There may be times when this is not a goal, but to the extent you want the interaction to return to civility, the following steps often will be helpful.

Win the Battle to Stay Calm. The early stage in a conflict is a critical period, as a lot is happening. Because we either are caught by surprise or have been anticipating an emotional interaction, we will be experiencing the first onset of physiological arousal. This means we will be at risk for doing or saying something regrettable, catching the other person's emotions, and so on. However, if we want to take control of the interaction, this critical period also represents an opportunity for us, one I actually learned about while playing tennis.

When I was growing up, John McEnroe was one of the most famous tennis players on the tour. For impressionable young tennis players, his behavior on the court made it seem like angry outbursts are good for one's game. However, while anger sometimes worked for him, it usually doesn't work for most players. During this time I learned something interesting. If I could stay calm after making mistakes, while opponents "went ballistic" or "pulled a McEnroe" after making their mistakes, I would have an advantage. While they were focused on anger, I was able to maintain my focus on each point.

A similar thing happens during conflict. If we can stay calmer than the other person, we have an advantage for several reasons. First, we may **avoid "catching"** the other person's intense emotions. In fact, we may even have begun the process by which we have helped the person's anger subside by enabling him or her to "catch" our calmness. Second, we **avoid doing/saying** anything we will regret. Third, we can **buy a little time** to listen to the other person and consider how we want to respond. Fourth, it puts us in a better position to **take control** of the interaction and direct it toward a constructive outcome. Fifth, for those of us who aren't likely to be in the mood to remain calm, we can think of **staying calm as a victory** over the other person. We outlasted the person, and while he or she are going crazy, we are in control. It might be a small victory, but if we are going to approach these situations like a battle, then the battle should be to remain calmer than the other person!

This step is not meant to suggest that we should avoid all emotion, as that is impossible. But to the extent that we can remain calmer than the other person, we will have some advantage in the interaction, and when the time is right we still will be free to express our feelings. I recognize that staying calm is a tough goal to achieve when we are angry and frustrated, but if we channel that frustration and resolve and think of it as winning a battle to stay calm, we can make some of our angst work to our benefit!

Although I've made a case for staying calmer than the other person, I haven't offered much advice on how to do it. Thompson (2004) does offer advice on this subject though. He is a former police officer who now trains police officers and other professionals (such as flight attendants) on how to defuse conflict situations. He outlines much of his approach in his book *Verbal Judo,* and although the title of his book might not inspire confidence in his ideas, his suggestions reflect an understanding of the emotional realities of conflict, and his ideas have helped a significant number of professionals whose jobs depend on staying calm in the face of angry people (police officers, flight attendants, etc.). Therefore, I will outline a few of his key ideas. First, he discusses the importance of **not interrupting** or of saying the first thoughts that come to mind when the conflict starts. Given our likely emotional state, and impaired ability to think and talk clearly and thoughtfully, it makes sense that we would want to hold off on saying the first thing that comes to mind. But what do we do when the other person says the first rude or cruel thing that comes to mind? Thompson suggests that when this happens we should not focus on the specific things being said literally. Remember, those comments probably are not informed by careful thought. Instead, we should interpret those comments as "I'm frustrated and I want you to hear what I have to say!" Although it can be hard to overlook the specific and hurtful things someone might say to us while, as

Thompson puts it, he or she is "under the influence" of anger, it is not a stretch to think that a message of frustration and wanting to be heard is at the root of an angry person's comments. Our willingness to hear angry comments in this light can be a key step to helping us stay calmer than the other person. If we stay focused on the global idea that a person is frustrated, we can focus more on problem solving than retaliating for a specific comment someone said when he or she was "under the influence" of anger.

The idea of having a **problem-solving attitude** also is an important part of staying calm, as not all versions of "calm" are equally good in conflict situations. If we are too calm and detached, we may appear to be apathetic, indifferent, or uninterested in what the other person has to say. If this happens at the same time the angry person wants to be heard, then our calmness could make the person more angry. Thompson suggests that during this time we should be nonverbally calm and project empathy. But given our earlier discussion of nonverbal behavior, rather than focusing on behaviors, expressions, or gestures to emulate, we should focus more on **attitudes** that can convey the appropriate amount of empathy and calmness. To do this we should consider the advice of Stone et al. (2000), who suggest that we should adopt a problem-solving attitude and be genuinely curious to learn the other person's perspective (they refer to it as the other person's "story" of the situation).

To consider this advice, think about what it would be like to approach a conflict situation with one of three very different attitudes. First, we try to win the altercation. We will do this by trying to answer whatever angry thing the person said, be louder than the person, and making sure that we win by assigning blame to the person. Second, you could have an attitude of remaining extremely calm. Our focus on being composed would result in our barely engaging the other person. By adopting the first attitude, you may "overpower" the other person and get your point across that he or she deserves blame. However, even if you get a public agreement from the person, you have done little to preserve a good working relationship with him or her (remember that this is one of our goals). More likely, you've helped ensure that her or she will resent you. He or she probably will regret letting you push him or her around. This person soon will be looking forward to "winning" the next altercation with you. It will be hard for you to trust each other and to work with each other. Solution two avoids much of this problem, but because it is indifferent to the other person's concerns, it is likely to do little to alleviate the person's anger. In fact, in order to get your attention to the person's concerns, this approach may make the person try even harder, and therefore intensify his or her anger (remember the demand-withdrawal pattern discussed earlier). Again, little has been done to move the situation toward a productive or constructive outcome. For a third approach, what if we approached the situation with some sincere curiosity and the intent to learn what is bothering the person, and on what can be done to solve the problem? With little effort on our part to manufacture the "correct" nonverbal behavior, we are likely to naturally project less defensiveness, and instead an openness to hearing what the other person has to say. This does not mean we have to agree with the person, but if we can begin the interaction with this kind of tone, we can make the first step toward a healthy outcome.

Still, beginning the interaction with empathy and a curious learning stance is only the first step. We will need to move the interaction to the point at which we can discuss the issue thoughtfully. To get to that point, we likely will have to let the other person say what's on his or her mind. That brings us to the next step.

Hear the Other Person Out. If a person is angry and intent on making sure we hear what he or she has to say, we are unlikely to make constructive progress with the interaction unless we let the person say whatever he or she has to say (this assumes it is not an emergency situation and that we can afford to hear the person out). Consider this from your point of view. When you are angry and venting to another person, do you want to be (1) interrupted, (2) blamed, or (3) argued with? I assume you want the person to sincerely hear what you have to say, and that if you are interrupted, blamed, or face a quick counterargument, you are not likely to be persuaded. There's little reason to think that these approaches would work any better with someone else. Therefore, I would advise **hearing the other person out** until everyone is calm enough to permit a "conversational opening," or a time in the conversation when everyone is calm enough to permit a reasonable, issue-focused discussion. This advice is consistent to that given by Thompson (2004), who suggests that it is important to make sure that the other person feels as though his or her concerns have been heard.

Although it is good to let the other person talk, it can be awkward to just sit or stand there in total silence, so what should we be doing while the other person is venting? First, remember the curious and learning attitudes mentioned above. Those should continue to characterize your demeanor throughout the entire interaction. In addition, according to many experts, there is one kind of message that is good to convey during this stage of the interaction: an attempt to understand the other person clearly. Thompson (2004) goes as far as to say that the only acceptable interruption is to say (in a calm tone), "Let me be sure I understand you clearly." Remember that, according to Stone et al. (2000), we should approach all of this with a sincerely curious learning attitude. Our goal should be to learn the other person's perspective. This explains why our initial participation in the conflict should involve sincerely asking questions to uncover the other person's "story." This does not mean we have to like or accept it, but simply reflects the reality that we won't make much constructive progress until we hear the other person out. The mechanics of actually doing this matter less than the attitude with which you approach the other person. Once we have a sincere interest in learning the other person's "story," we will be in a position to benefit from the use of three skills outlined by Stone et al. (2000): **Inquiry, Paraphrasing,** and **Acknowledgment.**

The point of inquiry is to learn the other person's perspective until it at least makes sense to us. We do not have to agree with the "story," but should understand it before trying to offer our own. Therefore, we should avoid questions that essentially "cross-examine" the other person, and instead use open-ended questions that are aimed at clarifying the situation. As each of these types of questions is discussed, imagine what it would be like to be questioned in that way, and also what kind of attitude is conveyed by each. Leading questions that cross-examine are not aimed at learning or clarifying: "But wasn't it really your fault?" "Don't you think that you should have handled the situation differently?" These questions will not help defuse a tense situation or truly "clear the air." Closed-ended questions (those that require the respondent to choose one of two or three answers) also should be avoided: "Do you think we should do _____ or _____?" Instead, we should favor open-ended questions, as they are more flexible and will permit a wider range of responses: "What are your thoughts on what we should do from here?" Once we have begun asking open-ended questions, we are on our way to understanding the other person's "story." Even if his or her initial answers aren't helpful and leave us confused, we can continue to ask for clarification using open-ended questions. These can be as simple as asking: "Could you explain a bit more what you mean?" "How did you feel when _____ happened?" "Could you help me understand a bit more what you mean, I'm still unclear about _____?" When delivered with an appropriate learning attitude and tone, questions like these make it clear that you are listening, and they give you information that will help you respond to the other person's concerns. These questions are useful because we can continue to use them constructively until the other person's story makes sense to us.

According to many experts on conflict, once we feel that we have heard what the other person has to say, it is important to verify our understanding by paraphrasing what the person has said (Stone et al., 2000; Thompson, 2004). Paraphrasing is when you "express to the other person, in your own words, your understanding of what they are saying" (Stone et al., 2000, p. 178). Paraphrasing provides direct evidence to the other person that we have made an attempt to hear his or her concerns, and it allows us to proceed with confidence that we have understood the other person. We can do this by briefly summarizing what we are hearing from the other person: "So it's frustrating you when I _____?" "For you the main issue seems to be _____?" If we are wrong, we always can ask additional open-ended questions for clarification. And if we are correct, then we are making progress.

Once we've asked questions and paraphrased, it is important that we acknowledge the other person's feelings before moving on to "fix" the problem. This step may not seem necessary, but let's briefly consider the effort it will have taken to get to this point in the conversation. We've managed to stay calm in the face of the other person's anger, we've resisted "catching" the person's anger, and we've bitten our tongue to hear the person out, ask questions, and to learn and paraphrase his or her story. All of this was necessary because the situation had reached a point when the person's anger was so intense that we could not reason with him or her. In other words, much of this has been about the other person's intense feelings, and their intensity. If we now proceed without having acknowledged those feelings, we will have missed much of the point. To acknowledge feelings, we just reflect the person's feelings back to him or her: "I can see how you would be so upset about this"; "It's frustrating when _____"; "You seem to feel really upset about _____." These reflections of feelings may seem obvious and overly simplified, but to the person who is feeling them, the validation will matter a great deal. If you try using phrases like these the next time you're in the presence of someone who is highly emotional (even if it's not a conflict situation), chances are the person will appreciate your acknowledgment of how he or she is feeling. It is important to point out that acknowledging another person's feelings does not mean that we are agreeing with the person or surrendering our own concerns or point of view. Instead, we are taking control of the interaction and helping create a conversational setting within which our concerns are more likely to be heard and considered.

Is All of This Really Necessary? Some of my favorite moments in the classroom are when students thoughtfully take issue with something I am covering, and it often happens when I am covering some of these ways of defusing conflict situations. Their concerns often reflect popular attitudes about standing up for ourselves, and not backing down from others (especially after someone has "crossed" us publicly). They advocate for a more direct approach of asserting ourselves until the other person backs down. As I've acknowledged earlier in this chapter, there are times when this approach might work. We might have higher status than the other person, or the other person's conflict style is less aggressive or self-concerned. Or, we may not care about the long-term consequences of the interaction. Finally, we may be in an emergency situation, and only have aggressiveness as an option. In each of these cases, a highly direct and intense approach might work well. But if we are faced with a very angry person, we cannot leave the scene, we have time available to us, and we want or need to achieve a constructive outcome, it is important for us to appreciate the reality of dealing with someone who is physiologically "under the influence" of anger. The other person is not likely to hear what we have to say until he or she calms down and is able to thoughtfully consider our concerns. If we argue before the other person is ready to hear us, we will have wasted our time and breath. It is with this reality in mind that the steps of defusing conflict have been offered.

How to Proceed Once the Anger Has Been Defused

Once we are at a point to share our issues and concerns, we can return to the principles of disagreement and negotiation that were outlined in the previous chapter. Along the way, we should remember what we have learned from this process of handling conflict. We should adopt a **learning and problem-solving attitude,** and hear the other person out and allow the person to save face, while still asserting our own perspective on the situation. To the extent that the other person is willing to participate in this kind of dialogue, we will have averted a potentially disastrous situation and maximized our chances for a successful and constructive outcome.

References

Abelson, R. (1981). Psychological status of the script concept. *American Psychologist, 36,* 715–729.

Bradfield, M., & Aquino, K. (1999). The effects of blame attributions and offender likableness on forgiveness and revenge in the workplace. *Journal of Management, 25,* 607–631.

Canary, D. J. (2003). Managing interpersonal conflict: A model of events related to strategic choices. In J. Green & B. Burleson (Eds.), *Handbook of communication and social interaction skills* (pp. 515–549). Mahwah, NJ: Lawrence Erlbaum.

Cannon, W. B. (1929). *Bodily changes in pain, hunger, fear and rage: An account of researches into the function of emotional excitement* (2nd ed.). New York, NY: Appleton-Century-Crofts.

Cissna, K. N. L., & Sieburg, E. (1995). Patterns of interactional confirmation and disconfirmation. In M. V. Redmond (Ed.), *Interpersonal communication: Readings in theory and research* (pp. 301–318). Orlando, FL: Harcourt Brace.

Cosmides, L., & Tooby, J. (2000). Evolutionary psychology and the emotions. In M. Lewis & J. M. Haviland-Jones (Eds.), *Handbook of emotions* (pp. 91–115). New York, NY: Guilford Press.

Cupach, W. R., & Canary, D. J. (2000). *Competence in interpersonal conflict.* Long Grove, IL: Waveland.

Fincham, F. D., Bradbury, T. N., and Scott, C. K. (1990). Cognition in marriage. In F. D. Fincham & T. N. Bradbury (Eds.), *The psychology of marriage: Basic issues and applications* (pp. 118–149). New York, NY: Guilford Press.

Fincham, F. D., Harold, G. T., & Gano-Phillips, S. (2000). The longitudinal association between attributions and marital satisfaction: Direction of effects and role of efficacy expectations. *Journal of Family Psychology, 14,* 267–285.

Folger, J. P., Scott Poole, M., & Stutman, R. K. (2005). *Working through conflict: Strategies for relationships, groups, and organizations* (5th ed.). Boston, MA: Pearson.

Goffman, E. (1955). On facework: An analysis of ritual elements in social interaction. *Psychiatry, 18,* 213–231.

Gottman, J. M. (1993). A theory of marital dissolution and stability. *Journal of Family Psychology, 7,* 57–75.

Hatfield, E., Cacioppo, J. T., & Rapson, R. L. (1994). *Emotional contagion.* New York, NY: Cambridge University Press.

Heider, F. (1958). *The psychology of interpersonal relations.* New York, NY: Wiley.

Korsgaard, M. A., Brodt, S. E., and Whitener, E. M. (2002). Trust in the face of conflict: The role of managerial trustworthy behavior and organizational context. *Journal of Applied Psychology, 87,* 312–319.

Richmond, V. P., & McCroskey, J. C. (2009). *Organizational communication for survival: Making work work* (4th ed.). Boston, MA: Allyn & Bacon.

Schachter, S., & Singer, J. E. (1962). Cognitive, social, and physiological determinants of emotional state. *Psychological Review, 69,* 379–399.

Seligman, M. E. (2006). *Learned optimism: How to change your mind and your life.* New York, NY: Random House.

Stone, D., Patton, B., & Heen, S. (2000). *Difficult conversations: How to discuss what matters most.* New York, NY: Penguin.

Thompson, G. (2004). *Verbal judo: The gentle art of persuasion.* New York, NY: HarperCollins.

Zillman, D. (1979). *Hostility and aggression.* Hillsdale, NJ: Erlbaum.

Zillman, D. (1988). Cognition-excitation interdependencies in aggressive behavior. *Aggressive Behavior, 14*(1), 51–64.

Zillman, D. (1990). The interplay of cognition and excitation in aggravated conflict among intimates. In D. D. Cahn (Ed.), *Intimates in conflict: A communication perspective* (pp. 187–208). Hillsdale, NJ: Erlbaum.

Chapter 12

Coaching and Being Coached

Think of something you do very well. You just get it, and can see what others miss. How would you go about teaching others to improve the skill? Or suppose you know someone else with such a skill. How should the person teach it to you? Or even if the person is not inclined to share it, how can you proactively learn it from him or her? With some skills, you might not care, but what if it's a seasoned coworker and you don't want to undergo ten years of mistakes to learn what she already knows about how to handle certain sales situations, management situations, or how to perform a task better than others? How could you learn from her?

This chapter explores these issues by examining the process of **coaching**. Before I go any further though, I have to explain what I mean by coaching, as the term is used in different ways throughout the literature. My treatment of coaching will focus on how coworkers can teach and learn from each other in one-on-one settings (or maybe with another couple of people present, but not large groups). I am not talking about executive coaching, in which an expert consultant helps an executive improve his or her skills. This is legitimate coaching, and executives could benefit from much of what I'm discussing throughout this book, but I don't presume that my readers are executives or that you are in a position to coach executives (at least not yet). It is more likely that you will need to coach and be coached by peers who are at or near your level in the organization. I also am not talking about coaching someone with performance deficiencies, though this often is necessary. If you find yourself needing to explain to a coworker why it is important to show up on time for work, I recommend you read Fournies's (2000) book on coaching to improve workplace performance. Instead I will focus on how you can improve your performance by learning the kind of hard-to-teach intuition that your more seasoned coworkers possess, so that you can develop your skills at a pace greater than experience typically allows.

For an example of the kind of intuitive skills I have in mind, consider the following example provided by Klein (2003). Darlene and Linda were nurses on a neonatal intensive care unit, which cared for babies who were born prematurely. These babies are high-maintenance, in that they have not developed more fully, and therefore are more at risk for various complications. Linda was a good and experienced nurse, but she was new to the neonatal unit. Darlene had spent six years on the NICU and was very experienced with babies. She handled the stress of the unit well. She was in charge of training new nurses, and had been training Linda for two months. At this point, she primarily was monitoring Linda, as less hands-on instruction was needed.

One evening, Linda was caring for an infant girl, "Melissa." Although Melissa was on the unit, she was not a highly complex case, and she had been steadily showing improvement. It was near the end of Linda's (and Darlene's shift), and at various times, Linda noticed a few symptoms with Melissa, though all still were within what could be considered as normal. Melissa was a little more tired than usual, but it was late at night, so this was normal. Her temperature was a little low, but still within normal range, so Linda increased the temperature of her isolette. She increased the temperature a couple of more times throughout the night when Melissa's temperature fell a bit more (though it still was within normal range). Babies on the unit often get blood tests via small heel sticks, and Linda noticed that Melissa was still bleeding a bit from hers. This isn't normal, but Linda assumed the heel stick may have been more messy than usual.

Then, according to Klein:

> But when Darlene walked past Melissa's isolette near the end of the shift, some-thing caught her eye. Something about the baby "just looked funny," as she later put it. Nothing major, nothing obvious, but to her the baby "didn't look good." Darlene had a closer look, now noticing specific details. She noticed the heel stick had not stopped bleeding. To Darlene, Melissa seemed a little "off color" and "mottled," and her belly seemed a little rounded. She noticed this even though every baby had a different complexion and body shape and Darlene was not particularly familiar with Melissa's normal state. A quick physical exam confirmed that Melissa still had an unusual amount of residual food in her stomach, causing bloating. Darlene checked Melissa's chart and noticed that the baby's temperature had dropped consistently over the shift. She called Linda over and asked her if the baby had seemed lethargic during the shift. When Linda replied, "yes," Darlene immediately raced to the phone and woke the duty physician.
>
> "We've got a baby in big trouble," she said. She explained the symptoms. The physician agreed with Darlene's assessment of a baby in crisis and immediately ordered antibiotics and a blood culture. Twenty-four hours later, the blood culture confirmed sepsis. If they had delayed giving the antibiotic until they had the results of the blood culture it probably would have been too late.
>
> (p. 16)

In this case, Linda and Darlene saw the same symptoms. As Klein (2003) notes: "Ultimately it was not so much the individual symptoms that were key, but a par-ticular constellation of symptoms. Linda could see all the signs, but she was unable to piece them together into a story that revealed the larger pattern" (p. 18). This is because Linda and Darlene were relying upon different kinds of knowledge. Linda was using *explicit knowledge,* or information she had learned in her training (appro-priate temperature range, how to handle lower body temperature, the normal range of fatigue for babies, normal color for babies, etc.). But Darlene was taking these same symptoms and noticing a much more sophisticated pattern, one that she learned from years of experience, not formal teaching. Darlene was using *tacit knowledge,* or the kind of intuition that enabled her to act, even though it would be difficult to explain to others how she fit the symptoms into a larger pattern. This tacit knowledge is what helped Darlene see what Linda was missing. Unfortunately, it's very hard to explain to others.

For a less dramatic example of tacit knowledge that we all possess, consider the act of walking through a parking lot, in terms of when we should stop and wait for cars, and when we should keep walking. Having two young children, I'm routinely confronted with their lack of tacit knowledge on this issue, and how difficult it is to share tacit knowledge. We tell children how to do this in a very by-the-book manner. Stop, look both ways, then cross. But adults often break these rules. We may stop some times but not others, and look sometimes, but not others. We may stop when no cars are coming, because we see someone in a car that might pull out. This is because of the tacit knowledge and intuition that adults have when walking through the parking lot. We *just* know when we need to pay greater attention, and when it is safe to cross. But notice that we don't rely on a formula to cross only when cars are a certain distance from us. Instead, we intuitively assess the car's distance and speed in determining whether to cross. We know what to listen for, how to look for tail lights that may signal someone is backing out, to look to see if someone is in the driver's seat, looking to back out. We also know to listen for different key sounds. If you want to appreciate your tacit knowledge on this issue, just try explaining these things to a small child. If you tell a child to stop and look both ways, he will stop and avoid crossing even if the nearest car is 100 yards away and moving slowly (to a child, this makes sense, because after all, he sees a car coming his way). Now try to explain how you determine at what distance and car speed it is safe to cross, at a level the child can understand. If you waited for one car, but later crossed when another car was at the same distance, why? And if speed is the reason, then how slow should a car be going before it is safe to cross? What is too fast or too close? Then explain why you will walk past one driver who is pulling out, but wait for another to pull out. Not easy, is it?

We encounter this exact same communication challenge in our workplace all of the time. Seasoned veterans know when to break the rules and when to follow them. Their performance is more efficient and effective (notice how quickly Darlene acted in the example above). The trick is to figure out how, as newer employees, we can learn this intuition from our coworkers without having to spend the years it typically takes to accumulate it. And once we develop this intuition, it is worthwhile to know how to help others develop it. Imagine the kinds of advantages you would have in your workplace if you could accelerate your learning of important job-related intuition, and share what you've learned with others. We will focus on these challenges in this chapter. To begin this process, we first will examine important characteristics of experts. What separates them from nonexperts?

How Experts See What Others Miss

Klein (1998) outlines a number of dimensions of expertise that help explain why experts see things that others miss. Although he offers a list of eight dimensions, I've grouped them into three general categories: *patterns, mental models,* and *action scripts and procedures.* As I cover each, I'll use examples from my teaching

Table 12.1 Things Experts See That the Rest of Us Miss

Patterns	• *Patterns:* They see how actions fit into a bigger pattern.
	• *Anomalies:* They notice when something is "off."
Mental Models	• *The Big Picture:* They see how all of the pieces fit together.
	• *Opportunities and Improvisations:* They can size up situations and identify possible courses of action more easily.
	• *Fine Discriminations:* They notice small details that can be very meaningful.
	• *They Know and Manage Their Limitations:* They made many mistakes on the way to becoming experts, so they've learned a lot about their abilities, and where they still are lacking.
Action Scripts and Procedures	• *The Way Things Work:* They can perform even complex tasks more effectively and efficiently than novices.
	• *The Past and the Future:* They have a good sense of how things will unfold in the future (with respect to their area of expertise, not the future in general) based on what they currently are seeing.

experience about things I might notice that a newer teacher may miss. It is not meant to brag or to suggest that I am an expert. But after 15 years of teaching, I should be able to notice a few things a first-year teacher would not notice. As I go through each of these, think of an area in which you may have some expertise, and notice how you can see these things that others miss (see Table 12.1).

Patterns

Experts are good at noticing both *patterns* and *anomalies.* In regard to patterns, experts are able to put different pieces of information together and see how they fit into a bigger pattern (as Darlene did in the earlier example). When teaching, I've gotten better at recognizing when a discussion is leading somewhere productive and when it is not. This helps me adjust my approach accordingly to keep a productive discussion going or redirect a less productive one. Earlier in my career I was less able to assess the flow of discussions—I was just happy students were talking! For another example, I'll mention that early in my career I used to get very frustrated with my students a few weeks into the semester (around October or March, depending on the semester). They would be far less responsive and it was harder to engage them, and that would annoy me. Eventually I learned that this was because it was right before mid-terms and they had to deal with a higher concentration of assignments and tests across various courses. Now I notice ebbs and flows in various student behaviors that occur throughout the semester. I don't excuse it and cancel class sessions, but at least I understand it better and can adjust without getting angry with students.

Experts also are good at noticing *anomalies,* or when something is "off" about a pattern. Because experts are good at developing reliable expectancies regarding what will happen, they are good at noticing when something expected does not happen. For example, there are various times when teaching that I notice students are not asking questions about things that normally generate questions. This cues me to stop and invite questions, and I usually receive the kinds of questions that I'm expecting. I learned to do this because in the past I found that students would struggle with certain types of material or assignments if certain questions were not addressed up front. It is natural to struggle with some things, so I tend to notice when students are not struggling. In the earlier example, Darlene noticed several anomalies with respect to Melissa's condition and appearance.

Mental Models

Mental models are "the stories we construct to understand how things work" (Klein, 2009). They represent the way we organize information, and when we need to perform certain tasks, we consult our mental models. When I was giving the parking lot example above, I consulted my mental model of the process of safely navigating a parking lot. I would not be surprised if you briefly consulted your own mental model on the process when reading the example. Klein (1998) outlines a number of characteristics of expertise that are related to mental models.

First, experts are aware of the *big picture*. When I first began teaching, I was focused on making it through one class session at a time. As I gained experience I developed a better sense of how the class sessions complement each other to build a coherent course, and eventually how they fit in with other courses in the curriculum. I also improved at seeing how my courses fit into my students' lives, in terms of preparing students for things they might encounter in the future. So compared to when I first began teaching, I have a better sense of a bigger picture. As a result, I am less likely to become overwhelmed with all of the details that fill in that big picture. If a particular class session doesn't go well, it is less stressful than it was at the beginning of my career, because I recognize that I can compensate during the next class. Similarly, while it can be overwhelming to be a new employee, as we gain experience, we start to see how all of the pieces of the "picture" fit together, and we're better able to handle all of the information we encounter.

Thanks to their mental models, experts also are tuned in to *opportunities and improvisations* that novices are likely to miss. They can size up situations and recognize when they can improvise and take advantage of opportunities presented by those situations. During class discussions, students sometimes offer a comment that I know can lead to a very in-depth discussion, and I'll pursue it. I've also improved at improvising in other ways. Sometimes an initial explanation or example doesn't work well and students will ask for me to explain more clearly. Often this involves coming up with a new explanation or example on-the-fly. At other times, during class sessions I might think of activities (that weren't prepared before the class session) that can help students apply material. After years of practice of translating complex ideas into the language of my students, I've also found that the same kind of skill comes in handy when explaining complex ideas to my young children. But earlier in my career, each of these tasks was more challenging to me and typically involved a greater amount of mental struggle.

Experts also can make *fine discriminations* between things that novices are not able to make. Klein (1998) uses examples of how expert wine tasters can "tell one type of grape from another and even one year of wine from another" (p. 157). In the earlier example, Darlene was able to notice something that made Melissa different from a healthy baby. In my teaching I am fortunate to watch presentations by many students who communicate very well. However, in the last couple of years, while watching presentations by strong presenters, I've started noticing a difference between presenters who are "performing" and those who are being more authentic and genuine with their audience. Both might be good, but the authentic ones are better in ways that I didn't really notice a few years ago.

Experts also are able to *know and manage their limitations*. This makes sense, as the path to expertise is paved in part by the many mistakes we make along the way, provided we admit those mistakes to ourselves and try to improve. Many of the teaching abilities I've described have developed partially because of mistakes I've made in the classroom. As a result, I've learned that I'm stronger with some aspects of teaching than I am with others. I know that there are some good approaches or types of assignments or activities that work for other teachers but would not work for me. I have a better sense of when I will be able to grade things quickly and when it would take me longer (this helps me decide when to have assignments due). I'm sure I will learn of many more limitations throughout my career, but it helps that I've become aware of many along the way.

Action Scripts and Procedures

As we learned earlier in this book, scripts represent our sense of how various behaviors are performed. We have scripts for first meeting someone, for how we handle conflict situations, and so on. Much of this book has been aimed at helping you improve your scripts for certain behaviors. Expertise is characterized by a couple of dimensions that are related to scripts.

Experts have a well-developed sense of *"the way things work"* (Klein, 1998, p. 152). They know how to perform certain tasks and are able to perform them more effectively and efficiently than novices. During my teaching career I have developed a good sense for how to take material from books and articles and to make it "come to life" in a lesson plan. I have done it enough that I can plan for class sessions more efficiently, where it once took me a lot longer to think my way through the process. Notice how this involves being able to do some things more efficiently than in the past. You may have learned to do something in a step-by-step manner, but as you gained experience, you may have developed a more fluid way of doing things. If it's in the workplace, it may include deviations from procedure or even bad habits. You wouldn't teach a beginner to do it that way, but it works for you.

A final characteristic of experts is their sense of *the past and the future*. Experts are able to sense how things will proceed in the near future, and also understand past conditions that led to the present one. I don't have a great teaching example, but since I've played drums for 20+ years, I can offer a drumming example related to this. With much of the popular music I hear on the radio, I typically can tell what a drummer is going to play and when. I have a sense of when he or she will hit a cymbal, do a long fill, or stop the beat. This comes from listening to and playing a lot of music over the years. I didn't have the same sense when I first started playing. A more profound example concerns when we all probably have experienced a lack of this sense when dealing with physicians who are helping us with some health problem. To us, the health problem is immediate and profound, and since our knowledge typically is limited, it can be overwhelming. But a physician often is able to tell with confidence that we are healing normally, or know when we will start feeling better. With regard to the past, the same physician may have a good idea of how we developed the ailment. And recall from our earlier example the ways in which Darlene had a clear sense of what was going to happen to Melissa, based on what already had happened to her.

These elements of the tacit knowledge that experts possess help them make better decisions (in areas related to their expertise), and this advantage is particularly noticeable when there is time pressure to make a decision quickly (such as in emergency or chaotic situations). In other words, experts are better able to think quickly "on their feet." Notice though that expertise is not about knowing more (facts, information, etc.) but instead about knowing how to perceive the things. Therefore, expertise in areas related to our job performance likely would benefit most of us on our own jobs. But how many of us pay attention to the experts in our workplace and try to learn from them? Or as Klein (1998) frames it:

> In organizations, much of the knowledge is held within the heads of the workers and is never shared. This is tacit knowledge. In most organizations, the culture seems to ignore the expertise that already exists, to take it for granted. If a skilled worker retired after thirty years on the job and tried to leave with a favorite personal computer, some programs, or a set of tools, he or she would be stopped. The organization knows the value of the equipment. But the organization lets the worker walk out with all of that expertise, which is worth far more than some minor equipment, and never says a word, never even notices the loss. Yet in an organization, knowledge is a resource and should be treated as such.
>
> (p. 170)

With this in mind, we will examine how we can learn this expertise from others in our workplace, and how we can coach others once we develop our own expertise. But first we will examine specifically how we can develop expertise on our own.

What Does It Take to Become an Expert?

Those who study expertise have a high standard for defining someone as an expert, and suggest that two criteria must be met: (1) expertise must lead to performance that consistently is superior to that of one's peers, and (2) expertise must produce concrete results (Ericsson, Prietula, & Cokely, 2007). In other words, assessment of expertise is based on performance and outcomes, rather than reputation. An athlete must win, and an employee, manager, or CEO must produce tangible results. Those who study experts and how they develop have identified fairly consistent findings. In reference to this research, Ericsson et al. (2007) indicate that "consistently and overwhelmingly, the evidence showed that *experts are always made, not born*" (p. 116, emphasis added). Although many people attribute performance to innate talent, the research suggests otherwise. Although size and height sometimes may play a role (such as in sports), expertise is born out of hard work. So how much practice does it take to become a world-class musician, athlete, chess player, or manager? Researchers in the area tend to agree that it takes approximately ten years (or 10,000 hours) of the right kind of practice and training in order to become an expert (Ericsson et al., 2007).

Notice that I said the "right kind" of training. It is not enough to simply perform a behavior for 10,000 hours or ten years. Instead, the development of expertise requires what is known as ***deliberate practice*** (Ericsson et al., 2007). Deliberate practice involves sustained and focused attention on something we are trying to do better. It is different than repeating something we already do well and going through the motions. It involves trying to push ourselves into areas where we struggle, and then carefully monitoring the feedback we receive from doing so. Deliberate practice takes a great deal of concentration, as it involves careful consideration about why each part of a skill is performed a certain way. Although many hours of practice are needed, because of this intense concentration, it is difficult to practice at this level for more than a few hours at a time. For example, after performing a task and making mistakes, we may back up and consider how we could have performed the task differently.

For example, an employee who wanted to become a good supervisor may engage in a number of deliberate practice behaviors, even before she becomes a supervisor. She will make a note of how the current supervisor spends his time, how he handles his employees, and other details of the position. She will try to consider his perspective (the things he has to focus on, in terms of how they are different from her area of focus). When observing, she will consider things he does that work well, and things that don't work so well. She will consider how she might do things differently, and why. And she will continue this kind of detailed thinking when she becomes a supervisor. She will analyze incidents and try to identify why they went well or poorly. She will venture into areas of less comfort (maybe giving critical feedback to employees), and monitor her progress in the same way she did with other activities. Clearly, she will spend a great deal of time thinking about supervising others, trying to build her skills, and paying careful attention to feedback she receives. Gradually over time, her performance will improve. And if she continues with it long enough, she is likely to be a very effective supervisor. She is able to make this progress on her own, but what if she received some kind of instruction in how to be a supervisor? In the following section, we will consider different ways that employees might learn to improve their skills in the workplace.

How Might We Learn From Others in the Workplace?

Before discussing different ways people learn, it is important to distinguish between types of learning outcomes. We can distinguish between ***hard skills, soft skills***, and ***expert-level intuition***. Hard skills are technical skills that involve working with machinery, hardware, and so on. Learning to use a computer system, software, or to operate equipment all are examples of hard skills. Soft skills are social skills, and involve working with people. This might include customer service, leaning to give feedback, or the communication skills discussed throughout this book. We can apply expert level intuition with both hard and soft skills. Some mechanics may be able to diagnose certain engine problems just by listening to the engine run (hard skill), and some people communicate so effectively that they display great tact, and know just what to say in challenging situations (soft skills). These distinctions will help inform this section on ways of learning in the workplace.

Observation involves learning by watching others. We can learn hard or soft skills by watching others and trying something ourselves. This can be problematic, as we may not observe the right aspects of performance (we may pay more attention to trivial aspects of a skill and miss essential ones), and we may fail to benefit from the kind of feedback others can give us if we are learning more directly from them. This method also may take more time than is realistically available to us, and in some cases it may not be safe to learn solely by observing (e.g., piloting an aircraft!). Therefore, other methods of instruction often are needed.

Training involves one or more individuals presenting information to a group of learners, and having the learners apply what is being learned. It is different than education in that the focus is on learning to perform skills, rather than just accumulating knowledge. For example, education about customer service might involve a discussion of different ways to handle customer complaints. But training would go further and have trainees actually practice different techniques. As a result, larger chunks of time typically are set aside for training sessions than are needed for lectures. A training session on customer service may involve one or more eight-hour days, in order to provide time for the trainers to cover content and allow trainees to apply it. Application may come in the form of discussing case studies, demonstrating skills, or performing role-plays. Training may be provided by members of the organization, but often is provided by outside contractors who bring their program to the organization. These consultants may work carefully with the organization to develop a training program that is tailored to the needs of the organization, or they may bring in a "canned" presentation (the same one-size-fits-all presentation that they give to all organizations).

Training can be good because it can reach a large number of people in a small amount of time. It may be better suited for hard skills than soft skills, at least if trainees can get reliable feedback. For example, software training may allow trainees to use the actual software, just as they would use it in their workplace. This is an ideal situation, as trainees are able to learn it in the context in which they will be using it, and they can get immediate and realistic feedback. In contrast, soft skills training often involves learning information out of context (in a group role-play in a classroom vs. in a real communication situation in the office), and therefore the feedback is not as realistic as it could be. In addition, when we learn in a different context than the one in which we will need to perform the skill on the job, we may not experience what is known as *skill transfer*. Transfer is when we are able to apply the skills we learn in one context (the training room) to another context (the workplace, where and when it counts). Transfer is very challenging to achieve. In one research project (Gentner, Loewenstein, & Thompson, 2003), participants learned about negotiation skills and read a case study in which those skills were demonstrated. Participants then read a new case with features that were very similar to the case they had learned. Even though little time had passed and the situations were very similar, very few participants applied the negotiation ideas they had learned to the new case. In other words, they didn't transfer what they had learned, at least unless they were prompted to apply it. This is important. Participants had just read about principles that would help them solve a novel problem, and yet did not think to apply those ideas to the problem. Based on this, it is likely that much of what we learn from training will fail to transfer unless the training does an excellent job representing the context in which we will need to apply the information, and unless we learn how to transfer the information to that context. For example, a training session on customer service will not necessarily lead to improved service. And even if all of this is achieved, another problem with training is that it won't do a great deal to help us develop our intuition with respect to a skill. It will teach us information and procedures, but not help us develop more sophisticated perspective and judgment about using the skills we are learning. Therefore, other methods are needed to promote the learning of intuition.

Coaching involves a knowledgeable coach working with a single learner. It may involve outside coaches (consultants), but also may involve current employees. It may involve a formal (created by the organization) or informal partnership. On one hand, it is less efficient than training, as it only addresses individuals rather than groups, but it does address some of the drawbacks of training. Coaching can more easily take place in the appropriate context (where one performs his or her job), and the learner can get immediate individual feedback that is tailored specifically to him or her. Coaching involves more dialogue than training, as the learner is able to more readily ask questions and receive answers. And when it comes to developing intuition, coaching can provide a considerable advantage. In fact, Ericsson et al. (2007) suggest that having a coach is an important aspect of becoming an expert, as coaches can help accelerate the process. Notice that many experts benefit from one or more people who are in a position to coach them (professional athletes, orchestra musicians, etc.). In keeping with the interpersonal focus of this book, we will focus on the interpersonal learning that takes place in the workplace, in the form of coaching. We will focus most specifically on going beyond basic tasks and trying to learn the expertise possessed by our more experienced colleagues. Then we will focus on how you can take the intuition you develop in your workplace and coach others on how to develop their own.

Getting Coached

It might seem odd to encounter a section on how to get coached, but it is worth noting that another key attribute of experts is that they were eager to receive critical feedback on their performance, so they could improve it (Ericsson et al., 2007). That idea will resonate with some readers, but not all. For those with an external locus of control or who otherwise refuse to acknowledge their mistakes, they probably do not think they need to be coached on anything. They already know it all, and mistakes are the fault of others around them. The ideas in this section will work for them only when they are ready to choose to allow them to work.

But what if you're ready, willing, and able to listen to others, and invite critical feedback? There still is one more problem: You need a decent coach. This may be problematic. The experts in your organization may not be inclined to coach others. In fairness, they probably wouldn't know how to share their expertise, as it is hard to describe to others. And even if they are willing, they may not be effective coaches.

Coaching is difficult. It takes patience, an ability to explain things, time (on top of one's normal duties), a decent relationship with the learner, and more patience (Klein, 2003). And frustrations from the learner's perspective include dealing with a poor coach, time, patience, and other factors (Klein, 2003). So that is our challenge: to learn from an expert who probably cannot explain his expertise, and may not want to. How can we overcome these issues?

The answer simply is that if you want to assure that you will accelerate your learning in the workplace, you will have to be proactive and take it upon yourself to be in command of your own development. Still, how can you get experts to share their hard-to-describe tacit knowledge with you? The answer may surprise you: Get them to tell stories about critical incidents in which their expertise was challenged and yet needed to navigate a challenging situation (Klein, 2003). We've already discussed many benefits of stories, but not how they help communicate tacit knowledge. **Critical incident stories** are useful because they can help uncover the sophisticated mental models that help experts diagnose challenging situations. They can help you identify the patterns, anomalies, big picture, and other elements of expertise discussed earlier in this chapter. For example, consider the emergency room story I shared a few chapters ago, about how a person's heart monitor could read a pulse, even if the heart wasn't beating. One story helped us gain an almost 3-D sense of what happened in that emergency room, and although our medical knowledge is limited, we understand what happened with impressive clarity. This is thanks to a detailed story of a critical incident. Klein and his colleagues have learned the value of critical incident stories (like the nursing example at the beginning of this chapter) by interviewing professionals in different lines of work, and have translated that tacit knowledge into coaching programs to help people accelerate the development of their expertise (Crandall, Klein, & Hoffman, 2006; Klein 1998, 2003, 2009). They have used critical incident interviewing to learn about the intuition of firemen, nurses, weather forecasters, and military specialists. Although they use a detailed research method known as cognitive task analysis, in this section I will outline how any of us can learn from the experts around us by getting them to tell key stories and asking the right questions in the process.

Getting Experts to Tell Stories

You may recall that earlier in the book I said that people generally will open up if you express an interest in what they do. We can take the same approach with experts by saying that we are interested in learning more about what they do, and then asking them for examples of key incidents. The incidents should be ones in which the expert was challenged and really needed to rely on expertise to navigate the situation. One might **ask for a story** of a time when the expert really struggled and was able to call on expertise to make it through the situation. In fact, the expert may not even know how he or she made it through the situation. From this point, you **ask the expert to describe the situation,** in enough detail that you can sense a general timeline of how things happened and when key decisions were made. Next, you will want to try to identify patterns or cues that guided the expert by **asking him or her about what he or she was thinking during key moments in the scenario** (Klein, 2003): "What caught your attention at this moment?" "What decisions did you make, and why?" "What patterns were you looking for during the incident?" "What important details did you notice?" Notice that these questions are designed to help you see the situation as it was seen through the expert's eyes. From here you dig further into the incident with **hypothetical "what if" questions** (Klein, 2003). This can be a very interesting part of the interview, because it allows you to basically throw "curve-balls" at the expert to see how he or she would have handled them. So if you were learning about how an excellent manager defused an angry meeting so that it could have been more productive, you might ask questions such as: "What if the most influential employee had yelled angrily at you during your first attempt to calm everyone down?" "What would you do if your first plan didn't work?" "What if the meeting had continued to escalate?" The responses to these questions will reveal a great deal about the expert's perspective. From here you can explore another very interesting angle, by asking how a novice would have handled various aspects of the situation (Klein, 2003). You can ask questions like: "What mistakes would I have made in interpreting that information? What would I have been likely to try here? What patterns did you see that would have confused me?" (Klein, 2003, p. 235). According to Klein, you should "press the expert to learn something while talking to you. Instead of allowing the expert to recite familiar material, try to get the expert to reflect on a challenging incident and see it from new perspectives" (Klein, 2003, p. 235).

This method has a few advantages over observation, training, or just asking experts "How do you do this?" You get rich details and you get to see how they relate to context (it is not an abstract training situation). You get to see how an expert views a challenge or task, which is a much more rich description than you will get from other methods. And if you have a reluctant coach who is not willing/able to coach you, using stories may pique his or her interest and encourage the expert to open up to you. And on your end, you get to hear one or more interesting stories, while getting to know your coworker and learning a great deal in the process. You still will have to work hard to develop your own intuition for the important tasks in your workplace, but you can do yourself a valuable service and accelerate your learning by learning how the experts around you have handled critical incidents. And by showing interest in a senior employee, you will be standing out as a highly motivated and proactive employee.

It should be noted that even if you are not able to get someone to talk about a specific incident, you have a couple of additional options. First, you could have the person walk you through a typical incident while asking some of the kinds of probing questions mentioned above. Or if the person is comfortable, you could have her walk you through failures that helped her learn important lessons, again while asking probing questions in an effort to uncover tacit knowledge.

Coaching Others

After spending time developing your skills, you may find yourself in a position to coach others. If you are approached by a motivated employee who is receptive to feedback, then you are off to a good start. But what if you are not approached, yet still feel someone would benefit from coaching? First you should consider whether the person is a good candidate for coaching. As we mentioned earlier, someone with an external locus of control, who does not feel he or she is doing anything wrong, may be less receptive to coaching. Also, someone with a very high self-esteem may feel that he or she is "above" being coached. You're welcome to try coaching these individuals, but understand that you may not be able to make meaningful progress with them.

Should you decide to coach someone, it is important to keep in mind that effective coaches have at least the following three things in common: (1) they help **create a good climate** for coaching and learning; (2) they **assess their learner and diagnose issues** *before* proceeding to change behavior; and (3) they **tailor instruction** to fit the individual characteristics of each learner (Klein, 2003). We will cover each of these elements in detail.

Creating a Good Learning Climate

According to Klein (2003), setting a climate means being respectful rather than demanding or evaluative. The focus is less on making someone prove herself and more on working together in a friendly, problem-solving way. This attitude can be demonstrated in a number of ways. For example, if someone needs coaching but doesn't approach you, how could you initiate coaching while maintaining a good learning climate? Rather than saying "That's not how you do it," "You need to do it differently," or "I can't believe you did it that way," you could offer a more welcome invitation, such as (all in a warm, understanding tone): "I used to struggle with that too, would you like me to show you some things that worked for me?" "What are you trying to do, I might be able to help?" Asking questions like this in the right tone demonstrates empathy and that others have struggled with the same tasks. This understanding tone should persist through the next two phases of coaching.

Assessing and Diagnosing

One burden of knowing enough to coach others is that we are at risk for just providing solutions, rather than helping the learners truly learn the reasons behind those solutions. I have been guilty of this, in that at times I've told other teachers how they might handle various problems, yet without helping them understand how I arrived at those solutions. I've tried to improve at this by getting better at assessing the learner's problem in these situations. The point is to try to assess why a person is struggling. What mistakes is he making? We may be able to do this by observing the learner performing the task in question, or by asking (again in an understanding tone) questions such as: "What is your reasoning for doing it that way?" or "What is the thinking behind doing it this way?" Or, you simply can instruct the learner to perform the task, but to talk you through each step, so that you will know what he or she is thinking while performing the task. This can help you reveal faulty assumptions or other problems with the learner's mental model. Once you have asked questions or had the learner walk through a task, you probably will have diagnosed one or more problems. At this stage, you may need to exercise discipline by making sure you focus only on one or two goals per coaching session. For example, if you see a person doing several things wrong, consider which one or two are most important and focus on those. If you try to focus on more, you will overwhelm the learner with too much information. Once you have diagnosed the problem and identified a couple of goals to pursue with the learner, you will be ready to offer instruction that is tailored to that learner's unique needs.

Tailoring Instruction to the Individual Learner

When coaching someone one-on-one, your first goal should be to avoid lecturing. You do not want to just tell someone everything, as the learner will need opportunities to gain experience in order to learn. Remember how experts learn to develop their intuition: a significant amount of deliberate *practice*, during which they receive feedback, either in the form of results they see, or from a coach. And remember that expertise is not about information, but patterns and mental models. While lecturing works great for delivering information, it does not work as well for helping people apply mental models to solve problems. So what kinds of things might a coach do during a session? Klein (2003) shared a number of effective coaching practices that his research team observed on various research projects.

Demonstrate the task yourself while thinking out loud. Notice that this strategy helps provide some of the same kinds of information as the learner would receive by interviewing you about critical incidents. You can describe important cues you're noticing, expected things that are absent, scripts you are using, and other relevant aspects of your mental model. Doing these things helps the learner see a problem through your eyes.

Discuss what could go wrong. By discussing things that could happen at different times during a process, and the cues you would look for as signs of trouble, you're helping the learner develop more sophisticated expectations for the process he is learning.

Let the trainee make mistakes. You probably weren't expecting to see this one. After all, our educational system conditions us to play it safe and avoid mistakes. However, I suspect that few of us know of anyone who learned something without making mistakes. In fact, when we are supported by an understanding and patient teacher or coach, it is an ideal time to make mistakes, as we will get valuable feedback, and if we really botch something, the coach can bail us out! Once a mistake is made, you can discuss why it might have been made (preferably by calmly asking the learner "What do you think happened?"), and by exploring the consequences of the mistake. And if it would be unsafe to allow a mistake, you still could walk the learner through the situation and explore what kinds of mistakes might be made (while also exploring their consequences).

Have the trainee think out loud while performing the task. Specifically, you should have the learner frequently tell you what she is doing and what she thinks will happen next. According to Klein (2003), this encourages learners to develop their intuition about how a process will unfold. This also works well when a trainee makes mistakes, as you can follow up with encouraging questions (in an understanding tone) such as: "What made you decide to approach it that way?" "What were you hoping/expecting to happen when you did that?" and "Why might it not have worked out as planned?" Notice in the last example that I used the word "might." This idea was passed to me by my colleague Dale Hartnett, who suggested that using "might" places less pressure on the learner for a correct answer. Anyone can guess why something might have happened more easily than having to have *the* one right answer to a question. So if you're having trouble getting someone to answer, you may benefit from replacing "why did" with "why might" in your question. Regardless of the approach you use, if you can get the trainee to think out loud while performing the task, you will have gained valuable information on why the trainee's approach is or is not working, and you will be in a better position to provide useful feedback.

Have the trainee instruct the coach. If you ask a trainee if he understands something, he may feel pressured to tell you "yes" when he really does not feel confident. Or even if a person feels she understands something, after trying it she may realize that she isn't completely able to do it. We probably all have been there. As a coach, watching the trainee perform a task can give you a sense of flaws in her mental models (Klein, 2003). This information will enable you to provide corrective feedback, or it will confirm that the trainee is able to perform the task effectively.

Help the trainee explore alternative action scripts. This involves asking the trainee for examples of other ways he could have accomplished the same result. According to Klein (2003), the benefit of doing this is to encourage the trainee to avoid following a single routine, and instead develop a richer mental model that enables him to solve problems with greater sophistication. And should the trainee encounter unexpected obstacles later on when performing the task on his own, he will be in a better position to overcome them.

Ask open-ended questions. Notice how this advice keeps showing up, as it applies to many communication situations. When coaching, an open-ended question has "more than one 'right' answer, and invites the trainee to reflect" (Klein, 2003, p. 232).

Notice improvements rather than just discussing weaknesses. It is easy to spot weaknesses and problems, but think of the last time someone pointed out an improvement. In teaching and parenting, we call this "catching them doing something good." This is a way to be encouraging and to help the learner see that his effort is leading to tangible improvements.

Manage time effectively. As mentioned earlier, we can manage our time effectively by focusing on just a couple of improvements in any one session. If we go beyond three things, we will overwhelm the learner, or he will forget at least some of what we've covered.

Go beyond procedures. Klein (2003) explains the importance of going beyond procedures:

> This is the core of coaching intuitive decision-making skills. You want them to gain an intuitive feel for the task instead of mechanically carrying out procedures. Master coaches are able to describe the cues, patterns, and action scripts they use for judging when procedures are not working. Or at least, they can show the trainees that it is possible to develop their intuitions.
>
> (p. 233)

This underscores the idea that coaching is less about imparting information (lecturing) and more about helping the learner see a task or problem with greater sophistication. Following these practices should help you coach others in your workplace more effectively. And if the experts in your organization are not blessed with these skills, you may be able to encourage them to share their expertise by having them discuss critical incidents they have faced.

References

Crandall, B., Klein, G., & Hoffman, R. R. (2006). *Working minds: A practitioner's guide to cognitive task analysis.* Cambridge, MA: MIT Press.

Ericsson, K. A., Prietula, M. J., & Cokely, E. T. (2007). The making of an expert-response. *Harvard Business Review, 85,* 146–147.

Fournies, F. F. (2000). *Coaching for improved work performance: How to get better results from your employees!* (Rev. ed.). New York, NY: McGraw-Hill.

Gentner, D., Loewenstein, J., & Thompson, L. (2003). Learning and transfer: A general role for analogical encoding. *Journal of Educational Psychology, 95*(2), 393–408.

Klein, G. (1998). *Sources of power: How people make decisions.* Cambridge, MA: MIT Press.

Klein, G. (2003). *The power of intuition.* New York, NY: A Currency Book/Doubleday.

Klein, G. (2009). *Streetlights and shadows: Searching for the keys to adaptive decision making.* Cambridge, MA: MIT Press.

Chapter 13

Navigating Organizational Politics

I'm going to begin this chapter on organizational politics with a scandalous story about . . . keyboards. Really. What if I told you that there was a keyboard layout available that takes much less time to learn than the current one, and is more ergonomic (so there are fewer repetitive strain injuries, like carpal tunnel syndrome). On top of this, you may find it interesting to know that the current keyboard layout we all use (QWERTY) actually was designed to slow typists down, by placing commonly used letters on the top and bottom rows (Rogers, 2003). It was developed at a time when typewriters could not support the speed of typists (when two keys were pressed to closely together, they would get jammed). So, we're all using a keyboard that was designed to slow us down, and there is a perfectly good alternative keyboard that nobody is using. If you want to Google it, it is known as the Dvorak keyboard. In fact, most computers will allow you to switch settings so you can use the Dvorak keyboard layout. So why has this idea not taken off? There are a few reasons. First, we have used the QWERTY layout for so long that it is hard to shift large numbers of people to an alternative. As for why the Dvorak layout didn't catch on back in the early 20th century when it was invented, it might be helpful to consider how many typing teachers would have been unemployed if it had caught on. Or as Rogers (2003) suggests: "vested interests are involved in hewing to the old design: manufacturers, sales outlets, typing teachers, and typists themselves" (p. 10). This brings me to the point of this entire chapter: In human systems, in which people have varied interests and motivations, *it is not necessarily good enough to be right or to have the best idea.*

I know keyboards aren't fascinating, so consider another example that had far greater consequences. It was first offered as an example of politics by Pfeffer (1992), and is based on the film *And the Band Played On,* which itself is based on a very well researched book of the same name, by Randy Shilts (1987). In the early 1980s the Centers for Disease Control (CDC) was faced with a challenge. An alarming number of people were starting to die from the disease we now know as AIDS. As early as 1981, some in the CDC had a sense that the disease was spread in the same ways as other blood borne diseases (such as hepatitis). People who were not in risk groups still were getting the disease, and the CDC believed they were getting it through blood transfusions. Within a couple of years, the CDC was confident that it could screen blood, and suggested that all blood be tested for AIDS before being used for transfusions. Representatives of the blood industry (blood banks, the Red Cross, etc.) opposed the test, and it was not implemented. A year later, in 1984, even though there was little doubt in the scientific community that AIDS was trans-mitted by blood, the blood industry still had not adopted a test. However, it did promise to form a task force to investigate the issue (Pfeffer, 1992). A test finally was approved in 1985, years after most people agreed that AIDS was transmitted via blood, and long after the CDC had begun advocating for the industry to adopt a test. According to Shilts (1987), "An estimated 12,000 Americans were infected from transfusions largely administered after the CDC had futilely begged the blood industry for action to prevent spread of the disease" (p. 599).

Once again, it is not good enough to be right or to have the right or best answer. The CDC was completely right, and yet it was not good enough. The situation was less about what was right/wrong, and more about the fact that CDC was advocating a test that would have been very expensive for the blood industry to implement. As Pfeffer (1992) suggests, the CDC was a group of scientists. In their world, the focus is on being right. They use science to study diseases, and the right answer prevails. But organizations like the Red Cross survive based on the quality of their PR and ability to navigate social systems for support. They were sophisticated at interacting with the media. In other words, they were much better political operators than the CDC. Regardless of what was right, they were able to spin things their way. Again, it is not good enough to be right. Until you accept this, you likely will find your professional work experience to be incredibly frustrating.

But in this chapter I will do my best to describe the reality of organizational poli-tics. If we want to have success in organizations, we likely will need to learn how to navigate the political landscape of our workplace. This chapter will focus in detail on how we might be more politically adept in our workplaces. I understand there may be resistance to learning about politics. After all, with examples like the one above, it's easy to have a distaste for politics and to dismiss it as needless game playing. However, I'm not sure what the alternative is. We can wish that people will act more sensibly, but I'm not sure why we should expect that to happen. So that leaves us to accept the reality of how people operate when there are resources, reputations, and various interests on the line. Still, this entire chapter will try to outline and argue for an approach to politics that is sincere and ethical, and that will leave our good reputation intact in the long run. Therefore, the focus will be on long-term integrity more so than on short-term gains or quick fixes. First we will examine what not to do, and then will shift our focus to more positive, yet realistic political strategies that reflect how people in organizations operate.

How to Alienate Others, Damage Our Reputation, and Compromise Our Integrity

DuBrin (2009) outlines a number of examples of negative political tactics that are worth avoiding, unless you want to encounter the kinds of negative consequences mentioned in the heading above (see Table 13.1). He provided a fairly long list, which I've narrowed down to a few categories. While I acknowledge that these approaches often can work in the short-term, we should be less optimistic about their potential to deliver us long-term success.

Aggressive tactics. There are a number of ways that aggression in the workplace can get the best of some people who will pursue their goals at all costs. **Machiavellianism**

Table 13.1 How to Lose Respect and the Ability to Have Lasting Influence with Others

Be Machiavellian
Bully Others
Engage in Bitter Rivalries
Hold a Grudge
Seek Revenge
"Backstab"
Humiliate Others

includes various types of manipulation. It might include being dishonest, giving false impressions, among other things. In one case, I had a colleague who might complain about something. If I were to agree with him (even if it was a quick nod to say "I hear you,") the colleague would then approach the target of the complaint and say "Not only do I think this, but it really bothers Joe and (any others who might have agreed)." I quickly learned to not agree with the person, based on the tactic the person was using. *Bullying* is another aggressive way some people try to get what they want. It ends up creating a great deal of stress for coworkers and resentment toward the bully. And think of the amount of time wasted in organizations to *bitter rivalries* and *holding a grudge/seeking revenge*. Again, these kinds of activities create a great deal of stress for coworkers and can be a distraction from getting things done. *Backstabbing* is when we pretend to be nice to a coworker at the same time we are doing/saying negative things behind his or her back (DuBrin, 2009). In an earlier chapter I mentioned that when I arrived at a new job, a coworker who was trying to take me under her wing badmouthed several of her colleagues. I assumed that she would do the same about me without hesitation, and I quickly learned to not trust her. Of course, some may take a more direct approach and engage in the *public humiliation* of others. This may be direct ("You're an idiot") or far more subtle. It might be as simple as insincerely asking a lot of questions of an individual's proposal during a meeting (only because the proposal belongs to that individual), being dismissive and condescending to an individual in public, or finding ways to embarrass someone without being direct. Some also might *abuse email in unprofessional ways*. This may include sending a negative message directed to one individual, yet including an entire group as recipients. Or it may involve taking a message that was meant for one recipient and forwarding it to others for whom it was not intended.

The above list of things to avoid is not complete, but it gives us a sample of negative things employees will do to get their way. I would hope that you would avoid engaging in these behaviors, even if they sometimes might feel good at the time, or work in the short-term. But I'm realistic enough to know that people do these things every day. I hope, though, you will see the connection between those behaviors and long-term damage to our relationships, reputation, and integrity and avoid them as much as possible. In their place, I will try to offer a perspective on organizational politics that will help you better understand and navigate your political landscape, yet with long-term positive outcomes in mind.

How Do Ideas Diffuse Through Large Groups?

To begin the process, we will examine a very useful theory that will help you understand why groups latch onto some ideas, while ignoring or rejecting others. The theory addresses two interesting questions: How do large groups of people come to adopt new ideas? and Why do some ideas catch on while others fail? Exploring these two issues using the concept of **Diffusion of Innovations** (Rogers, 2003) will help us better grasp how we can get others in organizations to adopt our ideas, proposals, and suggestions. Those of you familiar with the popular book/concept *The Tipping Point* (Gladwell, 2002) will recognize some of the ideas related to this theory. According to Rogers (2003), the diffusion of innovation "is the process in which an innovation is communicated through certain channels over time among the members of a social system" (p. 5). For our purposes, we can think of innovations as ideas we are trying to get others in our organization to support. First, it is important for me to set your expectations by stressing that:

> Getting a new idea adopted, even when it has obvious advantages, is difficult. Many innovations require a lengthy period of many years from the time when they become available to the time when they are widely adopted. Therefore, a common problem for many individuals and organizations is how to speed up the rate of diffusion of innovation.
>
> (Rogers, 2003, p. 1)

An innovation is an idea that is perceived as new, regardless of whether it actually is new (Rogers, 2003). Innovations have a number of attributes that help determine how readily they are adopted by others (Rogers, 2003). One is their *relative advantage,* or the extent to which an innovation is seen as better than the idea it is trying to replace. Notice that this is based on perception. We might have an idea that we know is better, but if it is not perceived as better by those whom we hope will adopt it, then our opinion, or even objective results (including those with credible scientific or research backing), won't matter much. Another characteristic of innovations is *compatibility,* or "the degree to which an innovation is perceived as being consistent with the existing values, past experiences, and needs of potential adopters" (p. 15). For example, if an innovation goes against the culture of an organization or would require a major shift in attitudes, it will be less compatible, and therefore it will be more difficult to get others to adopt it. A third dimension is *complexity,* which involves perceptions of how difficult the innovation is to comprehend or use.

Table 13.2 Characteristics Used to Judge Innovations

Relative Advantage	Is it better than the idea it is trying to replace?
Compatibility	Does it fit our existing values, needs, or the "way we do things"?
Complexity	How difficult is it to use, apply, enact, etc.?
Trialability	To what extent can we try it out on a limited basis without having to commit completely?
Observability	Can we actually see the results of the innovation?

Trialability is the extent to which individuals can test out the idea on a limited basis, so they can see if it works without having to adopt it completely. If we can try something out, we can reduce our uncertainty about an innovation, and this increases the chances that we will adopt it. A final characteristic of innovations, *observability,* is the extent to which the results of the innovation are visible to others. If we can see positive results, we will be more likely to adopt. In addition, we also will be more likely to talk about the results, and this makes it more likely that we will spread the idea to others. Based on these characteristics, Rogers (2003) concluded that "innovations that are perceived by individuals as having greater relative advantage, compatibility, trialability, and observability, and less complexity will be adopted more rapidly than other innovations" (p. 16).

For example, we can apply each of these characteristics to the Dvorak keyboard. It has a relative advantage over the QWERTY keyboard, trialability, and observability. But although it takes only a week to learn the Dvorak keyboard, until that happens, it is more complex than the keyboard with which most people now are familiar (and therefore less compatible). In addition, because we are so familiar with the QWERTY keyboard, it would take a major shift to adopt the Dvorak keyboard. So while the Dvorak keyboard is better in many respects, there still are barriers that have prevented its adoption. One approach might be to have those who haven't yet learned to type try it, as it would be easier for them to adopt it as their first keyboard than to switch from an established keyboard to a new one (overcoming the issues of complexity and compatibility).

In addition to characteristics of innovations, there are characteristics of potential adopters that also matter. Specifically, different people fit into different adopter categories: **innovators, early adopters, early majority, late majority, laggards.** *Innovators* (who constitute about 2.5% of a population) are forward-thinking, love to try new things, can tolerate uncertainty, are willing to take risks, and will work through initial setbacks. They often operate at the edges of a system, rather than being a central part of it. They're the ones often going against the status quo and trying new things. As a result, they're less likely to fit in with the crowd. But their approach helps them gain exposure to new ideas that they can bring into the system. Unfortunately, some of these advantages may make it difficult for innovators to communicate their ideas to others in the system who are less comfortable with risk, or less able to understand the innovation. *Early Adopters* (around 13.5% of the population)

Table 13.3 Categories of Adopters

Innovator	The first to try innovations. "It's something new, ok, I want in on it."
Early Adopter	Quick to adopt good ideas. Opinion leaders are in this group. "It didn't backfire on (the innovator) and seems like a good idea, so I'll try it."
Early Majority	Will take their cues from the early adoptors, whom they respect. "(early adopters) are trying it, so I should be doing it."
Late Majority	Will go along only when they have to in order to function. "Almost everyone is using email, I guess I have to also."
Laggards	Will hold out and resist as long as possible. "I'm not sure about this computer fad. I'm sticking with my typewriter."

are more linked to the social system and are highly respected by its members. They are open to new ideas, but will wait until they have been tested by innovators and will choose to adopt more carefully than innovators. Early adopters are important to the innovation process, because their adoption serves to endorse the innovation. Therefore, it is in the best interest of an innovator to gain the support of an early adopter, in order to increase the chances that an innovation will diffuse through a system. The *Early Majority* (34%) take longer to accept an idea, and usually do so slightly ahead of the average member of the system. They are more tentative than early adopters. However, once a significant number of the early majority adopt an idea, they help create what is called a critical mass (or tipping point), which is when an innovation has gained enough adopters to have taken off to the point that it can sustain itself. The *Late Majority* (34%) adopt ideas after the average member of the system has adopted them. They are skeptical and cautious, and will be on board only after most others have adopted the innovation. They are likely to adopt due to pressure from peers and the necessity of adopting the innovation (for example, having to use email because everyone else uses it and it is necessary to use it to do one's job). Finally, *laggards* (16%) are very resistant, and are the last to adopt the innovation. It takes a long time to get them to adopt an idea, as they prefer tradition over innovation.

There is one final key group that we will discuss, as they are key to the diffusion process: **opinion leaders.** According to Rogers (2003), "*Opinion Leadership* is the degree to which an individual is able to influence other individuals' attitudes or overt behavior informally in a desired way with relative frequency" (p. 27). People do not become opinion leaders because of any formal status, but rather earned by good performance, being a good fit for their particular social system, and accessibility. They earn the respect of their peers, as well as the kind of referent and expert power we explored earlier in this book. They are key to the diffusion process, because if an innovator can gain the support of one or more opinion leaders for an adoption, the opinion leaders will help legitimize and endorse the innovation. Where it used to be the crazy idea of some crackpot, now it's an idea worth checking out. Most opinion leaders are found in the early adopter category, and are important in helping an idea reach the early majority, and therefore, critical mass.

The above emphasis on different types of individuals suggests a final important implication related to the diffusion process: the importance of face-to-face communication. Notice that diffusion does not take place by just sending a single message out to a large group. If that happens, there are enough laggards, late majority, and early majority members who may be too cautious or risk averse to adopt the suggested innovation. Not all potential adopters are created equal. A single message sent to all potential adopters fails to utilize opinion leaders in a way that can give us the best chance of having our idea adopted.

So what does all of this information about diffusion mean for us if we have an idea and hope to get it adopted? First, it means we should seek out one or more opinion leaders to try to get them to support our idea. In the process we will have to demonstrate its relative advantages, compatibility, trialability, observability, and lack of complexity. Once we have one or more opinion leaders on board, the early majority is more likely to follow. Once enough of them are on board, we may reach critical mass, and the innovation may have enough momentum to sustain itself, to the point that the late majority will have to adopt it.

Let's reexamine the failure to adopt an AIDS blood test with this process in mind. That innovation was complex and not compatible with current procedures. It would have been expensive for the blood industry and would have required an additional step in their procedures. It also may have driven away some blood donors. Because the test initially was not 100% accurate, its relative advantage could be questioned. It could have been tried on a limited basis and the results could have been observed. So it is a mixed bag in terms of characteristics of the innovation. Now let's look at how the CDC communicated its ideas. It typically presented them at large meetings with those who would be voting on whether to change policy. This group likely was mixed in terms of adopter categories. Some may have been favorable to change, and others not favorable. And what about opinion leaders? It is unclear how well the CDC tried to appeal to opinion leaders, but it is possible that the greatest opposition to its proposed testing (the blood industry) may have been opinion leaders. For the CDC to have made greater progress, it would have had to win over one or more opinion leaders among the voting body (or who were connected to the voters). But the way things worked out, the idea to test was adopted only after many people had died and it was obvious that the idea had to be adopted. It was adopted because of its characteristics and out of necessity.

The diffusion process may be clear-cut, but when we try to apply it to having coworkers accept our ideas, we are left with a few challenges. Who are the opinion leaders? What if people have agendas and actively are against our ideas? How do we convince opinion leaders our ideas are good? To explore these issues we will examine a process outlined by Jeffrey Pfeffer (1992), which is built in some ways upon the diffusion process.

Pfeffer's Steps for Navigating Organizational Politics and Getting Things Done

Pfeffer (1992) makes an important distinction between decisions and the implementation of decisions. He says that while many people (and educational programs) focus on the process of making decisions, decisions by themselves change very little. For example, of those who decide at the beginning of a new year to lose weight, how many successfully implement that decision? Or in organizations, the decision to implement a new policy (say, friendly customer service) does not mean that everyone will follow the policy. Therefore, Pfeffer (1992) suggests that it is the *implementation* of decisions that matters. He notes that we spend more time living with the consequences of our decisions than we do making the decisions themselves, and argues that it is important to manage the consequences of our decisions. He argues that the effective use of politics will help us bridge the gap from the decision and actually being able to implement it effectively. In other words, he emphasizes the importance politics as a way of getting things done.

Step 1: Decide on Goals

This first step is fairly straightforward, and needs little explaining. But as Camp (2003) advises, you should focus less on outcomes you want and more on things within your control that you hope to do. So rather than aiming to "have my idea implemented," it would be preferable to focus on "convince my colleagues that my idea could benefit them and the organization."

Step 2: Diagnose Patterns of Dependence and Interdependence

Earlier I discussed the nature and importance of opinion leaders, but I did little to help you identify those who may be opinion leaders in your organization. This second step is about finding these key opinion leaders. However, for the moment our focus will be less on finding individuals and more on identifying key groups that can help make or break your efforts. Pfeffer (1992) refers to these groups as political subunits. A **subunit** is any way we can categorize a group of employees. Think of all of the ways you might group employees: age, rank, time at the organization, department, gender, race, religion, committee membership, ability, and others which may be relevant to your organization. Any of these groups may have some political power when it comes to certain issues. For much of the time, these groupings may not matter much. But on certain issues, they may matter considerably, and when this happens, we would consider these groups to be key political subunits related to our issue. For example, a few years ago when our college was exploring a key issue, one important subunit happened to relate to the size of departments. On this particular issue, those from smaller departments were very vocal and had a lot of influence over a particular issue, while larger departments had less influence. On many issues, department size probably doesn't matter. But on this one issue, department size was very important, and little progress on the issue would have been made without finding a way to win over the smaller departments.

So how do we determine which subunits are powerful with respect to an issue? Pfeffer (1992) suggests that we look at a variety of indicators: reputation, representation, consequences, and power symbols. First, we can ask around and assess which subunits have the *reputation* for having power on certain issues. This may be helpful, but since we are relying on others' perceptions, and those perceptions may be wrong, it is important to look at other indicators besides reputation. When we look at *representation,* we are examining whether certain subunits are disproportionately represented in certain organizational roles. For example, do key managers tend to come only from one or two departments? Are key committees made up only of people from certain departments? Answers to questions like these can give us a sense of who might be powerful in the organization. Related to the example I used above, at the time our college was exploring the issue I mentioned, a key committee in the process comprised mostly individuals from small departments. This is less likely due to some institutional bias than the fact that these departments were more active in seeking membership on the committee. Regardless of the reason, small departments had at least some advantage due to their representation on the key committee. Representation does not have to be based on department membership. It may be based on age, tenure in the organization, or other characteristics. We also can examine the power of subunits by assessing the *consequences* they experience. Consequences may include salaries, budget allocations to departments, or which departments get to hire new people or add new positions. If you examine consequences, you may find that some departments are benefitting most from decisions that are being made. Finally, *symbols of power* may include office location, office size, the building in which a department resides (if an organization has many buildings, and some are more coveted than others), or location within the building. An examination of several of these indicators (not just any one) may reveal very little, but it also may help you to identify certain subunits that have more power than otherwise would have been noticeable. If these subunits are relevant to what you are trying to accomplish, you likely will have to win them over to accomplish your goals.

Once you've identified key subunits, you can try to identify key individuals within those subunits. You may be able to use the same indicators mentioned above, but this time applied individually. What individuals have a reputation for being powerful, represent the unit with key assignments, experience the best outcomes (salary, perks, etc.), and display the greatest status symbols (office size, location, etc.)? You can consider additional questions, such as who seems to be the most respected (who has the strongest expert and referent power base?). Once you've identified one or more key individuals, you will know whom you will have to win over in order to accomplish your goals.

Step 3: Consider the Points of View of Key Individuals

In keeping with the audience-centered focus that has characterized much of this book, this next step is about getting a feel for where key individuals stand with respect to your initiative. Do they already support it or is there some opposition? Who can make or break your efforts, and what are they thinking and why? This step is akin to doing the kind of research that Camp (2003) advised when negotiating. This might seem obvious, but often when someone has an idea, the person proceeds to tell people what he or she thinks, rather than getting a sense of what others think. But if you first ask some questions (the types that have been advocated in this book: open-ended, etc.), you will learn valuable information that will help you develop your plan for getting others on board. Doing this will keep you from proceeding blindly.

Step 4: Consider the Power Bases of Key Individuals, as Well as Your Own Power Bases

The point of this step is to get a sense of our power relative to that of the key individuals who can make or break our efforts. I will focus on them from the point of view of different ways you can acquire various bases of power, but all of this applies to the power of the key individuals you are trying to win over. In this section we will explore many ways one might acquire power. Some will be ideas we have explored in earlier chapters, while others will be new. The ideas cluster into a few key categories.

Earn a Good Reputation

For all of the negative connotation that is attached to power and politics, it is worth noting that often we can gain power in the most legitimate of ways: We can earn a good reputation through our performance and by treating others well. As I discussed in an earlier chapter, it is important to start off with a good reputation, as it will lead to opportunities to enhance our reputation further. One element of our reputation will be based on our performance. Beyond doing our jobs well, we can enhance perceptions of our performance by taking initiative and going above and beyond our job description for the betterment of our coworkers or our organization. According to DuBrin (2009), there are additional ways we can demonstrate good performance. We can deliver dramatic and positive results quickly, which will establish our ability to solve problems. We also can take a situation that is problematic or even in a state of crisis, and turn it around. This shows our ability to overcome adversity and solve challenging problems.

We also can enhance our reputation by treating others well. Although it is possible to fake this behavior, my intention is to encourage you to do this with sincerity, as we already will encounter enough people in our professional lives who fake their way through this process. We treat others well in ways you may not have considered by pitching in and helping others out, providing support when others are stressed about something, providing supportive and encouraging coaching to others. And when we have disputes, we can handle them constructively. We can be tolerant of disagreement and negotiate in ways that do not put pressure on others. We can be supportive and agreeable and pick our fights carefully (DuBrin, 2009). And when we make mistakes, we can apologize (DuBrin, 2009). For what it's worth, in my own experience I have seen apologies have a considerable impact. We might wish people would apologize, but we rarely expect it and are very pleasantly surprised when it happens. The chances of us being right 100% of the time are slim. It is in our best interests to realize this now, and own up to our mistakes when we are wrong. We also can treat others well by praising them and making them feel valued and important (DuBrin, 2009). It sounds obvious, but how often do we stop to praise coworkers? It takes very little to make a big impact on others by doing this. If we are in a position of power over others, we can invite them to offer their ideas and feedback, and if possible, delegate some power and responsibility to them (DuBrin, 2009).

Still, in fairness to those of you who might be cynical about this, it is important to consider just how we can do this with sincerity if we are not that fond of some of our coworkers. The most useful way I have been able to do this is to realize that, from another person's perspective, his or her behavior makes sense (or at least more sense than it does from our perspective). For example, suppose I encounter a student whose behavior is frustrating. Maybe the student is missing too many classes, or is not participating much in class. Earlier in my career, students who exhibited this behavior used to frustrate me quite a bit. Over the years, I've learned to consider how this behavior might make sense from the student's perspective. If the student's perspective is unclear to me, I'll just ask in a warm tone: "I noticed you haven't been in class much lately, how is everything?" The answers I receive to this question help me better understand how the behavior is reasonable from the student's perspective. A student might be sick, having romantic troubles, having family troubles, or experiencing any other number of things. They probably are not trying to be challenging just for the sake of being difficult. Having this information enables me to better understand how the behaviors make sense from the student's perspective, and therefore, the absences are less frustrating. The student still will have to accept the consequences of the absences, but now this takes place without any animosity between us. And in some cases, I am able to provide support to help the student through a difficult situation. As Fournies (2000) suggests:

> People do not go through the world doing *illogical things* on purpose. They do what they believe to be the right thing at that moment in time. They have selected (they believe) the best alternatives for them, from those alternatives they see available to them. What they do appears illogical to them only when they find out it didn't work. It appears illogical to someone else who is watching because that someone else sees more alternatives, or knows the one selected will not work.
>
> (p. 56)

In other words, that coworker who does something that annoys you is selecting what he believes to be the best alternative. You don't have to like it or accept it, but you will be less frustrated if you realize that, from your coworker's perspective, the behavior makes sense. Realizing this will help you see the behavior in a different light and, even if you don't condone the behavior, you will be more able to treat the coworker with respect. To the extent you consistently treat coworkers well, and with respect, your reputation will be enhanced.

Gain Power Through Association and Allies

We also can develop power through our associations with others. You will recall that in the chapter on networking we discussed the ways in which our position in networks can provide us with advantages. And at times, we may gain an advantage simply by being in the right unit (Pfeffer, 1992). We also can develop alliances with powerful people or try to attract a mentor who is powerful (DuBrin, 2009). With these relationships you will gain valuable support, and learn a great deal about how things in your organization really work.

Be Good With Strategy

Strategy is about being skillful and creative enough to spot opportunities. It may be about opportunities to develop alliances, to merge your ideas with others' interests to get them to accept your ideas, to identify ways your organization can grow or improve, or to find compromises that can help solve problems. There is no one blueprint for doing this, other than being perceptive, paying attention, and, as was mentioned in the chapter on networking (Chapter 3), having a diverse network with structural holes in weak ties. Over time, as your vision of your organization and profession grows more sophisticated, so long as you remain flexible and avoid becoming rigid in your thinking, you may be better able to spot opportunities and think strategically.

Have Formal Authority

In some ways, this one is pretty obvious. Of course being in a position of authority is going to make it easier to have and exercise power. However, when I served as chair of our department for a few years, I noticed a few additional ways in which holding formal authority helps someone improve at gaining power through some of the other means mentioned on in this section. For example, as chair I met people from across campus and my network grew considerably. With it, my perspective on how things work in my organization broadened and I was able to develop a sense of whom I could approach for help with various kinds of tasks. This helped me have a more sophisticated strategy for solving various problems. Finally, I was able to develop relationships with various powerful people within our organization, and at times I benefitted considerably from the mentoring they provided. I should stress that I didn't seek any of these outcomes. I didn't try to work the system to gain any of these advantages. They were a function of my position and my ability to recognize the value of the people who were joining my network (or whose networks I was joining). In many ways, these benefits were far greater than the formal power I held in our department.

Have Resources and Control Their Allocation

It is no stretch to see how having a budget and control over its allocation can enhance our power. But even if we do not have such access, often there will be times when we can create resources that didn't previously exist. You may be able to control the flow of information with a company newsletter or by being in position to be a gatekeeper (for example, by occupying a structural hole that bridges two groups). Or you could be in control of others' time by leading a committee or a group of volunteers, or by being in charge of scheduling. You also may have control over important facilities. Notice that I am offering possibilities more than definite opportunities. This is because it will take some creativity on your part to spot potentially meaningful resources within your organization. The key is to be vigilant in observing your workplace and working to spot potential resources.

Table 13.4 Attributes Common Among Successful Political Operators

Energy and Physical Stamina	They work very hard and are persistent.
Focus	They commit to a narrow range of goals and stick with them.
Perceptiveness or Sensitivity to Others	They "read" people and situations very well.
Flexibility	If one plan fails, they will adjust and find other ways of meeting their goals.
Tolerance for Disagreement	They don't get offended when others disagree. It's just part of the process.
Can submerge their ego to get along	It puts others at ease, makes them less defensive, and helps build positive relationships.
Positive Attitude	They believe they will succeed, will not be discouraged by several "no" answers, and therefore, they often do succeed.

Possess Some Key Attributes

Pfeffer (1992) identified a number of attributes that he argues are displayed by people who are politically powerful. The first attribute is ***energy and physical stamina***. Notice the amount of work it would take to implement the steps we have discussed so far, in terms of assessing the political landscape of an organization, developing positive relationships with various constituencies, and so on. When you realize that getting things done in organizations requires a great deal more than stating our opinion or giving a speech and assuming others will agree with us, the need to have energy and stamina makes a great deal of sense.

The second individual attribute is *focus,* which involves narrowing our commitment to one or two goals and sticking to them. It is about not trying to accomplish too many things at once and having a scattered focus. In addition to hard work, it often takes time to gain approval for our initiatives. During this time, we can encounter many things that can distract us. Priorities may change, the profession may change, or new ideas may be presented. It is important to be able to maintain focus on one's goal.

The third attribute is ***sensitivity to others,*** or ***perceptiveness***. This type of sensitivity has nothing to do with being nice to others, and instead is about being able to read people and use that information to communicate effectively with them. It is about knowing that an aggressive approach may work with one person, but that a softer approach is needed with someone else. It also can be about sensitivity to timing, as in finding the right time to raise an issue, and when to wait instead. As for how to become more sensitive, Pfeffer (1992) suggests that it is about being interested in observing the behavior of others. One way to do this is to identify successful or unsuccessful communicators (in your mind, not out loud!), and watch how they communicate with others. What do they do that works, and that does not work? If you develop the habit of paying careful attention to others, you will improve your ability to read communication situations, and to handle them effectively.

The next characteristic is ***flexibility,*** which involves being able to modify our behavior and our approach to problems as needed. As opposed to being rigid, we will benefit by altering our approach to fit different people (so that we can take advantage of our sensitivity). Flexibility also is about adjusting our approach when we are faced with the inevitable obstacles we will face in gaining acceptance for our idea. People may oppose us, resources may disappear, personnel may change. Or, we may be confronted with the fact that there are legitimate flaws in our idea. An inflexible person will persist and defend an idea far too long. A flexible person will accept reality and adjust accordingly. Flexibility also can help us when we encounter "no" answers from others. Rather than just giving up, we may find ways to negotiate or alternative ways to accomplish our goal. You may have noticed that the political path to having our ideas accepted is not likely to be very smooth.

As a result, another important characteristic is having a ***tolerance for disagreement***. We discussed this in the conflict chapter (Chapter 11), but when it comes to politics, an unfortunate reality is that we may find that we need to work with people we don't particularly like in order to get things done. We can help this by trying to appreciate their perspective (as I outlined above), but we still may not like certain people very much. But what if these people are opinion leaders or other key people who can make or break our efforts? In these cases, it will be in our best interest to find areas of common ground, or to agree to disagree about some things (DuBrin, 2009). Even if you are dealing with people you like and respect, you should expect disagreement, and not be surprised by it. Based on what I've covered about negotiation and handling conflict, you should be in a better position to make things work, even when you encounter disagreement.

The final attribute mentioned by Pfeffer is *submerging one's ego and getting along*. This may seem odd to include in a chapter on power and politics, but consider the ways an inflated ego can get someone into trouble. We create distance between ourselves and others, alienate others, and encounter resistance. We may win on an issue, but gain enemies we don't need in the process. It is easy enough to make missteps and have blunders on our own. Who needs others to be cheering for this to happen to us? On the other hand, what happens when we keep our ego in check? It puts others at ease, helps endear us to them, and makes them more open to considering what we have to say. There may be some concern that it makes us appear weak, but if we are in control, asking the questions we want to ask, negotiating effectively, and experiencing success, then these appearances that suggest weakness are deceiving. This also is because it actually takes a fair amount of internal confidence to be self-assured enough to not always have to appear to be the smartest or most in-charge. Sometimes the polite person who holds her ground and gets others to answer her polite questions will have far more control than the person who is trying to display power and control others.

You may have noted the absence of one characteristic that sometimes is associated with power, success, and awe: charisma. Although charisma may help us gain power, there are plenty of noncharismatic people who are highly successful, well respected, and effective. If you are able to demonstrate the other attributes mentioned above, charisma may be a helpful addition, but lacking charisma is not likely to be problematic for you. In his review of personality and professional success, Hogan (2007) did not find charisma to be a meaningful factor that contributed to success. For example, notice that even in a dramatic business like football, some incredibly successful coaches are completely lacking in charisma (see: New England Patriots).

Earlier I mentioned the perspective I gained from being a department chair. Part of this perspective involved learning from some of the most astute political operators within our organization. When I think about the characteristics they displayed, I see considerable overlap with Pfeffer's list. The first thing that comes to mind is **hard work.** I was struck by how much work it takes to navigate organizational politics. These individuals were **astute in going to important events** (even when those events didn't interest them personally), getting to know people across campus. They also were very perceptive in **spotting strategic opportunities.** In addition, they had an **incredibly positive attitude about succeeding** in getting others to adopt their idea. They simply assumed that it would happen, even if it might take months or even years. Where many might be shocked or annoyed that others would disagree, or oppose their ideas, the best politicians in our organization recognized that these things just come with the territory. As a result, they were undeterred by setbacks and "no" answers (notice the stamina and focus they have at work here). One final characteristic separates the best politicians into two groups: those who were liked and those who were not. Some individuals helped others when they needed something. The best **helped others consistently,** even when they didn't need anything from them. These individuals are good examples of how one can navigate a political landscape in a positive and constructive way, and still succeed.

With this information on political power bases, you can gain a sense of ways in which key individuals have power in your organization, and you also will have a sense of power bases you can employ to gain support for your idea. An understanding of others' power bases will help you develop expectations about the likely success of different strategies you might choose to use. An understanding of your own power bases can help you spot opportunities to gain support, and possibly counter the power of others who are trying to oppose you.

Step 5: Consider the Strategies That You Might Be Able to Use

In this section we will cover a number of tactics that might be used to gain others' support for our ideas. Based on the assessment you've made from following the previous steps, you will have an idea of what would and would not work well in a specific situation, and for you personally. My goal is not to list all of the strategies that might work, as that would be a long list. However, I will cover a number of possible tactics, most of which come from earlier in this book. They can fit into three categories of influence that you might be able to use: your position, your relationship with others, and the skillful use of messages.

Using Your Position to Influence Others

There may be various ways we can use a position to our advantage. We may be able to exercise formal authority. We also may be able to benefit by bridging structural holes (Burt, 2005). In addition, we may have weak ties within the organization who can play a key role in helping us. We also may gain power from the department we are in and use that to our advantage. It also may be helpful to form coalitions with others who support your idea, as a coalition can overcome resistance by suggesting to others that there is broad support for your idea (DuBrin, 2009).

Using Relationships to Influence Others

We also may be able to appeal to our existing relationships, and benefit from the fact that we have treated others well for some time. Or if we have not established relationships with key individuals, we may be able to exchange favors and benefits with them (DuBrin, 2009). You will recall from an earlier chapter that I outlined the importance of participating in exchange relationships with others. We may be able to offer others something they need in turn for their support for our idea.

Using Messages Skillfully to Influence Others

Regardless of whether we use strategies related to position or relationships, at some point we will have to use messages skillfully. In this book I have described many ways this might be done. Notice that an important part of persuading others involves understanding our "target's" perspective and showing how we can provide what a person needs. DuBrin (2009) emphasizes this by advising us to focus on how others will benefit from adopting our plan. Camp (2003) talks about understanding your adversary's "pain" and showing how you can alleviate it. For example, we should address our idea's advantages, compatibility, trialability, observability, and lack of complexity (Rogers, 2003). These are examples of the kind of framing I discussed in an earlier chapter. We can increase our chances of being persuasive by framing our message in an optimal way. And as has been mentioned several times in previous chapters, by asking others open-ended questions, we can collect important information that will help us frame our message. And in order to help others envision our idea "in action" we may benefit from telling one or more stories. Also recall the other ways in which we can make our messages stick: make them simple, unexpected, concrete, credible, and emotional (Heath & Heath, 2007). Should we encounter disagreement or a "no" answer, we will be able to use the kind of negotiation skills outlined by Camp (2003). And if a situation broils into conflict, we have a sense of how we can defuse it so that we can get back to focusing on key issues. It is my hope that much of what has been discussed throughout this book will help you in these political situations so that you can find a way to get things done.

Notice that in this discussion of politics we have focused on positive and constructive means by which you might influence colleagues. Of course you can use other strategies, like intimidation, or using "dirt" on others, but I hope you recognize that you already have many more positive tools in your arsenal that will serve you better in the long run. To envision how all of these steps might work, I will walk you through a fictional yet realistic case that might require us to navigate the politics of our organization.

Suppose we came across a wellness program that might be good for our organization to adopt. It would involve tracking exercise and diet, and encourage people to adopt healthy habits (for example, taking a couple of breaks each day for walks, etc.). You have a lot of statistics on your side, in terms of exercise helping people focus better, reducing insurance costs for your company and possibly individuals (some companies now provide incentives to those who exercise). So how can you get others on board?

You could ask for time at an upcoming meeting and present your ideas. This approach often is implied as the way to do things (for example, public speaking courses often have a persuasive speech that involves this kind of advocacy). I used to think that it was good enough to craft a good presentation and win people over by delivering it well. While that can happen, often I have failed by relying solely on that approach. Why? Because often by the time we enter a meeting, people have talked about the issue and largely made up their minds on it. Even worse, opponents of the idea may have lobbied people before the meeting to "help" them make up their minds. In this context, walking in to give a speech on the topic when minds have been made up almost is a joke. This is not to say that speeches never are useful (after all, I've included a chapter on giving presentations), but if there is no need for a speech and people will have made up their minds before the speech, then it would be a waste of time to give one. Alternatively, we may have the authority to just implement the wellness program. However, if we don't work on implementing it well, it will be a joke and people will not take it seriously. In fact, they probably will mock it. This leaves us with Pfeffer's steps as a way of getting people on board with our proposal.

We know our goal: to convince others that it is a good idea for the organization to adopt a wellness program. Now we have to identify key subunits. One likely is based on who does/does not like to exercise regularly. As we examine other subunits, we may be able to learn more about those who do/do not exercise. Do those who exercise have all/few power positions, or control over the budget? This may or may not reveal any other key subunits. From there, we can consider who is likely to be for/against our idea, and why, as well as their bases of power. Among those who are opposed, do they control the budget, have positions of formal authority, or are they popular or a good old boy or girl? Or are opponents relatively absent of formal or relational power? We can use all of this valuable information to inform our strategy. We also can consider our own power bases. We may have good relationships with key people, some control over the budget, and authority, which we can use to our advantage. At this point, certain strategies may appear to be useful to us. Because finances may be an obstacle preventing the adoption of our idea, we can talk with those in control of finances about how a wellness program can lead to savings in various areas. And if some are concerned about the time it might take for such a program, we can talk about how productivity benefits when people are more healthy. Regardless of the specifics, notice that this is about getting key people on board with us (opinion leaders and early adopters) so that it will be easier to get everyone else on board. There is no guarantee this process will work, or work quickly. You may encounter considerable opposition, or uncontrollable circumstances (a rough economy). And you may have to wait months or years for conditions to change (economy improves; key people change their mind, change positions, retire, etc.). In other words, it may take a great amount of focus and stamina for you to see your idea implemented.

Switching to an example with more gravity, what could the CDC have done back in 1981 when it had a good idea that testing the nation's blood supply would save lives? First, notice what it did do: It assumed that if the staff went into meetings and presented the facts, people reasonably would accept them and agree. Obviously this didn't work. What might have worked? First, we know that, among the decision makers with respect to implementing a blood test, a key subunit consisted of the blood industry (Red Cross, blood banks, etc.). It does not seem that there was an equally strident subunit in favor of testing the blood. Why was the blood industry against the idea? It would have been an expensive hassle to implement. What were its power bases? It had strong public relations and was used to lobbying others for support, and as a result, it had a lot of clout (Pfeffer, 1992). The CDC's power bases were far less impressive. They were scientists who, because they were focused on being scientifically right and believed that was good enough, had little PR or political clout (Pfeffer, 1992). So what could the CDC have done? It could have tried to make connections with people within the "blood industry" subunit. Perhaps it could have convinced one or two key people on an individual level, and those key people could have influenced others within the subunit to change their position. This might have worked, but there is no guarantee, and it would have taken a long time. Alternatively, with a little effort, the CDC might have been able to secure a key power base simply by publicizing that the blood industry was against a test that would have made blood supplies safer. In other words, it could have exposed the blood industry's decision making to public scrutiny, by inspiring headlines such as "Would you want to receive blood that hasn't been tested?" Although a strength of the blood industry was its PR, its livelihood also was dependent upon it. By exposing its risky decisions publicly, the CDC would have been using a valuable leverage point that it had with respect to the blood industry. You may notice that there now are public relations efforts aimed at drawing attention to all kinds of diseases, including AIDS.

Ok, so I've given two different examples, and they suggested taking very different approaches. What can we conclude from this? We can conclude that when navigating organizational politics we need to be very flexible, as different circumstances warrant different approaches. So rather than assuming one approach is best, it is important to be good at surveying people and organizations, recognizing the various strategies we might use, and being able to employ a variety of strategies. I hope that after reading this book, you are in a better position to do all of these things.

References

Burt, R. S. (2005). *Brokerage and closure: An introduction to social capital.* New York, NY: Oxford University Press.

Camp, J. (2003). *Start with no: The negotiating tools that the pros don't want you to know.* New York, NY: Crown Business.

DuBrin, A. J. (2009). *Political behavior in organizations.* Thousand Oaks, CA: Sage.

Fournies, F. F. (2000). *Coaching for improved work performance: How to get better results from your employees!* (Rev. ed.). New York, NY: McGraw-Hill.

Gladwell, M. (2002). *The tipping point: How little things can make a big difference.* New York, NY: Little, Brown.

Heath, C., & Heath, D. (2007). *Made to stick: Why some ideas survive and others die.* New York, NY: Random House.

Hogan, R. (2007). *Personality and the fate of organizations.* Hillsdale, NJ: Erlbaum.

Pfeffer, J. (1992). *Managing with power.* Boston, MA: Harvard Business Press.

Rogers, E. M. (2003). *Diffusion of innovations* (5th ed.). New York, NY: Free Press.

Shilts, R. (1987). *And the band played on: Politics, people, and the AIDS epidemic.* New York, NY: St. Martin's Press.

Chapter 14

Giving Good Presentations

My goal in this chapter is to enable you to enjoy speaking in public and to do it well, even if you currently hate the thought of presenting to others. Or if you don't end up enjoying it, I at least hope that you will enjoy it more than you do now, or at least find it more bearable. And if you already have learned a lot about public speaking or have considerable experience with it, my hope is to offer you some things you haven't already learned. Finally and most important, my goal is to help you become much more effective when speaking in public. By "more effective," I mean that you will begin with more momentum, speak with energy, and actually be conversational with your audience, rather than reading to them or just dumping content on them.

These goals might sound like a stretch, but I often see my speaking students make this kind of progress by following the ideas I will outline in this chapter. Interestingly, rather than focusing on what to do *during* the presentation, I will focus mostly on what really makes or breaks most presentations: **the preparation we do *before*** we even open our mouths. If we really prepare enough for our presentations, the experience can be more like a conversation for us than a formal delivered address. To help us get to this point, I will begin by focusing on many of the mistakes we make when preparing, and then I will explain what we should do instead. Finally I'll discuss a few things that can be done during presentations to make them go more smoothly.

Much of what we know about effective speaking has not changed much. We're supposed to convince an audience why it needs to listen to us, and deliver a few clearly organized points on a level that is appropriate to the audience, preferably with a reasonable amount of enthusiasm, while looking at the audience as opposed to reading our notes. Although it definitely is challenging to do all of this, pause for a moment and consider how we already do much of this during conversation. We have to think of what to say (with less preparation than we're afforded for most speeches) and say it in a way that the listener will understand it. One difference is that in conversation we're likely more focused on whether the listener understands us, while during presentations we're often more focused on ourselves than the audience. Many of my suggestions in this chapter will be about making public speaking easier for us by shifting our focus to our audience and whether they understand us. In other words, I hope to show you a way to speak that is more natural and more like conversations. If you can move in this direction, I believe that speaking will become easier for you and that you will improve at it. This all starts with preparation. I firmly believe that much of the success/failure of speeches is rooted in preparation, and if you can prepare thoroughly by following the ideas in this next section, by the time you actually get around to delivering your presentation, most of the work will have been done and you will be more free to actually enjoy just speaking with your audience. With this in mind, let's consider some common mistakes people make when preparing for presentations.

How Do People Undermine Their Presentations Before They Even Begin Speaking?

We Are Distracted by Our Anxiety. Often, people struggle to prepare for their presentations because they are anxious about even the thought of presenting. This "fear or anxiety of real or anticipated communication" is known as *Communication Apprehension* (Richmond & McCroskey, 2009, p. 73). Notice that the fear is of real or anticipated communication. We can become anxious just thinking about it. Many people get anxious when preparing to speak. It's a perfectly natural reaction to being conspicuous and "evaluated" by so many listeners at once, especially since there likely is no easy way to exit if we make mistakes. So in general, the consequences are much greater than in most of the speaking situations we face. As a result, while preparing, some people might constantly get caught in "what if" thinking: "What if I forget what I'm saying, or lose my place, or drop my notes, or what if someone asks a question?" Spending time on these distressing thoughts keeps us from focusing on other aspects of preparation, and ironically it may make it more likely that some of our fears will come true.

I have a few suggestions for handling anxiety. First, do all of the things I suggest below in the next few sections in order to **prepare as well as possible.** All of them. They all will help. Then make sure you develop your introduction particularly well, so you can start with momentum. Our anxiety is most intense at the beginning of a presentation and gradually subsides, so if you can start strong (introduce yourself, convince the audience of the ways your topic is important to them, preview your presentation's two to three main points, and transition into the first point smoothly), you can handle the worst of it and the presentation will get easier (Whalen, 2007).

In addition, I encourage you to **think of some times** you recently experienced anxiety and feel like you were able to handle it well. We all have faced fears, so take those experiences and let them give you confidence in facing future fears. Think about the times that something wasn't as bad as you thought it would be or how you handled it well. These memories can be empowering.

You also can improve your comfort by using the idea **deep acting** (which I discussed in Chapter 7) by thinking positively about your audience (Grandey, 2003). Think about how easy it is to talk to someone one-on-one when you see that person in a positive light. We are less tense and self-conscious, and we look forward to talking with the person. Conversation takes a lot less effort. It might not be that easy when it comes to public speaking, but our attitude toward our audience can matter. To apply this idea to public speaking situations, think about what you like about your audience, whether it is specific individuals or the whole group. If they are strangers to you, then think about some of the characteristics of the group. What makes them a likeable audience? I learned this early in my teaching career when I would get frustrated with a particular class. Initially, I would bring that frustration into the class with me; it showed, and it led students to be more miserable with me. But eventually I started thinking about likeable aspects of the students in the class (they're so quiet because of the time the class is scheduled, or because it's around mid-terms, a tough time in the semester). This didn't lead me to lower my standards or give the students less work, but it did help me put their behavior in a more positive perspective. And once my perspective changed, I looked forward to class more, and was less anxious about the class when preparing to teach it. I also was less anxious while teaching, was more positive with students, and taught with more enthusiasm. Over time, I found that I was better able to establish good working relationships with my students. All of this happened simply because I changed the way I was looking at my audience. So if you find yourself being anxious, think of some legitimately positive things about your audience. It won't make your anxiety any worse, and it may be of some help with your anxiety.

So let's say you do all of these things and still feel anxious about what might go wrong in the presentation? My advice is to think of some of the most realistic fears, and simply **assume that they all will happen.** Give up on the idea of being perfect. If you speak long enough in front of audiences, mistakes will happen, even if you prepare well. So rather than worrying about "if," prepare for "when" and focus on challenges you could encounter during the presentation. And then consider what you can do to handle each smoothly. You can't prevent mistakes, but you can control your response to them, and if you plan in advance, you can take away some of the "power" of these mistakes you fear. And if you game plan for them, you will be caught less off-guard when they happen, and you will handle them more smoothly. If you handle them more smoothly, they will provoke less anxiety, and you even may gain confidence based on your ability to handle them. So for example, assume you will lose your place or forget what you have to say. Ok, what can you do about it? Assume that electronics aren't working. What can you do about it? What questions might the audience ask, and how can you answer them? Notice that these questions will help you prepare better in the process of reducing your anxiety. Just with these questions alone, you can prepare better by (1) having well-developed notes with font big enough that it's easy to find your place, (2) having handouts or other visuals as backup for PowerPoint or alternatives to videos you plan to use in case electronics aren't working, and (3) you may develop answers to questions you may face, or you may actually change your content to address possible questions. Notice what happens if you put this level of thought into preparing: We gain confidence and feel less anxiety. The trick is to make this kind of anticipation a routine part of your preparation. It is a big part of the "secret" to actually enjoying presentations.

We Don't Develop Our Content or We Try to Cover Too Much. When we know what we want to say, it is hard to appreciate how the audience might have trouble comprehending it or seeing how our ideas are linked. I often see people prepare as if they are creating a written document, even though a speech is much different. They will list a lot of points, each with their own subpoints. The way these points is linked is unclear. And the points often are not developed, so an idea may be mentioned with little elaboration. And often PowerPoint slides are flooded with content that is too hard to read. Or there's just so much of it that we don't bother reading it anyway. You've witnessed these presentations even among professionals, and you know how tough the experience is for the audience.

To improve in this area, stop for a moment and think about how many things you really remembered from even the best presentations you've seen. I would be surprised if you remembered more than three or four major ideas (unless they were organized into some kind of neumonic device to aid your memory). Contrast that with how we often prepare by developing a large number of points. There is a disconnect here and since I don't think audiences will change, it is up to the speaker to adjust. Therefore, I suggest that you try to **think of no more than two to three main points** for your presentation (Whalen, 2007). If you have more than that, try to fit them into two to three main points. If you abruptly were cut off and told, "We have one minute left, please just identify the two to three things we should remember most," what would you cover? Make those your main points. Unless you use a neumonic device to cover more than that, the audience won't remember more than that in one sitting, and they probably will get annoyed if you try to cram more than two to three points into their heads. *It's not about what you want to say, it's about what you want the audience to take with them.*

This idea also will help you decide what content to include/exclude. What do you want to accomplish with your audience? What do you want them to have gained from you? Really think about your audience and these questions, and use the answers to these questions to figure out what matters most.

Once you've decided on some of your key points, it's important to make sure you **cover them in enough depth.** Too often speakers think it is good enough to mention a point and move on. For obvious points, this may be enough, but for many points, more explanation is needed. Once you have a sense of the basic things you're hoping to say, you can develop them further by thinking of brief examples or longer stories. Recall all of the benefits of stories from Chapter 8. They can be a great way to make your point in a way that audiences will enjoy. And if you're in a less formal or more interactive speaking situation, you even can ask your audience questions. You can ask them for examples of times when they experienced whatever you're discussing. Or you can ask them for ideas on how they might handle something. Regardless of what you do, the point is that it is important to do more than just state a point and move on. Points need to be developed so that the audience can better understand what you want them to understand.

Once you have your content, it is important to then keep a few of these things in mind when **making presentation slides.** First, the point of slides is to complement your presentation, not replace you. You still are delivering the main content. The slides are just there to help your audience follow along (Whalen, 2007). So you don't need to include everything on your slide. With this in mind, try to use just a few (less than five) slides for your presentation. And then try to use no more than five lines on each slide, with no more than about seven words on each line. These should be sentence fragments and not complete sentences. And it helps if you can use a parallel structure for each line (so they all may begin with the same word, or same type of word and follow a similar format). Unless you want or need to include an incredibly profound passage word-for-word, avoid putting long passages on slides, unless you want your audience to zone out. As for fancy things like graphics and transitions, they are "icing on the cake," so worry about them only after you've followed all of the other preparation suggestions in this section.

We Create Notes That Will Make It More Difficult to Present. I see mistakes with notes related to both the amount and appearance of content. Students may script out an entire presentation so that on paper it doesn't look any different than a normal written essay. The problem with this is that the information is there, but in practice it is very hard to retrieve because it's all one long essay. None of the key points, main ideas, or that one thing we just forgot stand out. As a result, the presenter who uses notes like this is left to awkwardly dig to find the idea while becoming embarrassed because people are starting at him or her. This only makes anxiety worse.

Some students avoid this by using an outline format. This can help make key ideas stand out, but it is possible to also encounter problems with outlines. The main problem is that students sometimes put too much content on them, in the form of full sentences for both main ideas and subpoints. And often, all of this information is single-spaced and jumbled together. This creates problems similar to those I mentioned above: We can't retrieve the information we need when we need it.

Both complete scripts and highly detailed essays present an additional problem. They limit speakers by acting as too much of a "crutch" and in doing so they can act as a barrier between speakers and their audience. When speakers use detailed notes, they often focus too much on reading them verbatim. If it is a script the speaker may literally read the entire presentation. If it is an outline, the speaker may look up periodically, but often he or she awkwardly reads most of the presentation. This becomes especially problematic when a speaker is reading material that does not need to be read in precise language. For example, I've seen students look down to their notes to introduce themselves to the audience or to struggle reading through precise language to convey something they more easily could convey if they just looked up and told the audience. In this way, notes get in the way of just communicating directly with the audience using our own language (not something we wrote out that is unnatural to deliver in a public speaking situation).

The advice I offer to speakers is designed to overcome these problems I've outlined with notes, to make speaking with audiences more natural, and to make greater use of everyone's natural ability to use their own words to present to audiences. I suggest using **sentence fragment outlines** which contain enough information to guide you and jog your memory, but not so much that your content gets in the way. So rather than having several long sentences bunched together that are hard to follow, you should have **a few phrases** (approximately four to seven words each) that are spaced apart and easy to follow. This will be too few words to allow you to read them verbatim, but enough that they will cue you about what you want to talk about next. This will allow you to more naturally put ideas into your own words while looking at your audience, and not your notes. And then make sure you use boldface and spacing between topics in order to make ideas stand out more easily (for some examples note Table 14.1). I can understand that there may be concerns with following my advice, and particularly a concern about not having enough content to feel comfortable presenting. One answer to this is to prepare better, not in the sense of scripting or memorizing a presentation, but by limiting yourself to a small number of key points and then working to internalize them. As I will discuss

Table 14.1 First Example of Problematic Notes

First problematic type: completely scripted speech:

In this presentation I will cover several things that happen when we are perceiving conflict. These include that it is a threat to our face, that we become so physiologically aroused that we can't think clearly, that we experience anger flooding, and that we can "catch" others' emotions.

First I will discuss conflict as a threat to our face

A major potential threat we encounter in workplace conflict is a threat to our face. Our face is the identity we present publicly that we want to be accepted by others. Our public face is important to us, and we desire and expect that it will be validated or confirmed by others. We "lose face" when we perceive that our identity is being challenged or ignored. According to Goffman, there are several consequences of losing face in public, including shame and embarrassment, and feelings of diminished power. In response to this loss of face, we are motivated to save face, even if we have to be aggressive to do so. According to Folger et al., "face saving is an attempt to protect or repair relational images in response to threats, real or imagined, potential or actual." If you think about a time you were embarrassed by someone in public, you'll recognize that saving face is a kind of social "damage control," in which we try to address the threat to our face. Once we are in this "damage control" mode, our focus is narrowed to our face concerns, as our primary conversational goal now is about saving face. If we had been disagreeing about some issue, the interaction now has become personal, and likely emotionally charged. We no longer care about the original issue. Now the issue is about the person who crossed us. With our focus now on saving our face (and possibly on attacking another person's face), we have become less flexible in the range of conversational choices we are likely to make. And this presents one of the major challenges of conflict situations: working toward a constructive outcome with someone we believe has attacked our face. It is hard to want to work things out when someone has threatened our face. This is partly because we process the other person's actions as a social threat and physiologically we begin to become aroused. The nature and effects of this arousal are discussed below.

later, you can develop your points by thinking of examples or stories to tell that reinforce some of your ideas. In addition, if you're still concerned about just not having enough to help you out if you draw a blank, then I suggest preparing two sets of notes. Prepare a sentence fragment outline as I am suggesting here, but then prepare a backup outline that has more detail, but just enough that enables you to be more comfortable (see Tables 14.1–14.3).

We Fail to Sell Our Material to Ourselves. Too often I see people assume that as long as they have their ideas down on paper and any visual aids ready, they're all set to present. Then when they get up to present it often falls flat. The words and visual aids are there, but there is little emotion or enthusiasm. Traditional public speaking books address this issue by devoting a lot of space to explaining how to look enthusiastic. The advice is to use moderate gestures and facial expressions, as well as vocal variety. However, if this is what we pay attention to during our presentations, we will be distracted and self-centered speakers. Rather than focusing on our audience and whether we are reaching them, we are hoping our voice sounds right and that our hands are gesturing well, but not too much. But how often do you do these things during most conversations? Probably very little, unless you are self-conscious and in a stressful conversation. The traditional advice is problematic because it tries to awkwardly explain how to do something that will look awkward

Table 14.2 Second Example of Problematic Notes

Second problematic type: detailed sentence outline:

Introduction:

- In this presentation I will cover several things that happen when we are perceiving conflict.
- These include that it is a threat to our face, that we become so physiologically aroused that we can't think clearly, that we experience anger flooding, and that we can "catch" others' emotions.

Body

- First I will discuss face threats. A major potential threat we encounter in workplace conflict is a threat to our face. Our face is the identity we present publicly that we want to be accepted by others.
- Our public face is important to us, and we desire and expect that it will be validated or confirmed by others.
- We "lose face" when we perceive that our identity is being challenged or ignored.
- There are several consequences of losing face in public
    - shame and embarrassment, and feelings of diminished power.
- In response to this loss of face, we are motivated to save face, even if we have to be aggressive to do so.
- If you think about a time you were embarrassed by someone in public, you'll recognize that saving face is a kind of social "damage control," in which we try to address the threat to our face. Once we are in this "damage control" mode, our focus is narrowed to our face concerns, as our primary conversational goal now is about saving face.
- If we had been disagreeing about some issue, the interaction now has become personal, and likely emotionally charged. We no longer care about the original issue. Now the issue is about the person who crossed us.
- With our focus now on saving our face (and possibly on attacking another person's face), we have become less flexible in the range of conversational choices we are likely to make (Folger et al., 2005).
- And this presents one of the major challenges of conflict situations: working toward a constructive outcome with someone we believe has attacked our face. It is hard to want to work things out when someone has threatened our face. This is partly because we process the other person's actions as a social threat and physiologically we begin to become aroused.

My comments: There is too much content, it is too scripted, and it is too hard to follow. For example, key points don't stand out among lesser bullets.

if we follow that advice. Even worse, it is trying to explain something we all can do very naturally. When we are excited about something it is effortless to *look* enthusiastic (Whalen, 2007). Our voice naturally gains energy and in general we speak with greater emphasis.

The trick is to take this natural ability and make it work for us during presentations. Note that the difference between trying to look enthusiastic and actually becoming enthusiastic is an example of the difference between surface and **deep acting** I talked about in Chapter 7 (Grandey, 2003). Rather than using surface acting and trying to manufacture our gestures and enthusiasm during our presentations, we should use deep acting and change our attitude toward our topic so that our delivery

Table 14.3 Improved Notes

Improved Notes: sentence fragment outline:

Introduction:
- Ask them to think of a recent conflict they had, and have a couple people share their examples
- We will focus on what happens when we perceive conflict
- Will cover the following:
  - face threats
  - physiological arousal
  - anger flooding
  - emotional contagion

Transition into face threats

Face Threats – when our public identity is challenged
- why public face is important to us
  - it's how we want others to see us
    - **Give example from the meeting last week**
  - discuss the importance of our image
    - **Give example from the grocery store**
- what happens when we lose face: shame & embarrassment
  - tell the story about the waiter in the restaurant
- Think about face threats you have encountered
  - consider what it felt like & how you responded
  - if possible, have them share some examples
- When someone threatens our face:
  - we want to save face
  - the person who harmed our face is a threat
  - we must address the threat
    - tell the story about argument with Tim during meeting

My comments: This is easier to follow and it is easier to find important ideas. Rather than just reading these, you would use them to cue your memory so you can elaborate on each point. It will enable you to talk naturally with the audience. Also, to help make sure you explain things in enough detail, notice the reminders to give examples that I've put in **boldface** (I've only given a couple of examples, but you could insert these reminders in bold throughout your outline). And remember, if it looks like there aren't enough notes, you can have a second, more detailed outline as backup. But if you prepare enough with your main points and do the other things I'm advising, you probably won't need the backup.

---

will be naturally enthusiastic. So how can we do this when preparing for our presentation? There are a couple of approaches you might try. First, try to find something in the topic that you find fascinating, or at least interesting. **Answer questions to yourself like:** "What is fascinating about this?" and "What might others find fascinating about this?" The answers may lead you to interesting aspects of the topic that might not otherwise be covered. If it is a stretch to find something fascinating, then try to settle for finding something useful about it or something about it that may be helpful to the audience. Or try to relate it to an existing interest of yours or to members of your audience. Another approach is to be able to justify every bit of content you are covering. You can do this by assuming that at any moment a smart audience member will interrupt with the questions: "Why are you covering this? Why is this important to cover?" If you do this, you may find that it helps you select the most important content and omit the least important content. And if you really work hard to justify all of your content to yourself, just consider the effect it will have on you. You will believe in your content more and it will show in your presentation. Without having to fake any enthusiasm, you will look like someone who believes in the importance of his or her content. You will speak with conviction and greater confidence than you otherwise would have had. And if you do this while also finding the more fascinating aspects of your topic, you will be more likely to enjoy presenting about it, and that enjoyment will show. It sounds too simple to be true, but I've seen this approach work very well for students, and I've seen the opposite happen when students have failed to sell the content to themselves. Fortunately, it doesn't take a lot of skill or effort to give it a try, so the next time you prepare for a presentation I encourage you to sell it to yourself when you are preparing.

We Think About Ourselves, Not the Audience. There are a lot of things to do when preparing presentations, and it can be hard to remember to really consider our audience. I often hear students talk about rehearsing speeches in front of friends, and some may think it is good to present in front of a mirror. But these approaches focus mostly on how we look and sound when delivering, and not really on how well we are developing the key ideas in our presentation or reaching an audience. Instead of practicing our presentation, it would be better to spend our time strengthening the content, our attitude about the content and our audience, and then considering how we best can reach our audience. If we are very well prepared and have sold our material to ourselves, we are more likely to speak with confidence and enthusiasm. In other words, we improve those things with preparation, not delivery practice. The advice I've given to this point is consistent with this focus. It starts with what we cover, by asking key questions about what we want our audience to gain from our presentation. **What is most important for the audience to know?** What are the key points they should remember long after our presentation? When addressing your anxiety, you should consider questions or concerns the audience may raise. When selling content to yourself, you should consider what the audience might find fascinating or why it is critical for them to hear the information you are sharing. All of these aspects of presentation reinforce a point that is critical to remember about the process of presenting: *It's not about what you want to say, it's about what you want your audience to take away from your presentation.* If you prepare with this idea in mind and then keep it in mind when presenting, you will be a more effective speaker.

What Can We Do During the Presentation to Better Reach Our Audience?

Start Strong

In my courses I see many students who think that their presentation begins when I say "go." If they are standing at the front of the room waiting, they often are completely silent and then as soon as I say "go," it's almost as if a switch now has turned on and they begin talking. Or, before I say "go" they may be making small talk with a couple of audience members, which is great, but as soon as I tell them they can start, the comfort I saw ten seconds before is gone and they switch into a formal and distant speaking tone. Both of these situations are awkward and make it harder for students to begin their presentation with momentum. In this section I will offer a different way to approach this problem, at least when it is appropriate for the speaking occasion.

So the first point you should understand about presentations is that they often begin as soon as you walk into the room, not when you are told to "go." For many speaking occasions, you may have to just sit quietly and wait for your turn to speak. In these situations, you cannot really make small talk with the audience and you'll just have to sit and wait. This is common in formal ceremonial or professional situations at which different people take turns at a podium. In these situations, people might notice you while you're in the room, so you should be attentive of other speakers, but in general, your speech does begin only when you're told to begin.

But for less formal speaking occasions, there are many things you can do to "begin" your presentation before you are given the green light to start. You can take charge of your space by arranging the podium and any tables. You also can and should set up all of your visual aids before the presentation whenever possible. This will help you confirm that everything works and give you a chance to get something fixed if it is broken, or to adjust your presentation so you can give it without any aids. And if you've prepared in accordance with the previous section, then you will be ready to adjust should there be a problem with your visual aids. You also can mingle with members of the audience. Depending on the size of the audience, you can greet them at the door or just randomly go around the room (or not so randomly—pick out people who look more friendly!). Doing this has a couple of benefits. First, it helps you work off some of your nervous energy before you begin. Second, it helps you establish a little rapport with some audience members, and you now will have a couple of slightly familiar and friendly faces out there.

If you have to wait in front of the audience before beginning, and if the occasion is informal enough, you also can talk with the audience as a whole. This can be challenging, but you can use some of the principles from the networking chapter (Chapter 3) and just ask different questions to get the audience to open up. If you're visiting a particular organization, you can try to be curious and ask questions about the profession itself, or maybe a painting or piece of art you observed on the way in. This is less about memorizing questions to ask and more about being genuinely curious. Doing this also will allow you to work off nervous energy and establish rapport with the crowd. Finally, it will establish a conversational tone with the audience that you can carry over into your presentation.

And then when it is time to speak, you can make the transition less awkwardly than the examples I gave above. If your cue to begin is a certain time, you can watch the clock and simply transition by saying something like "Ok, we're going to get started," and then go into your presentation. If you do these things, there is no awkward silence at the beginning or no rough transition in style from before the presentation. In contrast to the students I've mentioned above, when students make a little small talk with at least some audience members and then transition as I've mentioned above, they find that they are less anxious at the beginning of their presentations and that they start with more momentum. From my perspective, these students also look considerably more professional and polished than those who silently wait or awkwardly change styles once they are told to begin.

Beyond beginning smoothly, there are a couple of additional things you must do in an introduction. Think about the last few times you have attended a presentation given by a stranger. What do you hope happens? Chances are you're thinking things like "I hope this isn't boring," and "I hope this is useful to me." I've already covered the use of deep acting to assure that you're presenting with enthusiasm, but it also is critical to devote time very early on to **answering an important question that will be on the minds of your audience members:** "What's in this for me?" In other words, why should they listen to you? What can they gain from your presentation? How will they be better off for their time with you? Rather than assuming that people will be interested in you, you would be better off assuming that they won't be interested unless you earn their interest. Think of how they will be better off after the presentation, in terms of what they will learn or be able to do, or how their lives will improve. Also consider the *Made to Stick* ideas that were discussed in Chapter 9 (Heath & Heath, 2007). However you handle this section, please remember that it is important to do. Note that I tried to do this at the beginning of this chapter.

Finally, in your introduction you should **establish your credibility** and **preview your main ideas.** There is no one way to establish credibility. You can be explicit and outline any credentials you may have, but if you want to be more subtle about it, you can do it simply by **referencing your experience,** providing examples of situations you've handled, or provide stories that showcase your credibility. Ideally, speak in terms of tangible activities you have done or things you have accomplished (saying "I'm trustworthy" won't get you very far, but a story that displays your trustworthiness will help). Although this sounds easy, it is easy to overlook or to think you don't have anything to offer. I see students with great experience fail to take advantage of it because they don't think it's relevant. So remember it doesn't have to be directly relevant. If you've never held a management position but you've been a captain of a sports team or head of an academic group, you probably will have some relevant experiences to share. The point isn't to stretch things too far, but don't prematurely discount experiences you may have had that are relevant and that can help enhance your credibility with your audience.

Finally, **preview your speech.** I know this is basic advice and it can feel silly to do it, but there are ways to do it that are more smooth. You can do the basic "First I'm going to talk about _____, then I'm going to talk about _____." However, you could frame them more in terms of what the audience will gain: "Today I'm going to share these three key points with you." As in your speech, your preview should cover a small number of main points (no more than four, ideally two to three). And then once you have offered a brief preview, you can transition into your first point in a way that the audience can "follow" you: "So as I said, the first thing we're going to cover is _____."

Use Notes Well

Many speakers struggle with notes and how to use them. I already discussed what to put on them, but here I will offer some ideas about actually using them. In a nutshell, my advice is this: *Do not talk and look at your notes at the same time.* You're not presenting to your notes, as they're not your audience, so why talk to them? When we do this the notes act as a barrier between us and our audience. When this happens, presenters end up focusing more on their notes and sometimes start looking at their audience less and less. To address these problems, just try to stop speaking any time you look down at your notes (or try to stop soon after you look down). Look down for a reminder of what you want to say next (this should be easy if you've formatted your notes clearly), then look back at the audience and start talking. If this approach is new to you, it likely will feel awkward at first; so don't be hard on yourself if you're still talking while looking at your notes. But if you can move in a direction of using them in the way I've outlined, you will be freer to connect with your audience without your notes getting in the way.

Finish Strong

We typically are most likely to remember what we hear first and last. So as you're nearing the end of your presentation, you should focus on ending with some momentum. I don't think you have to be too dramatic or cute in this section. It can be something as simple as reinforcing your main points ("Before wrapping up, I just want emphasize the main three things you should take away from today," with the three things being your main points) and then offering a sense of what the audience has gained. In other words, what can they do now that they couldn't before? What perspective have they gained that they didn't before? How are they better off now thanks to their time with you? Basically, think back to your preparation and what you hoped the audience would gain. And when closing, emphasize those things that were gained. An additional benefit of closing in this way is that it bookends your presentation nicely. If you opened by talking about outcomes and previewing your main points and you close with a quick review and emphasis on what has been gained, you've reinforced your points at the beginning and end, which likely will make your key ideas more memorable to your audience.

Putting It All Together

No single chapter can cover everything about public speaking, but I've tried to some offer some ideas to help make speaking more enjoyable and to help you improve at it. I sincerely believe that if you prepare completely using the ideas in the preparation section, your time in front of your audience will be much more bearable. You will feel better about your content and begin the presentation with more confidence. And if you start with this early momentum, it will help you overcome some of the natural anxiety you will experience. And if these things happen, you will be free to treat the presentation as a conversation with your audience, and that actually can be enjoyable. So if you take anything from this chapter, notice that very little of it focused on presenting and that most of it focused on preparation, and place most of your focus on preparation. And while I'd like to take credit for this focus on preparation, in fairness, it's really just an idea first expressed by Muhammad Ali that I've found applies incredibly well to public speaking. I'll leave you with his words and simply encourage you to appreciate all that preparation can do for your speaking:

The fight is won or lost far away from witnesses—behind the lines, in the gym, and out there on the road, long before I dance under those lights.

Table 14.4 Final Checklist for Good Presentations

1. Prepare considerably

- What 1–3 key things do you want your audience to remember? Let those be your main points.
- Create simple notes (sentence fragments) that allow you to talk with your audience.
- Sell the material to yourself—what about it makes it enjoyable to discuss with others?
- Game plan for anything that might go wrong. What will you do about each thing you fear might happen?

2. Start strong

- Connect with the audience before you even begin
- Have a strong intro that you've internalized
- Address what's in it for them
- Establish credibility
- Preview your ideas

3. Keep it going

- Use your notes well
- Focus not on what you have to say, but what you want them to hear
- Finish strong

References

Grandey, A. (2003). When "the show must go on": Surface and deep acting as determinants of emotional exhaustion and peer-rated service delivery. *Academy of Management Journal, 46*(1), 86–96.

Heath, C., & Heath, D. (2007). *Made to stick: Why some ideas survive and others die.* New York, NY: Random House.

Richmond, V. P., & McCroskey, J. C. (2009). *Organizational communication for survival: Making work work* (4th ed.). Boston, MA: Allyn & Bacon.

Whalen, D. J. (2007). *The professional communications toolkit.* Thousand Oaks, CA: Sage.

Index